15th International Conference on Interfaces and Human Computer Interaction (IHCI2021) and 14th International Conference on Game and Entertainment Technologies (GET2021)

Held at the 15th Multi-Conference on Computer Science and Information Systems (MCCSIS 2021)

Online
20 - 23 July 2021

ISBN: 978-1-7138-3581-3

Printed from e-media with permission by:

Curran Associates, Inc.
57 Morehouse Lane
Red Hook, NY 12571

Some format issues inherent in the e-media version may also appear in this print version.

International Association for Development of the Information Society (IADIS)
Rua Sao Sebastiao Da Pedreira
No. 100, 30, 1050-209
Lisbon, Portugal

Phone: 351 21 3151373
Fax: 351 21 3151244

secretariat@iadis.org

Additional copies of this publication are available from:

Curran Associates, Inc.
57 Morehouse Lane
Red Hook, NY 12571 USA
Phone: 845-758-0400
Fax: 845-758-2633
Email: curran@proceedings.com
Web: www.proceedings.com

TABLE OF CONTENTS

A NOVEL AUGMENTED REALITY SYSTEM TO SUPPORT VOLUMETRIC VISUALIZATION IN INDUSTRIAL PROCESS TOMOGRAPHY

Yuchong Zhang[1], Rahul Yadav[2], Adel Omrani[3] and Morten Fjeld[1]
[1]Chalmers University of Technology, Göteborg, Sweden
[2]University of Eastern Finland, Kuopio, Finland
[3]Karlsruhe Institute of Technology, Karlsruhe, Germany

ABSTRACT

Augmented Reality (AR), as a variation of Virtual Reality (VR), has been proved useful for decades. However, it is not widely utilized in most industries. To fill the gap between this technique and industrial usage, we propose a novel AR system in the context of industrial process tomography (IPT). As the pioneering AR deployment in IPT, this system offers a new solution to underpin the onsite data analysis regarding volumetric visualization. In our work, an endeavor to provide intelligent control for an industrial drying system is pursued by using microwave tomography (MWT), a breed of IPT, as an imaging modality. Here, the AR system is integrated with the MWT for post processing of its volumetric images, containing critical information of the industrial process. The core part of the AR system is implemented by an interactive mobile app that is supported on iOS/Android platforms. The overall system is generalized by four distinctive findings: interactivity, mobility, information richness, and mutual collaboration. Our proposed system opens the horizon of leveraging AR in IPT to benefit domain-related users regarding onsite data analysis and visualization.

KEYWORDS

Augmented Reality, Volumetric Visualization, Industrial Process Tomography, Microwave Tomography, Interactivity

1. INTRODUCTION

With the increasing pace of the fourth industrial revolution, industries are investigating and adopting new cutting-edge technologies for achieving higher efficiency and supporting decision-making procedures [de Souza Cardoso et al., 2020]. Augmented reality (AR), as a variation of virtual reality (VR), in which virtual objects are superimposed in the real environment [Azuma, 1997], is one of the leading techniques being proved and applied in numerous fields, like medicine and education [Billinghurst et al., 2015]. However, due to some specific deficiencies such as hardware limitations, computation power, and low knowledge convertibility, AR has still not become a prevalent tool in most industrial application domains [de Souza Cardoso et al., 2020, Teng et al., 2018]. Nonetheless, AR is capable of providing an interactive interface of displayed digital content, as well as offering ways to interact with information in a multimodal and collaborative manner [Ferrario et al., 2020]. It thus has a great potential to fill the gap between developer and industrial domain users by inciting novel mechanisms for underpinning onsite analysis.

Industrial process tomography (IPT), a non-invasive imaging technique, has been effectively employed in many manufacturing units for inspections, monitoring, product quality control, and safety issues, to name a few. Prominent examples are oil and gas processing [Ismail et al., 2005], chemical engineering [Tapp et al., 2003], seismology [Nolet, 2012], nuclear waste processing [Primrose, 2015], and flow inspection [Plaskowski et al., 1995]. Some typical types of IPT, such as microwave tomography (MWT) [Omrani et al., 2021, Yadav et al., 2020, Zhang et al., 2019, 2020a,b], electromagnetic induction tomography (MIT) [Soleimani et al., 2007], electrical resistance tomography (ERT) [Daily et al., 2004], and electrical capacitance tomography (ECT) [Nowak et al., 2019] are widely used for purposes such as moisture detection [Omrani et al., 2020, Yadav et al., 2021], crack detection and powder flow in pipes, and flow pattern detection of granules. In our study, we focus on a unique industrial drying process [Zhang and Fjeld, 2020] using precise drying and heating equipment with the aid of MWT, as displayed in Figure 1. The target of this drying process is detecting the moisture distribution in a polymer foam placed on a conveyor belt, by adopting the MWT technique. However, raw MWT data is often hard to interpret and may not be useful for intelligent control purposes. Thus, an AR system is proposed to be integrated with the MWT to visualize distinct moisture slices for efficient post-processing. Of the IPT engaged processes, the way to visualize the data as well as how the visualizations are displayed is central for hands-on users for further exploration.

Although a body of research has been implemented to bring the intelligence of AR into industrial domains, there is still a great scarcity of benefiting IPT by equipping AR. In this paper, we introduce a novel and preliminary AR system to support interactive and collaborative onsite analysis regarding volumetric visualization in IPT. Our system is capable of providing users an interactive way with high mobility to conduct the visualization analysis alongside the on-going industrial process. The critical information of the industrial process is visualized in our mobile AR App which is built on iOS/Android devices as an early-stage setup. The contributions of this paper can be summarized as follows.

- Propose a novel AR system in supporting onsite analysis with interactivity and mobility for IPT.
- Provide information richness of volumetric visualization regarding the IPT processes to support mutual collaboration of users.

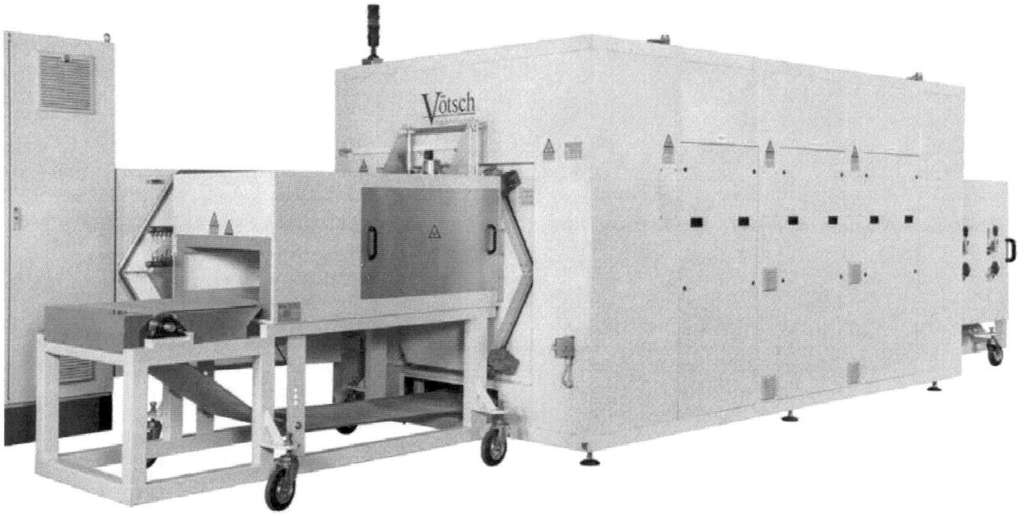

Figure 1. A side view of the precise equipment used in our study. The equipment is used for operating industrial microwave drying and heating for polymer materials using IPT (e.g., MWT), which is in laboratory HEPHAISTOS, Karlsruhe Institute of Technology, Karlsruhe, Germany

2. RELATED WORK

AR confers the advantages of interactivity and immersivity, enabling users to closely interact with the information needed by superimposing the elements in the physical reality [Ferrario et al., 2020, Teng et al., 2018]. That is, choosing the reasonable information to be visualized through AR interfaces is critical for both users and the on-going processes. In this regard, Cardoso et al. [de Souza Cardoso et al., 2020] have formulated an exhaustive survey paper describing the contemporary status of industrial AR, pointing out that most AR applications in the domain of industry are increasing as they provide a new and efficient way to convey the information needed. However, it is fair to note that there is still a great shortage of successful adoption of AR in IPT related systems. Nevertheless, some researchers have already begun harnessing this novel tool and compensating for the shortages to support visualization-related analysis in the domain of tomography [Draelos et al., 2018, Li et al., 2019, Mann et al., 2001, Nowak et al., 2019]. Dating back to 2001, Mann et al. [Mann et al., 2001] conceptualized an AR methodology to visualize the mixed fluid in stirred chemical reactors controlled by ECT. Recently, Nowak et. al [Nowak et al., 2019] pioneered a study regarding ECT, by proposing a novel AR; more precisely, a Mixed Reality (MR) system to support the in-situ collaborative analysis of numerical data in remote locations.

Volumetric visualization, as one of the objects of this study, has the capability to benefit the whole MWT processes by its exclusive properties which have been benchmarked by a small set of early research [Pereira et al., 2020]. For instance, Draelos et al. [Draelos et al., 2018] reported the first immersive VR viewer with stereo ray-casting volumetric rendering, to advance ophthalmic surgeries by using Optical coherence tomography (OCT). Currently, there is few existing research addressing adopting AR for onsite volumetric visualization in IPT system. Hence, how to effectively merge volumetric visuals with AR system to benefit targeted users in IPT areas becomes the main concern of this study.

3. METHODOLOGY

The proposed system is the first preliminary conceptualization to use AR/MR technology to support collaborative analysis on addressing volumetric visualization in the context of IPT. In our study, this system serves as an auxiliary tool to underpin the in-situ visualization analysis for an MWT related industrial microwave drying process.

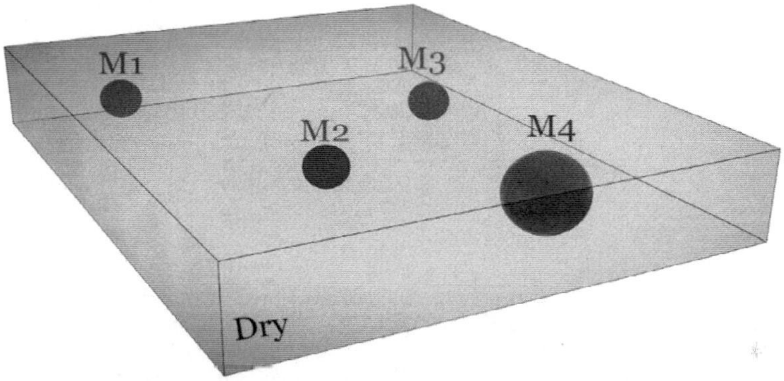

Figure 2. An example of an MWT qualitative volumetric reconstruction. Here M1, M2, M3, and M4 denote moisture hot spots (modeled in the numerical study as sphere) inside the polymer foam. The rest of the foam is modelled as dry

3.1 Microwave Tomography (MWT) Modality

In this industrial process, the objective is to dry the foam uniformly with the final target to keep the moisture under a certain level inside the complete volume at the end of the heating process. Often, those foams have non-uniform moisture distribution at the inlet, together with a nonuniform distribution of the electromagnetic field that leads to the formation of hotspots. Those hotspots might deform and destroy the foam respectively. Intelligent control of distributed microwave sources is a possibility that might efficiently address the non-uniform moisture distribution [Sun, 2016, Wu and Wang, 2017]. However, this requires the in-situ and non-invasive measurements of the unknown moisture distribution inside the material under test. Thus, to attain the moisture location and level inside the polymer foam in a running belt process, a MWT imaging method is integrated into the drying system [Omrani et al., 2021, Yadav et al., 2020]. The MWT imaging algorithm is used to estimate the moisture distribution and its level in the foam of infinite length and with large cross-sectional size. One numerical case of MWT reconstruction is visualized in Figure 2.

3.2 System Architecture

The proposed system has three main components, as displayed in Figure 3:

- Industrial process: This is a unique MWT-controlled industrial microwave drying process, operated in a confined chamber with sophisticated industrial settings. In our study, the target is a microwave drying process for polymer foams undergone by the precise equipment shown in Figure 1.
- Users: Operators who control and run the drying equipment, or researchers who take onsite observations and collect data for further analysis.
- AR App: The core part of our proposed system. As a preliminary stage, the application is manifested as a mobile App, run in iOS/Android mobile devices, and used for interactive and collaborative volumetric visualization and analysis. A floating interface overlaid in real environment containing different information is the main component of the application.

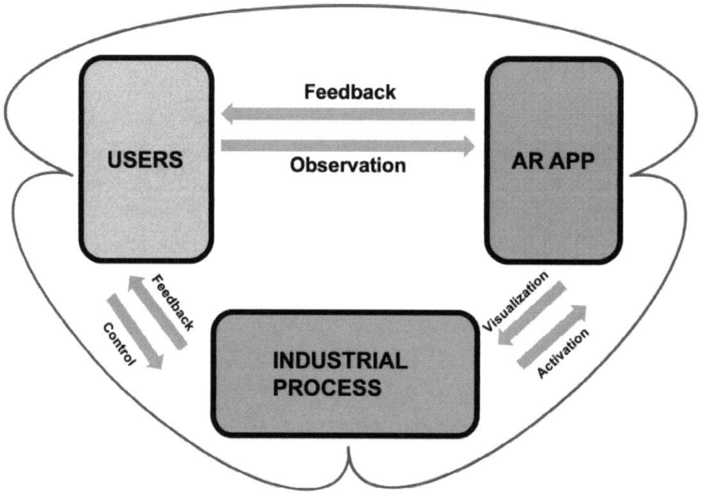

Figure 3. The proposed AR system framework. **Industrial process** block: This covers the whole running procedure of the industrial drying process, providing data and elements used for analysis. **Users** block: This represents the people involved in this context. The operators who control and run the process and the researchers who observe and analyze the process are the main composition of this part. **AR App** block: This entails the AR implementation, which was a mobile AR App developed on iOS/Android platform at the initial stage. The App allows different communities of people to get access to the volumetric data visualized interactively and to conduct the onsite analysis collaboratively

3.3 The AR Application

The central part of the AR system is a mobile AR App developed to visualize the necessary information and support interactive and collaborative onsite data analysis of volumetric input. This App serves as an intermediary tool between the operators and the precise equipment, which is used for displacing the visualized information regarding the ongoing process. The operators can interact with the visualizations projected on the AR interface, with the mobility of merely holding a mobile device alongside the bulky equipment. As Figure 4 illustrates, people from different communities, e.g., operators or researchers, have the capacity to interactively and instantly observe the information related to the process by simply activating the App without initiating other facilities. The App was developed via Unity and Vuforia engines, aiming at the present stage for iOS/Android portable devices such as smartphones and tablets. By pointing the camera of the devices at the precise equipment used for performing drying and heating, the App will then be activated, displaying a floating interface with the necessary information (figures, images, etc) virtually superimposed. The mobility of the AR interface provides users with available visualizations all the time when they move around the equipment which runs the designated process.

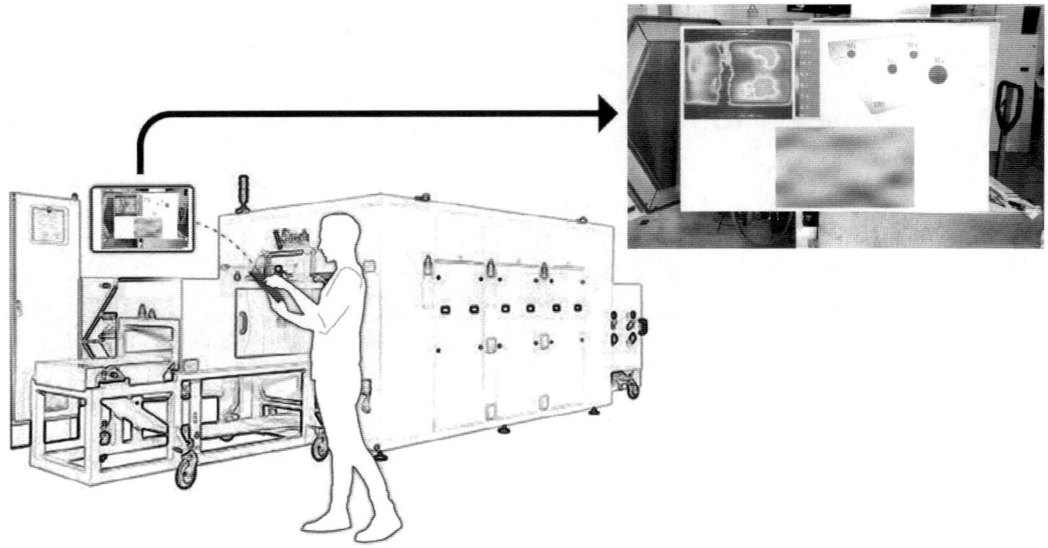

Figure 4. The realization of the proposed AR system. Users hold the handheld smartphones/tablets to run the AR App alongside the industrial setting. After the App activation, users can then observe the visualizations displayed on the AR interface. At present, the App is supported via iOS/Android mobile devices. The visualizations shown on the interface are multimodal, including the informative volumetric visualization (the upper right one)

4. FINDINGS

In our study, we present a preliminary AR framework to facilitate interactive and collaborative onsite data analysis regarding volumetric visualization in IPT systems. As a pioneer study in this context, our proposed AR system opens the new horizon of deploying this interactive technique into IPT by exemplifying an MWT-controlled microwave drying process.

Interactivity. The most prominent advantage of this system is that the information visualization by the AR interface is completely interactive. By using the AR App after activation, a user can easily get instant access to the visualized data by observing the interface which incorporates the information needed for decision-making. In addition, users are offered the option of focusing on different visualizations on the premise that we have projected different modalities of data into the virtual interface. Our AR system provides a new perspective of interactive data analysis for benefiting IPT related users.

Mobility. Another strength of this system manifests in its mobility. Generally, controlling and supervising an IPT related process requires implementation in specific and precise equipment and scientific laboratories, such as the drying apparatus and the HEPHAISTOS laboratory as mentioned before. Researchers who observe the data and analyze the ongoing process invariably conduct this work in dedicated computers located at different places. However, with this system they are empowered to hold a portable mobile device (a smartphone or tablet) with a running App to closely implement the data analysis beside the precise equipment. The mobility of our system highly reduces the time cost while improving the working efficiency.

Information richness. The AR interface is used for displaying the significant information needed for boosting the decision-making of the industrial process. In our example, we showcase the visualized data characterizing the specifications of the process. Especially, we report the first AR application of bringing volumetric visualizations which contain the key information used for further analysis in IPT systems. For instance, in our MWT microwave drying process, an up-to-date volumetric visualization has the capability to reveal the parameters of the material and the operating situation of the equipment.

Mutual collaboration. Our system enables in-situ collaboration by providing a virtual AR interface comprising different information (Figure 3). Under this setting, users from different communities, such as hands-on operators, academic researchers, and engineers, can independently conduct analysis by observing the corresponding visualizations and interact with each other on common problems as well. This shared mode breaks the gap of different communities working separately then integrates them into a complete working loop. Through our system, users concentrating on distinct targets originally can jointly interact and discuss at the same location, simultaneously having the access to the same interface containing visualizations.

5. LIMITATIONS

While we have listed the superiorities of the proposed AR system, we must also acknowledge some deficiencies in this preliminary framework. Foremost, though we have set a precedent for bringing the AR technique to benefit IPT, we have not yet evaluated our system through a systematic user study to gain constructive and critical feedback. Obtaining early-stage findings has not been sufficient for formulating a reliable AR system which should be deemed as a supportive tool in industrial settings. Only those prototypes which are established and improved based on proper usability testing can be the real-time applications at this stage. That is, a comprehensive experiment of user aspects is mandatory for a constructive human-in-the-loop system, which is not included in this study.

In addition, our preliminary system is implemented by a mobile App on portable smartphones or tablets. This setting can provide the fundamental AR experience for targeted users, but it limits the AR interface in small, bounded screens. Generally, a functional AR application elicits high interactivity and immersivity to users due to its property to put the virtual elements in front of people. The formulation of AR in handheld mobile devices to some extent hinders the essential advantages of AR, which should be tackled by introducing more advanced headsets that can make AR scenes more interactive and immersive.

6. CONCLUSION

In this paper, we present a preliminary AR system in the context of IPT to support volumetric visualization. The realization of the reported framework is conducted by a mobile AR App run on smartphones/tablets, aiding a specific MWT controlled industrial microwave drying process. We successfully prove that this novel system brings new conceptualization in this domain, by offering interactivity and mobility on users' in-situ data analysis and visualizations. Moreover, we emphasize that our AR system pioneers the volumetric visualization in IPT, thus increasing the information richness in this interdisciplinary area. The emergence of this system facilitates mutual collaboration by integrating different communities of users into joint discussions and interactions at the same location. This working mode greatly promotes the synergy pertaining to data analysis and visualization in IPT systems.

In future work, the priority will be involving constructive usability and usage testing, e.g., designing a systematic user study by engaging adequate people to perform specific tasks in our AR system, collecting feedback, and revising the system correspondingly. In addition, prototyping on advanced AR equipment such as Microsoft HoloLens or Magic Leap headsets will be another concentration, which should break the limit in screen displaying and yield higher interactivity and immersivity for targeted users.

ACKNOWLEDGEMENT

This project has received funding from the European Union's Horizon 2020 research and innovation programme under the Marie Sklodowska-Curie grant agreement No 764902.

REFERENCES

Azuma, R. T. [1997], 'A survey of augmented reality', *Presence: Teleoperators & Virtual Environments* 6(4), 355–385.

Billinghurst, M. et al, [2015], 'A survey of augmented reality', *Foundations and Trends in Human–Computer Interaction* 8(2-3), 73–272.

Daily, W. et al, [2004], 'Electrical resistance tomography', *The Leading Edge* 23(5), 438–442.

de Souza Cardoso, L. et al, [2020], 'A survey of industrial augmented reality', *Computers & Industrial Engineering* 139, 106159.

Draelos, M. et al, [2018], 'Real-time visualization and interaction with static and live optical coherence tomography volumes in immersive virtual reality', *Biomedical optics express* 9(6), 2825–2843.

Ferrario, A. et al, [2020], Aleedsa: Augmented reality for interactive machine learning, *in 'Extended Abstracts of the 2020 CHI Conference on Human Factors in Computing Systems'*, pp. 1–8.

Ismail, I. et al, [2005], 'Tomography for multi-phase flow measurement in the oil industry', *Flow measurement and instrumentation* 16(2-3), 145–155.

Li, R. et al, [2019], Augmented reality guided respiratory liver tumors punctures: A preliminary feasibility study, *in 'SIGGRAPH Asia 2019 Technical Briefs'*, pp. 114–117.

Mann, R. et al, [2001], 'Augmented-reality visualization of fluid mixing in stirred chemical reactors usingelectrical resistance tomography', *Journal of Electronic Imaging* 10(3), 620–630.

Nolet, G. [2012], Seismic tomography: with applications in global seismology and exploration geophysics, Vol. 5, *Springer Science & Business Media.*

Nowak, A. et al, [2019], Towards in-situ process tomography data processing usingaugmented reality technology, *in 'Adjunct Proceedings of the 2019 ACM International Joint Conference on Pervasive and Ubiquitous Computingand Proceedings of the 2019 ACM International Symposium on Wearable Computers'*, pp. 168–171.

Omrani, A. et al, [2020], A multistatic uniform diffraction tomographic algorithm for real-time moisture detection, *in '2020 IEEEAsia-Pacific Microwave Conference (APMC)'*, IEEE, pp. 437–439.

Omrani, A. et al, [2021], A combined microwave imaging algorithm for localization andmoisture level estimation in multilayered media, *in '2021 15th European Conference on Antennas and Propagation (EuCAP)'*, IEEE, pp. 1–5.

Pereira, M.et al, [2020], '3-d multi static ground penetrating radar imaging for augmented reality visualization', *IEEE Transactions on Geoscience and Remote Sensing* 58(8), 5666–5675.

Plaskowski, A. et al, [1995], Imaging industrial flows: applications of electrical process tomography, *CRC Press*.

Primrose, K. [2015], Application of process tomography in nuclear waste processing in 'Industrial Tomography', *Elsevier*, pp. 713–725.

Soleimani, M. et al, [2007], 'Dynamic imaging in electrical capacitance tomography andelectromagnetic induction tomography using a kalman filter', *Measurement Science and Technology* 18(11), 3287.

Sun, Y. [2016], *Adaptive and Intelligent Temperature Control of Microwave Heating Systems with Multiple Sources*, Vol. 8, KIT Scientific Publishing.

Tapp, H. et al, [2003], 'Chemical engineering applications of electrical process tomography', *Sensors and Actuators B: Chemical* 92(1-2), 17–24.

Teng, C.-C. et al, [2018], Interactive augmented live virtual reality streaming: a health careapplication, *in 'Proceedings of the 2nd International Conference on Medical and Health Informatics'*, pp. 143–147.

Wu, Z. and Wang, H. [2017], 'Microwave tomography for industrial process imaging: Example applications and experimental results.', *IEEE Antennasand Propagation Magazine* 59(5), 61–71.

Yadav, R. et al, [2021], Microwave tomography for moisture level estimation using Bayesian framework, *in '2021 15th European Conference on Antennas and Propagation (EuCAP)'*, IEEE, pp. 1–5.

Yadav, R. et al, [2020], Microwave tomography for estimating moisture content distribution in porous foam using neural networks, *in '2020 14th European Conference on Antennas and Propagation (EuCAP)'*, IEEE, pp. 1–5.

Zhang, Y. and Fjeld, M. [2020], Condition monitoring for confined industrial process based on infrared images by using deep neural network and variants, *in 'Proceedings of the 2020 2nd International Conference on Image, Video and Signal Processing'*, pp. 99–106.

Zhang, Y. et al, [2020], Task-based Colormap Design Supporting Visual Comprehension in Process Tomography, *in A. Kerren, C. Garth and G. E. Marai, eds, 'EuroVis 2020 - Short Papers'*, The Eurographics Association.

Zhang, Y. et al, [2019], Automatic image segmentation for microwave tomography (mwt) from implementation to comparative evaluation, *in 'Proceedings of the 12th International Symposium on Visual Information Communication and Interaction'*, pp. 1–2.

Zhang, Y. et al, [2020], 'Automated microwave tomography (mwt) image segmentation: State-of-the-art implementation and evaluation', *Journal of WSCG 2020*, 126–136.

CATEGORIES OF USER IMPAIRMENT

Till Halbach and Joschua Thomas Simon-Liedtke
Norwegian Computing Center
Oslo, Norway

ABSTRACT

This work presents a novel classification scheme for human impairments and aims at being as small as possible while simultaneously representing the vast diversity of users with impairments with sufficient accuracy. The scheme is based on the International Classification of Functioning, Disability, and Health of the WHO and consists of in total 21 impairment categories which are broadly grouped into the four main areas cognition, senses, voice, and movement. The classification scheme is of generic nature and can thus be applied to the design of human artifacts and environments in general, as it considers the plain interaction of the human body with its surroundings in multiple modalities. Simulation of user impairment is a primary application area.

KEYWORDS

Classification, Scheme, Disabilities, Personas, Expert, Artifacts, ICT

1. INTRODUCTION

On an international level, the WHO estimate that around 15% of the population have a moderate to severe disability (World Health Organization, 2011). For all ages, the estimate for Europe is 80 million or 16%, as compared to ~500 million citizens in total[1] (Eurostat, 2015a, 2015b). In Norway, 19% of the Norwegian population aged 18 and older is said to have a disability (The Norwegian Directorate for Children, 2013). The number of people with disabilities is expected to increase due to population ageing in many parts of the world. For instance, a 2015 prognosis in Europe for 2020 was 120 millions (European Commission, 2015).

When it comes to designing and implementing systems (services and products), information, and environments, it is therefore vital to ensure a high degree of accessibility and usability for the widest range of users possible, including people with disabilities. This applies to participation and co-creation as well as testing and evaluation likewise, and is often referred to as user-centred design or development. The use of actual users representing different user groups is generally considered as the best method to take user disabilities into account in a user-centred design process, not only with respect to user experience and usability but also accessibility (Petrie og Bevan, 2009; Fuglerud, 2014; Dumas og Salzman, 2006; Keates, 2006; Brajnik, 2008; Petrie og Bevan, 2009; Fuglerud, 2014). It has, however, also been pointed out that user participation often proves to be costly, time-intensive, and not straight-forward to apply (Petrie og Bevan, 2009; Røssvoll og Fuglerud, 2013; Petrie og Bevan, 2009). Challenges include recruiting the right population representing relevant user groups, finding and organizing the proper co-creating tools and methods, and conducting valid and useful trials.

To simulate user impairment[2] and thereby to partly reduce the need for user participation can be a good strategy to keep costs, time investment and complexity of design, development, and testing processes low. This work discusses which impairments should be considered. While we are targeting systems and applications in the realm of IT and ICT, the below discussion is of a generic nature and hence applicable not only to any technical artifacts, including self-service machines, museum and science center exhibits, smart-watches, smart homes, smart environments, etc., but to the design of everyday things in general (Norman, 2013).

---

1 The statistics consider 27 countries in 2012.

2 We prefer to use the term impairment over disability to focus on the reduction in function of the human body and not the consequence of someone not being able to do something.

The main contribution of this work is to unify previous work considering various impairment classifications with relevant standards and the WHO's International Classification of Functioning, Disability, and Health to a novel scheme.

The remainder of the article is straightforward: After a brief review of research related to expert testing and personas, the article continues with discussing various classification schemes in other works, before the novel set of categories is presented.

2. REPRESENTING USERS WITH IMPAIRMENTS

As detailed in the following, simulating user impairment (SUI) can be a good strategy to cut costs and complexity while meeting accessibility requirements in (agile) design and development processes and continuous testing. It is, however, stressed that SUI cannot replace the role of real users entirely, even though it can act as a substitute for involving users to some degree. Other research has recommended to combine SUI with methods that involve real users (Nielsen, 1994; Hwang og Salvendy, 2010). SUI can follow the chosen process as with normal user testing but replaces real users with dedicated testers, user advocates or experts who simulate any impairments real users might have. As a side note, any process should involve users from the very beginning and throughout the entire development (Røssvoll og Fuglerud, 2013; Bai *et al.*, 2019).

The research community uses multiple related and partly synonymous terms for SUI, including expert evaluation, expert inspection, empathetic walk-through, accessibility inspection, and others, but there are subtle differences. Expert testing can involve specialists who rely on their experience in the field, but it could also be that those experts follow particular guidelines (Petrie og Bevan, 2009). The main characteristic of SUI is that users with various functional impairments should be considered. The key motivation for this is that such testing is particularly efficient to indicate general usability and accessibility problems (Schmutz, Sonderegger og Sauer, 2016, 2017, 2018; Bai *et al.*, 2018; Stray *et al.*, 2019). Another reason is the necessity to mirror user diversity in development and testing based on population and impairment statistics.

SUI as a concept is also related to working with personas. Personas are fictional characters representing individual users or user groups, and different variants of persona methodologies exist (Fuglerud *et al.*, 2020). Persona testing and expert evaluations have both been considered to be insufficient because, as most variants are simple mental models, they are not representing users and their needs well enough (Sauer, Sonderegger og Schmutz, 2020). It is further argued that personas methodology can be made more robust by combining it with practical models and simulations (Petrie og Bevan, 2009).

3. IMPAIRMENTS TO CONSIDER

As previously mentioned, it is crucial that a great variety of individuals is represented when developing for instance technical solutions, and this includes individuals with impairments. However, there are many different impairments, and thus there is a large number of classification possibilities. The goal of the following discussion is to find the smallest set of categories that represents the diversity of user impairments with sufficient accuracy.

In ICT, it is common to use three broad categories of impairments on a high abstraction level: sensor, motor, and cognition (Fuglerud, 2014). Other research targeting (technical) science center exhibits has suggested to split up senses into vision and hearing, to differentiate between motor and mobility, and to account for voice, which results in six accessibility areas (Halbach og Tjøstheim, 2019). More precisely, the authors define mobility as everything related to the legs and lower extremities, whereas motor is everything related to the hands, arms, and upper extremities.

With the context of software development, a seven-category scheme has been proposed (Bai *et al.*, 2018). It consists of the areas auditory, attention and memory, higher-level logic, language and numbers, physical, speech, and visual. It is hence quite similar to the aforementioned six-category scheme for museum exhibits, but more detailed when it comes to subcategories in the cognition domain.

Early research from the creators of the principles of universal design proposes another seven-category scheme consisting of cognition, vision, hearing and speech, body function, arm function, hand function, and mobility (Story, Molly Follette and Mueller, James L. and Mace, Ronald L., 1998). We believe that hearing and speech should be separate, as the former for a human is about receiving signals / perception, whereas the latter is about sending / controlling. Lessons learned from exhibit evaluation advocates further to combine *arm function* and *hand function* without the loss of generality to *motor*. Also, the term *body function* could be more specific and clarify the difference to for instance *motor*, and this is why we prefer *touch*.

An even more fine-grained classification seems to be necessary, though, as for example there is substantial difference between measures that accommodate for low vision and measures that account for blindness. The European Standard EN 301 549 considers 10 different categories[3] (European Telecommunications Standards Institute, 2019): No vision, limited vision, no color perception, no hearing, limited hearing, no vocals, limited manipulation/strength, limited reach, no photosensitive triggers, and limited cognition. This list seems to have a fair level of differentiation, but it is argued here that it has three important shortcomings. One is the lack of mobility as a category. This is useful as reach and mobility are different (but related) concepts: Mobility is needed for instance to come close to user interfaces, and in situations where the interaction relies on a functioning foot or feets, such as controlling the gas pedal in cars or stepping on a dance mat in some video games. Next is the notion of photosensitive triggers, which is limited in meaning to flashes of light. General photosensitivity, on the other hand, is a much broader term, as it includes impairments related to the brightness of a screen and single user interface elements, and it addresses in addition technical features like dark color schemes. EN 301 549 also mentions "limited cognition, language, and learning[4]". This appears to be too little detailed, as cognition is a quite broad term, and there is a wide range of neurodiversity[5].

The World Wide Web Consortium speaks of neurological disorders and enlists additionally the following examples (W3C Web Accessibility Initiative (WAI)): focus / attention deficits, limited social communication and interaction, and memory impairments. This list can be expanded, as proposed in another work, by the categories orientation deficits, and limited coordination and planning abilities (Halbach og Tjøstheim, 2019). Yet other research has mentioned lingual (text and language) comprehension, which includes reading and writing, and partly speaking, as well as visual comprehension (Halbach, 2010; Røssvoll og Solheim, 2010).

A preliminary conclusion is that multiple schemes have been proposed so far, and the research community does not agree upon which of these schemes is most appropriate to represent the diversity of human impairments. It may hence be helpful to turn to the classification framework used by the World Health Organization, called International Classification of Functioning, Disability, and Health / ICF (International Classification of Functioning, Disability and Health). The ICF framework links body functions and structures that might be affected by particular conditions and disabilities with contextual parameters like environmental and personal factors, such as human activities and participation in the society, as well as barriers. The WHO emphasize that an individual's functioning consists of interactions between a health condition and contextual factors, and that these interactions are multi-directional.

The WHO propose eight major categories to classify these body functions and impairments. Of these categories, some are in our opinion not relevant for a user's access to technical assets: a) Functions of the cardiovascular, hematological, immunological and respiratory systems (ICF no. 4), b) functions of the digestive, metabolic and endocrine systems (ICF no. 5), c) genitourinary and reproductive functions (ICF no. 6), and d) functions of the skin and related structures (ICF no. 8). Touch is already covered by sensory functions. In addition, we have experienced from exhibits that it makes sense to divide the category neuromusculoskeletal and movement-related functions of movement and mobility (ICF no. 7) into functions related to the lower body extremities and functions related to the upper body extremities. The same strategy is employed for example in the statistics of the US Census Bureau (The US Census Bureau, 2012, 2018).

Relevant ICF categories are thus (our labeling in parenthesis):

---

3 The category privacy is disregarded here as it is not a functional impairment of humans.

4 In the literature in general, multiple terms are used as synonymous to learning disability: intellectual disability, reasoning disability, limited processing ability, and limited problem solving ability.

5 In fact, there cannot be a clear distinction between physical and neurological functioning. Complex biological processes like vision are rooted deeply inside basic brain processes, and mental disorders may affect the sensory and physical system as well. The classification in this work is only a simplification to ease the discussion of the impact of impairments.

1. Mental functions (cognition)
   - Global functions: orientation, intellectual, temperament and personality, etc.
   - Specific functions: attention, memory, emotional, perceptual, calculation, etc.
2. Sensory and pain functions of the human senses (senses)
   - Seeing and related functions (vision)
   - Hearing and vestibular functions (hearing)
   - Additional sensory functions, including smell, taste, and touch (touch)
3. Voice functions to produce sounds and speech (voice)
4. Not applicable (Functions of the cardiovascular, hematological, immunological and respiratory systems)
5. NA (Functions of the digestive, metabolic and endocrine systems)
6. NA (Genitourinary and reproductive functions)
7. Neuromusculoskeletal and movement-related functions of movement and mobility
   - Functions related to the lower body extremities (mobility)
   - Functions related to the upper body extremities (motor)
8. NA (Functions of the skin and related structures)

Moreover, cognition should in our opinion be split up into multiple subtopics, and we propose the following eight impairment classifications: Language, reasoning, attention, communication and interaction, memory, orientation, coordination and planning, and mental health and behavior. The reason for this differentiation is threefold. Each of these classifications typically requires 1) separate inclusion measures during the development of technical solutions, 2) the participation of a separate interest organization in user trials, and 3) the simulation of a separate user group in expert testing.

For instance, *language* targets organizations for people with a migrational or foreign background. *Reasoning* aims at organizations for people with general intellectual impairments. Organizations for individuals with ADHD is a good example for the category *attention*, and organizations for people with Autism Spectrum Disorder / ASD can be mapped to the category *communication and interaction*. Interest organizations for elderly are often involved when *memory* impairment is targeted. And while organizations for individuals with dementia exemplify *orientation*, the category *coordination and planning* targets organizations for people with Downs' syndrome. Finally, the category *mental health and behavior* is well exemplified by organizations for people with bipolar disorder. These eight subtopics seem necessary to cover as much as possible within the range of cognitive impairments. However, we have to admit that some user groups cover multiple areas. For example, the Norwegian Association for Persons with Intellectual Disabilities can be involved in user trials targeting memory, orientation, and reasoning, among others.

When it comes to taking into account individuals with low vision, there is a substantial difference between designing / testing for *lack of vision* and *limited vision*. That is, somebody entirely blind typically uses a screen reader, while many with low vision simply prefer to increase the screen zoom to increase readability. Next, people with color vision deficits are usually neither dependent on screen reader nor zoom, so developing for that user group typically involves measures and tests that check that the meaning of interface elements is not signaled by color alone. Individuals with light sensitivity is a category / area of its own, too, which in most cases relates to oversensitivity to light stimulus. In the hearing domain, we propose to differentiate between l*ack of hearing* and *limited hearing*. While the former considers deaf people with a focus on visual communication, the latter means that audio and sound in fact can be used in interfaces, while there should be measures to account for low volume levels, noise or distracting background music, to give a few examples. Likewise, there is a substantial difference in *lack of voice* and *limited voice*. In the former situation, user interaction has to rely on non-verbal schemes. *Limited voice* covers situations with an unclear or low voice, multiple speakers, background noises, and the like. In the movement domain, it is important to handle *limited reach*, as often experienced by people with a wheelchair, crutches, and similar, separate from *limited strength*, which targets situations where somebody controls an artifact by their feet without moving anywhere else. *Motor* is a corresponding domain for the upper-body functions: There is a significant difference between *reach* and *strength*. The former deals with whether interaction elements can be reached by arms, hands, and fingers, and the latter concerns for instance whether a button can be easily pushed or not. It therefore makes sense to give each of these particular areas an own category.

We propose to merge the ICF categories, diversified for subtopics, with the modified EN 301 549 standard, as well as altered own and other research, as discussed above, to a novel categorization scheme with a total of 21 categories, as enlisted in Table 1 below. A graphical illustration is depicted in .

Table 1. Proposed categories of user impairment and related ICF reference

This novel scheme may serve as an aid during planning, development and testing of human artifacts in general and technical assets in particular, including the simulation of user impairment. A major advantage of such a scheme is that it is generically applicable and globally comparable. Another benefit is that, with the aforementioned mapping of categories to interest organizations, it will be possible to obtain statistical data from those organizations to be used during considerations regarding which interest group to prioritize during development or testing. Also, the approach answers the WHO's recommendation to improve statistical data by adapting the ICF to specific areas (World Health Organization (WHO), 2011)

No.	ICF no.	Category	No.	ICF no.	Category
	1	Cognition		2.2	Hearing
1		Attention	13		Lack of hearing
2		Memory	14		Limited hearing
3		Orientation	15	2.3	Touch
4		Reasoning		3	Voice
5		Coordination & planning	16		Lack of voice
6		Linguistics & speech	17		Limited voice
7		Social communication & interaction		4	Movement
8		Mental health & behavior		4.1	Mobility (lower-body functions)
	2	Senses	18		Limited mobility reach
	2.1	Vision	19		Limited mobility strength / manipulation
9		Lack of vision		4.2	Motor (upper-body functions)
10		Low vision	20		Limited motor reach
11		Reduced color vision	21		Limited motor strength / manipulation
12		Light sensitivity			

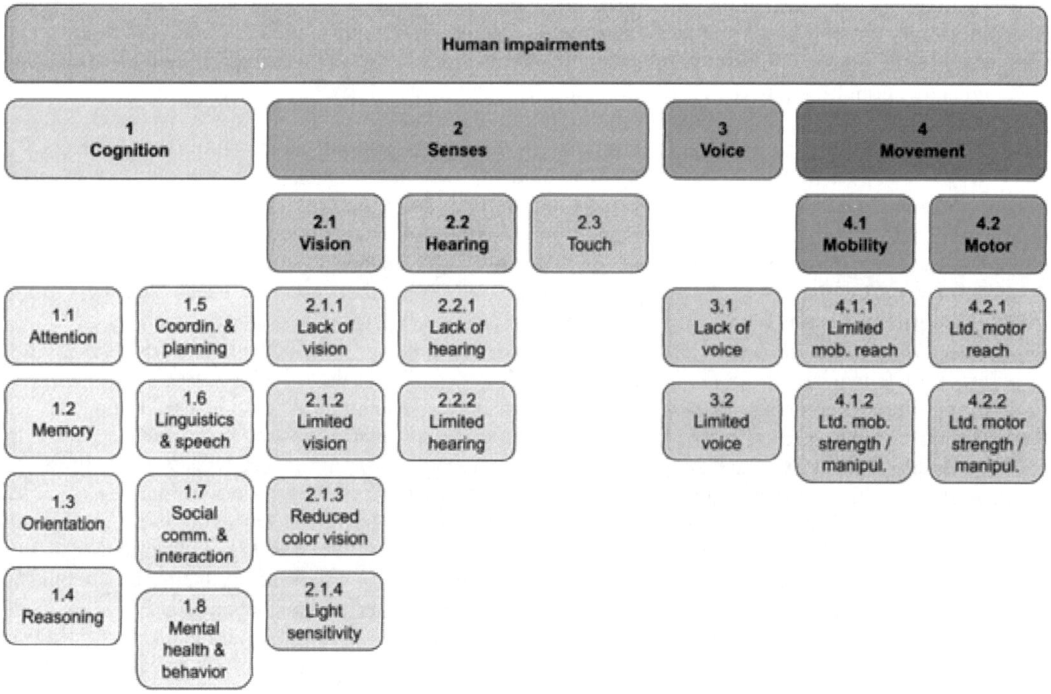

Figure 1. Proposed categories of human impairments relevant for technical artifacts

There are multiple implications of this work. ICT researchers, designers, developers, and others have hopefully been given additional aids to take into account human impairment in their work. Also, the wide range of human impairment has been underlined. Universal design is much more than a screen reader accessibility and a wheel chair ramp. We further hope that those who plan, develop, and test technology start to think of diversity in broader terms. The high number of various impairments underlines the importance of involving more users in the technology development than what is practiced today, or at least to simulate user impairment to a wider extent. Our vision is that a greater share of technology is becoming more inclusive for a wider range of human diversity.

The results in this work are limited by the following considerations. The objective of the literature review has not been to give a complete overview of all related research; however, we are confident that we have covered a sufficiently large share of the literature to develop this new classification scheme. Moreover, the nature of this work has been theoretical, and it needs to be verified in for instance user trials whether the scheme has just about the right number of categories (not too few or too many). It is also stressed that the scheme is not based on any statistics of impairment, which might be a good suggestion for future research.

4. CONCLUSION

By reviewing and discussing relevant work from the literature as well as related standards, we have developed a classification of impairments which we believe finds the right balance between being as small as possible and representing the vast diversity of users with impairments with sufficient accuracy. The scheme consists of 21 impairment categories in total which are broadly grouped into the four main areas cognition, senses, voice, and movement.

While the classification scheme is derived mainly with technical artifacts in mind, it is generic enough to be applicable to the design of human artifacts and environments in general, as it considers the plain interaction of the human body with its surroundings in multiple modalities. The classification scheme can be used in a variety of situations where real users or users with simulated impairments need to be represented in a systematic manner, such as planning and conceptualization, design and co-creation sessions, test iterations, and other development cycles.

We hope that the impairment categories are useful for all stakeholders of design and development processes, primarily usability and accessibility experts, but also graphic designers, interaction designers, developers, testers, architects, curators, carpenters, and more.

ACKNOWLEDGEMENT

This work was supported by the UnIKT program of the Norwegian Directorate for Children, Youth and Family Affairs.

REFERENCES

Bai, A. *et al.* (2018) «Categorization and Comparison of Accessibility Testing Methods for Software Development», *Studies in health technology and informatics*, 256, s. 821–831.

Bai, A. *et al.* (2019) «Evaluating accessibility testing in automated software build processes», *Norsk IKT-konferanse for forskning og utdanning*. Tilgjengelig på: https://ojs.bibsys.no/index.php/NIK/article/view/646.

Brajnik, G. (2008) «Beyond conformance: the role of accessibility evaluation methods», i *International Conference on Web Information Systems Engineering*. Springer, s. 63–80.

Dumas, J. S. og Salzman, M. C. (2006) «Usability Assessment Methods», *Reviews of Human Factors and Ergonomics*, 2(1), s. 109–140.

European Commission (2015) *Commission proposes to make products and services more accessible to the disabled persons*. Tilgjengelig på: http://europa.eu/rapid/press-release_IP-15-6147_en.htm.

European Telecommunications Standards Institute (2019) *Accessibility requirements for ICT products and services*. EN 301 549 v3.1.1.

Eurostat (2015a) *Disability statistics - prevalence and demographics*. Tilgjengelig på: http://ec.europa.eu/eurostat/statistics-explained/index.php/Disability_statistics_-_prevalence_and_demographics.

Eurostat (2015b) *Population and population change statistics*. Tilgjengelig på: http://ec.europa.eu/eurostat/statistics-explained/index.php/Population_and_population_change_statistics.

Fuglerud, K. S. (2014) *Inclusive design of ICT: The challenge of diversity*. University of Oslo, Faculty of Humanities, s. 282. doi: 10.13140/2.1.4471.5844.

Fuglerud, K. S. *et al.* (2020) «Co-creating Persona Scenarios with Diverse Users Enriching Inclusive Design», i *Universal Access in Human-Computer Interaction. Design Approaches and Supporting Technologies*. Springer International Publishing, s. 48–59.

Halbach, T. (2010) «Towards Cognitively Accessible Web Pages», i *Proceedings of Third International Conferences on Advances in Computer-Human Interactions (ACHI-2010)*. St. Maarten (Netherlands Antilles): International Academy, Research, and Industry Association (IARIA). Tilgjengelig på: http://publ.nr.no/5236.

Halbach, T. og Tjøstheim, I. (2019) «Towards Reliable Accessibility Assessments of Science Center Exhibits», i *Human-Computer Interaction – INTERACT 2019*. Springer International Publishing, s. 33–41.

Hwang, W. og Salvendy, G. (2010) «Number of people required for usability evaluation: the 10±2 rule», *Communications of the ACM*, 53(5), s. 130–133.

International Classification of Functioning, Disability and Health (ICF) (no date). Tilgjengelig på: https://www.who.int/standards/classifications/international-classification-of-functioning-disability-and-health (Åpnet: 30. mars 2021).

Keates, S. (2006) *Designing for Accessibility: A Business Guide to Countering Design Exclusion*. CRC Press.

Nielsen, J. (1994) *Usability Engineering*. Morgan Kaufmann.

Norman, D. (2013) *The design of everyday things: Revised and expanded edition*. Basic books.

Petrie, H. og Bevan, N. (2009) «The Evaluation of Accessibility, Usability, and User Experience», *The universal access handbook*, 1, s. 1–16.

Røssvoll, T. H. og Fuglerud, K. S. (2013) «Best Practice for Efficient Development of Inclusive ICT», i Stephanidis, C. og Antona, M. (red.) *Universal Access in Human-Computer Interaction. Design Methods, Tools, and Interaction Techniques for eInclusion*. Springer Berlin Heidelberg (Lecture Notes in Computer Science), s. 97–106.

Røssvoll, T. H. og Solheim, I. (2010) «Design of Cognitively Accessible Web Pages», *International Journal on Advances in Intelligent Systems*, 3(3&4), s. 303–312.

Sauer, J., Sonderegger, A. og Schmutz, S. (2020) «Usability, user experience and accessibility: towards an integrative model», *Ergonomics*, 63(10), s. 1207–1220.

Schmutz, S., Sonderegger, A. og Sauer, J. (2016) «Implementing Recommendations From Web Accessibility Guidelines: Would They Also Provide Benefits to Nondisabled Users», *Human factors*, 58(4), s. 611–629.

Schmutz, S., Sonderegger, A. og Sauer, J. (2017) «Implementing Recommendations From Web Accessibility Guidelines: A Comparative Study of Nondisabled Users and Users With Visual Impairments», *Human factors*, 59(6), s. 956–972.

Schmutz, S., Sonderegger, A. og Sauer, J. (2018) «Effects of accessible website design on nondisabled users: age and device as moderating factors», *Ergonomics*, 61(5), s. 697–709.

Story, Molly Follette and Mueller, James L. and Mace, Ronald L. (1998) *The Universal Design File: Designing for People of All Ages and Abilities*. NC State University, Center for Universal Design.

Stray, V. *et al.* (2019) «Empowering agile project members with accessibility testing tools: a case study», i *International Conference on Agile Software Development*. Springer, Cham, s. 86–101.

The Norwegian Directorate for Children, Y. A. F. A. (2013) *Slik har jeg det i dag*, s. 117.

The US Census Bureau (2012) «Americans with Disabilities: 2010», *The United States Census Bureau*. Tilgjengelig på: https://www.census.gov/library/publications/2012/demo/p70-131.html.

The US Census Bureau (2018) «Americans with Disabilities: 2014», *The United States Census Bureau*. Tilgjengelig på: https://www.census.gov/library/publications/2018/demo/p70-152.html.

W3C Web Accessibility Initiative (WAI) (no date) *Diverse Abilities and Barriers*. Tilgjengelig på: https://www.w3.org/WAI/people-use-web/abilities-barriers/ (Åpnet: 25. september 2020).

World Health Organization (2011) *World report on disability*, s. 350.

World Health Organization (WHO) (2011) «World report on disability». Tilgjengelig på: https://www.who.int/publications/i/item/9789241564182.

A SERVICE-DOMINANT LOGIC BASED FRAMEWORK FOR TEACHING INNOVATION IN HCI

Amela Karahasanović[1] and Alma Leora Culén[2]
[1]SINTEF Digital, Forskningsveien 1, Oslo, Norway
[2]Department of Informatics, University of Oslo, Gaustadalléen 23 B, Oslo, Norway

ABSTRACT

While Human-Computer Interaction (HCI) has successfully contributed to innovation, HCI education has made only moderate efforts to include innovation as part of the curriculum. In this paper, therefore, we propose a service-dominant logic-informed framework for teaching innovation in the context of HCI education. Our approach combines service-dominant logic from the field of marketing with experiential and constructivist learning, leveraging value co-creation as the primary method of connecting diverse actors within the service ecology. This aligns with the current conceptualization of central university activities as a triad of research, education, and entrepreneurship. The paper illustrates our framework with experiences from a project-based, bachelor's-level HCI course in the computer science department and shows how value co-creation brings a new dimension to HCI education. The proposed framework and our experience described herein can be useful for teachers designing and improving project-based HCI courses.

KEYWORDS

HCI Education, Innovation, Service-Dominant Logic, Value Co-Creation

1. INTRODUCTION

The HCI community has long recognized the need for continuously updated HCI curricula focused on what is a 'must' for the curriculum, choosing among diverse theories, frameworks, and exemplars. For example, the ACM SIGCHI Executive Committee sponsored a project (see Churchill et al., 2014, 2016) to investigate the present and future of HCI education. The project ran from 2011 to 2014, and the findings pointed to the desire among HCI scholars and educators to share and collaborate on the development of course outlines, curricula, and teaching materials, calling this the HCI living curricula. With fast-changing technologies and continued rapid expansion of the field, HCI education is particularly sensitive to issues of relevance and balance between theoretical and practical professional knowledge and skills. Thus, what should be taught and how to do it best (Churchill et al., 2013; Culén et al., 2014; St-Cyr et al., 2019) has been difficult to establish.

HCI researchers have also increasingly recognized that framing design activity, which is at the core of innovation, no longer relies on the traditional pairing of users with designers in today's mainstream participatory and co-design activities. Instead, approaches that value the full complexity of stakeholders in each design situation are recommended (Gray et al., 2019; Irwin, 2018; Rosenberg, 2016). Furthermore, recent awareness related to sustainability has highlighted the need to consider how the course design might help reach the university's aim to contribute more directly to the positive social changes that are needed today.

Since we consider deeper involvement with value creation for the public good (both at the institutional level and the level of instructional practice), we wanted to explore if and how Service-Dominant Logic (S-DL; Vargo and Lusch, 2008) might help teach innovation in HCI. S-DL proposes service as central to any exchange, whether for business purposes or otherwise (Vargo and Lusch, 2008). In (Hollebeek et al. (2019), the authors proposed an S-DL-informed model for customer engagement that views resource integration as a required antecedent of customer engagement and co-creation as its key outcome. In addition, work such as (Lusch and Nambisan (2015) and Ordanini and Parasuraman (2011) explicitly used S-DL to frame service innovation and highlight the importance of exploring the integrative interfaces between customer engagement and service innovation (Hollebeek and Andreassen, 2018). According to these views, innovation is a result of resource-integrating activities that create new resource configurations, thus paving the way for innovation. In line with S-DL, the main components of this perspective include the following:

- *Service platforms*: Structures of tangible and intangible resources that facilitate the undertaking of interactions between the involved actors (Breidbach et al., 2014).
- *Value co-creation*: The extraction of actor-perceived value from focal service innovation-related interactions (e.g., customer–firm, employee–firm).
- *Service ecosystems*: Networked actors connected through service exchanges that serve as the environment within which service innovation takes place. While some ecosystem actors may make direct innovation-related contributions, others may make indirect ones (e.g., by virtue of their connections to other actors).

S-DL has previously been applied to understand higher education as a customer experience (Ng and Forbes, 2009). A study by Ng and Forbes (2009) showed that the core service in a university experience is a learning experience that is cocreated, and that the value is emergent, unstructured, interactive, uncertain, and possessing a hedonic dimension. Additionally, Jarvis et al. (2014) applied S-DL to conceptualize engagement in large flipped classes. They provided an S-DL-based framework that was implemented in undergraduate marketing courses and showed that the approach fostered co-creation and enhanced the learning experience as well as the learning outcomes, even in very large classes. This framework was used for the evaluation and iterative improvements of an HCI course that we taught until 2017.

This paper contributes to HCI education by proposing a framework based on S-DL that fits the needs for active collaboration with industrial partners and experiential learning when teaching technology-based innovation, including social innovation. The paper is organized as follows. Section 2 describes the course and the key elements that we used for shaping and improving the course. Section 3 proposes an S-DL-based framework for teaching innovation in HCI and describes its main components. Section 4 describes how this framework was used to move our teaching in a more socially responsible direction, respond promptly to changes in the world around us, and bring a new dimension to teaching and learning HCI through value co-creation. Section 5 provides concluding remarks.

2. TEACHING CONTEXT

We taught a project-based HCI course jointly from 2011 until the present. In 2018, the course was fundamentally redesigned and split into two courses, one of which we have continued to teach under the same premises discussed in this paper but with more explicit involvement with the sustainability, social responsibility, and political aspects of innovation in HCI. The second course is taught by others and offers a deeper theoretical grounding in research methods in HCI. From 2011–2017, the course was the third class on interaction design in our bachelor's program in the interaction, use, and design of technology (the prerequisites for taking the course were the introductory course in interaction design based on Sharp et al. (2007) and use-oriented design), and now, it is the fourth course (with a research methods course using Lazar et al. (2010) as an additional prerequisite), offered during the last semester of students' bachelor's education. Until 2017, the course had about 80 students. At present, the course has an upper limit of 40 students. Due to the outbreak of COVID-19 at the start of the 2020 spring semester, the course had to be updated on-the-fly and adjusted to the new situation, while in 2021, it was offered as an online course.

Our original motivation was to provide our students with real-life and meaningful project experiences. Thus, before the start of the course each year, we discussed and identified a set of relevant problems. Once we decided on the potential topics, we recruited organizations, startups, or research organizations participating in large EU or Norwegian Research Council-financed research projects with related and relevant themes. Due to the large number of students in the class until 2017, we needed to recruit at least 10 outside collaborators each year, who were encouraged to provide two distinct project opportunities each. Each year offered both old and new collaborators, engaging over 30 organizations of different sizes and natures (from both the public and private sectors). The students typically worked in teams of four people, in line with the established optimum for experiential team-based learning (Kayes et al., 2005). In what follows, we focus on the opportunities that S-DL thinking and value co-creation in particular allowed us to incrementally transform the course with a deeper awareness of values and their visibility in the course outcomes in the context of the collaborative project.

3. S-DL-BASED FRAMEWORK FOR TEACHING INNOVATION IN HCI

After several years of working with this course, we needed an analytical tool to help us continuously improve the course and adapt it to social and educational changes in a structural way. We thus developed a conceptual framework for teaching innovation in HCI based on Service-Dominant Logic.

Table 1. SLE-based framework for teaching innovation in HCI

Component	Definition	Main issues
Service Ecosystem	A relatively self-adjusting system of industrial and educational actors and beneficiaries of services connected by shared interest in innovation and mutual value co-creation through the development of new technologies and exchange of services.	(1) The service ecosystem needs to consider diverse actors, such as the university, instructors, individual students, student teams, companies/organizations that own the problem, regulatory bodies (NSD), and end-users of proposed solutions as well as the broader society and the environment as parts of the system. (2) The actors need to understand the service ecology. (3) The actors need to understand the situated context of each project. (4) The need to develop a shared system of value expectations and understandings among actors.
Service Platforms	Structures facilitating actors' interactions with resources and/or other factors.	(1) The need to provide structured and efficient approaches for interactions (shared work platforms, blogs, emails, calendars, etc.). (2) The ability to adapt interaction to online-only communication. (3) The need to define clear rules for exchanges (confidentiality and intellectual property agreements among universities, companies, and students), the frequency and content of the supervision provided by companies, and ethics/privacy in contact with end-users and deliveries in the project (the platform for uploading the deliveries and informing the students). (4) Learn to communicate effectively. (5) Learn to relate concrete experiences to more abstract levels of knowledge and the converse. (6) Inclusion, trust, and safety need to be addressed. (7) The need to learn and develop professional conduct.
Value Co-creation	Jointly creating value through interactivity (within a student team, between the team and project stakeholders, and other actors in the ecology).	(1) Define key roles in the project (including roles within the team) and the nature of value co-creation. (2) The need to clearly communicate values and expectations among the involved actors. (3) Use diverse learning pedagogies, including peer-to-peer learning. (4) Assign tasks to different team members according to their skills or learning needs. (5) Discuss the purpose (identify benefits) of the project. (6) Utilize differences and diversity of perspectives and knowledge among design team members. (7) Engage with instructional staff to support design and new knowledge creation. (8) Teams take charge of the process.

Our concern was not about a specific curriculum, but how to use the above key elements of S-DL to design a course that reflected the values that we wanted to impart. Inspired by (Hollebeek and Andreassen (2018), Lusch and Nambisan, (2015), and Vargo and Lusch (2008), using teaching goals for the course and experiences gained from previous courses, we elucidated the following three components of the framework:

service ecosystem (including a broader network of participants than stakeholders e.g., the university strategy makers and social groups), service platforms (representing the set of technologies and platforms used), and value co-creation (covering a broader set of values than just the learning benefits for the students and the potential value of the project outcomes for partner organizations). This is summarized in Table 1. While the framework can be used for other courses, such as project-based engineering courses, we believe that it fits the complexity of the ecosystem needed for teaching innovation to HCI students particularly well.

4. EVALUATING AND IMPROVING THE COURSE

The S-DL-based framework was used as a tool to systematically evaluate and improve the course. It was used to get a bird's-eye perspective of the whole ecosystem and to assess the strengths and weaknesses of our course design for each version of the course. Each year, after the semester and exams were over, we collected feedback from the students, partners, and others contributing to the teaching (teaching assistants and supervisors) on the processes that unfolded in the work on the projects. We also served as supervisors for some of the projects, the ones that were directly related to our own research, which gave us the opportunity to observe students directly in action and make note of any challenging points that might need improvement. Some years, we also felt that we needed to make deeper inquiries to better understand how teams worked with value co-creation and how different actors collaborated and used service platforms. In 2015, we interviewed eight of our industrial and research partners and conducted a survey among all 18 student teams. In 2021, we conducted interviews with partners and students (four groups and three individual interviews: 13 students and three partners in total).

The interviews were conducted in Norwegian or English (depending on the students' preference). The collected qualitative data, including notes, observations, and interviews, were analyzed by the authors of the papers using a simple coding schema matching the framework elements. It should be noted that this evaluation was done in addition to the regular course evaluation completed by an independent student body at the end of each semester. This standard evaluation targets students and cannot reveal the views of other stakeholders, such as industrial and research partners, which are central to the success of such a project-based course. In what follows, we relate the three components of the framework to our course. We then explain how the framework helped us identify strengths and points of improvement in the course design.

4.1 The Service Ecosystem

Our course and the projects included actors such as the university with its teachers and other helpers, administrators, and students (individuals and teams) as well as other actors, such as participating research and industry partners, the Norwegian Data Protection Service (NSD), those people who might benefit from the outcomes of these projects, and, for some projects, others with governance knowledge, law, or expertise. The project beneficiaries represented diverse social groups. Some projects involved children, while others included people with special needs (e.g., patients and such users needed to be met with special care and perhaps additional consents or permits). There were also those who were difficult to recruit for participation for project work due to their busy schedules, such as air traffic controllers, police, oil-engineers, or firemen. This posed additional challenges for design teams and often departed from students' expectations of having situations prearranged for them. Additionally, student teams often had to master new and rather complex domain knowledge, both to support their design processes and to be able to communicate efficiently with field experts. This often presented additional workloads for instructors, internal supervisors, and contact persons in participating organizations. However, we did not find any evidence that students preferred projects in domains that were easier to understand or where the users were more accessible.

Almost always (with a couple of exceptions among 125 projects), the actors in service ecology gained a good understanding of the context for collaboration. Still, for some actors, it was more difficult to respond to the needs of some projects. For example, the regulatory body (NSD) could not change its routines to accommodate student projects, even understanding the project needs. Normally, it takes about four weeks from the submission of the notification form (for projects that require the processing of personal data) to its approval, which is too long for projects where students had only five weeks to deliver the first prototypes or solution sketches. This is an example of a challenge that we could not solve. It was addressed by workarounds—by either avoiding the collection of personal data altogether (for example, taking notes instead of audio recording interviews) or by postponing data collection that involved sensitive data.

4.2 Service Platforms

Apart from the possibilities for face-to-face meetings with instructional staff, students could share their project-related processes with the instructional staff as well as the industrial partners, using blog posts to share their progress regularly. Finding an adequate platform was left up to the students. Many teams preferred simple blogging platforms, such as Tumblr for external communications and Google Docs for internal work. Various scheduling tools, such as Doodle, were frequently used. E-mail was still one of the primary communication channels with partner organizations.

During the pandemic, the communication moved to Zoom and Teams. Figma (the collaborative interface design tool) and Miro (online whiteboard tool) were used for prototyping and sharing ideas. As the first lockdown in Norway began in the middle of the spring semester (March 2020), the students as well as the teachers, partners, and user groups had one week to completely change their project plans. The workshops and focus groups that had already been prepared were replaced with online studies.

Students often thought of partner organizations as clients and themselves as design consultants. Many students remarked that it was motivational to think that way and that it helped them to develop a professional attitude as well as to take the extra mile to learn. For example, they were willing to learn how to use sophisticated platforms that their clients carried out their work on, even if they required extra time and effort, and even if they were not likely to use these programs after the project is over. This was often the case for large organizations with proprietary platforms and specialized work tools.

4.3 Value Co-Creation

Value creation, and later value co-creation, was the most central focus of our efforts when shaping the course. At the start, our goal was to design a course that would benefit students (to create value for students primarily) by providing real-life experiential learning that granted self-efficacy and self-management while providing a good safety network should one be needed. However, through iterative improvements in the course design and formulation of the framework, we started to note more clearly the potential benefits of collaboration for diverse organizations. This enabled us to be clearer and more convincing in getting organizations to partner with us and to actively build and expand networks of potential project contributors, for example, by sharing success stories from previous projects and pointing out their impact. The main motivational factor for the organizations to engage in this collaboration was the possibility of exploring students' novel ideas or the ideas that they had but could not explore due to time or resource constraints.

However, when asked about the benefits of working with students after experiencing the collaboration, the organizations frequently highlighted the importance of students' creativity and the value of their activities for the organization. Many organizations became repeat participants, emphasizing that the projects generated significant value to the organization. The importance of the outcomes of collaborations for organizations could be classified as (1) significant experimental and conceptual explorations, (2) directly or indirectly generated larger research collaborations, and (3) outcomes that were interesting in their own right, either as usable products or experiences. With time, it became clear that beyond creating value for the students and learning only, we could actually talk about the co-creation of values for actors within the ecology, including the public and the university at large. Addressing the latter, every one of the participating organizations said that they would recommend such collaboration with the university to others.

To illustrate how the values were cocreated for diverse actors within the service ecology and how they intended to provide values for social groups or the society at large, Figure 1 gives an example of a project. It addressed the needs of people living in rural, scarcely populated areas for sustainable, convenient, and low-cost transport. It was a part of the research consortium consisting of two universities: a municipality and a hospital.

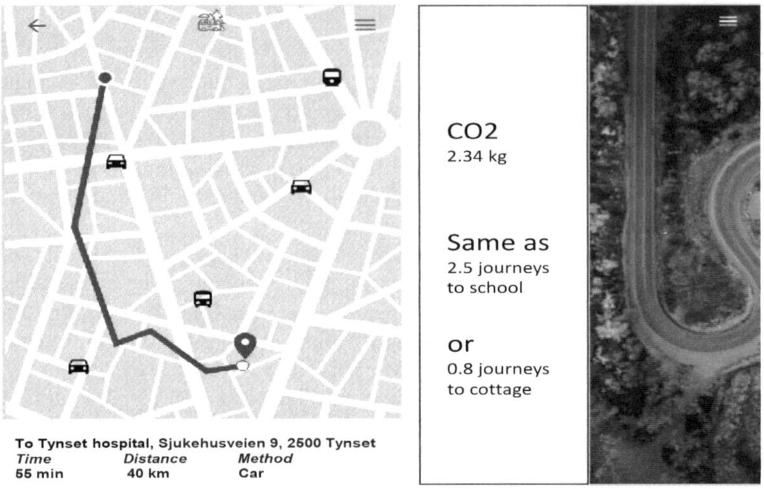

Figure 1. The picture on the left presents the neighbor function of the app. All available cars within a 1-km radius are shown on the map. The picture on the right shows the environmental impact of the selected journey (Ulshagen et al. 2020)

Mobility-as-a-Service (MaaS) is a type of service enabling users to plan, book and pay for different mobility services through a single digital platform. The MaaS app tailored to the transport needs specific to rural areas was developed (see Figure 1). The app uses an optimization tool that calculates possible journeys from point A to point B and the impact of the journey on the environment. Users of transport services can then select their journeys based on different criteria, such as waiting time, travel time, or CO_2 emissions. In their design, the student team considered both the impact on the environment and the impact on the local community.

To make the impact of the projects and co-created value more visible, for the benefit of all involved, we turned the final course presentations into a competition, where, as mentioned, a jury of experts evaluated the projects by novelty, impact, user engagement, and the ability to clearly communicate the central challenges and outcomes of the projects. The competition was followed by a social event, enabling students to meet diverse industrial partners, experts, faculty, and other guests. In this context, we would like to point out that this was also a way to network and identify potential openings for employment (something that happened on several occasions). Trying out a different opportunity regarding the same goal, we organized an open seminar featuring student innovators. Alongside their talks, the seminar included talks by organizations that participated in student projects, startups (some launched by our former students), and the Norwegian Business Association. For the cohorts with smaller numbers of groups (2020 and 2021), instead of having a competition, we invited all the external partners as well as guests from another European university teaching transition design to the presentations of the students' projects at the end of the semester.

4.4 Use of the Framework to Identify Strengths of the Course Design

The framework clearly leveraged value as a tool to evaluate and identify possible pathways to the co-creation of values through different partnerships with external actors. It also helped to compare the expected and actual outcomes of the co-creation. Students, the instructional team, and the industrial partners shared positive feedback on the significance of the projects and, specifically, on the opportunity to co-create values. For example, in a survey conducted in 2015, we asked each student team if it was valuable to collaborate with an industrial partner. The majority of teams found it to be valuable (MED 1; AVG 2.3 on the scale of 1 [totally agree] to 7 [totally disagree]; N = 18 groups). A corresponding question posed to eight partner organizations was answered affirmatively by all. In the interviews conducted in 2021, the students emphasized that a main value from the course, both for them and for the partners, was a gained understanding of how designers can make a real change toward a sustainable future and take the first steps toward such a change. The project results (different prototypes and tools developed in the projects) were of great value to both the students and the partners.

On a smaller scale, the framework allowed us to re-evaluate the course requirements and platforms (e.g., time investments for various actors) and outline how changes that we made affected the course (e.g., one year, we specified that the blog was an obligatory communication platform but found out that while this worked well for some teams, it did not work for others, resulting in just a recommendation to blog the year after). Paying attention to interactions among different actors within the ecology helped us gain insight into the amount of work and time needed by different actors to support the projects effectively (e.g., how many hours for teaching assistants, internal supervisors, etc.). It also enabled us to make clear agreements on working conditions and to attempt to make the conditions equal for all projects.

Among individual elements, the purpose of the project, learning from teammates, and the openness of many on the project, allowing for creative solutions, were most appreciated. In their post-course surveys, post-exam surveys, and the conducted interviews, the students stated that the diversity of skills, knowledge, and experiences within the team created additional value for them and increased both creativity and learning. They found teamwork in real-life settings to be both motivating and fun. One team described their teamwork experiences as follows: "We have a group of different people with different ways of thinking, stirred together in a creative pot, it's awesome!" Another said, "Working in a group has been a good learning experience and really helped us to explore the different ways to design." Still another team found that "It [teamwork] really helps. Quite often you have some ideas, but you need help to be able to explain them. So, in our group we really understood how each other was thinking, and we could really help each other describe and realize our ideas and creativity." The students also emphasized the importance of safe teamwork guidelines and "not killing each other's ideas."

4.5 Use of the Framework to Identify Points of Improvement

The framework helped to elucidate that while diversity (of knowledge, skills, thinking styles) in teams was appreciated and important for value co-creation, diversity in projects had a positive impact but at a sizable time cost. The ecosystems included many actors, leading to an increased workload for the instructional team related to project management. Due to the diversity of the projects, methodologies, eagerness, and skills of the teams, among other factors, the workload grew for students and partners, which we tried to compensate for by providing extra supervision. This added further hours for the instructional team, students, and sometimes the partner organizations as well. In terms of the workload among student teams, those who had the highest motivation and the best results often ended up using a lot more time than expected. The expected workload in the course was 13.5 hours per week, including lectures, work on assignments, readings, and projects. The actual self-reported average workload was as expected (MED: 40 hours per week for all group members [3-4]; MIN: 6; MAX: 70), but for those highly motivated students, the average of 70 hours was too high. The workload became a clear point of improvement, and this is one of the reasons for splitting the course in 2018 and scaling it down. The second reason for the split also emerged clearly from working with our S-DL-based framework—we felt that the situation in the world and in the field of HCI is changing—calling for responsible innovation and responsible teaching of innovation (Bates et al., 2019), and the new course design needed to have a substantially strengthened focus on social values and how to enact positive changes at scale (how to think about enacting changes at scale) toward more sustainable development.

We also decided that the new course would have all the projects dedicated to the same overall topic. For example, the topic in 2020 was 'Artificial Intelligence for Sustainability,' and our partners were invited to come with project proposals addressing this topic in different ways, ranging from healthcare chatbots to AI agents, enabling smart transport in rural areas or waste management. With these more complex projects, the issues of how to teach and learn about responsible innovation come to the forefront. Another point of improvement that emerged was related to first-time partners. It was difficult for us to know exactly how they would work, even when we communicated well about the course and saw great potential for value co-creation. The student feedback on some first-time partners was often somewhat lower, with the main complaint that they sometimes did not dedicate enough time to projects.

On the other hand, some partners also had suggestions for improvement. They expressed a desire to be better informed (by us) about students' abilities regarding their programming experience, design experience,

HCI methods, and other skills. While we recognized the importance and potential challenges that the lack of such information might cause, we could not provide this information in a timely fashion at the start of the course. Massification and mobility in education certainly had an impact on this, as we often had students from other institutions as well as international students. Although we asked all students to describe relevant experiences, skills, and knowledge when selecting a project to work on, their self-assessments did not always match the reality. Also, they often did not always have the skills that we expected (e.g., even though everyone had to have a programming course, not everyone was actually able to program). One of the partners, for example, told us that their team had no programming skills whatsoever, though they expected informatics students to be able to do well with programming. The students, however, were quite creative and delivered a range of ideas and explorations that were highly appreciated. If the partner had possessed this insight, they informed us that they would have written a very different brief to start with. Our master's students had especially varied educational backgrounds (e.g., bachelor's in education, music, art, design, and/or psychology), sometimes to the great benefit of teamwork. However, this made it difficult in terms of course planning in two ways: how to best connect the experiential learning path with a more theoretical and methodological one and how to determine how much work the extra supervision would take.

5. CONCLUDING REMARKS

We believe that the proposed framework fits well with HCI education in times of global change. Our work bears similarities to the research mentioned above on S-DL in higher education, as it focuses on the co-creation of value and the desire to create an engaging and positive learning environment. However, our framework considers multiple factors, where, in addition to the university and students, industrial partners and possibly their customers contribute to the co-creation of value through joint innovation efforts and experiential learning in design teams. It also provides more specific details, enabling its direct application in course design and evaluation. Collaboration with industrial partners brings a current and relevant industry focus to HCI education in a way that is concrete, experiential, and centered on what is of growing importance: co-creating values for all—the students, the partners, the university, and the public—through education. The students also become better prepared for professional practice. With the flipped classroom elements of the course and focus on critical thinking, students felt empowered and more confident in the skills they gained through the course and, most importantly, through the project work. The survey, the course evaluations completed by an independent student body, and interviews with participating organizations all showed that it is precisely the co-creating value that was the most productive aspect of this form of learning. When the projects were successful, students felt a sense of pride and that they were actually contributing to society. In some instances, the student projects have been recognized as innovations and have motivated companies to research, seek grants, or develop products in collaborations across the service ecology. Notably, at the moment, the framework and the iterative approach to making a course allowed us to align with our institute's and university's strategies to scaffold active collaborations between academia and the industry to provide timely, relevant, and responsible contributions to mounting social challenges. As an analytical tool, the framework helped us iteratively to improve the course and adapt it to different challenges in a structured way. For example, it helped us to identify and address the need to shift the focus toward sustainable innovation and the need to quickly adapt work and communication platforms due to the pandemic. In terms of the limitations of the work, the main one is that we can only report on our own experiences with the proposed framework. This limitation also frames opportunities for future work. We hope to be able to observe others using the same framework in their courses to gain a more objective assessment of its usefulness.

ACKNOWLEDGEMENT

We are grateful to all the students and partners who contributed over the years to the work described in this paper. This research was, in part, funded by EEA grant no. EHP-CZ-ICP-2-019 for the project 'Transition Design: A new challenge to service and interaction design education' and by the Research Council of Norway, grant no. 296639, for the project 'Smart Transport in Rural Areas.'

REFERENCES

Bates, O., New, K., Mitchell-Finnigan, S., Mauriello, M.L., Remy, C., Bendor, R., Mann, S., Chopra, S., Clear, A.K., Preist, C., 2019. Towards a Responsible Innovation Agenda for HCI, in: Extended Abstracts of the 2019 *CHI Conference on Human Factors in Computing Systems, CHI EA '19*. ACM, New York, NY, USA, pp. W24:1-W24:8. doi: 10.1145/3290607.3299017

Churchill, E., Preece, J., Bowser, A., 2014. Developing a Living HCI Curriculum to Support a Global Community, in: CHI '14 Extended Abstracts of the 2014 *CHI Conference on Human Factors in Computing Systems, CHI EA '14*. ACM, New York, NY, USA, pp. 135–138. doi: 10.1145/2559206.2559236

Churchill, E.F., Bowser, A., Preece, J., 2016. The future of HCI education: a flexible, global, living curriculum. *interactions 23*, pp. 70–73. doi: 10.1145/2888574

Churchill, E.F., Bowser, A., Preece, J., 2013. Teaching and Learning Human-computer Interaction: Past, Present, and Future. *interactions 20*, pp. 44–53. doi: 10.1145/2427076.2427086

Culén, A.L., Mainsah, H.N., Finken, S., 2014. Design, Creativity and Human Computer Interaction Design Education. *J. Adv. Life Sci.* V 6 N 34 2014 6, pp. 97–106.

Breidbach, F.C., Brodie, R., Hollebeek, L., 2014. Beyond virtuality: from engagement platforms to engagement ecosystems. *Manag. Serv. Qual.* 24, pp. 592–611.

Gray, C.M., Toombs, A.L., Owczarzak, M., Watkins, C., 2019. Digital civics goes abroad. *interactions 26*, pp. 74–77. doi: 10.1145/3301661

Hollebeek, L.D., Andreassen, T.W., 2018. The SD logic-informed "hamburger" model of service innovation and its implications for engagement and value. *J. Serv. Mark.* 32, pp. 1–7.

Hollebeek, L.D., Srivastava, R.K., Chen, T., 2019. S-D logic–informed customer engagement: integrative framework, revised fundamental propositions, and application to CRM. *J. Acad. Mark. Sci.* 47, pp. 161–185.

Irwin, T., 2018. The Emerging Transition Design Approach, in: *Design Research Society 2018: Catalyst*, pp. 968–989. doi: 10.21606/drs.2018.210

Jarvis, W., Halvorson, W., Sadeque, S., Johnston, S., 2014. A large class engagement (LCE) model based on service-dominant logic (SDL) and flipped classrooms. *Educ. Res. Perspect.* 41, pp. 1.

Kayes, A.B., Kayes, D.C., Kolb, D.A., 2005. Experiential learning in teams. *Simul. Gaming* 36, pp. 330–354. doi: 10.1177/1046878105279012

Lazar, J., Feng, D.J.H., Hochheiser, D.H., 2010. *Research Methods in Human-Computer Interaction.* John Wiley & Sons.

Lusch, R.F., Nambisan, S., 2015. Service innovation: A service-dominant logic perspective. MIS Q. 39.

Ng, I.C.L., Forbes, J., 2009. Education as Service: The Understanding of University Experience Through the Service Logic. *J. Mark. High. Educ.* 19, pp. 38–64. https://doi.org/10.1080/08841240902904703

Ordanini, A., Parasuraman, A., 2011. Service innovation viewed through a service-dominant logic lens: a conceptual framework and empirical analysis. *J. Serv. Res.* 14, pp. 3–23.

Rosenberg, D., 2016. Educating for HCI at scale. *interactions 23*, pp. 72–75. doi: 10.1145/2931081

Sharp, H., Rogers, Y., Preece, J., 2007. *Interaction Design: Beyond Human-Computer Interaction*, 2nd ed. Wiley.

St-Cyr, O., MacDonald, C.M., Churchill, E.F., 2019. EduCHI 2019 Symposium: Global Perspectives on HCI Education, in: Extended Abstracts of the 2019 CHI Conference on Human Factors in Computing Systems, CHI EA '19. Association for Computing Machinery, New York, NY, USA, pp. 1–7. doi: 10.1145/3290607.3298994

Ulshagen, A., Justnæs, N.S., Walmann, J.C., Nagafi, B.Y., TiD, Transport i distriktene, Rapport IN3010 - Transformativt design, 2020. (in Norwegian)

Vargo, S.L., Lusch, R.F., 2008. Service-dominant logic: continuing the evolution. *J. Acad. Mark. Sci.* 36, pp. 1–10.

WEB-BASED REMOTE SHIP HANDLING SUPPORT SYSTEM USING MOBILE DATA COMMUNICATION

Tsuyoshi Miyashita[1], Ryota Imai[1], Masaki Kondo[2] and Tadasuke Furuya[3]
[1] *Graduate School of Marine Science and Technology, Tokyo University of Marine Science and Technology, 2-1-6, Etchujima, Koto-ku, Tokyo, Japan*
[2] *National Institute of Technology, Toba College, 1-1 Ikegamicho, Toba, Mie, Japan*
[3] *Tokyo University of Marine Science and Technology, 2-1-6, Etchujima, Koto-ku, Tokyo, Japan*

ABSTRACT

Nowadays, in Japan, the coastal shipping industry has problems reducing the ship's crew and aging. The closed sea areas in central bays and ports in Japan are navigated by many ships. In these waters, an inexperienced ship operator may make a mistake in judgment due to extreme tension, which may cause a marine accident. In this study, as a proposal for such a situation, the authors made a prototype to provide ship operators on board with maneuvering assistance from shore. It was developed by using wireless and mobile communication, VPN, and web browser. We conducted an actual ship experiment in the actual sea as a verification, and its effectiveness was discussed. It was shown that maneuvering about the same level as onboard as possible. As a result, it was confirmed that this method could be effective by future improvements.

KEYWORDS

ICT, Computer Application, Information Support

1. INTRODUCTION

Approximately 85% of the marine accidents of cargo ships in Japan were caused by human factors such as inadequate lookout and improper maneuvering (Japan Coast Guards, 2019 Status and Countermeasures for Marine Accidents, 2020). Also, 54% of accidents were attributable to human actions (European Maritime Safety Agency, Annual Overview of Marine Casualties and Incidents 2020, 2020), illustrating a similar trend in other parts of the world. In addition, the steady increase in the world's marine transport volume suggests that the number of seafarers worldwide will become tighter in the future.

Under these circumstances, the spread of Automatic Identification System (AIS) for tracking ships and Electronic Chart Display and Information System (ECDIS) for displaying nautical charts, as well as rapid advances in maritime broadband communication, IoT, AI, and big data processing technologies, especially in Europe, have stimulated efforts to realize autonomous ships. MUNIN (MUNIN, 2016) and AAWA (AAWA, 2016) have conducted conceptual studies mainly as part of an industry-academia-government collaboration project. At the same time, the primary corporate efforts toward practical application include SVAN (SVAN, 2018) by Rolls-Royce Commercial Marine (now Kongsberg Maritime), Yara International, and Yara Birkeland by Kongsberg.

In Japan, on the other hand, the Ministry of Land, Infrastructure, Transport and Tourism's roadmap for the commercialization of autonomous ships indicates that Phase II will proceed after 2020 (Ministry of Land, Infrastructure, Transport and Tourism, follow-up to June 3, 2016 report, 2018). A feature of Phase II autonomous ships is that, while the final decision-maker will still be the ship's crew, they will be more closely linked to shore and will be able to directly operate onboard equipment as well as monitor it from shore. In addition, the onboard computer and network environments will be further enhanced and integrated. The amount of data collected by various sensors is expected to be greater than that of Phase I autonomous ships.

The closed waters of Tokyo Bay and other significant bays and harbors in Japan are navigated by many ships. It is a crucial traffic area where incoming and outgoing vessels and shipping routes intersect. In addition to the complex submarine topography and narrow waters, many fishing grounds are in the bay. These waters can quickly become a source of maritime accidents for inexperienced navigators due to maneuvering errors and carelessness caused by tension and stress. Navigators are trained over a long period through joint work and instruction on board with knowledgeable and experienced navigators. However, coastal shipping faces a severe problem of an aging seafarer population and a shortage of seafarers. They do not have as much time to work together and teach as before. To ensure navigation safety and provide a place to gain experience, the authors are researching ways an older but more experienced person can assist an inexperienced navigator onboard a ship from shore.

There has been a lot of research on autonomous ships and remote control of ships from shore, as described above. The ultimate goal of these studies is to develop autonomous ocean-going vessels. While this is ideal, there are problems with the cost of construction, modification, and operation. For example, even though AIS is becoming more and more popular, many small vessels are not required to be equipped with AIS. Satellite communication, which can cover the entire ocean, has the problem of high communication costs. Under these circumstances, rather than aiming for autonomous ships, it is more practical and effective to provide ship handling support from the shore for safe navigation while constantly exchanging and providing information through two-way communication with vessels within the range of mobile communication.

LTE and 3G wireless communications are available in coastal waters within a few kilometers of land. With this in mind, the signal strength and status of mobile communications in Tokyo Bay have been continuously surveyed (Ohshima, 2015, Ohshima, 2020). From the results of these surveys, it has been confirmed that there are areas where high-quality communications are not available. It is currently challenging to ensure stable and sufficient communication speed at sea. Since the final decision-maker is the navigator on board the ship, if the disruption of mobile communications is temporary, the navigator on board can navigate the vessel with authority to steer. We believe that a work-around is possible, in which the ship's navigation rights are transferred to shore when communications are restored.

This study designed and fabricated a prototype system that can transmit ship handling assistance and steering signals from shore. Mobile data communication is used for communication. Navigational information, engine information, and ship circumference images are displayed on a web browser. Maneuvering instructions are also given via the web browser. The system enables ship handling support with the Internet and a Web browser without being restricted to a specific location or device. In addition, we verified the remote control of the rudder (heading) and CPP (speed and velocity) on an actual ship sailing in Tokyo Bay and examined its effectiveness.

2. REMOTE SHIP HANDLING SUPPORT SYSTEM

We constructed our prototype system between the training ship "SHIOJI MARU" owned by the Faculty of Marine Engineering, Tokyo University of Marine Science and Technology, and the Number 3 Research Building on the Etchujima Campus of the same university and tried to display the voyage/engine data of SHIOJI MARU during the voyage and to realize remote ship handling support. This chapter describes the configuration of the prototype system.

Figure 1 shows the outline of the prototype system. The upper part of the figure is the SHIOJI MARU side, and the lower part is the land side. The data collection program of the experimental server of the prototype system (hereinafter referred to as the ship server) placed on SHIOJI MARU side in the figure collected AIS, GPS (Global Positioning System), ARPA (Automatic Radar Plotting Aids), voyage/engine data, etc., and sent them to the experimental building via WebSocket communication using mobile data communication. In addition, the image of the surroundings of the ship acquired from the camera, the image of radar echo, and the image of ECDIS were transmitted by HTTP streaming. A total of about 155 kbps data (Oishi, 2016), 144.6 kbps video data JPEG-compressed with a frame rate of about 15 fps and a resolution of 1500 x 300, 2.7 kbps voyage/engine data, and about 6.8 kbps AIS received data, were transmitted from the ship to land.

On the contrary, WebSocket communication was also used to send the hull control message for maneuvering from the experimental building to SHIOJI MARU. Mobile data communication in this case is consumer mobile data communication. The transmission speed is about 150 Mbps for downlink and 50 Mbps for uplink according to the catalog specifications, and there is no bandwidth guarantee due to the best effort method, communication restrictions, and communication regulations.

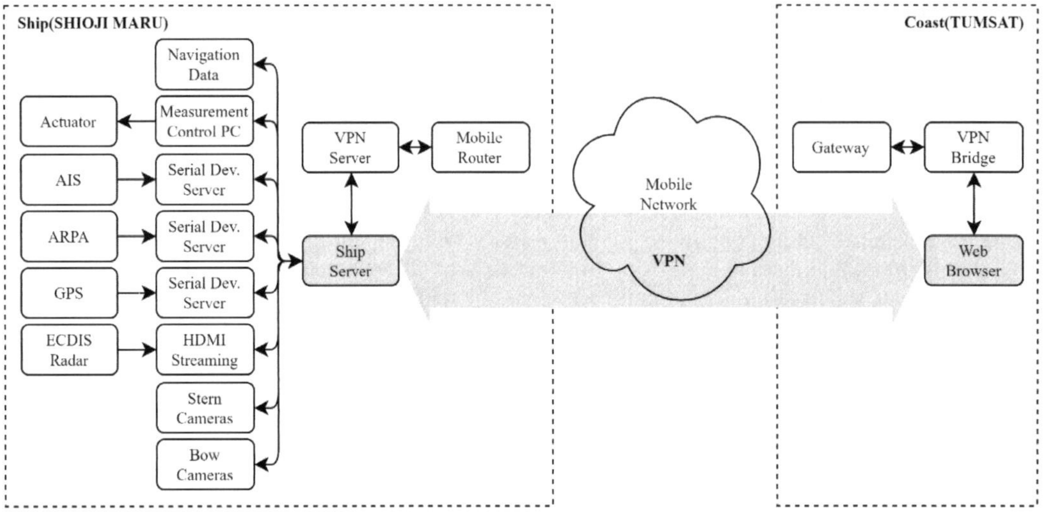

Figure 1. Configuration of remote ship handling support system

SHIOJI MARU is equipped with a measurement control server PC that aggregates the information measured by the navigation instrument and can control the rudder angle, CPP, and thruster (hereinafter referred to as a measurement control PC). By connecting this measurement control PC and the server of the prototype system via LAN and performing UDP communication, the state variables of the hull and the response values such as rudder and CPP required for maneuvering can be input to the ship server. Conversely, by sending a control message (64 bytes binary data) including the rudder angle and CPP control values from the ship server to the measurement control PC, the rudder of SHIOJI MARU can be controlled since the rudder angle and CPP can be input to the steering panel of the bridge via the measurement control PC.

2.1 Display of Voyage/Engine Data

When maneuvering a ship, it is necessary to know the data on which the decision is based. If you are a ship officer, you will monitor various navigation instruments inside the bridge. Of these, data essential for remote monitoring and decision-making during maneuvering is selected and displayed. A general Web browser is used for the display. As one of the communication standards for computer networks called WebSocket (IETF RFC6455, The WebSocket Protocol, 2011), it was newly added in HTML5 (HTML Living Standard: 9.3 Web sockets, The WebSocket Protocol, 2019) and is supported mainly by recent Web browsers. By using this communication standard, two-way communication between the server and client is possible in real-time. This communication is conditional on use in a VPN environment to prevent attacks from the outside to intentionally damage the browser.

HTTP communication from the Web browser is used for the initial request processing, and the subsequent processing is handed over by WebSocket and used for the sequential display of voyage/engine data. At this time, it is not necessary to reload the screen of the Web browser each time. In addition, there will be a screen where the land and ship can send canned messages to each other to let each other know what is going on, and a screen that displays a real-time graph of the round-trip delay time of the ping to keep track of the current communication status. Figure 2 shows an example of a web browser screen for remote control support. The top row is a browser screen displaying images of the ship's surroundings taken by a camera. To the right of the middle row is a browser screen displaying navigation and engine data, which collects information measured by various navigation devices. To the left of this is the browser screen used for ship handling instructions. For example, by selecting or inputting the rudder angle and CPP and clicking on the button on the browser, the control signals for rudder angle and CPP are sent to control the ship. Finally, the bottom row shows the ECDIS and radar screen streaming.

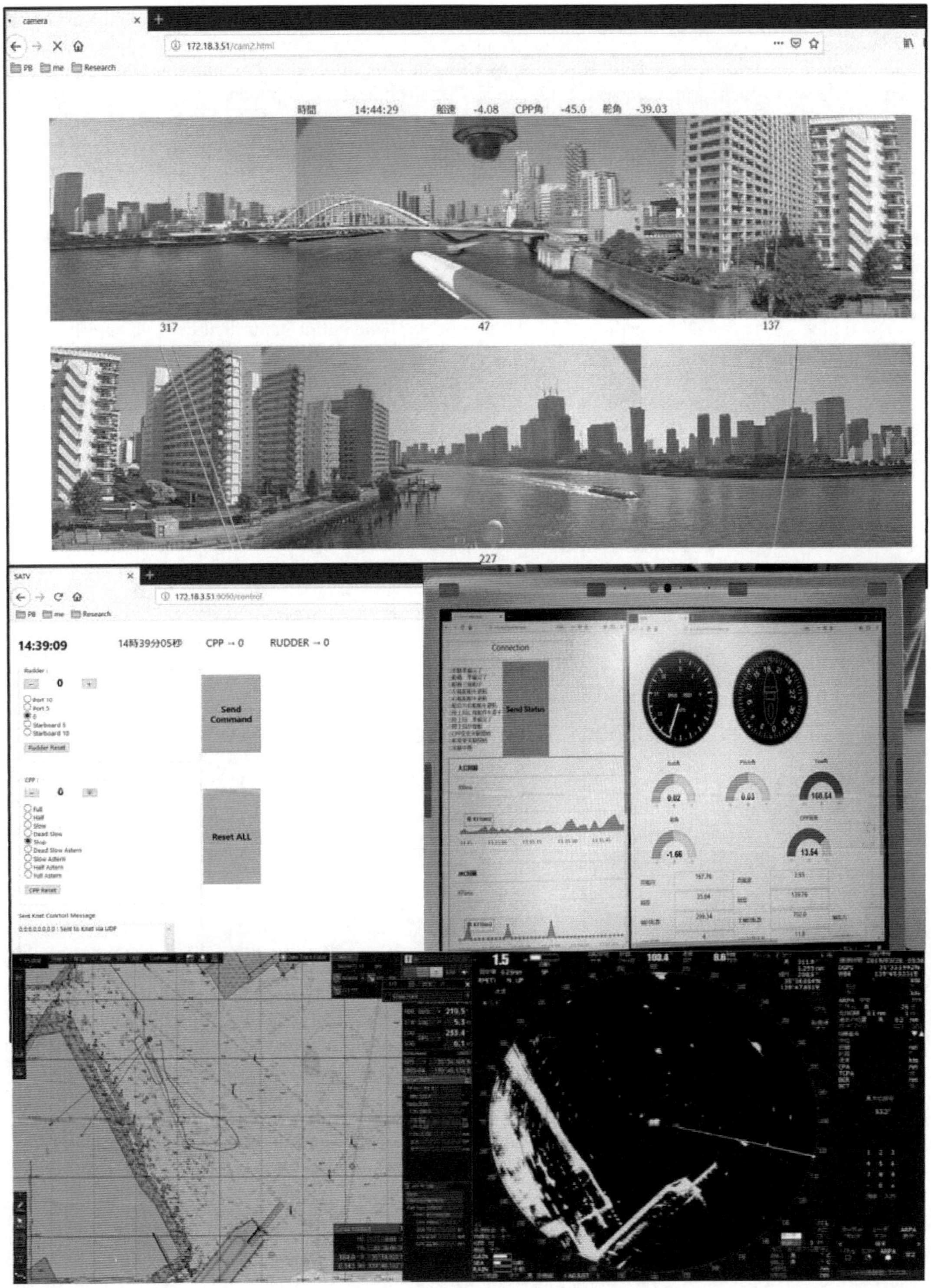

Figure 2. Example of a browser screen used during remote ship operation

On the actual bridge, the navigators must approach each instrument on board to obtain information. Sometimes, they observe the movements of other ships that they can watch windows. Therefore, multiple navigators are active on the bridge. However, by consolidating information on one console, it is possible to navigate a ship with a small number of navigators. To transition from traditional operations less cumbersome for the navigator, building an interface with a computer screen with steering and watching the ship is necessary. We created and modified the interface based on interviews with experienced captains. In addition, in a real ship, the navigator can feel the effects of sway and wind. Therefore, we have created a visual interface that allows the navigator to intuitively understand the ship's state, which cannot be felt in remote areas.

2.2 Hull Control

The proposed system enables remote maneuvering in an emergency. We are using bidirectional communication between the server and client made possible by WebSocket. The hull is controlled by sending a fixed-length binary message of 64 bytes, including control values such as rudder angle and CPP to the actuator command program of SHIOJI MARU measurement control PC from a Web browser. Communication to the actuator command program to control SHIOJI MARU hull is limited to 64 bytes fixed-length binary messages by UDP to a specific port according to the manufacturer's specifications.

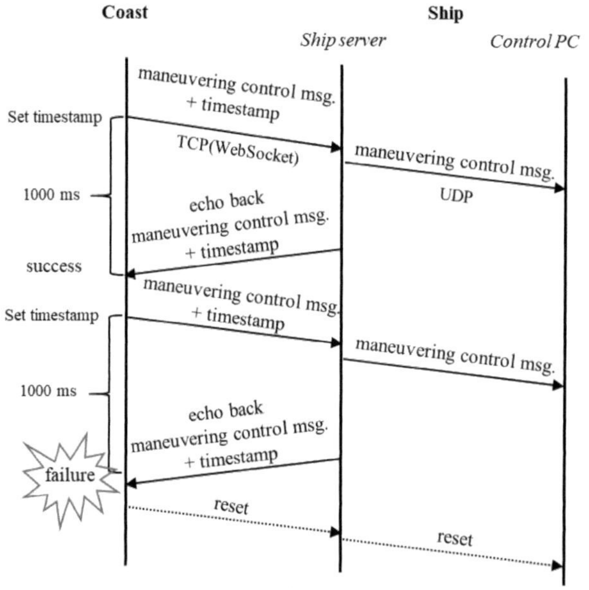

Figure 3. Configuration of remote ship handling support system

When using mobile data communication at sea, the occurrence of communication interruption cannot be ignored depending on the ship's position. In particular, care must be taken in handling when a communication interruption occurs during the transmission of a control signal. Therefore, keepalive messages are exchanged between ships and land. If the response cannot be received within a certain period, it is judged that the communication is interrupted, and the reconnection process is performed.

Furthermore, to ensure that the control message reaches the experimental server at the application layer, the control is shown in Figure 3 is implemented. First, the control message is sent with a timestamp generated by the client's JavaScript. The experimental server returns the received control message and time stamp to the client as an ACK. If the client gets the ACK within 1 second, it considers it successful and prepares to send the following control message. If ACK is returned for more than 1 second, a control message with all zeros is sent, and an alert is displayed on the browser. The ACK restriction is set to 1 second or less because it was found in the experiment that the average round-trip delay time of the control message was about 0.3 seconds in Section 3.3.

3. EXPERIMENT

In the system prototyped in this study, an actual ship experiment was conducted to examine the usefulness of remote control. The ship used for the experiment is the training ship "SHIOJI MARU" owned by the Faculty of Marine Engineering, Tokyo University of Marine Science and Technology. In this experiment, first, the left turn was performed by inputting the rudder angle by remote control, and the speed was increased by inputting CPP. It was confirmed whether the bow direction and the shipping speed changed according to the input. Next, the round-trip delay time of the ship handling control message between the ship server was measured from the Web browser between the ship and land. A seamen's competency certificate holder carried out ship handling. Figure 4 shows the maneuvering scenery.

Figure 4. Remote control scenery

Figure 5 illustrates the track and route displayed on the ECDIS during remote maneuvering and the route with the course change points and course annotated. The counterclockwise experiment at point B in Figure 5 is described in Section 3.1, and the acceleration experiment by CPP from point A is described in Section 3.2, although the order is reversed.

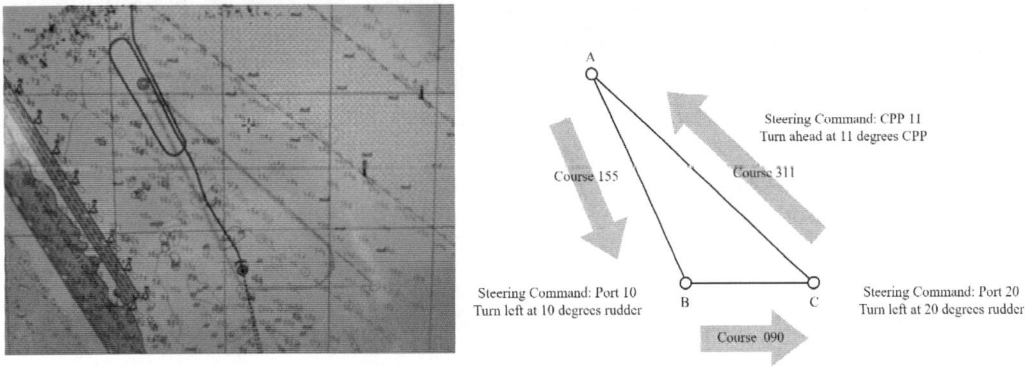

Figure 5. Routes / tracks by ECDIS and route illustrations

3.1 Left Rotation Experiment by Rudder Angle Input

In remote maneuvering using mobile data communication, a left rotation experiment using Port 10° was conducted to examine whether it is possible to achieve the same level of rudder angle input to the steering panel inside the bridge. The results of turning left are shown in Figure 6. Figure 6 shows the relationship between the rudder angle and the bow direction according to the time series on the horizontal axis. The solid bathtub line indicates the rudder angle, and the dashed line that descends to the right shows the bow direction. It can be seen from the response value of the measurement control PC that the rudder is responding within 2 seconds after the control message is transmitted when turning counterclockwise. In addition, it can be said that the direction of the bow is changing without causing any particular delay in the change of course itself.

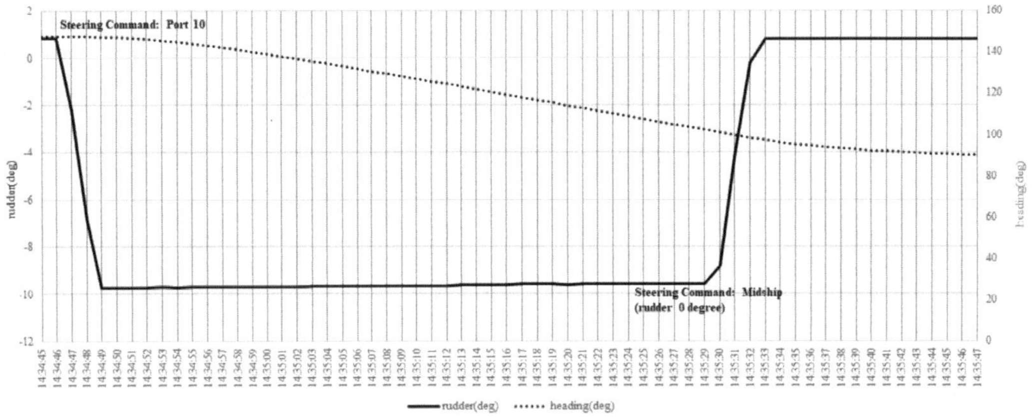

Figure 6. Rudder angle and bow direction

3.2 Acceleration Experiment by CPP Input

Next, a speed-up experiment with Pitch 11° of CPP was conducted in the manner of 3.1. CPP stands for controllable pitch propeller, and by changing the blade angle, the ship's speed can be increased or decreased. The results are shown in Figure 7. Figure 7 shows the relationship between CPP and ship speed according to the time series on the horizontal axis. The solid line at the top shows the CPP, and the dashed line at the bottom shows the ship's speed.

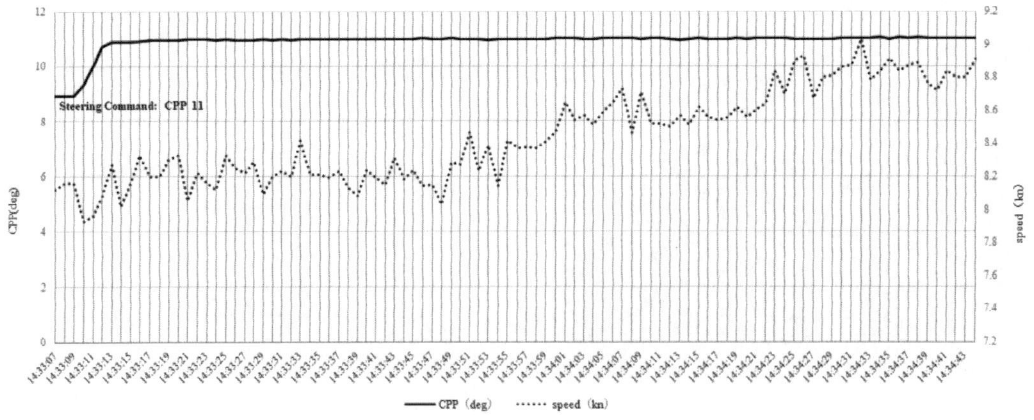

Figure 7. CPP and ship speed

As in 3.1, it can be seen from the response value of the measurement control PC that the CPP is responding within 2 seconds after sending the control message. It can also be seen that the shipping speed is also increasing in chronological order.

3.3 Round-Trip Delay Time for Maneuvering Control Messages

To investigate the round-trip delay time of mobile data communication between SHIOJI MARU ship server from the Web browser, the round-trip delay time of the 72-bytes ship handling control message, including the time stamp at the time of transmission, as measured by the following procedure. First, the ship handling screen of the Web browser is operated to send a maneuvering control message with a rudder angle of 1° to the experiment server. This maneuver control message contains a timestamp of the time the Web browser submit button was clicked. The ship server that received the ship handling control message extracts the 64 bytes required to control the hull by sending it to the measurement control PC from the received message and then sends it to the measurement control PC as binary data via UDP.

At the same time, the received message is sent back to the Web browser as it is. The Web browser records the time when the echo back from the experiment server is received as a time stamp. To determine that the echoed back maneuvering control message is the same as the one transmitted, it is determined whether or not the timestamps in the message are equal. In this experiment, the difference between the time recorded at the time of transmission and the time at which the Web browser received the echo back was measured as the round-trip delay time. iperf is a benchmarking tool for round trips. Although we used iperf for the measurements, we also used our measurement program to understand the round-trip delay time between the web browser and the server on the ship.

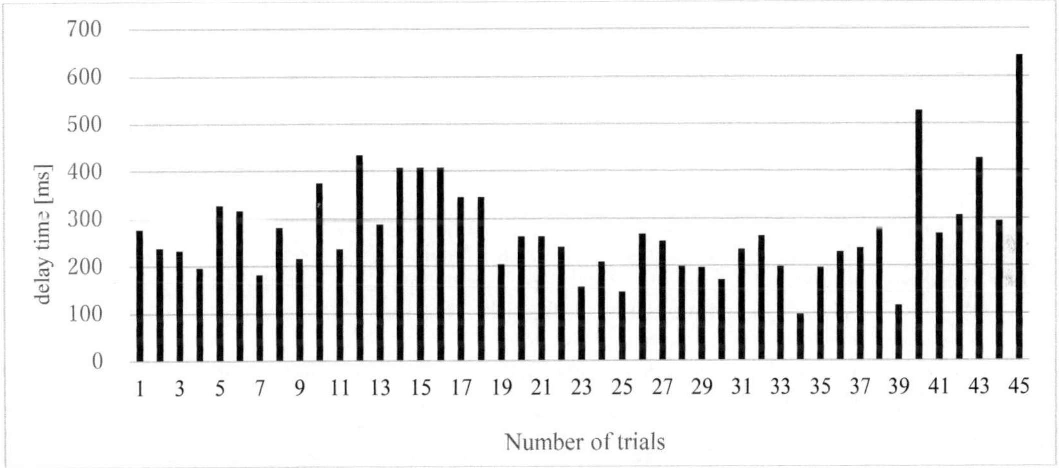

Figure 8. Round-trip delay time between ship and land

The measurement results are shown in Figure 8. The horizontal axis is the number of trials, and the vertical axis is the round-trip delay time. Around 21:00 on June 18, 2019, when trying to send and receive dummy messages 45 times between SHIOJI MARU and a web browser while anchored off Tateyama, the round-trip delay time was 0.3 seconds on average, 0.7 seconds maximum, and 0.1 seconds minimum.

4. CONCLUSION

In this research, we built a prototype system that enables advanced information sharing and ship handling support between ship and land from various locations using mobile data communication and general-purpose software such as Web browsers toward the practical application of autonomous ships. In addition, we conducted a field experiment to investigate the feasibility of providing ship handling support by issuing steering commands from the coast.

First, experienced captains who used this system evaluated it as a good interface for ship handling. They also believe that the ship operation using this interface is also good. The main functions that we specifically realized are shown below.

- A screen that allows non-follow-up steering (without using Helm)
- A screen to grasp the communication status
- Display of the bow direction together with the camera image

Next, from these experiments, the following main conclusions were obtained.

A) It is possible to transfer information necessary for navigation between land and sea using mobile data communication. However, the communication state may become unstable and interrupted due to the influence of other communications in the sea area. In the future, it is necessary to ensure good communication at all times through the spread of 5G communication and the installation of high-precision communication antennas.

B) The main navigational information necessary for ship operation collected at sea was generally reproduced on land.

C) The maneuvering control message sent from land can be received on board, and the response can be confirmed by the voyage information sent from the ship.

D) Real-time transmission of images by web cameras and radar is not possible at present because of the large data capacity. However, it was found that there was no significant problem in remote ship handling support even if images were transmitted at regular time intervals.

E) The transmission of navigational information about other ships, such as AIS, GPS and ECDIS/Radar Streaming, is good. The information displayed on the ship could be reproduced on land.

F) A left rotation experiment with rudder angle input and a speed-up experiment with CPP input were conducted by remote control, and the rudder and CPP responded within 2 seconds. Course change and speed increase can be controlled without any delay.

G) The possible effect of a delay of up to 2 seconds is when changing course; on the scale of SHOJI MARU, a course change of 10 degrees will lead to a delay in the decision to maneuver because of the fast-turning response. However, large angle course changes are not made in actual ship operations. However, large angle course changes are not made in actual ship operations, because a route with small course changes is selected. Therefore, a delay of 2 seconds is acceptable.

H) As a result of the measurement experiment of the round-trip delay time between the ship (ship server) and the land (Web browser), the average round-trip delay time by mobile data communication is 0.3 seconds. The Web browser is required to receive the arrival confirmation of the control message for maneuvering within 1 second, but since the ACK response can be received within the range, the effect on remote maneuvering is small.

The above shows the possibility of remote ship handling support using a web browser as an interface and mobile data communication between ship and shore. However, in this experiment, the rudder and CPP are mainly verified. In the future, it will be necessary to increase the number of functions to be verified in consultation with the training ship and evaluate its effectiveness.

As a future issue, adding the function to display the received AIS data on the browser can be considered. As an alternative, we are streaming ECDIS video, but we would like to eliminate this. Furthermore, AIS-equipped ship information will be superimposed and displayed on the voyage image displayed on the browser, and the display of AIS-non-equipped ships detected by image recognition will be examined in the future.

ACKNOWLEDGEMENT

We would like to express our gratitude to the crew members of SHIOJI MARU, who cooperated in the experiment in advancing this research.

REFERENCES

AAWA, 2016, Remote and Autonomous Ships The next steps, [online] Available at https://www.rolls-royce.com/~/media/Files/R/Rolls-Royce/documents/customers/marine/ship-intel/aawa-whitepaper-210616.pdf [Accessed 25 Jun. 2021].

European Maritime Safety Agency, 2020. Annual Overview of Marine Casualties and Incidents, [online] Available at http://emsa.europa.eu/publications/reports/item/4266-annual-overview-of-marine-casualties-and-incidents-2020.html [Accessed 21 May. 2021].

HTML Living Standard: 9.3 Web sockets, 2019. The WebSocket Protocol, [online] Available at https://html.spec.whatwg.org/multipage/web-sockets.html#network [Accessed 21 May. 2021].

IETF RFC6455, 2011. The WebSocket Protocol, [online] Available at https://tools.ietf.org/html/rfc6455 [Accessed 21 May. 2021].

Japan Coast Guards, 2020. 2019 Status and Countermeasures for Marine Accidents, [online] Available at https://www6.kaiho.mlit.go.jp/info/keihatsu/20200511_state_measure01.pdf [Accessed 21 May. 2021]. (in Japanese)

Kuroda, H. et al, 2020, LTE Radio Field Intensity Investigation for Improving Multipath Communication at Sea. In The journal of Japan Institute of Navigation, Vol. 142, pp 67-78. (in Japanese)

Ministry of Land, Institute, Transport and Tourism, 2018. Initiatives to be Promoted for Deepening the Productivity Revolution in the Maritime Industry - Follow-up to the Report of June 3, 2016, [online] Available at https://www.mlit.go.jp/common/001237409.pdf [Accessed 21 May. 2021]. (in Japanese)

MUNIN Project, 2016, MUNIN Final Brochure, [online] Available at http://www.unmanned-ship.org/munin/wp-content/uploads/2016/02/MUNIN-final-brochure.pdf [Accessed 25 Jun. 2021].

Ohshima, K. et al, 2015, 3G Radio Field Intensity Measurement Experiment in Coastal Waters of Tokyo. In The journal of Japan Institute of Navigation, Vol. 136, pp 72-79. (in Japanese)

Oishi, H. et al, 2016. Navigational Data Display System between Ships and Land Using Mobile Data Communication. *In IEEE Transactions on Data and Knowledge Engineering*, Vol. 135, pp 156-165. (in Japanese)

SVAN, 2018, Rolls-Royce and Finferries demonstrate world's first Fully Autonomous Ferry, [online] Available at https://www.rolls-royce.com/media/press-releases/2018/03-12-2018-rr-and-finferries-demonstrate-worlds-first-fully-autonomous-ferry.aspx [Accessed 25 Jun. 2021].

MAGVI: TOWARDS SALIENCY-DRIVEN VIDEO MAGNIFICATION APPLICATION FOR THE PEOPLE WITH LOW VISION

Prajakta Thakur, Tanay Dalvi, Varun John and Swati Chandna
SRH University Heidelberg, Germany

ABSTRACT

Interacting with dynamic content such as videos, movies is very challenging for people with low vision. While screen magnifier software enables visually impaired people to pan and zoom the static content, such as text and images. They still lack efficient and intuitive means to pan and zoom over the dynamic content such as videos, movies, or YouTube videos. Therefore, a new approach is needed to enable people with low vision to interact with the dynamic content with ease. This paper presents a concept of the fully integrated application called as MagVi which aims towards making dynamic content accessible. This is composed of two main components; the first component is the video magnification application that uses the video saliency models to automatically identify the salient Region of Interests (ROI) in different videos. The second component of this application allows visually impaired users to view the identified ROI in a mobile application and also to dynamically pan and zoom, change the font size of the text throughout the application.
The quantitative and qualitative evaluation with five low vision people revealed that the application was considered effective and efficient to use. Our approach has enabled people with low vision to pan and zoom over the dynamic content from a mobile phone which indicates the potential of making videos accessible to visually impaired people.

KEYWORDS

Low Vision, Intelligent User Interface, Video Magnification, Video Saliency

1. INTRODUCTION

Low Vision is defined by the National Eye Institute as a bilateral visual impairment that is defined as visual acuity of less than 0.3 (6/18, 0.5 logMAR) but better than 0.05 (3/60, 1.3log MAR) (Crossland et. al. 2011). Enhancing the vision through low vision aids helps people with low vision lead a better life. Magnification is one such way that helps objects appear better. In low vision practice, the magnification increases the size of the retinal image outside the damaged area to enable patients to see and read.

A substantial amount of data in the form of videos has been generated in recent years at an incredible speed to provide accessibility of dynamic content to people. The major challenge lies in addressing one of the fundamental questions "How to enable people with low vision to watch dynamically changing content". The heterogeneous nature and size of the videos and the need to watch these videos in a magnified mode is the main challenge.

There exist various screen magnifiers, such as ZoomText. These magnifiers magnify the original content but lack the ability to watch the enlarged content without using keyboard or mouse actions. Therefore, this paper develops an intelligent user interface called MagVi - Video Magnification Application for people with low vision. This interface supports the idea of making dynamic content accessible. The main objective of MagVi is to identify the regions of interest in the video and show these identified regions in a magnified form directly in a mobile interface.

2. RELATED WORK

There exist various magnification aids for people with low vision. These include low-tech optical magnifiers, desktop video systems, and now the cameras of the smartphones are used recently to serve the purpose. Closed-circuit television (CCTV) project images from a static image onto a large screen. Such systems allow users to adjust the position, magnification level. But, the actual content differs from the content which is magnified. Also, these devices are not portable; this causes difficulty in reading longer text and also searching for specific text. Smartphones also increasingly support magnification for low vision users. Apple and Android phones now include a built-in magnifier, and numerous free or low-cost third-party apps are available in the Apple or Google stores. Unlike dedicated handheld magnifiers, these smartphone-based solutions are cheaper, do not require carrying an additional device, and are likely to draw less attention to the user. However, they present other similar disadvantages to dedicated handheld magnifiers. The focus of all the aforementioned screen magnifier applications is either on static content or requiring the user to adjust the magnifier manually. SViM, a magnifier interface, is utilized to show the distinctive recognized ROIs, and move the focal point of the magnifier to these ROIs on user's demands mouse clicks. (Aydin et. al. 2000) addressed a few of these limitations by introducing SViM screen magnifier which could show distinctive recognized ROIs and move the focal point of the magnifier to these ROIs on user's demands by mouse clicks. In contrast, MagVi automatically identifies regions of interest in videos. It pushes these regions to MagVi smartphone application, allowing users to view the identified ROI in magnified mode.

3. MAGVI DESIGN AND IMPLEMENTATION

MagVi application is designed through a user-centered process to make videos more accessible to visually impaired or low vision people who use screen magnifiers. It is composed of several components that first determines the ROIs and then these ROIs are exhibited in a mobile application to ensure the effortless transition between the detected regions of interest when the video is watched.

The overview of the MagVi design is shown in Figure 1. It is composed of two major components: *the backend cloud* that uses the video saliency model to underline the salient aspects of the video, *the MagiVi app* that fetches the video from the file explorer/Assets/URL and pushes the video to backend to detect the regions of interest. Later, these detected ROIs are received by the *MagiVi app* to perform zooming and panning or switching between the detected ROIs.

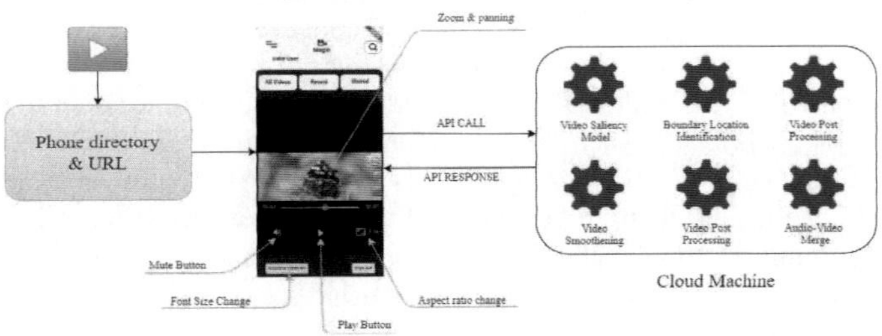

Figure 1. The overview of the MagVi Application Interface

3.1 Video Saliency in Backend

The human visual system employs visual attention mechanisms to effectively deal with huge amount of information by focusing only on attention-grabbing parts of a scene. These parts of a scene are called salient parts (Jiang et. al. 2018) Video saliency models aim to predict attention grabbing or salient parts of a video. Initially, saliency models were simply extensions of static saliency approaches like (Guo et. al. 2008), (Cui et al. 2009), (Seo et. al. 2009). These methods used static scenes for initial processing and applied the processed result on 3D feature maps, or optical flow images. These works were followed up by dynamic saliency detection methods which employed either data-driven techniques or spatio-temporal features to learn relevant features. Some examples of these methods include methods proposed by (Mathe et. al. 2012), (Rudoy et. al. 2013) and (Leboran et. al. 2017). The current state-of-the-art for video saliency models employs deep learning models which are trained to predict saliency in images and videos. Two such models which use CNNs trained on human fixation maps were proposed by (Huang et. al. 2015) and (Pan et. al. 2016). Another method that uses the long short-term memory (LSTM) model for sequential modelling of video frames was proposed by (Hochreiter et. al. 1997).

This paper uses DeepVS (Jiang et. al. 2018) which is an object-to-motion CNN that contains two subnets, one for modeling objectness and another for modeling motion respectively; the combined outputs of the two subnets are then provided as input to an LSTM model. Figure 2 shows the basic flow of the Video Saliency backend. It consists of three main functionalities.

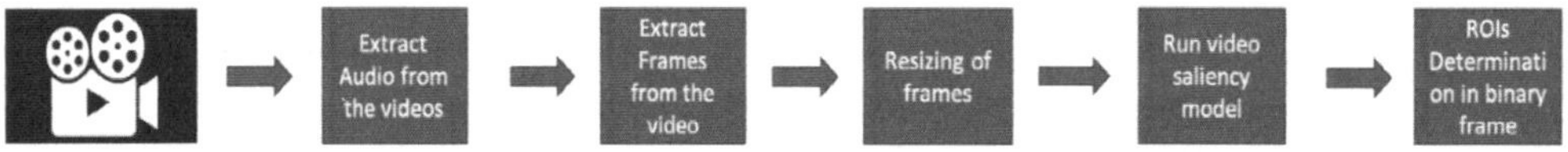

Figure 2. Overview of video saliency backend

3.1.1 Extracting Audio from the Original Video

The first step which the MagVi backend performs after receiving the file from the front end is to extract the audio from the original video file. This process is conducted due to the usage of OpenCV package in the zoom functionality of the backend application. OpenCV removes the audio part of the video during its processing, which makes saving the audio part of the original video saved individually essential.

Audio extraction is conducted using FFmpeg (FFmpeg Developers, 2016) software which is open-source software for handling multimedia files. FFmpeg uses a demultiplexer to read the video file which helps it to extract different parts of the video like video frame and raw audio. Further, it uses a decoder to decode the encoded file based on the format of the video. For audio extraction, FFmpeg then filters the raw audio from the input file. After the filtration audio file is created using a multiplexer and encoder. Magvi uses the audio filter application of FFmpeg to extract raw audio from the original video by making a command line call to the software.

3.1.2 Zoom Frames and ROI Detection

This step extract frames from the video and then put them through a video saliency model to identify the ROI in the frame. MagVi uses the DeepVS video saliency model (Jiang et. al. 2018) which is also used as used by SViM. DeepVS is a deep learning-based video prediction model which has been trained on the LEDOV dataset (Jiang et. al. 2018). DeepVs takes the frame of size 448x448 as input and then return a binary frame of size 112x112 where pixel with 1 represent ROIs. After extracting frames for the zoom frame functionality MagVi first resizes them to 448x448 size. Then the frames are sent to the DeepVS model for saliency prediction. DeepVS return frames of size 112x112 which are binary masked. Pixels with 1 represent ROI identified by the model. MagVi then identifies ROIs from the masked frames by identifying contours of the lit-up pixels, after which boundary points are identified of the contours. Based on the boundary points of the contour MagVi crops the original frame and writes them in a video file that only has frames and no audio.

3.1.3 Merging of Audio and Video File

The next functionality performed by MagVi is to merge the individual audio and video frames into one file. Magvi performed this action by using FFmpeg to merge the files. FFmpeg uses its multiplexer to merge both files. After, processing in the multiplexer FFmpeg saves it in a video file.

3.2 MagVi User Interface

The Video saliency part plays as the core of MagVi User Interface. On top of this core, we can create various magnification interfaces. The simplest MagVi setup is a handheld interface with a video player magnification that allows users to zoom and pan with assistive zooming and panning depending on the determined ROIs. Users may also adjust the aspect ratio of videos depending on their needs using the interface.

The workflow in the MagVi magnifier interface is as follows: The user enters the app and sees a list of videos, as well as a customizable menu called the *dynamic menu.* This menu allows the user to change font size and layout. If the user wishes to see a specific video, he must first log in. With this magnifier, the user begins watching a video. While watching the video, the user can use pinch-zoom to zoom in and out. The MagVi interface has a light and dark mode known to help those with low vision done for Display Customization. The font size and design of the whole interface could be changed using a dynamic menu on any interface tab.

We have implemented our designs based on different design principles. There are six individual principles commonly associated with gestalt theory: similarity, continuation, closure, proximity, figure/ground, and symmetry & order. Gestalt concepts are relatively simple to integrate into almost any design. They can quickly elevate a design that seems haphazard or as if it's competing for a user's interest to one that provides a smooth, regular interaction that directs users toward the action you want them to take (Soegaard, 2002).

We began with various user interface design phases as the first step. Prototyping, which is a draft version of a project that helped us to explore our thoughts and demonstrate the purpose behind a feature in the UI stages (Prototyping, 2020). Prototyping was helpful in application design—beginning with (low fidelity) and moving to an utterly usable platform that can allow targeted users to browse through the prototype(high-fidelity).

3.2.1 Low Fidelity Prototype

Our Low-Fidelity configuration started with a paper model or sketch, where the emphasis was on the position of the features in our application. We drafted a fundamental plan for some visual attributes of our final application.

This sketch was then changed over into a clickable wireframe with the assistance of wireframe tool (Adobe XD). The wireframes were intended to interactively test the application components and revamp them accordingly.

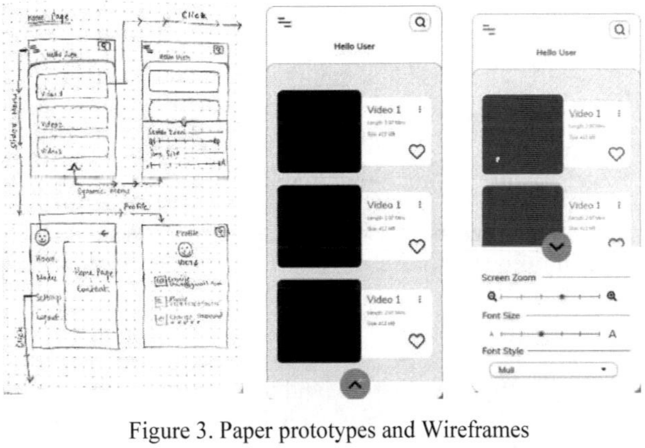

Figure 3. Paper prototypes and Wireframes

3.2.2 High Fidelity Prototype

After having a solid understanding of how our application works with the assistance of a mock-up, we planned a model. This prototype is shown in Figure 4. It is a detailed and realistic design of our application that we used to test it with 5 different low vision participants. The basic flow of the MagVi user interface consists of three main functionalities: 1. Fetching Videos 2. Transfer to Video Saliency Backend 3. Processed ROIs.

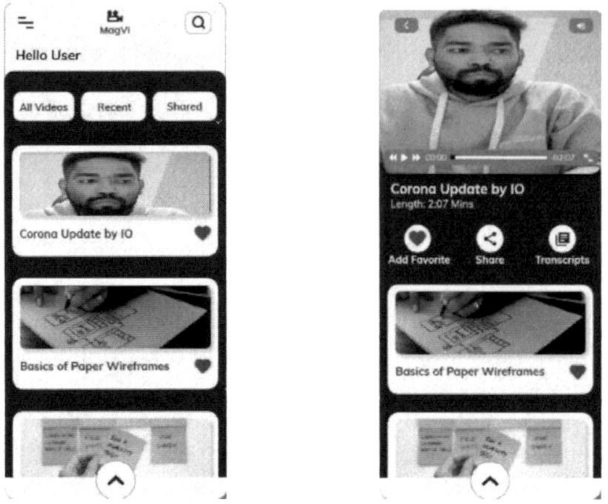

Figure 4. High Fidelity Prototype

3.2.3 Fetching Videos

The primary function of our user interface is to retrieve video from file explorer. The video is fetched using the flutter assets or the file explorer of the application itself. For this, a flutter-based video player kit based on *Mx player* is used. *mx_player_plugin* is a flutter plugin to open video records utilizing mx player with caption and VLC player. We were able to fetch videos in our flutter program by adding dependencies such as video_player (Flutter Dev, 2021) and video_player_flutter in *pubspec.ymal* file of application. *pubspec_yaml* is a dart library to get to and control substance of pubpec.yaml files. It is a data type representing data stored in pubspec.yaml files (Pubspec, 2020). Pubpec.ymal file in flutter: The package's metadata is included in the pubspec. A kit can also include pubspec-listed dependencies, Dart libraries, applications, tools, samples, photos, and videos.

3.2.4 Processed ROIs

The mobile app receives the video from an API call after detecting the ROI, and the user can monitor it and concentrate on the ROI by zooming or panning the video. We were able to zoom and pan video according to the user's wishes by using the same video player plugin in flutter and wrapping it with high-level playback control. The ROI detected by the backend mechanism can be zoomed in on by the user. The aspect video of the video player is being improved to improve the user interface. The user can mute, unmute, pause, and play the video while watching.

3.2.5 Dynamic Menu

The dynamic menu allows adjusting of the font size and style and the overall contrast of the application. When changing the font size, a default size is chosen based on the mobile device specifications, stored in a variable, and alter its value according to the size change. This is performed with the assistance of asynchronous void functions, and the variable is then called from within the style part of a text or a button. This application follows a similar process for font style change for the entire application. The Magvi program can also be switched to a dark mode for improved visibility; this was accomplished using flutter plugins to fit the dark colors to the software. Font change, dark/light mode and Firebase for login feature dependencies were added to the pubspec.yaml file. The build.gradle file was also modified to bind the database (Firebase) to the application interface (Flutter Fire, 2017).

4. USER STUDY

We conducted usability testing with a non-government organization named Enable India which helps people with disabilities. EnAble India (Enable India, 2017), a non-profit organization is bringing changes to the lives of PwDs through technology innovations, breakthroughs in skill trainings and behavioral change tools. Enable India has changed the mindset of 729 business houses and built frameworks of inclusion in universities and government agencies, thus creating a robust business case for employing PwDs in formal and informal sectors across India.

Participants: The usability testing which we conducted had 5 participants from different low vision categories that helped us to test our application thoroughly. Other types of users here were far-sighted, color blind.

Apparatus: We performed this usability testing via video conference call, considering the COVID situation and international participants. We used our roles as moderators, observers, and data loggers to dig deeper into our mobile app, for which a video conference was recorded, and a data logger framework was used.

Procedure: We began this procedure with a quick introduction of our application and methodology to the participants. We attempted to comfort the participants before clarifying the methodology. A portion of the participants had an idea about the usability testing, so it wasn't that hard to simplify them on the methodology.

Results:

- The navigation bar is not visible on the video: The video's navigation bar was grey in colour with buttons, making it difficult for users to navigate.
- Button colors of the videos are too light: The light-colored buttons on the video navigation bar made it impossible for users to navigate.
- Dark mode is more adaptable. In our application, we had two modes: light mode and dark mode, but dark mode was preferred by users.
- Icon size can be increased: A few users suggested that the application's icon size for the menu bar be increased.

5. RESULTS

According to Jakob Nielsen when doing usability testing, if you reach five users per segment, you tend to hear so much duplicate material that the time and cost of doing more research outweighs the rare possibility of discovering a new result. Details such as task execution, task completion rate, task error rate, comments, and notes were obtained from audio recordings of the testing.

Below are few participants from Usability Testing:

Participant	Name	Age	Gender	Type of Low Vision
1	Naveenkumar	22	Male	Having only center vision
2	Narendra VG	29	Male	Retinitis pigmentosa
3	Anisha Mahanta	32	Female	Optic atrophy

The tasks given to participants are:

1. You are a grandmother/Grandfather and want to knit a sweater for your grandchild, so you want to learn a knitting. Can you watch knitting video and magnify it yourself?
2. Your friend has difficulty watching videos. He wants some application that can magnify videos while watching. You as a friend decided to help him and stumble upon MagVi, so you try it and for that, you need to create an account. Can you create an account in this application?
3. You are a mother/Father of two kids, one of them is farsighted and has difficulties in using light mode of MagVi. Can you help your child in changing the theme of the application?
4. You are a teenager who uses MagVi to watch videos but wants to view the description of the video. Can you go to a video and open video description?
5. You've added list of favorite videos and want to see them, can you navigate yourself to the favorite list of videos.

Efficiency: Indicators of efficiency include task completion time and learning time (Frokjaer et. al. 2020). In this testing, we use task completion time as the primary indicator of efficiency (Frokjaer et. al. 2020). As shown in *Table 1*, task 3 and task 5 have the least task completion time. Tasks 2 and 4 are complex for users to complete while consuming the maximum amount of time. Task 1 was performed in average time compared to the other tasks since it revolved around the application's core purpose.

Table 1. Indicators of efficiency

Participants	Task 1	Task 2	Task 3	Task 4	Task 5
1	101	208	32	-	21
2	89	288	47	389	38
3	124	269	27	412	17
4	156	233	52	-	27
5	145	306	35	397	29
Average	123	260.8	38.6	310.4	26.4
Standard Deviation	28.34	40.03	10.50	77.45	8.04

Effectiveness: Two different ways to assess effectiveness are task execution efficiency and the number of errors made during the interaction. *Table 2* represents the effectiveness of each task. Users, apart from task 4, were able to complete all tasks taking their time.

Table 2. Indicators of effectiveness

Participants	Task 1	Task 2	Task 3	Task 4	Task 5
1	100%	100%	100%	-	100%
2	100%	100%	100%	100%	100%
3	100%	100%	100%	100%	100%
4	100%	100%	100%	-	100%
5	100%	100%	100%	100%	100%
Average	100%	100%	100%	60%	100%

6. DISCUSSION

Video availability for individuals with low vision has generally stayed neglected. With the Video Saliency and GUI, this paper has ventured out toward this path. MagVi's user experiments with the target audience, i.e., people with different types of low vision, indicate that it can meet a long-standing usability need in the sense of video magnification. DeepVS model was trained on smaller datasets, and therefore, a large set of data could be helpful in testing the saliency model to improve the generalization of this whole concept. With the functionality that MagVi already has taken into consideration, several additional features can support people with low vision. Some additional features like text and context contrast, application zoom, and a desktop edition for MagVi can be included to make the experience more comfortable for users while watching the dynamically changing content, i.e., videos. Time taken to identify the ROI of a video can be significantly decreased with the help of advanced cloud machinery.

7. CONCLUSION

With screen magnifiers, individuals with low vision who need magnification have a troublesome time watching videos. Everything comes down to experiencing issues in videos without magnifying them, which can be debilitating for individuals with low vision. MagVi gives an answer for these challenges which are faced by people with low vision in their daily lives. MagVi employs machine learning to identify the ROI and magnify it for users in order to improve their digital experience. In an era where learning is aided by visual representations such as videos, a platform like MagVi can have a significant and positive effect on the lives of individuals with low vision.

REFERENCES

Aydin, A., Feiz, S., Ashok, V. and Ramakrishnan, I., 2020. Towards making videos accessible for low vision screen magnifier users. Proceedings of the 25th International Conference on Intelligent User Interfaces. 2020, pp. 10-21.

Crossland, M., Gustaffson, J., Rumney, N., Verezen, A., Low Vision (Position Paper). ECOO. https://www.ecoo.info/wp-content/uploads/2012/09/ECOO-Position-Paper-Low-Vision-FINAL.pdf

Cui, X., Liu, Q. and Metaxas, D., 2009. Temporal spectral residual. Proceedings of the seventeen ACM international conference on Multimedia - MM '09, pp. 617–620.

Enable India. https://www.enableindia.org

FFmpeg tool (Version be1d324) [Software]. http://ffmpeg.org/

Video Player plugin for Flutter https://pub.dev/packages/video_player

Flutter fire. https://firebase.flutter.dev/docs/auth/usage/

Frokjaer, E., Hertzum, M. and Hornbaek, K., 2000. Measuring usability. Proceedings of the SIGCHI conference on Human factors in computing systems - CHI '00, pp. 345-352.

C. Guo, Q. Ma, and L. Zhang , 2008. Spatio-temporal Saliency detection using phase spectrum of quaternion fourier transform. 2008 IEEE Conference on Computer Vision and Pattern Recognition, 2008, pp. 1-8.

Hochreiter, S. and Schmidhuber, J., 1997. Long Short-Term Memory. Neural Computation, 9(8), pp. 1735-1780.

Huang, X., Shen, C., Boix, X. and Zhao, Q., 2015. SALICON: Reducing the Semantic Gap in Saliency Prediction by Adapting Deep Neural Networks. 2015 IEEE International Conference on Computer Vision (ICCV), pp. 262–270.

Jiang, L., Xu, M., Liu, T., Qiao, M. and Wang, Z., 2018. DeepVS: A Deep Learning Based Video Saliency Prediction Approach. Computer Vision – ECCV 2018, pp. 625-642

Leboran, V., Garcia-Diaz, A., Fdez-Vidal, X. and Pardo, X., 2017. Dynamic Whitening Saliency. IEEE Transactions on Pattern Analysis and Machine Intelligence, 39(5), pp. 893-907.

Mathe, S. and Sminchisescu, C., 2012. Dynamic Eye Movement Datasets and Learnt Saliency Models for Visual Action Recognition. Computer Vision – ECCV 2012, pp. 842-856.

Pan, J., Sayrol, E., Giro-I-Nieto, X., McGuinness, K. and OConnor, N., 2016. Shallow and Deep Convolutional Networks for Saliency Prediction. 2016 IEEE Conference on Computer Vision and Pattern Recognition (CVPR), pp. 598–606.

pub.dev. https://pub.dev/packages/pubspec_yaml

Rudoy, D., Goldman, D., Shechtman, E. and Zelnik-Manor, L., 2013. Learning Video Saliency from Human Gaze Using Candidate Selection. 2013 IEEE Conference on Computer Vision and Pattern Recognition, pp. 1147–1154.

Seo, H. and Milanfar, P., 2009. Static and space-time visual saliency detection by self-resemblance. Journal of Vision, 9(12), pp. 15-15.

Soegaard, M., The Glossary of Human Computer Interaction Chapter 22 - The Glossary of Human Computer Interaction edited by Mads Soegaard. https://www.interaction-design.org/literature/book/the-glossary-of-human-computer-interaction/gestalt-principles-of-form-perception

usability.gov. https://www.usability.gov/how-to-and-tools/methods/prototyping.html

RESEARCH ON THE INTERFACE USABILITY OF HOSPITAL WECHAT PUBLIC PLATFORM IN THE FORM OF INTERNET

Chen-Rao Zhong[1], Chien-Hsiung Chen[2] and Jin-Long Lin[3]
[1]*Master's student / Department of Design, National Taiwan University of Science and Technology*
[2]*Professor / Department of Design, National Taiwan University of Science and Technology*
No.43, Keelung Rd., Sec.4, Da'an Dist., Taipei City, Taiwan
[3]*Master's student / Department of Industrial Design, National Cheng Kung University*
No.1, Daxue Rd., East Dist., Tainan City 701, Taiwan

ABSTRACT

This study explores whether the Chinese Hospital WeChat Public Platform interface conforms to the user's operating habits and behavioral needs at the present stage by investigating the interface usability of Hospital WeChat Public Platform. Firstly, in the literature review, this study refers to the four usability principles of ISO 9241-11 (1998) and Nielsen (1994) summarized by Young et al. (2006) and regards these principles as the criteria for the WeChat Public Platform evaluation in hospital samples. Secondly, using the performance measurement method to conduct a quantitative analysis of the data, it is concluded that there are significant differences among the three hospital samples of the three task interfaces. Then, the design suggestions are obtained through four usability principles: (1) The interface's presentation should have primary and secondary levels and be arranged orderly to enable users to operate effectively and quickly. (2) Besides providing an excellent operation system, simplifying interface levels and steps is also one way to improve efficiency. (3) The interface is the most intuitive presentation of information, so its interface presentation should be concise and consistent, and the function level distribution should be reasonable to improve user's degree of satisfaction. (4) On the design of Hospital WeChat Public Platform interface, designers should pay more attention to the users who haven't used WeChat applications and design a standard interface to meet the need of user's learnability. Thus, the interface design should conform to the four principles of usability, and the user's demand is the key to the design.

KEYWORDS

Hospital Registration System, WeChat Public Platform, Interface Design, Usability Principle, Performance Measures, One-way ANOVA Between Groups

1. INTRODUCTION

With the advent of the age of big data and popularity of social software, China has derived a new registration method that you can register immediately if you follow the WeChat Public Platform. Major hospitals keep pace with the times and use the WeChat Public Platform to create new model of mobile Internet registration, and promote new forms of Internet development. In the era of "Internet+," various industries actively optimize and upgrade themselves by utilizing the Internet platform, and the medical industry is no exception. Based on the Internet, the "Internet+ medical treatment" is deeply integrated with the traditional medical and health services to form a new type of medical through the mobile Internet, Internet of Things, cloud computing, big data and other information technologies, and thus to promotes mobile information services and intelligent medical services that benefit all people (Meng et al., 2016). According to Tencent's official data, in China, WeChat is currently the communication and social platform with the largest user base. By 2020, the number of monthly active accounts of WeChat is up to 1.2025 billion, and the number of accounts of WeChat Public Platform has exceeded 20 million. WeChat Public Platform has become the preferred channel for hospitals to develop information construction and optimize the medical treatment process due to its richness of contents, the accuracy of message transmission, and the mobility of functional operation. Therefore, with the alternation of the Internet era and the promotion of WeChat Public Platforms, the medical industry actively builds a Hospital

WeChat Public Platform in the context of the needs of patients and hospital reforms. This will help improve hospital service quality, promote the hospital information construction, optimize the medical treatment process, and improve patients' medical treatment efficiency.

To sum up, making the Hospital WeChat Public Platform's interface easier to understand and operate has become an important topic. This study explores whether the Hospital WeChat Public Platform interface presentation conforms to users' cognition and behavior. The research objectives are summarized as follows:

(1) Assess the Hospital WeChat Public Platform interface design and understand users' interaction requirements when they operate the interface.

(2) Investigate the relationship between the user's operation experience of registration and the Hospital WeChat Public Platform interface to explore the usability factors that affect the user's operation.

(3) Explore the usability principles and put forward suggestions on the Hospital WeChat Public Platform interface design elements.

2. BRIEF LITERATURE REVIEW

Based on the function of WeChat application, WeChat Public Platform is one of the most important instant communication platforms in mobile Internet era, which has wide range of communication methods, strong user stickiness, high acceptance and accessibility. It implements a new model of online and offline access and establishes relations with users mainly through the interactive forms (Deng, 2020). To this end, mobile medical will become a new way to seek medical treatment in the future, which can alleviate the contradiction between doctors and patients and promote medical service quality. So, the WeChat Public Platform is the best medium (Huang et al., 2017). With the help of the medium WeChat Public Platform, hospital mobile medical service system can not only improve the stability of medical treatment and improve the patient's convenience and satisfaction, but also reduce hospital development costs (Xiong, 2020). Then, WeChat Public Platform is the most direct way for users to contact. Its interface design will directly affect the user's appreciation, browsing, and adhesiveness. The design elements such as text, graphics, color, navigation, and other information are combined to present to the users (Shen, 2016).

For this reason, many Chinese scholars have put forward relevant researches on the design of the hospital system interface of the WeChat Public Platform. He et al. (2020) used the UTAUT model to study patient satisfaction. They analyzed that effort expectation, performance expectations, facilitating factors, service pricing and individual innovation positively affect patients' satisfaction and these factors are used as the basis for the design of mini-program prototype. Sun (2018) used the five elements of user experience as the standard of hospital system's interface design and tested the system's function and its usability. Combined with the characteristics of young and middle-aged users using medical applications, Liu (2018) considered that a minimalist interface should include the recognizability of graphics, the order of structure, and the interaction of animations to improve the user's adhesiveness, which coincides with this article's viewpoint.

In terms of usability, ISO 9241-11 (1998) defines usability as: Effectiveness, Efficiency, and Satisfaction of a system for specific users and specific uses in a specific operational environment. Nielsen's (1994) five usability principles are often cited by scholars, including Learnability, Efficiency, Memorability, Errors, and Satisfaction. To this end, Young et al. (2006) summarized the three attributes defined by ISO 9241-11 (1998) and the usability attributes proposed by Nielsen (1994). They listed four usability principles as well as their measurement methods. Referring to the four usability principles summarized by Young et al., this study will discuss the usability of the Hospital WeChat Public Platform interface design elements. In summary, the following is a list of four usability principle definitions and measurement methods:

(1) Effectiveness: It refers to the user's accuracy and completion rate when completing specific operational tasks and objectives. The evaluation method is the task completion rate.

(2) Efficiency: It refers to the ratio of the user's task completion rate to time, which is evaluated by the time spent on task performance.

(3) Satisfaction: It refers to the participant's feeling and acceptance degree of users when operating the interface. The evaluation method is the score obtained by users' rating the scale.

(4) Learnability: It refers to whether users can effectively and quickly learn the interface's operation. The evaluation method is to find out whether the operation behavior is easy to learn through non-participatory observation.

3. RESEARCH METHOD

3.1 Methods and Architecture

This study aims to explore the comprehensive influencing factors when users operates the Hospital WeChat Public Platform. Therefore, the experiment will focus on the hospital registration system's different functional interfaces on the WeChat Public Platform. Through online research, the hospital registration systems of the WeChat Public Platform of three first-class hospitals in Shenzhen, Guangdong Province are selected as the experimental samples to explore the differences, advantages, and disadvantages of different interface designs bringing for users. Using SPSS statistical software to analyze the experiment's significance and supplemented by non-participatory observation, the experiment mainly adopts One-way ANOVA and focuses on the quantitative study of task performance and System Usability Scale (Starting now referred to as SUS) to explore users' operation experience and usage needs for the Hospital WeChat Public Platform interface. The specific experimental process is as follows:

Experiment A: Questionnaire survey and task design

(1) First, the participant is asked to fill out an online questionnaire, including name, gender, age, education level, past registration methods, and functional preferences.

(2) Summarize and sort out the questionnaire; select functions considered important by the participants in the questionnaire; use these functions selected and the main functions explored in the literature as the experimental operation task's functional items.

Experiment B: Task operation and SUS measurement

(1) Invite the participants to operate the experiment task, and explain the experiment content and process briefly to them, including the introduction of the participant, the introduction of the experiment sample, and the introduction of the task content.

(2) Ask the participants whether they know the task or not, and start the task operation after getting the oral response. Observe the problems occurred during their operation on the interface without disturbing them and record the time of each task's operation with a timer while the participants operate the tasks.

(3) After the task, introduce the scale's content to the participants before guiding them to fill in the SUS, and then explore the participants' scoring criteria and reasons.

(4) After completing the operation task and SUS, learn about the participants' operation feelings and feedback.

3.2 Participants

After screening the questionnaire survey of Experiment A, 30 participants who have never used the three experimental samples are invited to participate Experiment B. Among them, there are 11 males and 19 females, and their ages range from 18 to 31. Each Participant participates in one Hospital WeChat Public Platform operation and carried out five tasks aiming at the interface design's usability. All participants use the same experimental equipment, and the network environment connected in the same field. In addition, the operation information and content received are the same to ensure the comparability of experiments.

3.3 Equipment and Samples

The device used in the experiment is a smartphone made by an Apple company. The model is an iPhone XR, with a 6.1-inch touch screen and 1792 × 828 pixels, and an LCD screen is used. The dimension is 150.9mm × 75.7mm × 8.3mm (length × width × thickness), and the system is IOS operating system. The performance timer uses the stopwatch function of the smartphone.

The experiment selects Shenzhen, China, which has the development needs for medical information construction and digitalization, as the city of tested sample hospitals. Taking the authority and representativeness of the sample comparison into account, this experiment selects the top six tertiary general public hospitals in 2018 (Shen Chuang Zong He, 2019). Then, from the perspectives of satisfaction, public welfare, competitiveness, and design style, we choose three WeChat Public Platforms as experimental samples tested, and finally select "Hospital sample 1", "Hospital sample 2", "Hospital sample 3". The design style and functional level layout of these three Hospital WeChat Public Platforms are different. The following figure shows the first page of the operation interface of the three Hospital WeChat Public Platforms:

Figure 1. Interface home pages of three hospital samples
(Hospital sample 1 on the left, Hospital sample 2 in the middle, Hospital sample 3 on the right)

3.4 Task Design

Because the experimental operation cannot disrupt the hospital's regular registration order, there is no actual registration in this experiment, so individual functions cannot be explored. Deng (2020) and Xiong (2020) classified "Intelligent diagnosis guidance" and "Appointment registration" as the main functions of the Hospital WeChat Public Platform. While Zhou and Shao (2020) divided "Appointment registration" into "Patient management," "Appointment registration," and "Appointment record." Li (2015) tested the main functions of the hospital registration system, including "Interactive guidance," "Medical card management," "Doctor management," and "Inquiry appointment registration." Through the questionnaire survey, users consider that the four functions of "Appointment registration," "Appointment inquiry," "Order inquiry and payment," and "Doctor list" are essential. Through literature and questionnaire, the functions of "Intelligent diagnosis guidance," "Appointment registration," "Medical card management," and "Doctor list" are selected as the functional items of experimental operational tasks.

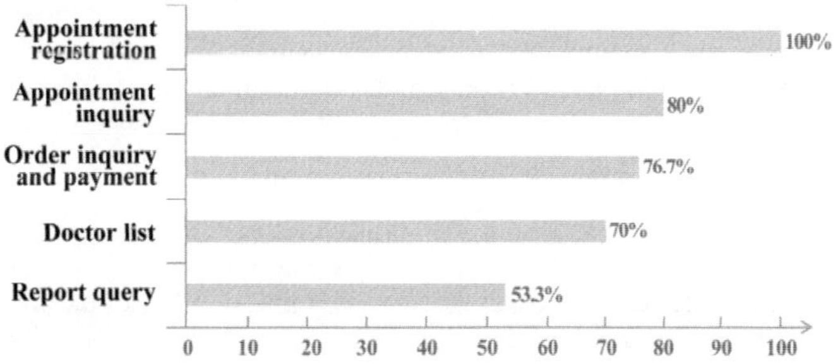

Figure 2. Questionnaire survey on functional preferences of Hospital WeChat Public Platform

To sum up, this experiment will focus on the four functions including "Intelligent diagnosis guidance", "Appointment registration", "Medical card management" and "Doctor list", and according to the medical treatment and registration process, the task themes will be designed as follows: Intelligent diagnosis guidance - Medical card management - Appointment registration - Setting attention - Viewing the doctors' list. The specific task content and purpose are shown in Table 1.

Table 1. Task content and purpose description

Task	Task theme	Task content	Task purpose
1	Intelligent diagnosis guidance	Enter the medical guidance AI system to fill in the date of birth and gender information, enter the disease's condition, check the recommended department, and return to the home page.	Understand whether it is easy for user to operate the AI diagnosis system
2	Medical card management	Find the medical card management page, add name/ID/mobile phone number to bind the medical card, then delete it and return to the home page.	Explore whether the function of the management account conforms to the user's operational awareness and behavioral cognition
3	Appointment registration	Enter the appointment registration area, select the department/physician/date, and select the time available for the appointment to view the registration information. Return to the home page without clicking the registration.	To explore the differences of registration levels and interface presentation of different public platforms
4	Setting attention	Follow three doctors with five stars in the clinic, and finally return to the home page.	investigate whether the function fits the user's needs by the behavior of following the physicians
5	Viewing the list of doctors	Please unfollow the three physicians just followed from the physician list and return to the homepage.	To explore the user's intuition and learnability of information transmission in personal accounts

4. RESEARCH RESULTS

4.1 Task Performance Results

One-way ANOVA analysis is conducted by SPSS statistical software. The shorter the time it takes, the better the performance. The significant standard α value is set as 0.05, and $P < 0.05$ indicates a significant difference. As shown in Table 2, there are significant differences in Task 1 ($F=3.681$, $P=0.039<0.05$), Task 4 ($F=8.800$, $P=0.001<0.05$) and Task 5 ($F=3.682$, $P=0.039<0.05$), while there are no significant differences in Task 2 ($F=0.679$, $P=0.516>0.05$) and Task 3 ($F=2.046$, $P= 0.149>0.05$). The detailed results are as follows:

Table 2. ANOVA test results of five task performance

Task theme	Hospital sample 1 M(SD)	Hospital sample 2 M(SD)	Hospital sample 3 M(SD)	F value	P value
1. Intelligent diagnosis guidance	141.71 (22.67)	164.73 (68.73)	109.72 (31.35)	3.681	0.039*
2. Medical card management	136.70 (43.60)	160.00 (77.36)	133.90 (34.42)	0.679	0.516
3. Appointment registration	80.64 (31.73)	118.70 (86.92)	71.82 (23.20)	2.046	0.149
4. Setting attention	63.86 (26.13)	142.89 (71.13)	74.72 (22.64)	8.800	0.001*
5. Viewing the list of doctors	29.68 (12.13)	34.75 (11.22)	65.87 (53.44)	3.682	0.039*

* Table $P<0.05$, there is a significant difference between the three samples (unit: second)

4.1.1 Task 1: Intelligent Diagnosis Guidance

Task 1(F=3.681, P=0.039<0.05) has a significant difference in task performance. As shown in Table 3, there is a significant difference between Hospital sample 3 (M=109.72, SD=31.35) and Hospital sample 2(M=164.73, SD=68.73), but there is no significant difference between Hospital sample 1 (M=141.71, SD=22.67) and Hospital sample 2(M=164.73, SD=68.73) as well as Hospital sample 3 (M=109.72, SD=31.35). The task performance of Hospital sample 3 (M = 109.72, SD = 31.35) is better than that of the other two hospitals samples. The AI system's response speed and guidance are the factors that affect the performance of this task. Intelligent diagnosis guidance is a new function developed. The system completion degrees of the three samples are not high, and their reaction speeds are slow. However, the guidance mode of Hospital sample 3 is optional, and its guidance is better. In the other two samples, it needs to input disease keywords manually to identify, so the participants spend more time inputting disease keywords. Therefore, the guidance of the system is the key to the performance of this task.

Table 3. The LSD post hoc results of Task 1

Experimental sample	Hospital sample 1	Hospital sample 2	Hospital sample 3
Hospital sample 1	—	0.268	0.128
Hospital sample 2	—	—	0.012*
Hospital sample 3	—	—	—

4.1.2 Task 4: Setting Attention

Task 4 (F=8.800, P=0.001<0.05) has a significant difference in task performance. As shown in Table 4, there are significant differences between Hospital sample 2 (M=142.89, SD=71.13) and Hospital sample 1 (M=63.86, SD=26.13) as well as Hospital sample 3 (M=74.72, SD=22.64), while there are no significant differences between Hospital sample 1 (M=63.86, SD=26.13) and Hospital sample 3 (M=74.72, SD=22.64). Hospital sample 2 (M=142.89, SD=71.13) costs the longest time, so its task performance is the worst. This function makes it convenient for patients to find their favorite doctor for a consultation quickly. The main reason affecting task performance is the recognition degree of text and icons. The degree of recognition is mainly related to the position, the expression of the text and the design of the icons. In Hospital sample 2, the icon is too complex and is situated at the bottom, what's more, the meaning conveyed by words is not clear, so the participants cannot quickly understand the icon's intention and spend more time looking for the icon.

Table 4. The LSD post hoc results of Task 4

Experimental sample	Hospital sample 1	Hospital sample 2	Hospital sample 3
Hospital sample 1	—	0.001*	0.599
Hospital sample 2	—	—	0.002*
Hospital sample 3	—	—	—

4.1.3 Task 5: Viewing the List of Doctors

Task 5 (F=3.682, P=0.039<0.05) has a significant difference in task performance. It can be seen from Table 5 that there are significant differences between Hospital sample 3 (M=65.87, SD=53.44) and Hospital sample 1 (M=29.68, SD=12.13) as well as Hospital sample 2 (M=34.75, SD=11.22). Simultaneously, there are no significant differences between Hospital sample 1 (M=29.68, SD=12.13) and Hospital sample 2 (M=34.75, SD=11.22). Hospital sample 3 (M=65.87, SD=53.44) takes the longest time, so its task performance is the worst. The number of functional operation levels is the main reason that affects this task: the fewer operation levels, the simpler the using process. Hospital sample 1 only has three levels to view the doctors' list, while Hospital sample 3 has five levels, making the operation more complicated.

Table 5. The LSD post hoc results of Task 5

Experimental sample	Hospital sample 1	Hospital sample 2	Hospital sample 3
Hospital sample 1	—	0.728	0.019*
Hospital sample 2	—	—	0.040*
Hospital sample 3	—	—	—

4.2 System Usability Scale Results

SUS was proposed by John Brooke (1996) to test the usability of the interface. Since its establishment, it has been widely used in rapid scoring and testing the usability. The three hospital samples' scores are analyzed by One way ANOVA, and the following results are obtained (see Table 6). There is no significant difference in SUS evaluation among the three hospital samples (F=2.180, P=0.133>0.05). The participants said that the usage experience and the aesthetics of the interface were their criteria. The interface design of Hospital sample 3 is relatively consistent, and the white background with black text makes them feel simple and legible, which is consistent with Padda's (2003) view of interface readability. However, there are still some aspects to be adjusted in the use of functions.

Table 6. ANOVA Test Results of SUS

Task theme	Hospital sample 1 M(SD)	Hospital sample 2 M(SD)	Hospital sample 3 M(SD)	F value	P value
SUS	56.75 (19.04)	52.00 (18.55)	70.50 (23.74)	2.180	0.133

Using the SUS score scale proposed by Bangor and Kortum (2009), the usability of three Hospitals' WeChat Public Platforms are explored. As shown in Figure 3, Hospital sample 3 (M=70.50, SD=23.74) has passed the qualifying standard of usability (that is, the mean score reaches 68 or more); and hospital sample 2 (M=52.00, SD=18.55), hospital sample 1 (M=56.75, SD=19.04) have not reached the qualifying standard of usability. It can be concluded that there is no significant difference among the WeChat Public Platforms of these three Hospitals. All of them belong to the qualified range according to the SUS score scale. They cannot meet users' needs, and there is still room for improvement.

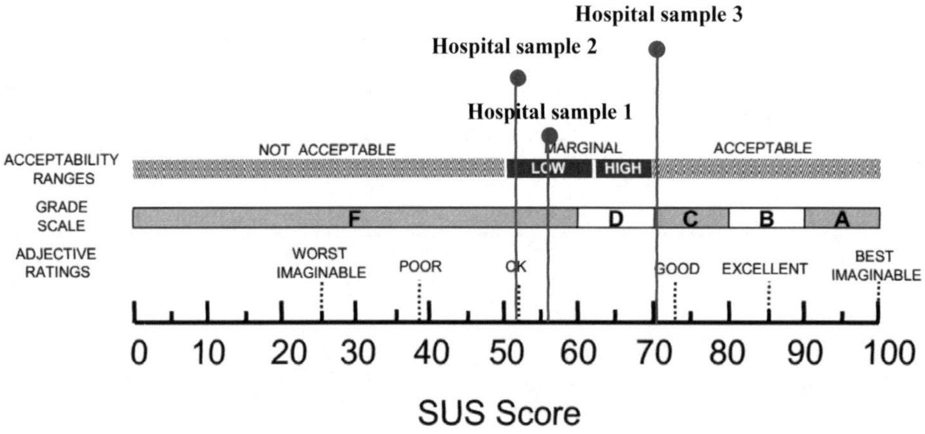

Figure 3. Comparison of SUS scores of three Hospital WeChat Public Platform

5. DISCUSSION

Combined with literature review and research results, the four usability principles, respectively Effectiveness, Efficiency, Satisfaction, and Learnability, will be taken as the directions of discussion:

(1) Effectiveness: In this experiment, all of the 30 participants complete the five specific tasks and goals. Therefore, the interface design of the three Hospital WeChat Public Platforms meets the basic functional requirements of users. However, there are significant differences in three tasks' performance, which is worthy of further exploration.

(2) Efficiency: Through the ANOVA analysis, there are significant differences in task 1, task 4, and task 5. Hospital sample 3 has the highest efficiency in Task 1, while Hospital sample 1 has the highest efficiency in task 4 and task 5. Comparing the three operational tasks, it can be found that in task 1, "Intelligent diagnosis guidance" is the least efficient. The experiment shows that the reason is that the AI system in task 1 “intelligent diagnosis guidance” is slow in response and low in guidance, which significantly affects the operation on the interface. Therefore, in the interface design, the speed of system operation and the guiding intention will significantly affect the interface's ease of use.

(3) Satisfaction: After operating the interface, the user's feeling and experience on the interface can be quantified through the scale. In the SUS analysis, Hospital sample 3 is more in line with the users’ satisfaction standard than the other two hospital samples. After the experiment, through the participants' feedback, most of them think that the interface of Hospital sample 3 is more concise and consistent than other samples. However, Hospital sample 3 is not the best in task performance. Therefore, it can be inferred that the influencing factor of the satisfaction of Hospital WeChat Public Platform is interface presentation rather than task performance.

(4) Learnability: In this experiment, all the participants have not used these three hospital samples before, but the participants who have used the WeChat application operate more smoothly and find the task target more quickly than those who have not used the WeChat application. Therefore, the learnability of Hospital WeChat Public Platform is related to the fact that whether the participants have used the WeChat application before. This is consistent with Wang and Huang's (2015) point of view that "ease of use depends on the user's previous experience in interactive functions" in their study on mobile e-books’ ease of use.

6. CONCLUSION

This study aims to explore the comprehensive influencing factors when users operates the Hospital WeChat Public Platform. The literature and experimental results provide a more specific design basis for the Hospital WeChat Public Platform interface. According to the discussion on four principles of ease of use, this study puts forward some design suggestions of usability on the interface of the Hospital WeChat Public Platform: (1) The interface's presentation should have primary and secondary levels and be arranged orderly to enable users to operate effectively and quickly. (2) Besides providing an excellent operation system, simplifying interface levels and steps is also one way to improve efficiency. (3) The interface is the most intuitive presentation of information, so its interface presentation should be concise and consistent, and the function level distribution should be reasonable to improve user’s degree of satisfaction. (4) On the design of Hospital WeChat Public Platform interface, designers should pay more attention to the users who haven’t used WeChat applications and design a standard interface to meet the need of user's learnability. The findings of this study contribute to the research on the interface usability of the Hospital WeChat Public Platform and are expected to give relevant designers more consideration. To meet the needs of the age of aging in China, we will conduct more experiments on the middle-aged and elderly groups in the subsequent studies.

REFERENCES

Bangor, A., & Kortum, P., 2009. Determining what individual SUS scores mean: Adding an adjective rating scale. *Journal of Usability Studies*, Vol. 4, No. 3, pp. 114-123.

Brooke, J., 1996. Sus: a ‘quick and dirty’ usability. *Usability evaluation in industry*, pp. 189.

Deng Lu, 2020. Exploration of medical treatment mode on WeChat Public Platform of a tertiary hospital. *Business Information Magazine*, No. 13, pp. 127-129+138.

HE Hui-qian .et al., 2020. Analysis and Research on Influencing Factors of Internet Medical Patient Satisfaction. Packaging Engineering, Network debut.

Huang Yong-gang. et al., 2017. Design of hospital appointment registration process based on WeChat Public Platform. *Chinese Medical Equipment Journal*, Vol. 38, No. 5, pp. 53-55.

Iso, W., 1998. 9241-11. Ergonomic requirements for office work with visual display terminals (VDTs). *The international organization for standardization*, Vol. 45, No. 9.

Lee, Y. S. et al., 2006. Systematic evaluation methodology for cell phone user interfaces. *Interacting with Computers*, Vol. 18, No. 2, pp. 304-325.

Li Jin-cheng, 2015. The design and implementation of a clinic system based on WeChat platform . Master's dissertation, Harbin Institute of Technology, Harbin.

Liu Min, 2018. Research on the design and study of user medical mobile phone APP- “EASY MEDICAL TREATMENT”. Master's dissertation, Xi'an University of Technology, Xi'an.

Meng Qun. et al., 2016. Development Status and Reflection of Chinese Internet plus Healthcare. *Chinese Journal of Health Informatics and Management*, Vol. 13, No. 4, pp. 356-363.

Nielsen, J. 1994. *Usability Engineering*. Morgan Kaufmann Publishers, San Diego, CA, USA.

Padda, H. K., 2003. QUIM map: a repository for usability/quality in use measurement . Doctoral dissertation, Concordia University, Montreal.

Shen Chuang Zong He, April 28, 2019. The latest list of Shenzhen's 50 public hospitals. URL: https://city.shenchuang.com/yl/20190428/1489565.shtml

Shen Jian, 2016. Brief analysis on the interface design of WeChat Public Platform. *Art Education Research*, No. 23, pp. 98+106.

Sun Ya-qi, 2018. Design and implementation of hospital registration APP. Master's dissertation, Nanjing University of Science and Technology, Nanjing.

Wang, C. M., & Huang, C. H., 2015. A study of usability principles and interface design for mobile e-books. *Ergonomics*, Vol. 58, No. 8, pp. 1253-1265.

Xiong Ding-guo, 2020. Research on the Construction of Hospital Mobile Medical Service System Based on WeChat Public Platform. *Information&Communications*, No. 6, pp. 121-123.

Zhou Miao-liang, & Shao Hong-hong, 2020. Use WeChat Public Platform to Improve Hospital Medical Services. *China Health Industry*, Vol. 17, No. 2, pp. 177-179.

ACOUSMA: UBIQUITOUS & INTELLIGENT AUDITORY DISPLAYS

Andreas Michelakis[1], Emmanouil Zidianakis[1], Asterios Leonidis[1], Stavroula Ntoa[1], Margherita Antona[1] and Constantine Stephanidis[1,2]

[1] *Institute of Computer Science, Foundation for Research and Technology - Hellas, Heraklion, Greece*

[2] *University of Crete, Heraklion, Greece*

ABSTRACT

ACOUSMA is a platform based on micro-services architecture developed to allow effortless enhancement of Ambient Intelligence (AmI) environments with personalized auditory displays. ACOUSMA consists of two system packages designed for interaction with three groups of users: auditory display experts, AmI application developers and AmI environment inhabitants. Auditory display experts can generate, upload and share their designed auditory representations using an intuitive Content Management System (CMS). AmI application developers with no prior knowledge on the field can integrate personalized auditory displays in any AmI environment with minimum effort using a simple application programming interface. An intelligent module was developed to adapt and grow to user preferences in real time, enabling conversion of semantic information into meaningful, user-tailored auditory displays. Finally, AmI environment inhabitants experience auditory displays that occur in the right place at the right time and are adjustable to their preferences. Usability evaluation from both experts and final users has shown that the target user groups can benefit from using ACOUSMA as a platform to store and share auditory representations, as well as to provide personalized, meaningful and context-sensitive auditory displays. Moreover, users could successfully and efficiently communicate their needs and adjust auditory displays using the intelligent module.

KEYWORDS

Auditory Display, Ambient Intelligence Environment, Recommendation System

1. INTRODUCTION

Interaction multimodality is often claimed to be a fundamental feature of Ambient Intelligence environments and related applications (Aarts & Wichert, Ambient intelligence, 2009). However, in practice, for the majority of applications, the focus is on the visual channel to display information. Due to such focus on visual displays results the auditory channel is often not efficiently utilized by AmI applications, as developers have limited specific domain knowledge and lack tools to provide meaningful, personalized auditory displays. To address this issue, this paper introduces ACOUSMA, a complete framework and suite of tools designed to aid AmI developers and Auditory Display experts in enhancing AmI environment applications with information-rich auditory displays that are personalized to inhabitant's preferences and adapt according to environment and inhabitant context. The system provides: (i) A standardized way of storing and sharing created auditory representations, (ii) A standardized way to deploy and control auditory display playback, (iii) Flexibility in use and monitoring of hardware (output devices), (iv) Auditory displays that are in harmony with user and environment context (occurring at the right place, at the right time), (v) Auditory displays that can be adjusted in real time to user preferences, (vi) Dynamic evaluation of environment context before and during playback of an auditory display, (vii) Meaningful and personalized auditory displays for any given AmI environment data or event.

2. BACKGROUND & RELATED WORK

2.1 Background

ACOUSMA is built upon the AmI paradigm and the background theory of auditory representations, auditory displays and sonification. **The AmI paradigm**'s realization is a result of microprocessors decreasing in size, the high computing power to user ratio and the successful user experience with mobile devices and technological artifacts (Adelstein, Gupta, & Richard, 2015). An AmI environment is characterized by five primary features (Aarts & Encarnação, 2006) (Schmidt, Kranz, & Holleis, 2005): *Embeddable* - It is built upon technological advancements of computer networks, sensors, actuators and distributed computing. *Context-aware* - Utilizes contextual information regarding users, creating profiles, recognizing user activities, situation and location. *Personalizable* - It is customizable according to user preferences. *Adaptive* - It adapts dynamically to change in user preferences and context. *Anticipatory* - Uses artificial intelligence to predict user intentions. ACOUSMA as a platform for AmI environments inherits those characteristics. **Auditory representation** is defined as a technique or design approach that aims to the creation of a sound that can be used to communicate and represent information or a meaning (Csapó & Wersényi, 2013) (Serafin, et al., 2011). In literature, auditory representations are summarized into three categories, basic, speech based and sonification based (Csapó & Wersényi, 2013). Basic auditory representations include auditory icons (Gaver, 1986) and Earcons (Blattner, Sumikawa, & Greenberg, 1989). Speech based representations include Spearcons (Walker, Nance, & Lindsay, 2006), Spindices (Jeon & Walker, 2009), Auditory Emoticons (Froehlich & Hammer, 2004) and Spemoticons (Nemeth, Olaszy, & Csapo, 2011). Sonification includes Auditory Warnings (Patterson, 1990), Morphocons (Parseihian & Katz, 2011) and Musicons (McGee-Lennon, Wolters, McLachlan, Brewster, & Hall, 2011). ACOUSMA integrates in its interfaces the majority of auditory representation types. **Auditory Displays**, as stated in (Walker & Kramer, Ecolological Psychoacoustics and Auditory Displays, 2004) is the field that examines the use of sound to depict information in computing environments. Four approaches for creating an auditory display are established in literature (Walker & Nees, Theory of sonification, 2011) (de Campo, 2007). Those are, Audification (Kramer, 1994), Event-Based – Parameter mapping (Grond & Berger, 2011), Continuous and Model Based (de Campo, 2007). Another, rather new approach is that of Blended Sonification (Tünnermann, Hammerschmidt, & Hermann, 2013) and has been used for ambient, calm auditory displays. ACOUSMA is designed to support playback of auditory displays generated with any approach.

2.2 Related Work

Only a limited amount of research work exists in the field of Auditory Display in the context of AmI environments. To the best of our knowledge, no platform or framework for the management and distribution of personalized, context sensitive auditory displays in AmI environments is currently available. The majority of Auditory Displays do not consider environment context and user preferences before deployment or during playback of auditory displays. Examined here are data sonification tools, programming interfaces and existing AmI auditory display applications.

Data sonification tools are used for generating auditory analogies to datasets and are mainly used for data analysis and exploration. Interaction with those systems is performed via a Graphical User Interface (GUI) and there is no requirement for programming skills. For inputting data, a tabular document is needed (text, csv), as the tools offer no database support. Sonification Sandbox (Davison & Walker, 2007) and xSonify (Candey, Schertenleib, & Merced, 2006) use the parameter-mapping approach for sonification and MIDI for sound output. Another promising sonification tool, Sonifyer (Dombois, Brodwolf, Friedli, Rennert, & Koenig, 2008), uses the Audification approach and a limited version of parameter-mapping (frequency modulation synthesis). A recent work, the Sonification Workstation (Phillips & Cabrera, 2019) is an open-source, multi-platform application designed for general sonification tasks. Functions covered by the tool are data exploration and art, while approaches available are mainly parameter mapping and Audification. The audible output of the tool can only be heard with the tool running and there are no options for audio file export.

Programming frameworks have been developed to allow sonification of data. Differently from sonification tools, such frameworks requires an adequate knowledge of sonification techniques and programming. Interaction with these frameworks happens in a text-based environment, a source code editor. SuperCollider (Wilson, Cottle, & Collins, 2011) is an open-source platform for audio synthesis and algorithmic composition, used by musicians, artists, and researchers working with sound. SoniPy (Worrall, Bylstra, Barrass, & Dean, 2007) is a publicly available framework based on the Python programming language. It uses components of Python for data acquisition, storage and analysis and adds modules for perceptual mappings and sound synthesis. Csound (Lazzarini, et al., 2016) is also a publicly available sound and music computing system.

Auditory display applications designed for intelligent environments draw real-time data produced by environment's sensors to generate meaningful auditory feedback. Systems use a variety of hardware and software tools (some already discussed here) in order to provide meaningful auditory displays. UPSTAIRS (Tünnermann, Leichsenring, Bovermann, & Hermann, 2015) and Knock 'Knock (Tünnermann, Hammerschmidt, & Hermann, 2013) are prototype systems that use the Blended Sonification approach with contact microphones placed in the environment to capture data and the SuperCollider engine to transform those data into meaningful auditory displays. In Powerchord (Lockton, Bowden, Brass, & Gheerawo, 2014) methods were examined to raise awareness for energy consumption. In the augmentation of a kitchen described in (Groß-Vogt, et al., 2018), the application used two loud speakers for playback and a laptop to receive data emerging from environment sensors.

Currently, there is no standardized hardware or software framework to deploy and control auditory displays in AmI environments. Context-awareness and personalization approaches are also missing. There is no flexibility in the usage of output devices (meaning that applications are bound to the hardware used). In AmI environments where an abundance of information arises from sensors and services, it is crucial that standardized methods exist for harnessing information as well as software and hardware infrastructure to support deployment of applications that create memorable user experiences. The rationale behind the design & development of ACOUSMA is precisely the gap found in literature and current applications. In detail, there is no system to allow management of auditory displays in AmI environments as well as no standardized way for providing auditory displays by AmI applications and non-expert users (application developers). Aligning with the AmI paradigm's major characteristics, ACOUSMA provides context-aware, personalizable and adaptive auditory displays. Moreover, ACOUSMA uses available network resources (devices and speakers) to direct and control auditory displays anywhere in the intelligent environment.

3. DESIGN PROCESS & USER REQUIREMENTS

A user center design process was followed to elicit functional and non-functional requirements for ACOUSMA. The platform is targeted to three target user groups: Auditory Display experts, AmI application developers and AmI environment inhabitants. Auditory Display experts can use sophisticated, domain specific tools to design, develop and deploy auditory displays. AmI application developers are involved in the creation of applications for multiple domains. They develop multimodal interfaces that use the environment's infrastructure (sensors, actuators & services) to provide information-rich user experiences. Finally, AmI environment inhabitants are people that live in and experience AmI environments, ranging from residents of a smart home to visitors of a museum. These users have extremely diverse needs and preferences, requiring multimodal interfaces capable to adapt in a natural way to their profile.

In the process of eliciting user requirements for ACOUSMA, Brainstorming, Group Discussion, Direct Observation & Scenarios were used. Experienced researchers in the field of HCI and AmI as well as UX/UI (user experience / user interface) experts and AmI application developers participated in two brainstorming sessions and group discussions. Multiple Direct Observation sessions with user representatives were also executed. As a main outcome, using ACOUSMA's interfaces, Auditory Display Experts should be able to store & share auditory representations, and quickly and easily test stored designs in an AmI environment; AmI application developers should be able to integrate and deploy personalized auditory displays, and allow the system to evaluate the right context to initiate and auditory display; AmI environment inhabitants should be able to experience personalized and adjustable auditory displays.

4. IMPLEMENTATION

The system consists of two distinct packages, the Speaker Director and the Auditory Display Director. Both packages combined aim to enhance Ambient Intelligence environments with personalized auditory displays. Auditory displays are deployed based on user, environment and application context, as well as user specific preferences regarding auditory representations and sound categories.

4.1 Speaker Director Package

In order to present an auditory display, the most basic requirement is an output device, a speaker. Therefore, output devices in an AmI environment are required to be ubiquitous, enabling the distribution of auditory displays anywhere and in every condition. The Speakers Director package was developed as a solution to support this requirement consisting of the following modules.

An AmI Audio Client can be a physical device (e.g., smartphone, TV) with one or more audio output devices, running software enabling playback control of these devices over network. A cross-platform software was developed enabling easy integration and over network playback control for any device usually found in AmI environments. Consequently, any device with audio output capabilities can be enhanced with the software and transformed into an AmI Audio client. In essence, through a network of AmI Audio Clients the seamless distribution of auditory displays in AmI environments is achieved. Every AmI Audio Client establishes a connection to the Speaker Server and sends real-time updates regarding output devices playback status, as well as the client's location (e.g. "kitchen" in a Smart Home).

The Speaker server is a RESTful API, developed for easy direction of a playback request to an AmI Audio Client. As mentioned above, the Speaker Server keeps track of each connected AmI Audio Client's output devices status, as well as the client's location, allowing an auditory display request to be directed to any of the available output devices.

AmI Speakers Explorer is a web application/user interface for testing auditory displays and monitoring the status of AmI Audio Clients. It was developed for Auditory Display experts and AmI application developers willing to quickly view available locations and output devices and deploy tests while developing an application for an AmI environment (see Figure 1, left). The information is made available in real-time by the Speakers Server. In case a developer or a technician would like to add a new AmI Audio Client, they need to run the provided software at a compatible device (see Figure 1, right).

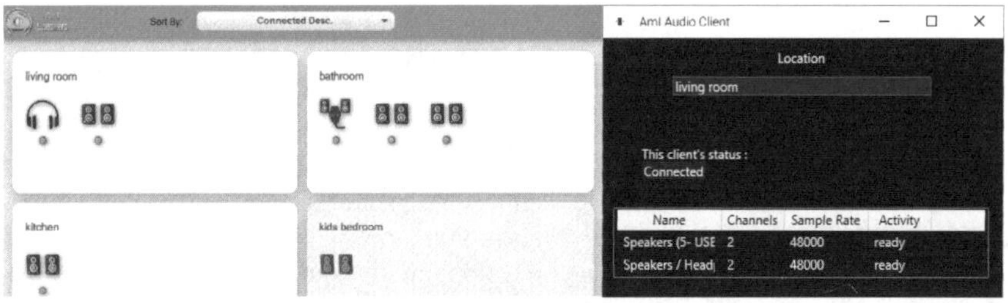

Figure 1. AmI Speakers Explorer (left) & AmI Audio Client (right) user interface

4.2 Auditory Display Director

The Auditory Display Director package's components provide an extensive suite of interfaces for AmI application developers and Auditory Display experts to deploy meaningful and personalized auditory displays to AmI environment inhabitants. The Auditory Display Director package consists of the following components:

The AmI Audio Library was developed as a cloud-based database structure to store the complete variety of auditory representations found in auditory display design. The structure in which database items are stored enables retrieval in the form of an audio stream, including information regarding the representation, sound category and information type, as well as a list of descriptors/tags describing the semantic content of the representation. Items stored in the database are retrieved and used from various other modules of ACOUSMA.

AmI Audio Library Explorer, a content management system (CMS), was developed for the AmI Audio Library to enable searching, listening, generating and uploading auditory representations. It is a responsive and easy to use web application for all devices (see Figure 2, left), intended to be used by auditory display experts. The application offers three main functions: *Searching*. The user can easily search for a specific auditory representation filtering database item by representation type, sound category, information type or tag. *Adding a new representation*. The user can either choose to upload a created representation to the database or generate a new auditory representation. Currently, only the generation of Spearcons is supported. The auditory display expert can upload a new auditory representation to the database and add additional tags or remove the extracted ones before uploading. *Bookmarking*. The user can choose to bookmark auditory representations. Apart from the ability to listen to bookmarked auditory representations, the Auditory Display expert can view and copy their unique IDs to be used for testing with AmI Speakers explorer.

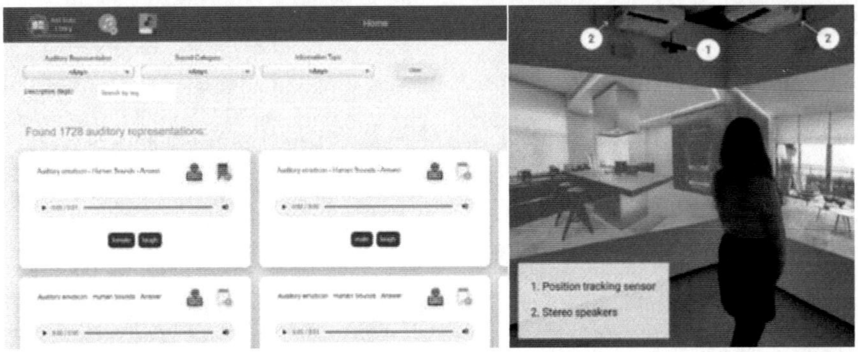

Figure 2. AmI Audio Library Explorer user interface (left). Simulation space infrastructure (right)

The Auditory Display Server, is a RESTful API which exposes functions that application developers can query to: (i) Start and control a specific auditory display playback, (ii) Request and control a recommended auditory display playback (for a specific user). After each query, a specific workflow is followed. In the case of (i), a specific representation is given with a playback action, location or user and urgency level. All these parameters are passed to the queue manager in order to be sent to the Speaker Director for playback. In the case of (ii), specific input for the recommender is given, as well as the desired playback action and urgency level. The recommender then produces a recommended representation which is passed to the queue manager in order to be then sent to the Speaker Director for playback. In order to better understand the two workflow directions, the individual components that take part in the process will be analyzed.

An **API Client Library** was established in order for application developers to easily query and use exposed functions of the Auditory Display Server API. Developers with applications in different programming languages can add language specific modules that ease communication with the RESTful API. Currently, modules for C# and Typescript programming languages have been designed and developed for developers ranging from zero to expert knowledge in auditory displays. Practically, experts in auditory displays may want to have better control using the specific auditory display playback functions, while developers with no knowledge of the field can use the recommender for producing auditory displays.

The Auditory Display Recommender is a knowledge-based recommendation system designed using current state-of-the-art approaches in auditory representations and displays as well as this type of recommender and technique (Aggarwal, 2016). The aim of the recommender is to return a single recommended auditory display for a given query-target while keeping the recommended item personalized to user preferences. The recommender runs a similarity function for each feature found in the expanded target (T), comparing it to each feature found in every item in the auditory representation database (X). The score of each similarity function is regulated by a specific weight configured by auditory display experts. Each function has a feature specific asymmetric reward configured by user's preferences. The refinement of the case-based recommender results works by using the technique of critiquing. Using different modalities provided by each AmI application, the user can critique the recommended auditory display. The critique is then used by the recommender to adjust the user's profile and therefore the produced auditory display. Usually, a list of recommended auditory display is presented to the user for further critiquing. If a user likes a recommended auditory display, then the respective case in the case history is adjusted.

The Queue manager component evaluates queues and directs playback requests to the Speaker Director. For every location in an AmI environment, a queue to hold incoming requests is initiated. Queues are evaluated according to requests' urgency. Effectively, that means that displays with higher urgency will precede those of lower urgency in the order of play. In the case of the emergency – urgency level, all current active displays will be superseded. Since multiple AmI applications may request different auditory displays for different users and locations at a single point in time, the Queue Manager ensures that those are handled appropriately and sent to the Speaker Director in an urgency-specific order. This, in combination with Speaker Director's evaluation of contextual information, prevents the scenario of a user getting overwhelmed and confused by auditory displays. Therefore, auditory displays are presented according to applications demands and according to users' activities and busyness of the auditory channel.

5. EVALUATION

Both a heuristic and a user-based usability evaluation were carried out for all modules of ACOUSMA. The ten well established heuristics by (Nielsen & Molich, 1990) were used and six experts in the field of HCI were invited to participate. The outcome of the evaluation indicated a total of 62 usability issues for the AmI Audio Library Explorer and 12 for the AmI Speakers Explorer interface. The major usability problems had to do with *Visibility of system status*, *Flexibility and efficiency of use*, and *Error prevention*. Those along with all minor issues were solved by adjusting or adding new functionality to both interfaces.

A weather application for an AmI environment was prepared for the user-based evaluation. A total of 17 people participated (7 people were assigned to the role of the auditory display expert, 6 to the role of the AmI environment inhabitant and 4 to the role of AmI application developer). The scenario was the following: "A construction company composed by architects, designers and programmers, builds apartments based on AmI technologies. With each purchased apartment, the company offers an interactive platform through which residents can install AmI applications. Those applications utilize shared resources and services provided by the apartment and display useful information in a variety of methods (audio, video) facilitating and improving the day-to-day lives of users. The company is currently utilizing a team of Auditory Display experts and AmI application developers to create a weather forecast application. The application, using audio, will promptly inform a user regarding the weather conditions at the location of a scheduled event on their calendar. For this purpose, the company uses the ACOUSMA system. Moreover, the company has a simulation space (simulating apartment rooms) to test applications before release. When complete, the application will be available for use through the apartments' interactive platform". Three use cases derive from this scenario: a) an auditory display expert using ACOUSMA to generate and test auditory representations for various weather conditions, b) an AmI application developer using the API client library module to initiate user-tailored auditory displays for various weather conditions, and c) an AmI environment inhabitant (apartment resident), experiencing the auditory result of the weather forecast application with the ability to critique. Each participant had to complete a number of tasks based on their role. In order to reenact the process of working on a weather forecast application, an interactive 3D space (see Figure 2, right) was utilized (Zidianakis, et al., 2021).

User-based evaluation for the role of Auditory Display Expert followed the think-aloud method (Someren, 1994) and through the completion of 11 tasks aimed at examining the usability of ACOUSMA. At the end, participants were asked to fill out the System Usability Scale (SUS) questionnaire (Brooke j. , 1996) (Brooke J. , 2013) and a number of additional questions that aimed at gathering statements regarding user's perception of both interfaces functions. Results were positive with a high average SUS score of 94.17 and with all users having a positive perception of AmI Audio Library Explorer functionality and 83% of them being positive about the functionality of the AmI Speakers explorer.

User-based evaluation for the role of AmI Environment Inhabitant was designed to measure the effectiveness of the Auditory Display Recommender module as well as the perceived usability of an application enhanced with ACOUSMA's features. To that end a blank preference profile was initiated letting the participant dynamically shape their profile through interaction with the weather forecast application and ACOUSMA. Participants followed 5 everyday scenarios that could take place in the smart home. According to each scenario, the participant would trigger events at the simulation space, initiating characteristic soundscapes, which were created to simulate real-life acoustic conditions. The weather forecast application would inform the participant about weather conditions according to each scenario. Moreover, the evaluator would collect comments regarding the understandability of the display. Also, the participant, using a tablet device, would critique the provided recommendation. At the end, participants were asked to fill the Usability Metric for User Experience (UMUX) (Finstad, 2010). The questionnaire was chosen as it has a high correlation to the SUS (Berkman & Karahoca, 2016), making it ideal to capture perceived usability for this user-group, as the evaluation was burdened with extensive questions and comments. The application scored an average UMUX score of 89.3/100. The poorest score indicated the need for improvements in the effectiveness and efficiency of the ACOUSMA's recommender. Additionally, 71.4% of participants could precisely understand the information being transmitted with the recommender having no prior knowledge of the user's preferences, while the percentage increased to 85.7% after participants used critiquing.

Finally, for the role of the AmI application developer, after the user-based evaluation, a number of comments regarding the documentation and overall usability of the API were gathered. Participants were given a template project of a web-application and were asked to complete certain tasks. Moreover, participants had to set up an AmI Audio Client. Afterwards, they were asked to fill in the SUS questionnaire and were interviewed individually. Overall, three out of four participants commented that the API was well documented. Also, only one participant had trouble finding the right function to use.

6. CONCLUSIONS

This paper has presented the design, implementation and usability evaluation of ACOUSMA, a platform that encapsulates all functions necessary to standardize the integration of context-aware, personalized auditory displays in Ambient Intelligence environments. Using ACOUSMA's interfaces and modules, auditory display experts can generate, upload, store and share auditory representations; AmI application developers can efficiently integrate meaningful auditory displays that are personalized and context-aware; AmI environment inhabitants can use the intelligent mechanism to critique and adjust auditory displays to their preferences at any time. The user-based evaluation of ACOUSMA yielded positive evidence that user requirements were successfully met. It is of course evident that, in order to ensure the fulfilment of all user requirements and usability of ACOUSMA, AmI applications must be developed to integrate its features. Results of the user-based evaluation have shown that ACOUSMA is ready to be used by AmI applications to enhance any AmI environment with auditory displays. The next step of this work is therefore to further evaluate the effectiveness of all ACOUSMA's modules through the usage of ACOUSMA in AmI applications of various domains.

REFERENCES

Aarts, E., & Encarnação, J. (2006). Into Ambient Intelligence. *True Visions*, 1–16. doi:10.1007/978-3-540-28974-6_1

Aarts, E., & Wichert, R. (2009). Ambient intelligence. *Technology Guide*, 244–249. doi:10.1007/978-3-540-88546-7_47

Adelstein, F., Gupta, S., & Richard, G. (2015). Fundamentals of Mobile and Pervasive Computing, McGraw-Hill 2005. Retrieved from https://academic.microsoft.com/paper/2540045046

Aggarwal, C. C. (2016). Knowledge-Based Recommender Systems. *Recommender Systems*, 167–197. doi:10.1007/978-3-319-29659-3_5

Berkman, M., & Karahoca, D. (2016). Re-assessing the usability metric for user experience (UMUX) scale. *Journal of Usability Studies archive, 11*(3), 89-109. Retrieved from https://academic.microsoft.com/paper/2513654055

Blattner, M., Sumikawa, D., & Greenberg, R. (1989, 3). Earcons and Icons: Their Structure and Common Design Principles. *Human-Computer Interaction, 4*, 11–44. doi:10.1207/s15327051hci0401_1

Brooke, j. (1996). SUS: A 'Quick and Dirty' Usability Scale. 207-212. Retrieved from https://academic.microsoft.com/paper/19399978

Brooke, J. (2013). SUS: a retrospective. *Journal of Usability Studies archive, 8*(2), 29-40. Retrieved from https://academic.microsoft.com/paper/2252211299

Candey, R., Schertenleib, A., & Merced, W. (2006). Xsonify sonification tool for space physics. Retrieved from https://academic.microsoft.com/paper/2100685825

Csapó, Á., & Wersényi, G. (2013, 11). Overview of auditory representations in human-machine interfaces. *ACM Computing Surveys, 46*, 1–23. doi:10.1145/2543581.2543586

Davison, B., & Walker, B. (2007). Sonification Sandbox Reconstruction: Software Standard for Auditory Graphs. Retrieved from https://academic.microsoft.com/paper/2108893166

de Campo, A. (2007). A data sonification design space map. *Proc. of the 2nd International Workshop on Interactive Sonification, York, UK.*

Dombois, F., Brodwolf, O., Friedli, O., Rennert, I., & Koenig, T. (2008). SONIFYER A Concept, a Software, a Platform. Retrieved from https://academic.microsoft.com/paper/2437944523

Finstad, K. (2010, 9). The Usability Metric for User Experience. *Interacting with Computers, 22*, 323–327. doi:10.1016/j.intcom.2010.04.004

Froehlich, P., & Hammer, F. (2004). Expressive Text-to-Speech: A user-centred approach to sound design in voice-enabled mobile applications. *Proc. Second Symposium on Sound Design.*

Gaver, W. (1986, 6). Auditory Icons: Using Sound in Computer Interfaces. *Human-Computer Interaction, 2*, 167–177. doi:10.1207/s15327051hci0202_3

Grond, F., & Berger, J. (2011). Parameter mapping sonification. In *The sonification handbook.*

Groß-Vogt, K., Weger, M., Höldrich, R., Hermann, T., Bovermann, T., & Reichmann, S. (2018, 6). Augmentation of an Institute's Kitchen: An Ambient Auditory Display of Electric Power Consumption. The International Community for Auditory Display. doi:10.21785/icad2018.027

Jeon, M., & Walker, B. N. (2009, 10). "Spindex": Accelerated Initial Speech Sounds Improve Navigation Performance in Auditory Menus. *Proceedings of the Human Factors and Ergonomics Society Annual Meeting, 53*, 1081–1085. doi:10.1177/154193120905301708

Kramer, G. (1994). *Auditory Display: Sonification, Audification, And Auditory Interfaces.* Retrieved from https://academic.microsoft.com/paper/2037001540

Lazzarini, V., Yi, S., Ffitch, J., Heintz, J., Brandtsegg, Ø., & McCurdy, I. (2016). *Csound: A Sound and Music Computing System.* Retrieved from https://academic.microsoft.com/paper/2625119159

Lewis, J. R. (2013, 3). Critical Review of 'The Usability Metric for User Experience'. *Interacting with Computers, 25*, 320–324. doi:10.1093/iwc/iwt013

Lockton, D., Bowden, F., Brass, C., & Gheerawo, R. (2014). Powerchord: Towards Ambient Appliance-Level Electricity Use Feedback through Real-Time Sonification. *Ubiquitous Computing and Ambient Intelligence. Personalisation and User Adapted Services*, 48–51. doi:10.1007/978-3-319-13102-3_10

McGee-Lennon, M., Wolters, M., McLachlan, R., Brewster, S., & Hall, C. (2011). Name that tune. ACM Press. doi:10.1145/1978942.1979357

Nemeth, G., Olaszy, G., & Csapo, T. (2011). Spemoticons: Text to Speech Based Emotional Auditory Cues. Retrieved from https://academic.microsoft.com/paper/2561770656

Nielsen, J., & Molich, R. (1990). Heuristic evaluation of user interfaces. ACM Press. doi:10.1145/97243.97281

Parseihian, G., & Katz, B. F. (2011, 10). Rapid Auditory System Adaptation Using a Virtual Auditory Environment. *i-Perception, 2*, 805–805. doi:10.1068/ic805

Patterson, R. (1990). Auditory warning sounds in the work environment. *Philosophical Transactions of the Royal Society B, 327*(1241), 485-492. Retrieved from https://academic.microsoft.com/paper/2029418069

Phillips, S., & Cabrera, A. (2019). Sonification workstation.

Schmidt, A., Kranz, M., & Holleis, P. (2005). Interacting with the ubiquitous computer. ACM Press. doi:10.1145/1107548.1107588

Serafin, S., Franinovic, K., Hermann, T., Lemaitre, G., RInott, M., & Rocchesso, D. (2011). *The Sonification Handbook.* Retrieved from https://academic.microsoft.com/paper/2184854514

Someren, M. (1994). The think aloud method : a practical guide to modelling cognitive processes. Retrieved from https://academic.microsoft.com/paper/2149617571

Tünnermann, R., Hammerschmidt, J., & Hermann, T. (2013). Blended Sonification –Sonification For Casual Information Interaction. Retrieved from https://academic.microsoft.com/paper/2595908185

Tünnermann, R., Leichsenring, C., Bovermann, T., & Hermann, T. (2015). Upstairs: A calm auditory communication and presence system. Retrieved from https://academic.microsoft.com/paper/2604127400

Walker, B. N., & Kramer, G. (2004). Ecolological Psychoacoustics and Auditory Displays. *Ecological Psychoacoustics*, 149–174. doi:10.1016/b978-012515851-0/50007-2

Walker, B. N., & Nees, M. A. (2011). Theory of sonification. *The sonification handbook*, 9–39.

Walker, B., Nance, A., & Lindsay, J. (2006). Spearcons: Speech-Based Earcons Improve Navigation Performance in Auditory Menus. Retrieved from https://academic.microsoft.com/paper/2134632849

Wilson, S., Cottle, D., & Collins, N. (2011). The SuperCollider Book. https://academic.microsoft.com/paper/1510634195

Worrall, D., Bylstra, M., Barrass, S., & Dean, R. (2007). Sonipy : the design of an extendable software framework for sonification research and auditory display. *ICAD 2007 : Immersed in Organized Sound : Proceedings of the 13th International Conference on Auditory Display, June 26-29 2007, Montreal, Quebec, Canada.* Retrieved from https://academic.microsoft.com/paper/1581350311

Zidianakis, E., Chatziantoniou, A., Dimopoulos, A., Galanakis, G., Michelakis, A., Neroutsou, V., ... Stephanidis, C. (2021). A technological framework for rapid prototyping of X-reality applications for interactive 3D spaces. *4th International Conference on Human Interaction & Emerging Technologies: Future Applications, IHIET-AI 2021.* Strasbourg, France: Springer.

PROPOSAL FOR SURROUNDING INFORMATION PRESENTATION SYSTEM FOR THE VISUALLY IMPAIRED

Honomi Chiba and Yutaka Miyaji
Department of Social Informatics, Graduate School of Social Informatics, Aoyama Gakuin University
5-10-1 Fuchinobe, Chuo-ku, Sagamihara, Kanagawa, Japan

ABSTRACT

Since people obtain more than 80% of their information from their sense of sight, visually impaired are limited in the information they can obtain. Nowadays, there can be 2.2 billion people who are visually impaired in the world. Generally, it is hard for those who have limited or weak eyesight to obtain the information about surroundings. However, there is little information using sound or Braille in public. In this research, we proposed a system that presents object information, character information, and their directions audibly to visually impaired people who have difficulty obtaining information about their surroundings, using an omnidirectional camera and a glasses-type wearable device. In this system, information about the surrounding area can be individually presented at any desired timing, regardless of the location. In addition, the system can be used by people who do not know where the information is because it uses omnidirectional cameras. To verify the accuracy of this system, we selected vertical and horizontal outdoor sign boards as the target objects and conducted an experiment to see if the system could actually recognize them. In addition, when the system was actually used by the experiment collaborators, we were able to obtain good evaluations for the high accuracy and ease of operation and were able to demonstrate the effectiveness of the system.

KEYWORDS

Wearable Interface, Information Presentation System, Visually Impaired

1. INTRODUCTION

More than 80% of the information we receive comes from our sense of sight (Educational Equipment Editorial Board, 1972) so visually impaired have limited access to information. However, it is estimated that there are at least 2.2 billion people in the world who have visually impaired (World Health Organization, 2019), and among them, those with limited or weak vision have a difficult time obtaining information about their surroundings. Since the aging of the population has been cited as the main reason for the increase in the number of people with visual disabilities (World Health Organization, 2019) it is expected to continue increasing in the future.

It is valid that the visually impaired read Braille as a means to obtain information other than through the sense of sight. However, only 10% of the Japanese visually impaired are able to use it because it requires training to learn (NEXT VISION, 2015). In addition, there is also the problem that there are few places where. As other means of obtaining information, sound signs and voice announcements can be mentioned. Sound sign represented by an acoustic signal generator has the problem of coexistence with the living environment such as noise(Japan Federation of the Visually Impaire, 2014). Also, the operation time of acoustic traffic signals is limited. Higashiyama(2002) researched what visually impaired people find inconvenient, some people expressed dissatisfaction with the operation time of acoustic signals(Higashiyama, A., 2002). In addition, the sound that allows the information to be read by the human voice is also a source of noise because the repeated sound is played and it is played at a loud volume regardless of the surrounding sound volume (Maekawa, M., 2007).

As a solution to this kind of noise in voice guidance, a system that uses a small transmitter/receiver signal aid (Japan Federation of the Visually Impaired, 2006) to provide voice information individually has been proposed. This system consists of a signal aid carried by the user and a voice guiding device installed at the point where the voice guidance is needed. When the user enters the receiving range of the radio waves emitted from the voice guidance device, the signal aid emits an electronic sound. Thus, the user is informed that they can receive voice guidance. If the user needs information, they can press the button on the signal aid. When the button is pressed, the signal aid transmits a radio wave within a range of 10 to 15 meters. After this radio wave is received by the voice guiding device, specific voice guidance is provided (Japan Federation of the Visually Impaired, 2013). This method of voice guidance is limited to the visually impaired who have a signal aid. Therefore, it is a measure against noise due to the guidance that is not provided when it is not needed. But there is a problem that the places where voice guidance is available are limited.

In this way, the time and place to obtain information is limited because it is insufficient that braille and sound provide the visually impaired with the information by means of Braille and sound is insufficient. In order to improve these problems, we thought that it is necessary to have a system that can present information to the visually impaired by sound at any time and in any place.

There have been many studies on the provision of information around the visually impaired. One such product is the OTON GLASS, which is researched, developed, manufactured, and sold. This is a pair of glasses that reads the text out loud for the user (Shimakage, 2018). When the user puts on the glasses, faces the text and presses the button on the frame, the text is converted into speech and presented. This is an interface for people who have difficulty reading the character, but who know where the character information such as dyslexics and weakness. However, it is difficult to use for people who do not know where the character information is. Miyata et al. (2016) proposed a wearable interface that uses an omnidirectional camera and a position sensor to present recognized character information in an audio format. The information can be obtained from 360° around and can be used by people who do not know where the information is due to using an omnidirectional camera. However, the interface is heavy and it is uncomfortable to wear it for a long time (Miyata, et al, 2016).

The purpose of this research is to evaluate its effectiveness in constructing a system that displays the surrounding object information, character information, and its direction by voice. Using the constructed system, we will conduct operational verification. After that, we will have the participants of the experiment use this system and evaluate its effectiveness through questionnaire surveys.

2. SURROUNDING INFORMATION PRESENTATION SYSTEM

In this chapter, we will specifically describe the surrounding information presentation system we have built in this research.

2.1 Figures and Tables

This system uses the omnidirectional camera "THETA V" and the glasses-type wearable device "JINS MEME" (Figure 1). JINS MEME can acquire the user's blink, the angle of the face, and the direction the user is facing. The user wears a hat to which THETA V is fixed, wears JINS MEME, put on earphones that do not block their ears, put on their neck Android, and to use this system. In this system, applications created using "Monaca", an application development platform, are used on Android. HTML, CSS, and JavaScript are used to develop this application.

The operation of the system is as follows.

Shooting

1. The user nods.
2. JINS MEME detects the user nods.
3. The app instructs THETA V to release the shutter after 2 seconds.
4. The user moves their face back to the front within 2 seconds.
5. THETA V's shutter is released.
6. The user can also use the buttons on the app screen to take a picture.
7. When the user turns up, the reset is performed and they can shoot again.

Obtaining object(character) information

1. After taking a picture, the user turns to the direction where the object(character) information they want to know is located.
2. The user tilts the face to the right(left).
3. JINS MEME detects the user tilts the face.
4. The app presents information on the object(character) in that direction through the earphone.
5. On the app screen, the user can also check the object(character) information in text.
6. The user can also use the buttons on the app screen to get object(character) information.
7. When the user turns up, the reset is performed and they listen to the object(character) information voice again.

For the font of the application, we adopted a gothic body that is easy to read for visually impaired people, based on the research (Ishida, H. and Amano, K., 2009). The colors of the buttons were yellow and blue based on color universal design (Bureau of Social Welfare and Public Health. 2011).

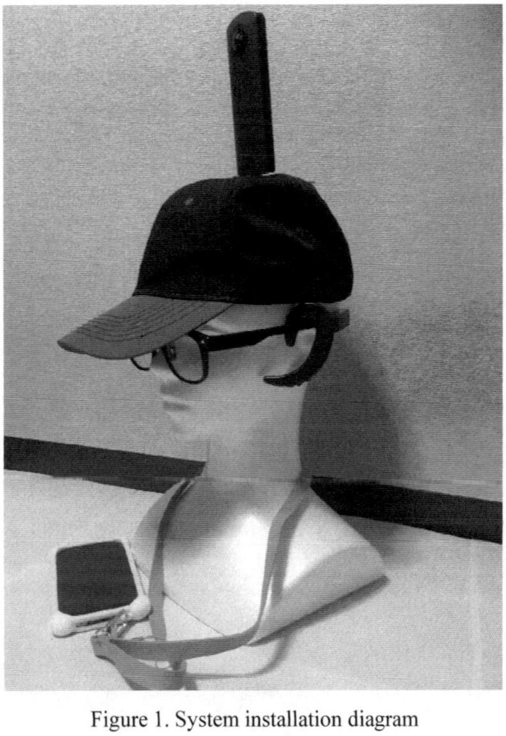

Figure 1. System installation diagram

2.2 System Configuration

In this section, the components of this system are described. The system consists of four parts: the image capture part, the direction update part, the object recognition and character recognition part, and the voice presentation part (Figure 2).

2.2.1 Image Capture Part

Using THETA V to capture an omnidirectional image. The image is taken by nodding or by pressing the button on the smartphone screen. The captured equirectangular cylindrical image will be divided into four images: front, back, left, and right. The divided images will be displayed on the screen of the smartphone. Each time a picture is taken, the displayed image will be updated.

2.2.2 Direction Update Part

Using JINS MEME to update the direction the user is facing. If there is a change of 45 degrees or more, the direction the user is facing is considered to have changed. Since the information presented audibly is always in front of the user, the information presented will change when the orientation changes. And the orientation display on the screen of the smartphone will also change.

2.2.3 Object Recognition and character Recognition Part

The recognition of object and character appearing in the four images that were taken and divided is performed in a server built in Python. In this research, we use the Computer Vision API provided by Microsoft Azure Cognitive Services to analyze the images, and receive the cognitive information of the front, back, left, and right sides in the form of texts. Since the object recognition results are in English, we will obtain the results in Japanese by using googletrans, which is a package for using global translation in Python. Object information can also be checked in text on the screen of a smartphone. Similarly, the character information can also be checked. Recognition is performed each time an image is taken.

2.2.4 Voice Presentation Part

The voice presentation part converts the Japanese language information obtained by the object recognition and character recognition part into voice. When the user tilts their face to the right, the object information in front of them is presented through earphones that do not block their ears. Similarly, when the user tilts their face to the left character information is presented.

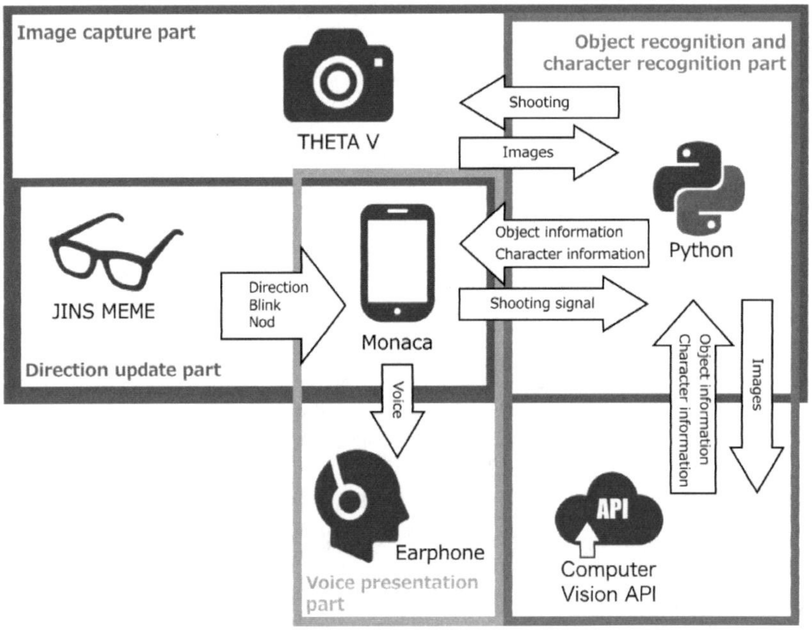

Figure 2. System configuration diagram

3. EVALUATION OF THE SYSTEM

In this chapter, we describe the experiment conducted to evaluate the effectiveness of the surrounding information presentation system constructed in this research.

3.1 Objectives

The purpose of this experiment is to confirm the accuracy and effectiveness of the information display system that we have constructed. First, we conducted an operation test outside to verify whether the target object and the character contained in it could be recognized correctly. Next, the system is used by the experiment collaborators, and a questionnaire is conducted to show the effectiveness of the proposed interface.

3.2 Methods

The method of the experiment conducted to evaluate the effectiveness of this system is described.

3.2.1 Experiment 1: Verifying the Operation of Object Recognition and Character Recognition

In Experiment 1, behavioral verification is conducted to confirm that the object and the character contained in it can be recognized correctly. Since this system is intended to be used outside, we selected horizontal signs and vertical signs located outside the house for verification. Each sign was photographed twice at 11:00 a.m. and 5:00 p.m. with the camera positioned in four directions (front, back, left, and right) to verify that the object and character were correctly recognized.

3.2.2 Experiment 2: Evaluating the Effectiveness of the Proposed Interface

In Experiment 2, we will have students in their teens and twenties use the system and conduct a questionnaire survey to evaluate the effectiveness of the proposed interface. The experiment will be conducted with eyes closed and with a clear file to narrow the field of vision from the periphery to the center. The questionnaire consists of 13 multiple-choice questions and 3 free-response questions. In the question of choice, the worst evaluation was 1 point and the best evaluation was 5 points. The contents of the questions are as follows.
Question 1: Is it uncomfortable to wear this interface for a long time?
Question 2: Is this interface heavy to wear?
Question 3: Is it embarrassing to wear this interface when going out?
Question 4: Is it dangerous to wear this interface when going out?
Question 5: Does this interface make you deaf to the sounds around you?
Question 6: Is it difficult to move when wearing this interface?
Question 7: Is the presented object information easy to understand?
Question 8: Is the presented character information easy to understand?
Question 9: Is the presented object information useful when peripheral information is not available?
Question 10: Is the presented character information useful when peripheral information is not available?
Question 11: Is the information on the application screen useful when my vision is poor?
Question 12: Is this system easy to operate?
Question 13: Can you operate this system as you want?
Question 14: What do you think is good about this system?
Question 15: What do you think should be improved in this system?
Question 16: Do you have any other comments or suggestions?

3.3 Results

In this section, we show the results of each experiment.

3.3.1 Experiment 1

The result of object recognition is that both horizontal and vertical signs were correctly identified as "signs" at both 11:00 and 17:00 in all directions. On the other hand, the results of character recognition were sometimes incorrectly recognized for both vertically and horizontally written signs. The misrecognized characters are shown in Figure 3. In the case of Japanese hiragana characters that are similar to each other, the cloud point was not recognized. In the case of similar characters between Chinese characters, the dot on the right-upper was not recognized.

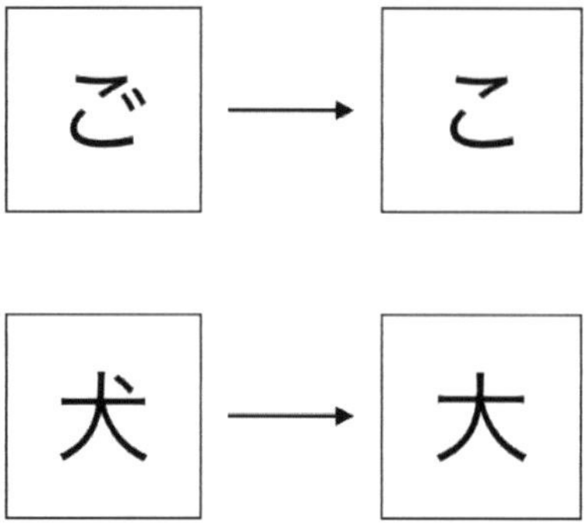

Figure 3. Experiment 2 - The misrecognized characters

3.3.2 Experiment 2

Table 1 shows the average and variance values of the questionnaires that were evaluated with the worst evaluation as 1 point and the best evaluation as 5 points of Experiment 2. In this experiment, 10 students used the system and answered the questionnaire afterwards. The experiment was conducted outside. Ten respondents were in their teens or twenties, two were male, and eight were female. In the open-ended questions from Question 14 to Question 16, many respondents commented on the accuracy and operability of the system. In addition, some respondents were concerned about the time it takes to get the information.

Table 1. Experiment 2 - Questionnaire results

Item	Average value	Variance value
Q1: Is it uncomfortable to wear this interface for a long time?	4.50	0.28
Q2: Is this interface heavy to wear?	4.30	0.68
Q3: Is it embarrassing to wear this interface when going out?	3.50	1.83
Q4: Is it dangerous to wear this interface when going out?	4.40	0.49
Q5: Does this interface make you deaf to the sounds around you?	5.00	0.00
Q6: Is it difficult to move when wearing this interface?	4.00	1.33
Q7: Is the presented object information easy to understand?	4.60	0.27
Q8: Is the presented character information easy to understand?	4.40	0.27
Q9: Is the presented object information useful when peripheral information is not available?	4.70	0.23
Q10: Is the presented character information useful when peripheral information is not available?	4.80	0.18
Q11: Is the information on the application screen useful when my vision is poor?	4.90	0.10
Q12: Is this system easy to operate?	4.50	0.28
Q13: Can you operate this system as you want?	4.30	0.46

3.4 Discussion

In this section, we will discuss the objective based on the results of the two experiments.

3.4.1 Experiment 1

Conduct a discussion of Experiment 1. The purpose of this experiment is to verify the operation of the object recognition and character recognition parts of this system. In the operation verification, investigated whether they could actually be recognized as we selected vertical and horizontal signs outdoors as the target objects.

According to the results of Experiment 1, both the horizontal and vertical signs were correctly recognized as "signs" at 11:00 and 17:00 in all directions. Which means that the accuracy of object recognition is high. On the other hand, some of the characters in the signs could not be recognized correctly.

However, the number of unrecognized characters is at most one character per signboard. Additionally the characters that could not be recognized correctly are mistaken for similar characters. Therefore, the character recognition has been achieved with some accuracy.

The characters in the horizontal signboard were all correctly recognized at 11:00, but some of them could not be correctly recognized at 17:00. The reason for this may be that the signboard was placed facing west and was backlit during the shooting. Therefore, it is an issue for the future to install a light on the camera so that the system can be used at any time of the day without any loss of accuracy.

3.4.2 Experiment 2

Conduct a discussion of Experiment 2. The purpose of this experiment is to evaluate the effectiveness of the proposed interface by having the experiment collaborators actually use the system and conducting a questionnaire survey.

According to the results of Experiment 2, a good evaluation was obtained in general. On the other hand, in response to question 3, "Is it embarrassing to wear this interface when going out?" with some respondents saying they were not embarrassed at all, while others said they were embarrassed. In addition, there was an opinion that "What do you think should be improved in this system?" in question 15 was "not fashionable". From this it is conceivable that some people did not like the interface in which the camera was fixed to the baseball cap used in this research. Also, in response to question 6, "Is it difficult to move when wearing this interface?", there was a comment that it was "difficult to move". This may have been unstable due to the fact that the camera and the cap were secured by only one screw.

Therefore, changing the type of cap that secures the camera is an issue to be addressed in the future. In addition, "The information was not immediate because there was a time lag between the recognition of the image and its display" was mentioned in the question 15. In this research, object recognition and character recognition were performed in all the quadrants of the captured images. In other words, it takes time from the time the photograph is taken to the time the information is presented due to the recognition being done 8 times in a single photograph. Therefore, it is necessary to examine the improvement of speed by also performing character recognition only when the results of object recognition include signs and other objects that may contain character.

4. CONCLUSION AND FUTURE WORK

In this research, we proposed a system that presents object information, character information, and their directions audibly to visually impaired who have difficulty in obtaining information about their surroundings using omnidirectional cameras and glasses-type wearable devices. This system addresses the problem that the time and place for obtaining information on the current Braille and sound support are limited because the surrounding information is presented in any timing to each individual without choosing the place. In addition, it can be used by people who do not know where to find the information due to the system using an omnidirectional camera.

In Experiment 1 of this research, to verify the operation of the object recognition and character recognition parts of the system, horizontal and vertical signs outside were photographed twice at 11:00 and 17:00 so that they were positioned in the four directions of front, back, left, and right of the camera to verify whether the object and character could be recognized correctly. As a result, both the horizontal and vertical signs were correctly recognized as "signs" at 11:00 and 17:00 in all directions, and it was confirmed that the accuracy of object recognition was high. In addition, it was confirmed that character recognition can be performed with a certain degree of accuracy. But some of the characters in the signboards could not be recognized because of turbid marks or dots on the right shoulder of Chinese characters. So although there is room for improvement such as the use of light.

In Experiment 2, the effectiveness of the proposed interface was evaluated by having the experiment collaborators actually use the system. As a result, we were able to obtain good evaluations for the high accuracy and ease of operation.

Through this research we evaluated the effectiveness of a system that presents object information, character information, and their directions audibly to the visually impaired. We were able to confirm the effectiveness of the system presented in this research.

There are three issues to be addressed in the future. The first point is to consider adding a light to the camera. In this experiment, it was confirmed that the accuracy of character recognition was lower when the camera was backlit. Therefore, it is necessary to investigate how the accuracy of character recognition changes when the light is turned on in a dark place or at a time. The second point is the consideration of the type of cap for the proposed interface. In this experiment, a baseball cap was used to fix the camera on the head, but some people said it was "embarrassing" and "difficult to move". So it is necessary to change or add the type of cap to make the interface suitable for oneself. The third point is about improving the speed of information presentation. In this research, since object recognition and character recognition were performed on all of the quadrants of the images taken, it took a long time for the information to be presented. Therefore, when object recognition is performed, only when a character is included, character recognition is performed to reduce the processing time. By doing so the speed of information presentation may be improved.

REFERENCES

Bureau of Social Welfare and Public Health. 2011. Tokyo Metropolitan Government Color Universal Design Guidelines. Available at: www.fukushihoken.metro.tokyo.lg.jp/kiban/machizukuri/kanren/color.files/colorudguideline.pdf (Accessed December 1, 2020).

Educational Equipment Editorial Board, 1972. *Industrial Education Equipment System Handbook.* Japan Science and Technology Press, Tokyo, Japan.

Higashiyama, A., 2002. Everyday Troubles Confronting the Individuals with Visual Impairment. *In Ritsumeikan journal of human sciences*. No. 4, pp 99-111.

Ishida, H. and Amano, K., 2009. Legible Fonts for Students with Visual Impairments. *In Tsukuba college of technology techno report*. Vol. 17, No. 1, pp 6-10.

Japan Federation of the Visually Impaired. 2014. Current status of sound signature, Available at: http://nichimou.org/impaired-vision/barrier-free/sound-sign/ (Accessed November 24, 2020).

Japan Federation of the Visually Impaired. 2006. Product name Signal aid. Available at: www.normanet.ne.jp/~nichimo/yogu/product/category/c10/c10-1_signal.html (Accessed November 24, 2020).

Japan Federation of the Visually Impaired. 2013. Report on a research project to establish a system to comprehensively guarantee the safety of the visually impaired when they go out. Available at: http://nichimou.org/wp-content/uploads/2014/02/9aff1483649e8747de10bfbd5c8bca55.pdf (Accessed November 10, 2020).

Maekawa, M., 2007. Development of a Noise-conscious Voice Guide System. *In Industrial research institute of ishikawa*. Vol. 57, pp 17-20.

Miyata, T. et al, 2016. Omnidirectional Word Detection System for Teaching with Stereophonic Sound. *In IEICE technical report*, Vol. 115, No. 516, pp 179-184.

NEXT VISION. 2015. A public interest incorporated association. Available at: http://isee-movement.org/real/life#anchor2 (Accessed November 24, 2020).

Shimakage, K.. 2018. Bring the joy of reading to the blind with OTON GLASS, glasses that read text out loud! Available at: https://camp-fire.jp/projects/view/25370 (Accessed November 10, 2020).

World Health Organization, 2019. *World report on vision.* World Health Organization, Geneva, Switzerland.

EFFECT OF WEBSITE COLOUR SATURATION ON TRUSTWORTHINESS AND VISUAL APPEAL IMPRESSIONS

Weronika Kaczmarek-Gajewska and Marian McDonnell
Institute of Art, Design & Technology, Kill Avenue, Dun Laoghaire, Co Dublin, Ireland

ABSTRACT

Initial impressions of websites can be formed in a matter of milliseconds. Colour is one of the most prominent features of a website, especially the saturation of colours. The present study investigated how colour saturation affected user perception of trustworthiness and visual appeal of websites. 122 participants were recruited and randomly divided into one of the three conditions (desaturated, control, saturated). Only 108 participants were included in the analysis, as 18 participants did not pass the Ishihara colour blindness test. Participants rated the trustworthiness and visual appeal of thirty website screenshots on a seven-point Likert scale. Two one-way ANOVAs and a Pearson's correlation were carried out to investigate user ratings of trustworthiness and visual appeal of websites based on the websites' colour saturation. Results found that colour saturation had no significant impact on visual appeal. Desaturated websites had a negative effect on perceptions of trustworthiness compared to the control group. Visual appeal and trustworthiness were positively highly correlated. Further research should be carried out, where only certain items on a website are manipulated, and investigation into gender is also recommended.

KEYWORDS

User Perception, Saturation, Visual Appeal, Trustworthiness

1. INTRODUCTION

1.1 Visual User Perception

User perceptions are vital to design (Lindgaard et al., 2011). Studies show that humans form impressions of websites in a matter of seconds (Reinecke et al., 2013). This underlines the importance of good web design. Furthermore, initial impressions outweigh subsequent stimuli. Therefore, the first impression may outweigh usability issues (Lindgaard, 2007). People may not interact with a website if they deem it visually unappealing or difficult to use (Cheshire et al., 2010). Additionally, user perceptions influence judgments such as perceived reliability, usability, information quality, usefulness, user satisfaction and trustworthiness (Lindgaard et al., 2011). Visual perception is an important concept in web design as websites are mainly interacted with visually. Perceptions are formed when light hits the retina in the eye, and the brain processes the information.

Visual design, content design and social-cue design are essential for establishing trust in websites (Fimberg & Sousa, 2020). Visual design is concerned with aesthetic appeal and considers colour, font type, space and layout. Content design includes brand information, news, product information, grammar, and social-cue design is concerned with customer service and social presence. Fimbreg and Sousa (2020) found that among visual design features, colour, font and images establish the most trust. Moreover, Thielsch et al. (2014) show that, in initial website impressions, aesthetics have the most influence. Moshagen and Thielsch (2010) show how visual aesthetics in web design influence perceived usability, satisfaction, and pleasure. The split-second initial impression of visual appeal predicts opinions of website trustworthiness and usability (Reinecke et al., 2013). Lindgaard et al. (2011) link visual appeal, trustworthiness and perceived usability and display a positive relationship between these variables. However, Frik and Mittone (2019) demonstrate that visual appeal only has a marginal influence on website trust. Their study is more concerned with trustworthiness in the context of privacy and purchase intention, but it is still an interesting finding. Other studies highlight the importance of visual appeal and its influence on trust. However, such studies mainly focus on how general visual appeal influences trust, and they do not specify which variables may affect the outcomes.

1.2 Visual Appeal and Trustworthiness

The term visual appeal can be used interchangeably with visual aesthetics or beauty. It is defined as an instant pleasant experience aimed at an object and occurs at a precognitive level (Moshagen & Thielsch, 2010). Furthermore, Tractinsky et al. (2000) discuss how what is beautiful is usable, emphasising that visual appeal influences the perceived judgements of many aspects of web design. This is related to Thorndike's (1920) halo effect, where physical attractiveness influences judgements of personality.

Users rate visual appeal almost instantly. Due to the speed at which users appraise a website's visual appeal, their impressions form precognitively, using bottom-up processes which assess incoming stimuli without previous knowledge (Lindgaard et al., 2006). This may be attributed to the mere exposure effect, where visual appeal is an initial emotional impression, rather than a cognitive one, as shorter time-frames discovered higher scores than longer time-frames (Bornstein & D'agostino, 1992). The mere exposure effect implies that users may view websites with which they are familiar as more trustworthy and visually appealing than unfamiliar websites. Once an impression of a website is formed, users may employ confirmation bias, ignoring factors that contradict their opinion, such as usability issues or untrustworthy content (Lindgaard, 2007). This further emphasises the importance of visual appeal.

Trust is a vital factor when predicting user behaviour and interaction with websites (Cheshire et al., 2010). Trust is involved when assessing risks such as monetary risks when purchasing online or privacy risks in social media platforms. Lack of trust may negatively affect the willingness to interact with websites (Cheshire et al., 2010). Trust exists in situations where risk and uncertainty are present. Trust and trustworthiness may have different meanings: trust is developed over time, while trustworthiness is an attitude that is usually a precursor to trust (Chopra & Wallace, 2003). Cheshire et al. (2010) propose the term general website trust for context-independent attitudes about websites' trustworthiness. The present study assumes this definition when discussing trust and trustworthiness. This involves trusting a website without any prior knowledge about it, tying in with the mere exposure effect where a familiar website may be rated higher in trust (Lowry et al., 2007). Familiarity with a brand does indeed increase trustworthiness towards a website (Beldad et al., 2010).

Trustworthiness towards a website can be increased by good reviews, a favourable return policy or third-party certifications (Chang et al., 2013). Many factors may influence trust towards websites. However, most research is conducted on e-commerce websites (Beldad et al., 2010).

1.3 Colour Online

Lindgaard (2007) notes that colour is one of the most salient factors in websites; often, the background colour is displayed before content. Khuong et al. (2018) confirm that colours significantly affect trust in websites in a Vietnamese population, specifically the colour orange over grey. Colour can be considered as a cue for trustworthiness, with blue colour-schemed websites eliciting the highest amount of trust (Alberts & van der Geest, 2011). Lindgaard (2007) confirms this, reporting that students described colour as their main reason for disliking websites, considering blue and pastel colours most appropriate for websites. However, Cyr et al. (2010) find that website colour preferences differ across cultures. Therefore it is important to consider the cultural context when considering colour applications in web design. Seckler et al. (2015) divide colour based on its properties. These are hue (the pure spectral colour), saturation (the intensity of a colour), and brightness (the visually perceived luminance of a colour). When analysing the colourfulness of websites Nordhoff et al. (2018) found that the variable colourfulness was too broad and further specified sub metrics such as image amount, colour saturation defined as the average pixel value of saturation, and colourfulness, defining it as the average colour pixel differing from grey. The saturation of colour was the most significant amongst colourfulness variables for local websites. On the contrary, Seckler et al. (2015) find that colour is not as significant in affecting visual appeal in users as structural factors, such as vertical symmetry and visual complexity. However, manipulating colour affected the visual complexity. Therefore there is a link there nonetheless. Contrarily, Pengnate et al. (2018) found that visual complexity had no significant visual appeal effect. They note, however, that they only tested e-commerce websites, which may have lower visual complexity. According to Seckler et al. (2015), higher colour saturations were rated as having more visual appeal. Furthermore, Camgöz et al. (2004) show that images high in saturation and brightness attract the most attention. Skulmowski et al. (2016) find the contrary, that highly saturated websites have a negative effect on website trustworthiness and visual appeal. Lindgaard (2007) finds the same result, as pastel websites (low in saturation) were named the most visually appealing. As Nordhoff et al. (2018) have shown, colour saturation is the most significant amongst specific colour variables, such as colourfulness or image amount.

1.4 Present Study

Research rarely focuses on specific visual design factors that affect user impressions, such as the number of textboxes or images. Furthermore, studies exhibit mixed results as to the appeal and trustworthiness of colour saturation. Additionally, few studies focus on specific colour properties and have poor control over said properties (Seckler, Opwis & Tuch, 2015). Therefore, the current study aims to focus on the colour saturation of websites and their effect on visual appeal and trustworthiness.

Based on the previous research, the current study aims to investigate the effect of colour saturation on visual appeal and trustworthiness. The following research question is presented:

RQ: Is visual appeal and trustworthiness affected by website colour saturation?

The following hypotheses are proposed:

H1: There will be a significant difference for internet users in their visual appeal scores based on the website's colour saturation.

H2: There will be a significant difference for internet users on their trustworthiness scores based on the website's colour saturation.

H3: There will be a significant correlation between trustworthiness scores and visual appeal scores.

2. METHODOLOGY

2.1 Design

The current study employs a between-subjects experimental design. Colour saturation is the independent variable (k=3, desaturated -50%, saturated +50%, control 0%), and trustworthiness and visual appeal are the dependent variables. The current study employs a between-subjects design as studies find that, in website aesthetics research, participants may too easily detect the manipulation, possibly biasing their response (Thielsch & Hirschfeld, 2012). According to recommendations by Seckler et al. (2015), six website genres have been chosen for the experiment (e-commerce, online newspapers and news portals, search engines, social networking, company, and various websites).

2.2 Participants

A total of 122 participants took part in the experiment. However, of the 122 participants, 104 had normal colour vision and passed the shortened Ishihara Colour Test (Ishihara, 1987). The 18 participants who did not pass the test were removed from the analysis. Participants were recruited using convenience snowball sampling and were aged between 18 and 74 (M=29.82, SD=14.01). Of the 104 participants, 69.2% were female, and 30.8% were male. 80.8% of participants were born in Ireland. However, all participants were included as Ireland is a multicultural country. According to the 2016 census, 11.6% of the population is non-Irish (CSO, 2017). Most participants rated themselves to have above-average internet usage experience (72.7%), with only 4% rating themselves below-average. The study was approved by relevant Ethics Committee (DTPEC). All participants were treated according to the ethical standards set out by the Psychological Society of Ireland.

2.3 Materials

The stimulus materials consisted of 30 websites, 5 each across six different content domains (E-commerce, online newspapers and news portals, company websites, social networking websites, search engines, various types). These domains were based on the mental models found by Roth et al. (2010). The mental models describe where users expect to find web objects within a website. This was to allow for a wide variance between the websites presented to the participants. Screenshots were taken of existing web pages (always the main page) to ensure the experiment's high ecological validity. Furthermore, to control for the confounding effects of other features of websites (e.g., usability) and increase the study's internal validity, static images were used instead of functioning websites. However, this may have also negatively impacted the realism of the experiment.

The websites were rated using a 7 point Likert Scale. Previous research has shown that these single-item measurements are appropriate for initial aesthetic assessments (Jacobsen et al., 2004) and are regarded sufficiently reliable and valid for first-time perception judgements (Baumgartner et al., 2019). Single-item measures may be more optimal for measuring perceptions in a long battery of questions where participants may find multiple-item measures repetitive (Baumgartner et al., 2019).

All websites were checked for their page rank to control for the familiarity effect, using Google PageRank scores of 6 or less. Google PageRank scores range from 0 (very unpopular) to 10 (very popular)) using the online tool CheckPageRank (CheckPageRank.net, 2004). All 30 websites were screenshotted using Google Chrome Version 87.0.4280.109 (Official Build) (64-bit) in full-screen mode at a resolution of 1920 X 1080 pixels. Each screenshot was manipulated for colour saturation using Adobe Photoshop (Version 21). The desaturated condition was a -50% saturation, while the saturated version was a +50% saturation overlay to keep the saturation uniform (Skulmowski et al., 2016).

All materials were included in a Microsoft Forms questionnaire on a password-protected sever, which is a college requirement for GDPR data protection reasons. This included the Ishihara Test for Colour Blindness (1987). The study also included an information sheet, a consent form, and a debrief, all embedded into online Microsoft Forms. The information sheet included why the study was being carried out and how the participants' data would be collected and anonymised. The Microsoft Forms questionnaires were disseminated using an online tool to randomise the assigned conditions while still keeping the personal data on a secure server (Allocate Monster, 2021).

2.4 Procedure

A link invite to take part in the study was made available to the participants. When the participants clicked the link, they were directed to one of three Microsoft Forms (one of the three conditions). They were then welcomed and invited to participate in the experiment and asked to complete the questionnaire on a laptop or computer where possible. Each of the participants was randomly assigned to one of the three condition groups. Next, the participants were asked simple demographic questions, including age, gender, country of birth, and internet use habits. The participants were then required to participate in the shortened Ishihara Colour test, to control for possible colour blindness (Ishihara, 1987).

Then screenshots of websites were shown to the participants. A time limit did not restrain these viewings, as many studies show no significant difference between time conditions when measuring initial perceptions (Skulmowski et al., 2016). After the participants viewed the image, they rated the visual appeal and trustworthiness of the website on a seven-point Likert scale (1 being not at all trustworthy/visually appealing to 7 being very trustworthy/visually appealing).

3. RESULTS

3.1 Overview

IBM SPSS, Version 26 was used to perform two, between groups one-way analysis of variances (ANOVA) on the data collected. The dependent variables were trustworthiness and visual appeal. The independent variable was colour saturation of websites (desaturated -50%, control 0%, saturated +50%). Pearson's correlation was also conducted to test the relationship between two dependent variables. For all statistical tests, an alpha level of .05 was used. Participants were randomly assigned to one of the three conditions, where they rated 30 websites, and their scores were then averaged to conduct the analysis.

Preliminary tests were conducted to test assumptions. A Levene's Test of Homogeneity of Variance indicated that the assumption of homogeneity of variance had not been violated. The data was normally distributed. Outliers were detected and removed. Of the 122 participants that took part in the study, 18 were excluded for not meeting the colour blindness criteria. Furthermore, question 5 of the Ishihara test was excluded from analysis, as many participants typed in a number when there was none. Furthermore, 16 participants failed to complete the visual appeal questions due to a Microsoft Forms malfunction. However, their scores were still used for trustworthiness analysis but not for visual appeal analysis.

88 participants were included in the visual appeal analysis.H1 stated that the saturation would influence initial visual appeal impressions of websites. A one-way between-groups ANOVA was conducted to explore the impact of colour saturation on initial impressions of websites' visual appeal. Participants were randomly assigned to three groups according to the saturation level (Desaturated: -50%; Control: 0%; Saturated: +50%). There was no statistically significant difference in visual appeal for the three groups, F (2, 85) = 1.205, p = .305, eta=.02. Therefore, H1 was rejected.

A total of 104 participants took part in the trustworthiness analysis.H2 stated that the saturation would influence initial trustworthiness impressions of websites. A one-way between-groups ANOVA was conducted to explore the impact of colour saturation on initial impressions of websites' trustworthiness. Participants were divided into three groups according to the saturation level (Desaturated: -50%; Control: 0%; Saturated: +50%). There was a statistically significant difference in trustworthiness for the three groups, F (2, 85) = 4.161, p = .018, eta=.076. Post-hoc comparisons using the Tukey HSD test indicated that the mean trustworthiness score for the desaturated group was significantly lower than for the control group. Participants in the saturated group did not differ significantly from either the desaturated or control group. H2 was accepted.

H3 hypothesised that the visual appeal and trustworthiness of websites would have a significant linear correlation. A linear Pearson correlation was computed to investigate the relationship between initial impressions of visual appeal and trustworthiness. There was a strong positive linear relationship between visual appeal and trustworthiness, r (430) = .643, p<.0001. The higher the visual appeal, the higher the trustworthiness. 41% of the variance in the visual appeal is associated with trustworthiness. 36% of the variance in visual appeal is associated with trustworthiness in the saturated group, 39% for the desaturated group, and 46% for the control group.

4. DISCUSSION

4.1 Overview and Discussion

The present study investigated if initial perceptions of visual appeal and trustworthiness were affected by colour saturation. There was no difference between visual appeal scores across the conditions, therefore H1 was rejected. This is an interesting finding as research suggests that colour should influence visual appeal as it is the most salient website feature (Lindgaard, 2007). This may be due to the low power of the results and a lower number of participants. Unfortunately, due to software malfunctions, 16 out of 122 participants did not complete the study's visual appeal element. Another explanation for the non-significant result might be a lack of a time control variable. Lindgaard et al. (2006) show that aesthetic evaluations occur in 50ms evaluations. However, the longer the time allowed for evaluating aesthetics, the more thought processes are included in the evaluation process (Leder et al., 2004). Therefore, due to the time not being controlled as a variable, longer evaluations can see a shift in scores due to previous knowledge, domain expectations and personal preferences. Furthermore, the websites chosen for the experiment had a rank of 6 or lower on GoogleRank, which could have negatively influenced the visual appeal scores. Their design may not have been as good as high ranking websites.

Colour saturation had a significant influence on trustworthiness, and H2 was accepted. Interestingly, the desaturated and saturated groups did not significantly differ, but analysis shows that participants evaluate saturated websites slightly more positively than desaturated ones. This result is consistent with Seckler et al. (2015), who found that more saturated websites are more aesthetically pleasing. However, it contradicts Skulmowski et al. (2016), who found increased saturation negatively affects trustworthiness. However, the contrary results to high saturation in Skulmowski's et al. (2016) research may be due to websites already being highly saturated, so any increase created oversaturated images. Perhaps, the Irish population prefers more saturated websites, while desaturated websites do not spark interest or catch attention. Furthermore, the lack of a time control variable may have affected the results as trustworthiness is usually evaluated in a longer time frame. The evaluation of trustworthiness may involve a more top-down and deliberate process, which the experiment allowed with no time control.

H3, which stated that there would be a correlation between trustworthiness and visual appeal, was accepted. There was a strong positive correlation between the dependent variables. This shows that there is an indirect effect of colour saturation on visual appeal through trustworthiness. If the trustworthiness is high, the visual appeal is also high, but this effect is not directly due to the saturation.

4.2 Theoretical and Practical Implications

The implications of this study suggest that colour is a significant factor in website design. Website developers should consider how to use saturation to their advantage. Desaturated websites evoke less trustworthiness towards a website and should be avoided at the design stage. Users will be more likely to interact with and invest time on a website when it is more saturated. Hall and Hanna (2004) show that utilising user's preferred colours and greater aesthetic rating of websites led to higher intention to purchase online. Most prominently, saturation is important for colour blind people as contrasting saturations on a website help distinguish elements (Hall & Hanna, 2004). Furthermore, this project's results fill a research gap identified in the literature review. The results show that saturation is, in fact, a significant part of colour and aesthetic evaluations.Another theoretical implications is that colour saturation considerations should be part of visual design education. Furthermore, the results underline the need for more research to be completed on the colour factors (hue, brightness, saturation) as the present study found significant results. The present study strengthens the finding that lower saturation in websites has a negative effect on evaluations of visual appeal and trustworthiness.

One of this present study's strengths is that the contrast levels were both equal and consistent in differing from the control condition. Furthermore, the trustworthiness scale condition had a good power effect and had a sufficient amount of participants in each condition. The addition of the control group allowed the researcher to see the true results of saturation on user perceptions. This control group had not been used in previous studies. Another strength of the study is that the participants completed the experiment in non-lab controlled environments, positively influencing ecological validity. Participants viewed the screenshots as they would on an everyday basis, and therefore the results can be more valid.

The present study's main limitation was the website screenshots were not displayed full-screen, and therefore were viewed as smaller images, thus interfering with ecological validity. Furthermore, there were no time constraints in the experiment, which could have led to more positive ratings due to the familiarity effect.

No randomisation of images could be achieved due to the constraints of the software. Moreover, the websites had not been pre-tested for the prototypicality of the content domains. The websites were compiled according to the GoogleRank rating to avoid the familiarity effect. Another limitation is that no qualitative data was collected from the participants.

4.3 Future Research

In future research, it is recommended to control other website elements, such as website complexity, to gain true insight into the effect of colour saturation. Also, it is recommended that the experiment be carried out on equivalent computers to keep the conditions more constant. Unfortunately, due to Covid19, the study had to be carried out remotely. Despite asking participants to complete the study on a computer or laptop, nearly half completed the experiment on a mobile phone, which could have affected the results.

Furthermore, it would be interesting to investigate how the saturation of specific objects on a website would affect visual appeal and trustworthiness. In the present study, the whole websites' saturation had been adjusted. However, many websites may have only some elements more saturated. Therefore manipulating some items only within a website may create different results and produce more ecologically valid results.

4.4 Conclusion

In conclusion, the present study supports Seckler's et al. (2015) findings that websites with higher saturation are more visually appealing and trustworthy, and users negatively consider desaturated websites. While saturated websites were not significant, they were higher in ratings than desaturated ones for both trust and visual appeal. It seems that aesthetic choices may have important implications for website designers and developers, specifically colour saturation. Saturation can attract attention and may be helpful in creating accessible websites for colour blind people.

REFERENCES

Alberts, W. A., & van der Geest, T. M. (2011). Color matters: Color as trustworthiness cue in web sites. *Technical communication*, *58*(2), 149-160.

Allocate Monster. (2021, January). Allocate Monster. Retrieved January, 2021, from https://allocate.monster/

Baumgartner, J., Sonderegger, A., & Sauer, J. (2019). No need to read: Developing a pictorial single-item scale for measuring perceived usability. *International Journal of Human-Computer Studies*, *122*, 78-89.

Beldad, A., De Jong, M., & Steehouder, M. (2010). How shall I trust the faceless and the intangible? A literature review on the antecedents of online trust. *Computers in human behavior*, *26*(5), 857-869.

Bornstein, R. F., & D'agostino, P. R. (1992). Stimulus recognition and the mere exposure effect. *Journal of personality and social psychology*, *63*(4), 545.

Camgöz, N., Yener, C., & Güvenç, D. (2004). Effects of hue, saturation, and brightness: Part 2: Attention. *Color Research & Application*, *29*(1), 20-28.

Chang, M. K., Cheung, W., & Tang, M. (2013). Building trust online: Interactions among trust building mechanisms. *Information & management*, *50*(7), 439-445.

CheckPageRank.net. (2004). *Check Page Rank - Check Your PageRank Free!* CheckPageRank. https://checkpagerank.net/index.php

Cheshire, C., Antin, J., Cook, K. S., & Churchill, E. (2010). General and familiar trust in websites. *Knowledge, Technology & Policy*, *23*(3-4), 311-331.

Chopra, K., & Wallace, W. A. (2003, January). Trust in electronic environments. In *36th Annual Hawaii International Conference on System Sciences, 2003. Proceedings of the* (pp. 10-pp). IEEE.

CSO. (2017, September 25). *Census of Population 2016 – Profile 7 Migration and Diversity - CSO - Central Statistics Office.* https://www.cso.ie/en/releasesandpublications/ep/p-cp7md/p7md/

Cyr, D., Head, M., & Larios, H. (2010). Colour appeal in website design within and across cultures: A multi-method evaluation. *International journal of human-computer studies*, *68*(1-2), 1-21.

Fimberg, K., & Sousa, S. (2020, July). The Impact of Website Design on Users' Trust Perceptions. In *International Conference on Applied Human Factors and Ergonomics* (pp. 267-274). Springer, Cham.

Frik, A., & Mittone, L. (2019). Factors influencing the perception of website privacy trustworthiness and users' purchasing intentions: The behavioral economics perspective. *Journal of theoretical and applied electronic commerce research*, *14*(3), 0-0.

Hall, R. H., & Hanna, P. (2004). The impact of web page text-background colour combinations on readability, retention, aesthetics and behavioural intention. *Behaviour & information technology*, *23*(3), 183-195.

Ishihara, S. (1987). *Test for colour-blindness*. Tokyo, Japan: Kanehara.

Jacobsen, T., Buchta, K., Köhler, M., & Schröger, E. (2004). The primacy of beauty in judging the aesthetics of objects. *Psychological Reports*, *94*(3_suppl), 1253-1260.

Khuong, T. T., Nhi, P. Y., Nhan, D. T., & Thuan, N. H. (2018, February). Colour, trust, satisfaction, and E-loyalty: the vietnamese experience of website design. In *Proceedings of the 2nd International Conference on Machine Learning and Soft Computing* (pp. 140-144).

Leder, H., Belke, B., Oeberst, A., & Augustin, D. (2004). A model of aesthetic appreciation and aesthetic judgments. *British Journal of Psychology*, *95*(4), 489e508. http://dx.doi.org/10.1348/0007126042369811.

Lindgaard, G. (2007). Aesthetics, visual appeal, usability and user satisfaction: what do the user's eyes tell the user's brain? *Australian Journal of Emerging Technologies & Society, 5(1).*

Lindgaard, G., Dudek, C., Sen, D., Sumegi, L., & Noonan, P. (2011). An exploration of relations between visual appeal, trustworthiness and perceived usability of homepages. *ACM Transactions on Computer-Human Interaction, 18(1), 1–30.* doi:10.1145/1959022.1959023

Lindgaard, G., Fernandes, G., Dudek, C., & Brown, J. (2006). Attention web designers: You have 50 milliseconds to make a good first impression!. *Behaviour & information technology*, *25*(2), 115-126.

Lowry, P. B., Roberts, T. L., & Higbee, T. (2007, July). First impressions with websites: the effect of the familiarity and credibility of corporate logos on perceived consumer swift trust of websites. In *International Conference on Human-Computer Interaction* (pp. 77-85). Springer, Berlin, Heidelberg.

Moshagen, M., & Thielsch, M. T. (2010). Facets of visual aesthetics. *International Journal of Human-Computer Studies, 68(10), 689–709.* doi:10.1016/j.ijhcs.2010.05.006

Nordhoff, M., August, T., Oliveira, N. A., & Reinecke, K. (2018, April). A case for design localization: Diversity of website aesthetics in 44 countries. In *Proceedings of the 2018 CHI Conference on Human Factors in Computing Systems* (pp. 1-12).

Pengnate, S. (Fone), Sarathy, R., & Lee, J. (2018). The Engagement of Website Initial Aesthetic Impressions: An Experimental Investigation. *International Journal of Human-Computer Interaction,* 1–15. doi:10.1080/10447318.2018.1554319

Reinecke, K., & Gajos, K. Z. (2014). Quantifying visual preferences around the world. *Proceedings of the 32nd Annual ACM Conference on Human Factors in Computing Systems - CHI '14.* doi:10.1145/2556288.2557052

Reinecke, K., Yeh, T., Miratrix, L., Mardiko, R., Zhao, Y., Liu, J., & Gajos, K. Z. (2013). Predicting users' first impressions of website aesthetics with a quantification of perceived visual complexity and colorfulness. *Proceedings of the SIGCHI Conference on Human Factors in Computing Systems - CHI '13.* doi:10.1145/2470654.2481281

Roth, S. P., Schmutz, P., Pauwels, S. L., Bargas-Avila, J. A., & Opwis, K. (2010). Mental models for web objects: Where do users expect to find the most frequent objects in online shops, news portals, and company web pages? *Interacting with Computers, 22*(2), 140–152. doi:10.1016/j.intcom.2009.10.004

Seckler, M., Opwis, K., & Tuch, A. N. (2015). Linking objective design factors with subjective aesthetics: An experimental study on how structure and color of websites affect the facets of users' visual aesthetic perception. *Computers in Human Behavior, 49,* 375–389. doi:10.1016/j.chb.2015.02.056

Skulmowski, A., Augustin, Y., Pradel, S., Nebel, S., Schneider, S., & Rey, G. D. (2016). The negative impact of saturation on website trustworthiness and appeal: A temporal model of aesthetic website perception. *Computers in Human Behavior, 61,* 386-393. https://doi.org/10.1016/j.chb.2016.03.054

Thorndike, E.L. (1920). A constant error in psychological ratings. *Journal of Applied Psychology*, *4*(1), 25–29. https://doi.org/10.1037/h0071663

Thielsch, M. T., Blotenberg, I., & Jaron, R. (2014). User evaluation of websites: From first impression to recommendation. *Interacting with Computers*, *26*(1), 89-102.

Tractinsky, N., Katz, A. ., & Ikar, D. (2000). What is beautiful is usable. *Interacting with Computers, 13(2), 127–145.* Doi: 10.1016/s0953-5438(00)00031-x

BIOBIASED: A SPECULATIVE NEWS APP FOR SYNTHETIC BIOLOGY

Amalia Kallergi
Institute for Science in Society, Radboud University, Heyendaalseweg 135, 6525 AJ, Nijmegen, The Netherlands

ABSTRACT

BioBiased is a mobile application that uses the format of fictive news to promote reflection over synthetic biology. The app introduces interested citizens to the benefits and risks of synthetic biology, the different application contexts in which synthetic biology might be deployed, and the different views and perspectives that may affect our responses to it. The work is motivated by an interest to exploit relevant HCI methods, namely design fiction and speculative design, to promote engagement with emerging technologies. Our work contributes a concrete digital artifact with a societally relevant purpose as well as a flexible framework to operationalize speculation in other emerging technologies too.

KEYWORDS

Design Fiction, Speculative Design, Mobile App, Synthetic Biology

1. INTRODUCTION

Today's emerging technologies, from AI and big data to synthetic biology, are negotiated with the acknowledgment that science and technology must be developed *for* and *with* society. Recent shifts in research and innovation practices (Zwart *et al.*, 2014) are characterized by increased attention to the impacts of a technology and by increasing degrees of public and stakeholder participation. Consider as an example the framework of Responsible research and innovation (RRI) (von Schomberg, 2013), and its emphasis on innovation processes that are anticipatory, reflective, responsive and inclusive (Stilgoe *et al.*, 2013). This social turn has also highlighted the prominent role of values. On the one hand, values shape science and innovation. On the other, they underlie our perceptions of new technologies and new technological risks.

The requirements of responsible innovation are not easy to meet. Nor can public engagement with science be universally catered by a single intervention. Nevertheless, we believe that such objectives are a worthwhile challenge for HCI expertise. Technological artifacts such as games, mobile applications and online platforms can be used to organize public engagement activities with qualities and affordances that are lacking in traditional, co-located formats. Moreover, HCI's rich methodological toolkit can be of relevance to practitioners faced with comparable challenges. Our shared challenges range from supporting participation to supporting ethical reflection. As Grimpe *et al.* (2014) note, methods of a more critical edge such as critical design (Erlhoff and Marshall, 2007) may be HCI's most timely contribution to responsible innovation.

This work appropriates a set of attractive HCI methods, namely design fiction and speculative design, to promote public engagement with an emerging technology. Specifically, we apply the strategy of speculation to promote reflection over synthetic biology, an emerging technology of substantial societal and ethical implications. Building on our earlier work in analogue games (Kallergi, 2016), we design a mobile application (*BioBiased*) that makes extensive use of speculative fiction in the form of fictive news about speculative synthetic biology products. *BioBased* is thus an example of an app with a societally relevant purpose in a domain where digital interventions have much to offer. It is also an example on how to operationalize speculation into a usable framework that can be easily applied to other emerging technologies too.

The remainder of this paper is organized as follows: In Section 2, we introduce the methodologies of design fiction and speculative design, highlight their potential to engage us with emerging technologies and review related work that uses speculation in the context of synthetic biology. In Section 3, we describe the making of the *BioBiased* mobile app, paying particular attention to the generation (i.e., composition and visualization) of its speculative content. Section 4 concludes this paper and provides directions for future work.

2. BACKGROUND

2.1 Design Fiction and Speculative Design

Design fiction is a productive coming-together of the cultural forms of design and fiction (Hales, 2013). It produces stories about technologies and the fictive world they inhabit. From fully-fledged science fiction (Johnson, 2009) to vignettes, videos, mixed media or appropriations of mass media, these stories activate the imagination and trigger their audiences to recreate and populate a world in which the artifact resides. Sterling (2009)'s much cited definition refers to the "deliberate use of diergetic prototypes to suspend disbelief about change", a definition that was further dissected into three constituting elements: a story world, a prototype existing in this story world, and a discursive space (Lindley and Coulton, 2015). Bleecker (2009)'s equally influential essay refers to the "conflation of design, science fact and science fiction" into objects that tell stories about possible futures. Hales (2013) addresses the multidimensionality of design fictions and emphasizes their speculative capacity. For the purposes of this paper, it suffices to say that design fiction involves the embedding of a technological artifact into a story world situated in the future. The practice is motivated by the firm belief that stories can facilitate discussion and reflection over, among others, the ethics and values surrounding a technology (Tanenbaum, 2014). It is also motivated by the desire to discuss and explore possible technological futures rather than the need to make a specific future happen. As others have noted (Linehan *et al.*, 2014), design fiction is a useful way to reflect about the implications of emerging technologies and it has been successfully applied by HCI practitioners in fields such as AI or robotics.

Design fiction can refer to both text-based and object-based (re)constructions of a story world. In the first case, an imagined technological artifact is embedded in a narrative structure: It may be described, depicted or implied in a story delivered in a textual, visual or mixed media format. Differences between design fictions and more traditional story-based HCI methods (e.g. scenarios) are discussed by Blythe (2014) who further explores a peculiar textual format, i.e. academic abstracts. In object-based fictions, the story is embedded in the imagined artifact, which is present in its material form. Object-based design fictions are often discussed alongside critical and speculative design for they all share an interest in the capacity of physical artifacts to enact the context in which this artifact is seemingly used. The question whether speculative design is a subset of design fiction or *vice versa* is not of immediate relevance to this paper.

Speculative design and critical design are practices that expand the practice of design beyond its traditional role as a problem-solving enterprise. Dunne and Raby (2013)'s influential book (and studio practice) set the agenda for design practitioners to critically engage with scientific and technological developments. At their core, critical design and speculative design emphasize both *criticality*, as the questioning of prevailing values, and *speculation*, as a way to navigate the many possible technological futures that lie ahead. Critical design is, thus, defined as a practice that "uses speculative design proposals to challenge narrow assumptions, preconceptions, and givens about the role products play in everyday life" (Erlhoff and Marshall, 2007). This aim is unmistakably a socially engaged one and one that strives to raise awareness and provoke debate. To this end, it uses speculation accompanied by humor, parody, provocation and disruption. Malpass (2013) offers a useful analysis of speculative and critical design in terms of their use of satirical devices and further highlights the use of humor and satire, in its many forms, as an instrument for reflection and debate. Helms and Fernaeus (2018) further remind us that humor is of dual nature, i.e., parodic and comedic, and that both elements can be useful for the construction of a design fiction.

Design fictions are often delivered in recognizable media formats, while speculative/critical designs are more often than not accompanied by similar supportive documentation (Malpass, 2013). Newspapers, product catalogues, advertisements and online platforms have been repeatedly employed to (better) situate speculative technological artifacts. For some (Auger, 2013), design fictions may be better conceptualized as "design factions", i.e. speculations in search of plausibility. The author further emphasizes the need for a context that is relatable, familiar and not too "science fiction"-like and suggests that familiar media formats can add to plausibility and familiarity. Others, however, note that familiarity with a format may cause misunderstandings and, eventually, deception (Coulton *et al.*, 2016).

This short overview reminds us of the qualities of fiction (understood here as both narration and fictiveness) and speculation (understood here as the design of what-if worlds) as a means to meaningfully engage with emerging technologies. This rich tradition provides us with strategies that can challenge assumptions, positively and productively surprise users and stakeholders, and stimulate discussion by situating and "domesticating" technologies into a (story) context.

2.2 Fiction and Speculation in Synthetic Biology

Synthetic biology is a heterogeneous practice that abounds with hope and hype. The integration of engineering principles with biological research is expected to deliver new-to-nature organisms for human use. Partially due to the resistance of EU publics to genetically engineered food and feed and partially due to the historical circumstance, ethical and societal aspects of synthetic biology are being examined already at the onset of the field. Some of these investigations play with fiction and speculation, either implicitly or explicitly.

Practices such as technology assessment, public engagement with science, or RRI often employ participatory activities familiar to HCI practitioners. In their various incarnations, workshops, focus groups and other deliberation events are likely to involve some narrative or speculative stimuli as a prompt for discussion. For example, short provocative statements about synthetic biology were used to facilitate discussion during synthetic biology futures workshops with conducted with experts (Frow and Calvert, 2013). These statements announce a plausible yet unrealized expectation about synthetic biology occurring at an unspecified moment in the future. Furthermore, participatory forms of technology assessment often make use of future scenarios to explore the ethical dilemmas and value conflicts accompanying emerging technologies (Lucivero, 2016). The format of techno-moral vignettes (Boenink *et al.*, 2010), i.e. future "snapshots" (Stemerding *et al.*, 2019) illustrating the moral conflicts associated with emerging technologies, have been employed in a number of investigations on the ethics of synthetic biology. Consider as an example the collection of stories generated by Rathenau institute (*SynBio Politics | Rathenau Instituut*), the Dutch office for technology assessment and science system assessment, based on vignettes by life science students participating in the iGEM[1] competition (Betten *et al.*, 2018).

The subject matter of synthetic biology has attracted significant attention from speculative designers. Dunne and Raby (2013) dedicate a chapter to examples from the life sciences. Out of the many exhibitions around the life sciences, we wish to mention the 2013 exhibition "Grow your own" (*Grow Your Own... | Science Gallery*, 2013), hosted by the Science Gallery at Trinity College Dublin. The exhibition was dedicated to synthetic biology and synthetic life and featured, among others, the notorious "E.chromi" (Ginsberg *et al.*, 2009), a speculative work by A. Ginsberg created in collaboration with the Cambridge University iGEM team. A conscious effort to involve creative forces in understanding the implications of synthetic biology was undertaken by the "Synthetic Aesthetics" initiative. The project coupled 6 pairs of speculative designers and synthetic biologists for a 2-week residency (Calvert and Schyfter, 2017), resulting in co-produced, speculative works and a book publication (Ginsberg *et al.*, 2014). The organizers highlight the shared interests between STS (Science and Technology studies) scholarship and critical design, including the investigation of alternative futures and the exposure of assumptions, and emphasize the playful and tangible qualities of speculative designs. Lastly, when it comes to the use of speculative narratives in the debate surrounding synthetic biology, a mention is due to the Bio:Fiction initiative (Schmidt *et al.*, 2015). Bio:Fiction is a short film festival on emerging scientific topics, with synthetic biology featuring in the festival's first (2011) and second (2014) editions. The organizers analyze the depicted futures of synthetic biology as envisioned by the participating filmmakers and note that such speculations can suggest new framings for debating synthetic biology.

3. BIOBIASED: A SPECULATIVE NEWS APP

3.1 Concept and Implementation

BioBiased is a mobile app based on a collection of fictive cases about synthetic biology. Users can draw a case, choose between two opposing arguments and influence with their answers the collective state of the fictive world (cf. Figure 1). Each case consists of two elements (cf. Figure 1):

- A fictive news story, featuring a speculative synthetic biology application, situated in a world where synthetic biology is widespread and commonplace

[1] The iGEM (International Genetically Engineered Machine) competition (*igem.org*) is an annual event in which teams of undergraduate students propose and implement novel synthetic biology solutions.

- Two opposing arguments, for and against the featured application

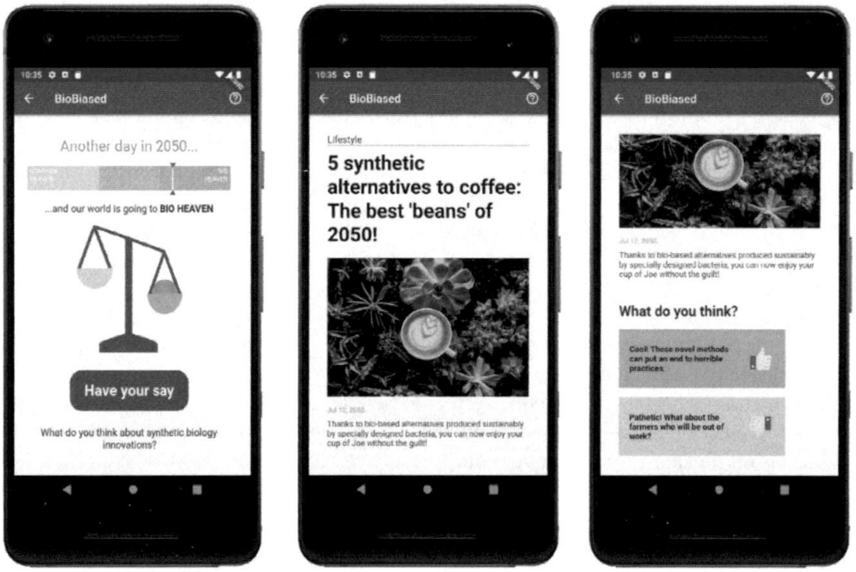

Figure 1. Start screen and case example. Opposing arguments are provided in relation to the fictive news story

The format of new stories allows us to represent speculative synthetic biology applications in a short and recognizable manner. Naturally, the stories capture the hype of synthetic biology and the hopes associated with it, not its scientific reality. Moreover, they allow us to represent the broader context of the envisioned applications. Although brief, our news stories activate a setting to be populated by one's existing knowledge and imagination and a milieu of human practices around the featured application. Opposing arguments, on the other hand, capture the range of concerns surrounding biotechnology and the multiplicity of issues that different stakeholders may find relevant. As such, they provide additional depth to the activated context: the news story is complemented by personal views that often bring to our attention neglected or ignored aspects. At the same time, the opposing arguments also illustrate the complexity of the debate and the inadequacy of absolute, polarized positions.

BioBiased was produced in the context of *SafeChassis*, a synthetic biology research project with a strong commitment to RRI. The bioengineers of *SafeChassis* work towards integrating built-in safety mechanisms ("genetic safeguards") in the genome of the Pseudomonas Putida (*P. Putida*) bacteria. These "safelocked" bacteria could then be used to implement safer synthetic biology products of commercial and societal relevance. *BioBiased* was designed as a public outreach initiative for (young) adults. Interested citizens are introduced to the benefits and risks of synthetic biology, the different application contexts in which synthetic biology might be deployed, and the different views and perspectives that may affect our responses to it.

A prototype of *BioBiased* was developed in the Flutter framework. In its present version, the application contains 21 cases. As a first step to capture the views of its users, the app also supports additional comments regarding one's argument of choice. Presently, the app is available via the Google app store for invited users only. The generation of the app's speculative concept was core to its development and it is described in detail in the remainder of this subsection.

3.1.1 Writing Speculative News Stories

To generate our news stories, we reviewed applications specific to *P. Putida* (Poblete-Castro *et al.*, 2012; Loeschcke and Thies, 2015; Nikel and de Lorenzo, 2018), i.e., the organism under investigation in *SafeChassis*. *P. Putida* is an industrially relevant bacterium, presently used for the manufacturing of useful chemicals in industrial settings. The potential of bio-based economy to provide a more sustainable mode of manufacturing was emphasized in our stories. Secondly, *P. Putida* is an attractive candidate for environmental applications such as bioremediation, i.e., the use of living organisms to detoxify polluted environments, and biocontrol, i.e., use of living organisms to control pest insects, weeds, or plant diseases. Novel, not yet realized applications as discussed in scientific literature on genetic safeguards were also considered (Moe-Behrens *et al.*, 2013; Schmidt and de Lorenzo, 2016). Finally, our set of examples was enriched by informal exchanges with project partners during the project's duration. Table 1 summarizes the application domains used for the generation of our stories.

Table 1. List of application domains for synthetic biology with corresponding applications. *NB*: Applications indicated in square brackets partially overlap with others in the list

Domain	Applications
Medical	[Drug production]
	New therapies, new drug delivery methods
	Microbiome enhancement, human enhancement
	Bio-sensing
Agricultural	Food security, new crops (drought – resistant, pest- resistant)
	Biocontrol
	Bio-sensing
Industrial, Material	Sustainable production, bio-based economy
production	Biodegradable materials
Environmental	Bioremediation
	CO2 reduction
	Waste management
	Energy, biofuels
	[Bio-sensing]

Our news stories are delivered in the form of online content. Visual resemblance with online posts was used to increase realism. Nevertheless, we wish our stories to be clearly perceived as fictive: Our examples are inspired by current scientific developments but are not yet realistically possible and should *not* be understood as such. To this end, all stories were labeled with a future date (*2050*) while the home and help page of the app indicate that users enter a fictive future world. To increase visibility, we incorporated references to a future year in the headline or description of the stories as appropriate. The format of the app is also expected to be sufficiently different from typical news outlets such as news websites or newsfeed apps. In addition to interface elements, an exaggerated, over-the-top tone and word puns such as paraphrasing recognizable brand names and toponyms were used to emphasize the speculative character of the story. Note that our news stories are not about synthetic biology *per se* but about the broader context of its applications. Therefore, we organized them into familiar news categories such as economy, local news or lifestyle blog posts. In the present implementation, the distribution of cases per application domain is as follows: environmental (7), medical (5), industrial (4), agricultural (3). The cases appear under the following new sections: lifestyle (4), economy (3), environment (3), health (2), local news (2), politics (2), advertorial (1), science (1), sport (1), world (1).

3.1.2 Generating Arguments: Technological Heaven or Conservative Haven?

To generate arguments for and against the featured applications, we compiled a list of ethical and societal issues associated with synthetic biology (Parens *et al.*, 2009; Schmidt *et al.*, 2009; Presidential Commission for the Study of Bioethical Issues, 2010; Newson, 2011; Rerimassie and Stemerding, 2014; Gregorowius and Deplazes-Zemp, 2016). Biosafety and biosecurity risks were only minimally represented. This corresponds with a vision of the fictive world in which genetic safeguards (i.e., the research products of *SafeChassis*) are successful and operational. Table 2 summarizes the broader issues that informed our arguments. Admittedly, these issues tend to be interpreted as sources of arguments *against* synthetic biology while arguments *for* a featured application typically emphasize its benefits. We are aware of this limitation and, whenever possible, tried to identify positive interpretations of the issues at stake and to emphasize different types of benefits (i.e. societal, economic, scientific and environmental).

Arguments are provided in a personal and informal tone implying uninhibited and uncensored reactions. They personify everyday responders with emotions, imperfections and daily concerns. Moreover, our arguments do not try to be balanced, watertight or convincing. On the contrary, they often express overly optimistic or overly suspicious positions in a tone that makes them hard to endorse fully. When examined in conjunction, we expect these exaggerated positions to become both hard to relate to and hard to dismiss.

Table 2. List of ethical and societal issues referenced in the arguments

Issue	Potential harms
Notion of life	a. Hubris of creating life b. Intrinsic value of life; commodification of life c. Reductionist view on life
Notion of unnaturalness	a. "Unnatural" products and processes b. Tampering with nature
Justice	a. Fair distribution of benefits; access to knowledge and tools; equity; divide haves/ have-nots b. Patents, ownership, intellectual property, monopolies c. Fair distribution of risks and benefits Sustainability; land and water use; overuse

3.2 Preliminary Evaluation

At early stages of development, we conducted a card sort activity with three members of our research group (experts in synthetic biology ethics) to check the appropriateness of our story fragments. Participants were asked to organize our news headlines first according to their own categories and then according to newspaper sections. While our final set of cases differs slightly from the one used in this card sort, the exercise was informative for two reasons. Firstly, it confirmed that the format of headlines is recognizable and that the referenced synthetic biology applications are, at minimum, perceived. Secondly, it highlighted productive conflicts in the categorization: The same application was perceived as either a solution to a grand societal challenge or a marketing trick. We tried to accommodate this plurality by using different news sections for comparable applications.

The visual and interface design of the mobile app was iteratively informed by rapid, informal evaluations. Early mockups and clickables were created in Illustrator and InVision and informally inspected by close affiliates who recommended a more light-weighted visual style. A deployed version of the app was informally inspected by one usability expert and formally tested by two casual users; the latter were observed while interacting with the app for as long as they deemed relevant. These evaluations revealed issues with the visibility of the future date and with the visualization of the world state. Suggestions and improvements in the form of interface and textual tweaks (cf. subsection 3.1.1) were implemented as appropriate in the present version. The casual users were also asked to select five adjectives out of a subset of 25 words (c.f. Microsoft Product Reaction cards method). Both participants described the app as meaningful, creative and relevant.

4. CONCLUSION

BioBiased is a speculative work insofar as it speculates how life in a future powered by synthetic biology could be. It is also a design fiction insofar as it situates synthetic biology applications (what is being prototyped) in a future world by means of narrative (news fragments). In effect, the what-if question we ask is: What if our society made widespread use of synthetic biology? What practices would emerge? What questions would be (still) troubling us? Many of our envisioned applications are direct translations of the present hype: What if all the promises of synthetic biology were technically achievable? Like speculative design, our stories 'domesticate' synthetic biology and dis-place it from the lab into everyday life. The broader context and multiple implications of an emerging technology are encapsulated both in the news stories and in the accompanying arguments. Our work, thus, contributes a flexible narrative framework that makes extensive use of speculation but can be easily applied to other emerging technologies. *BioBiased* is a concrete implementation that nicely showcases this while creating opportunities to empirically evaluate the effects of speculation.

During the composition of our fictive news, we were confronted with the risk of (too much) plausibility and, subsequently, with our own responsibility as researchers representing an academic organization. Preliminary results suggest that interface and textual tweaks can increase visibility of the future world and prevent misunderstandings. Futurist visuals were also suggested as a means to increase visibility (what Coulton *et al.* (2016) refer to as "signposts" for obvious fictions), a design choice that is worth considering further. Coulton *et al.* (2016) warn that familiarity with a fiction's format (in our case, online news) may lead to ambiguity and misunderstandings. We wonder if their observation still holds true in a time of increased awareness of fake news. Then again, synthetic biology is complex, unfamiliar and, in times, contested subject. We are curious to see how familiarity with synthetic biology may influence the perceived plausibility of our stories.

Presently, our app offers only limited opportunities for users to voice their opinions and concerns. Emphasis is more on encountering multiple perspectives than in articulating them. One can certainly question the representativeness of these perspectives, produced exclusively via desk research. Arguably, the conscious choice to exaggerate some of the arguments may result in an oversimplification of the debate or even in the reinforcement of stereotypes. We expect that the overarching humorous tone of the app and the juxtaposition of polarized positions can prevent this risk. Nevertheless, many opportunities reside in co-creating the application's content. Design fictions are identified by the HCI community as valuable tools for participatory design (Lyckvi *et al.*, 2018), also in the case of emerging technologies. Given also Strachan (2016)'s criticism on speculative design's lack of participatory elements, we are eager to explore more ways to incorporate user insights into the app. For example, submitted user comments could be integrated as accompanying arguments. This form of co-creation best suits the online and distributed character of the app. Co-creating news stories, on the other hand, is likely to require some facilitation and /or an offline setting. Given also the extent of research and fine-tuning that was required for the composition of news stories, some form of expert involvement will remain compulsory.

ACKNOWLEDGEMENT

This work is part of the research program SafeChassis: Implementing and Assessing Safeguards for Lifestyle Engineering of a Versatile Industrial Chassis with project number 15814, which is financed by the Dutch Research Council (NWO).

REFERENCES

Auger, J. (2013) 'Speculative design: crafting the speculation', *Digital Creativity*, 24(1), pp. 11-35.

Betten, A. W., Rerimassie, V., Broerse, J. E., Stemerding, D. and Kupper, F. (2018) 'Constructing future scenarios as a tool to foster responsible research and innovation among future synthetic biologists', *Life sciences, society and policy*, *14*(1), p. 21.

Bleecker, J. (2009) *Design Fiction: A short essay on design, science, fact and fiction.* (29). Near future laboratory.

Blythe, M. (2014) 'Research through design fiction: narrative in real and imaginary abstracts', *Proceedings of the SIGCHI conference on human factors in computing systems*. pp. 703-712.

Boenink, M., Swierstra, T., Stemerding, D. J. S. i. E., Law, and Technology (2010) 'Anticipating the interaction between technology and morality: A scenario study of experimenting with humans in bionanotechnology', 4(2).

Calvert, J. and Schyfter, P. (2017) 'What can science and technology studies learn from art and design? Reflections on 'Synthetic Aesthetics'', *Social studies of science*, 47(2), pp. 195-215.

Coulton, P., Lindley, J. and Akmal, H. A. (2016) 'Design Fiction: Does the search for plausibility lead to deception?'.

Dunne, A. and Raby, F. (2013) *Speculative everything: design, fiction, and social dreaming*. MIT press.

Erlhoff, M. and Marshall, T. (2007) 'Critical design' *Design dictionary: perspectives on design terminology*. Walter de Gruyter, pp. 94-96.

Frow, E. and Calvert, J. (2013) 'Opening up the future (s) of synthetic biology', *Futures*, 48, pp. 32-43.

Ginsberg, A. D., Calvert, J., Schyfter, P., Elfick, A. and Endy, D. (2014) *Synthetic aesthetics: investigating synthetic biology's designs on nature*. MIT press.

Ginsberg, A. D., King, J. and University of Cambridge iGEM 2009 team (2009) *E.chromi.*

Gregorowius, D. and Deplazes-Zemp, A. (2016) 'Societal impact of synthetic biology: responsible research and innovation (RRI)', *Essays in biochemistry*, 60(4), pp. 371-379.

Grimpe, B., Hartswood, M. and Jirotka, M. (2014) 'Towards a closer dialogue between policy and practice: responsible design in HCI', *Proceedings of the SIGCHI Conference on Human Factors in Computing Systems*. pp. 2965-2974.

Grow Your Own... | Science Gallery (2013). Available at: https://dublin.sciencegallery.com/growyourown/ (Accessed: Feb 07, 2020).

Hales, D. (2013) 'Design fictions an introduction and provisional taxonomy', *Digital Creativity*, *24*(1), pp. 1-10.

Helms, K. and Fernaeus, Y. (2018) 'Humor in design fiction to suspend disbelief and belief', *Proceedings of the 10th Nordic Conference on Human-Computer Interaction*. pp. 801-818.

igem.org. Available at: https://igem.org/Main_Page (Accessed: March 31, 2021).

Johnson, B. D. (2009) 'Science Fiction Prototypes Or: How I Learned to Stop Worrying about the Future and Love Science Fiction', *Intelligent Environments*, 2, pp. 3-8.

Kallergi, A. (2016) 'BIO-CHASE', *Abstracts of the Papers Presented at the 10th European Conference on Games Based Learning, ECGBL 2016*.

Lindley, J. and Coulton, P. (2015) 'Back to the future: 10 years of design fiction', *Proceedings of the 2015 British HCI Conference*. pp. 210-211.

Linehan, C., Kirman, B. J., Reeves, S., Blythe, M. A., Tanenbaum, J. G., Desjardins, A. and Wakkary, R. (2014) 'Alternate endings: using fiction to explore design futures', in *CHI'14 Extended Abstracts on Human Factors in Computing Systems*. pp. 45-48.

Loeschcke, A. and Thies, S. (2015) 'Pseudomonas putida—a versatile host for the production of natural products', *Applied microbiology and biotechnology*, 99(15), pp. 6197-6214.

Lucivero, F. (2016) 'Scenarios as "Grounded Explorations". Designing Tools for Discussing the Desirability of Emerging Technologies', in *Ethical assessments of emerging technologies*. Springer, pp. 155-190.

Lyckvi, S., Roto, V., Buie, E. and Wu, Y. (2018) *Proceedings of the 10th Nordic Conference on Human-Computer Interaction*.

Malpass, M. (2013) 'Between wit and reason: Defining associative, speculative, and critical design in practice', *Design and Culture*, 5(3), pp. 333-356.

Moe-Behrens, G. H., Davis, R. and Haynes, K. A. (2013) 'Preparing synthetic biology for the world', *Frontiers in microbiology*, 4, p. 5.

Newson, A. J. (2011) 'Current ethical issues in synthetic biology: Where should we go from here?', *Accountability in research*, 18(3), pp. 181-193.

Nikel, P. I. and de Lorenzo, V. (2018) 'Pseudomonas putida as a functional chassis for industrial biocatalysis: from native biochemistry to trans-metabolism', *Metabolic engineering*, 50, pp. 142-155.

Parens, E., Johnston, J. and Moses, J. (2009) *Ethical issues in synthetic biology: An overview of the debates*.

Poblete-Castro, I., Becker, J., Dohnt, K., Dos Santos, V. M. and Wittmann, C. (2012) 'Industrial biotechnology of Pseudomonas putida and related species', *Applied microbiology and biotechnology*, 93(6), pp. 2279-2290.

Presidential Commission for the Study of Bioethical Issues (2010) *New directions: The ethics of synthetic biology and emerging technologies*. Washington, D.C., US.

Rerimassie, V. and Stemerding, D. (2014) *SynBio politics- Bringing synthetic biology into debate*. The Hague.

Schmidt, M. and de Lorenzo, V. (2016) 'Synthetic bugs on the loose: containment options for deeply engineered (micro) organisms', *Current opinion in biotechnology*, 38, pp. 90-96.

Schmidt, M., Ganguli-Mitra, A., Torgersen, H., Kelle, A., Deplazes, A. and Biller-Andorno, N. (2009) 'A priority paper for the societal and ethical aspects of synthetic biology', *Systems and synthetic biology*, 3(1-4), p. 3.

Schmidt, M., Meyer, A. and Cserer, A. (2015) 'The Bio: Fiction film festival: Sensing how a debate about synthetic biology might evolve', *Public Understanding of Science*, 24(5), pp. 619-635.

Stemerding, D., Betten, W., Rerimassie, V., Robaey, Z. and Kupper, F. J. F. (2019) 'Future making and responsible governance of innovation in synthetic biology', 109, pp. 213-226.

Sterling, B. (2009) 'Design fiction', *Interactions*, 16(3), pp. 20–24.

Stilgoe, J., Owen, R. and Macnaghten, P. (2013) 'Developing a framework for responsible innovation', *Research policy*, 42(9), pp. 1568-1580.

Strachan, C. G. (2016) 'Design, fiction and the medical humanities', *Medical humanities*, 42(4), pp. e15-e19.

SynBio Politics | Rathenau Instituut. Available at: https://www.rathenau.nl/en/making-perfect-lives/synbio-politics (Accessed: March 31, 2021).

Tanenbaum, J. (2014) 'Design fictional interactions: why HCI should care about stories', *interactions*, 21(5), pp. 22-23.

von Schomberg, R. (2013) 'A vision of responsible research and innovation', in Owen, R., Bessant, J. and Heintz, M. (eds.) *Responsible innovation: Managing the responsible emergence of science and innovation in society*. Wiley, pp. 51-74.

Zwart, H., Landeweerd, L. and van Rooij, A. (2014) 'Adapt or perish? Assessing the recent shift in the European research funding arena from 'ELSA' to 'RRI'', *Life Sciences, Society and Policy*, 10(1), p. 11.

EL MERCADITO WEB: AN ALTERNATIVE FOR REMOTE SALES FROM LOCAL MERCHANTS

Alejandra Del Prado Zetina, Teresa Guadalupe Escamilla Paredes, Ixzel Jiménez Zamora, Alma Delia Sánchez Carbajal and Rocío Abascal Mena
Maestría en Diseño, Información y Comunicación (MADIC)
Universidad Autónoma Metropolitana (UAM), Unidad Cuajimalpa, México
Avenida Vasco de Quiroga 4871, Col. Santa Fe Cuajimalpa. Alcaldía Cuajimalpa de Morelos, C.P. 05348, Ciudad de México

ABSTRACT

This article presents the problem of the effects on local trade and sales of micro and small entrepreneurs in Mexico City (CDMX), which arise from the COVID-19 pandemic. It raises the development of a proposal for a solution for distance sales of users not assiduous to the use of technology for sales. Also, it explains the development of an interface called El Mercadito Web, whose objective is to contribute to maintaining sales in neighborhoods using different communication channels, concentrated in a simple interface free and easy to use. The development process responds to stages of User Centered Design (UCD). Finally, the scope and limitations are described, as well as the proposals to improve the prototype designed from its evaluation with the users.

KEYWORDS

Local Commerce, Distance Sales, COVID-19, Human-Computer Interaction, User Centered Design, Prototyping

1. INTRODUCTION

As a result of the global pandemic caused by COVID-19, trade in Mexico suffered a destabilization, mainly affecting micro, small and medium-sized enterprises (MSME), some of which had to close their businesses or seek other alternatives for sale. For the Mexican context, it was very difficult to think that local merchants would continue to be unable to sell since it is through them that jobs are generated and families that are up to date are sustained. Along with the crisis, a new way of selling at a distance emerged; online sales have become an option for MSME, rescuing traditional and local commerce.

The purpose of this article is to show the development of a prototype that arises from the use of an interactive systems design approach: User Centered Design (UCD). The platform called El Mercadito Web is proposed as a solution to the difficulty of continuing to sell. A site developed for local merchants with the purpose of promoting their distance sales; easy to use and intuitive, avoiding user uncertainty, integrating some of the existing sales forms or those that have been used organically such as WhatsApp and Facebook.

This article is organized as follows. Section 2 contextualizes the current situation in Mexico, specifically Mexico City (CDMX); local commerce and sales derived from confinement by COVID-19 are also retaken; then, the relevance of the El Mercadito Web proposal as an HCI project is explained, where the use of these tools is justified according to UX Design and UI Design; as well as the objective for which it was created is described. In section 3, a state of the question is presented regarding platforms focused on distance sales and which served as inspiration for the development of the El Mercadito Web interface. In section 4, the process and methodology used for the development of a pretotype and prototype are described, as well as the main results of the tests carried out on users. Finally, in section 5, the conclusions are presented showing if the project to be developed was viable, why, and what future work is intended to be carried out with it.

2. MAIN PROBLEM

The world is experiencing a humanitarian, health and economic crisis. Following the COVID-19 pandemic, the economies closed and stalled. According to the Confederación Patronal de la República Mexicana [(Confederation of Employers of the Mexican Republic (COPARMEX cited in Infobae, 2020))], the health crisis the country is in has caused eight jobs to be lost per minute; likewise, the president of the Confederación de Cámaras Nacionales de Comercio, Servicios y Turismo [(Confederation of National Chambers of Commerce, Services and Tourism (CONCANACO))], José Manuel López Campos, indicated the urgency of implementing strategies that help more than 4.1 million micro, small and medium-sized companies.

By the end of March, CONCANACO reported that the losses due to the closure of 64,758 establishments in Mexico City, derived from the containment measures announced by the government before the contingency, amounted to 3 billion pesos (Forbes, 2020). The most affected industries, according to CONCANACO and INEGI estimates (cited in Saldaña, 2020) were the commerce, services and tourism sector. For May, the situation of MSME became more acute, since they had a loss of sales of 112 billion pesos, which represented a decrease in sales of 83 percent, compared to the period last year. According to the Organización Acción Ciudadana Frente a la Pobreza [(Citizen Action Organization Against Poverty (cited in Arista and Ortega, 2020))], 12.4 million people in Mexico are self-employed and 21 million work in micro and small economic units.

Derived from this situation, alternatives arose that had aim to help small businesses, with the aim of restoring the economic dynamics by connecting businesses that have distance sales with potential customers. Online sales or e-commerce have become an option for MSME to continue selling their products remotely, whether through home delivery, WhatsApp groups, Facebook, or even partnering with companies like Amazon, to be able to offer their products. For the Alianza Nacional de Pequeños Comerciantes [(National Alliance of Small Merchants (ANPEC))] during the quarantine, local sales grew by 20 percent, as people began to head to the stores in the neighborhood (Mex Newz, 2020). In the words of Cuauhtémoc Rivera, president of ANPEC, "traditional commerce has found digital commerce to complement each other, which encourages the local economy to move".

For this reason, El Mercadito Web appears as an alternative to support local commerce; this with the purpose of helping sellers not see their income affected and continue to cover their expenses, with a view to that even after the pandemic this platform can continue to be used.

3. STATE OF THE ART

WhatsApp (founded in 2009) is an application whose main function is communication and instant messaging between users through chat. During the confinement of the COVID-19 pandemic, the creation of sales groups in limited areas, such as the colonies, proliferated in Mexico City to offer products in a delimited area. This tool began to be used because there is easy of delivery due to the distance between users, it creates a network of trust between neighbors and it is considered that it supports the local economy and those merchants who, due to various situations, had to close their stores, as well as people who entered the world of sales or services when they became unemployed. WhatsApp facilitates direct communication between the buyer and the seller, as well as the contact for deliveries and shipping locations. However, one of the limitations is that there is no order to offer products or consult a specific one. There is no catalog, nor categorization of products or services.

Other of the applications or platforms that exist or are used for sales is Facebook (founded in 2004). Facebook has various channels to sale such as Fan pages, Marketplace or groups, like WhatsApp. Facebook enables direct communication between seller and buyer; Marketplace or the store section of Fan pages, allow to upload products in an orderly way and consulted more easily than on WhatsApp. The downside of Facebook is that it requires creating an account or profile and having a grasp of how it works.

Another platform that served as inspiration and that is more related to the sale of local trade products is Red Maceta (http://www.redmaceta.com/). It works through a web page, where both producers and customers can enter and find products by category. Merge the use of WhatsApp, Facebook, email and the online store. It has hours to make purchases and notifies the user if they are out of it. It has a video tutorial that explains how it works and how to make purchases or register as a seller. Use simple and colloquial language to point out the sections and take the user easily through the page. It appeals to the idea of creating community and supporting the local, so it does not only focus on a user design based on business needs.

In addition to the previous examples, there are consolidated platforms for the sale of products at a distance. However, it seeks to generate a platform that inspires trust among users who are not experts in the use of applications or the Internet and who have the need to continue selling despite the closure of shops, markets or street markets, offering as a first option to do so in an area close to your premises or business, where they don't even need to hire a delivery man. In addition, it is sought that they do not lose part of their sales in the payment of commissions for managing a platform and that they do not need the use of data or Internet access.

4. DEVELOPMENT PROCESS OF EL MERCADITO WEB

Since its inception, El Mercadito Web was thought of as a user-friendly interface, so always the comments made during the observations and evaluations of the tool were considered. With the evaluation of the prototype, the level of usability and ease of navigation that the user had with it was detected, as well as usability aspects were taken into account as a pleasant and intuitive design, facilitating the user to move within the page, without this it will either stress or make the user to feel inefficient. Basing the project on HCI helped prioritize user needs and avoid developer bias, as it was constantly used to resolve user and navigation conflicts. The main process of development included the next steps which are going to be explained below: detection of needs, storyboard, inspiration board and point of view, prototype, digital prototype and heuristic evaluation.

4.1 Detection of Needs

As explained in the problem section, the pandemic generated by COVID-19 has brought social and economic consequences. The dynamics of buying and selling have had to be adapted due to social distancing measures. For this reason, as a first approach to detect changes in people's routines during quarantine, a group of users was observed through video calls or face-to-face observations with relatives or acquaintances. A brief semi-structured interview was applied to them and from this some profiles emerged, among which, there were users dedicated to trade, who faced the difficulties of having to sell remotely through technological platforms. Added to the fact that some WhatsApp groups created from the pandemic were observed, as a local initiative of neighbors to promote consumption in their surround.

A detection of the main needs of the observed users was made and by means of brainstorming only fifteen of them were extracted, highlighting: sales revenue, the possibility of selling remotely with due precautions, taking advantage of technological tools that were not complicated to use, nor need more experience to use them. They also sought to sell through calls or messages and that they did not cost or charge a commission, as some platforms that already exist do, which were discussed in a previous section.

From these observations, a type of user was defined: local merchants, not experts in the use of technology and whose businesses have not entered the market for distance or Internet sales, but who were forced to think about to do so in order to continue obtaining economic income.

4.2 Communication Exercise with the Team: Storyboard

Once the types of users were defined, the problems to be addressed and the main needs of these, various storyboards were developed among the members of the research team, to determine if they agreed on the way the solution was visualized. For this, the user was visualized and how he felt facing the problem of selling from a distance, his emotions, concerns or feelings, as well as a scenario of his day to day. The storyboard together with the previous interviews with the users, helped to generate a narrative of the problem, the knot or climax of the situation and the outcome. When working on HCI projects, it is important not to start with the researchers' preconceptions, but to really think about the user, recognize what they are concerned about, what they feel, and thus be able to offer them a solution, rather than a technological one, focused on enabling them to fulfill an objective that helps them feel fulfilled.

4.3 Inspiration Board and Point of View

After the storyboards were reviewed, the team discussed what keywords had to be considered to generate a platform that was mainly intuitive and that facilitated the main detected need: selling remotely. In order to delimit these ideas, the inspirational words and their meaning were discussed, then we looked for existing platforms (although they were not explicitly dedicated to sales) that would help in visualizing what the El Mercadito Web platform would look like. These platforms inspire design option and some of the main functions for the interface proposal. Inspirational words were: free, confident, intuitive, quality, visually attractive, interaction, upgradeable, and diversification.

In addition, a point of view that encompasses the needs of users was determined, which was: *an interface that can be used from a mobile phone and that facilitates remote sales, in which local merchants can increase their customers and sales.*

4.4 Pretotype

According to Pretotype Labs LLC co-founder Alberto Savoia (quoted in the leader summaries digital library), "*pretotyping is focused on answering a basic and important question: what is there to build?*" Pretotypes make it possible to gather valuable user data and interface functionality, this in order to continue or not with the development of the proposed idea, using less time and cost than a prototype (Savoia, 2013).

For the development of the pretoype we focus on two techniques: Minimum Viable Product (MVP) and False Door; in the first, we return to basic characteristics that the final interface would have, such as user registration, product registration and sale; in the second, the technique allowed us to show what the final product would look like, the interaction that could exist between the user and the interface, and whether the design would capture the attention of the same. The way we used these techniques was with a video, which was uploaded to the YouTube platform; this video was shared on WhatsApp to users that we already had identified, they were asked to watch it and answer the questions: would you use this website? And why?

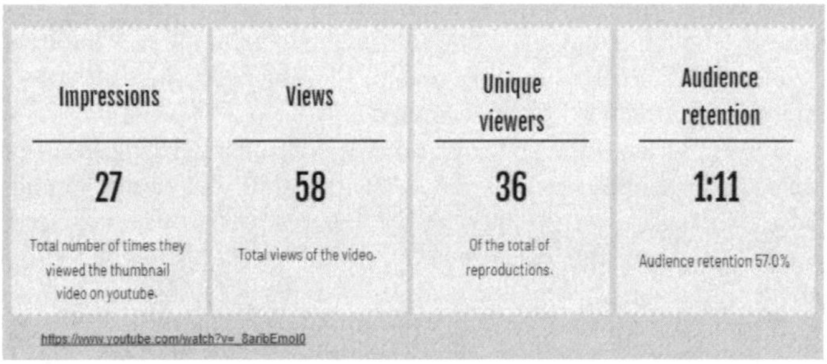

Figure 1. Youtube Analytics for the pretotype activity

The results obtained by the users were favorable, the video was attractive to them and in some way El Mercadito Web solved the need to follow or start remote sales (see Figure 1). Some of the suggested comments were considered for the development of the final prototype and others remain as future work, which will be explained later. It is worth mentioning that when the video was uploaded on a platform like YouTube, we had more visits than we expected, which led us to the conclusion that the pretotype was of interest to other users than ours.

4.5 Digital Prototype

The development of the prototype was divided into two facets; in the first, the Genially (Online software that allows you to create animated and interactive presentations) tool was used; this software allowed the user to navigate, basically, through screens, which contained interaction with start buttons, return, next, sell product, register product, among others (https://view.genial.ly/5edb191c3498730d8f39a54e/interactive-content-mi-mercadito-atari).

From this first test for users, the following improvements were obtained:

- Interface focused especially on users who sell products from the basic basket.
- The layout of the registration and payment process was modified to make it more intuitive.
- Sizes and font types, color palette and menu type were approved.

Once the previous suggestions were included, the second and last facet of the final prototype was carried out. Genially is a limited tool for interaction, for this reason the final version of the prototype was developed in adobe XD, which allowed greater control of the functions and the final design. Sketches with different interactions and transitions were generated that improved the usability of the prototype.

Likewise, when developing the prototype, the 10 heuristics of Jakob Nielsen (https://www.nngroup.com/articles/ten-usability-heuristics/) were considered, which in the next point will evaluate the relevance of the prototype with the user.

Figure 2. Customer record

Figure 3. Menu

Figure 4. Confirm order

Figure 5. Orders issued

Figure 6. Welcome to El Mercadito Web

Figure 7. Personal data registration

Figure 8. Payment forms

Figure 9. Contact

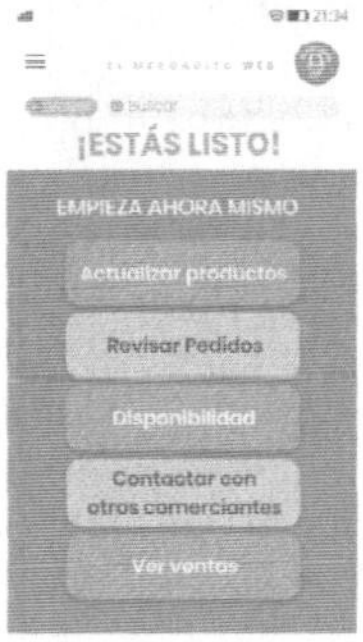

Figure 10. Main menu

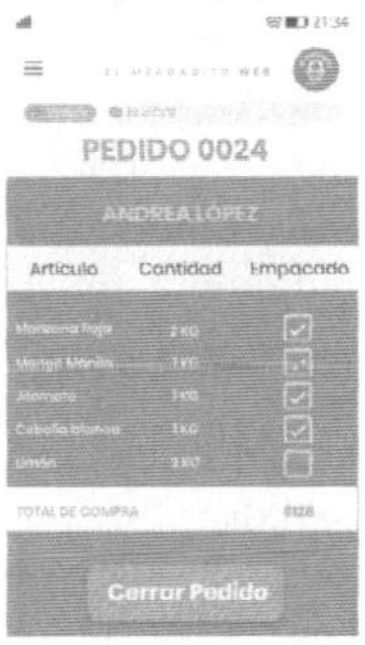

Figure 11. Order

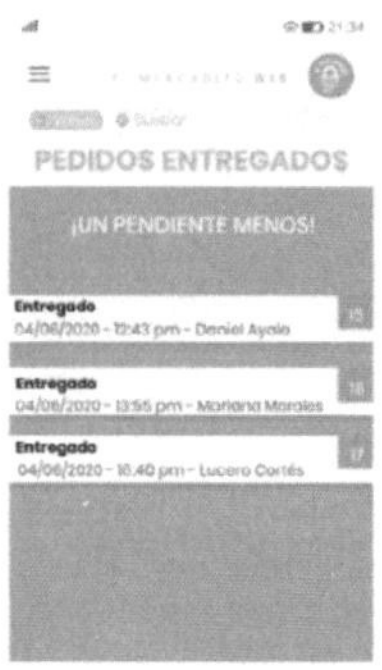

Figure 12. Stock   Figure 13. Orders Issued   Figure 14. Day's sales

4.6 Heuristic Evaluation

According to Mónica Gimenez (2017), a heuristic analysis is *"a technique to evaluate the usability of a system of interfaces and processes by an expert, based on the principles of the discipline of human-computer interaction"*. This analysis, in which the user experience intervenes, helps us find usability errors in the system, obtaining conclusions and proposals for improvements that should be implemented. The criteria to evaluate within the prototype were as follows: 1) Show system status, 2) Family metaphors and language, 3) Control and freedom, 4) Consistency, 5) Error prevention, 6) Memory recognition, 7) Flexibility and efficiency, 8) Aesthetic and minimalist design, 9) Recognition, diagnosis and recovery from errors and 10) Help. The way in which the functionality of the interface was determined was through an interview with users, in which they evaluated two activities: browsing the El Mercadito Web and placing an order.

To evaluate the heuristics, descriptions of actions were made that were related to each one, in such a way that they were easier to understand for those who were evaluating Mi Mercadito Web. Subsequently, questions were asked about them, which allowed obtaining important data on the usability of the prototype. The heuristics in which the users agreed that they were not within the interface or were not easy to identify were: 1) Control and freedom, 2) Family metaphors and language, 3) Help, 4) Memory recognition, 5) Show system status and 6) Consistency.

One of the modifications that was made after the evaluation had to do with the heuristic control and freedom of the user; based on user feedback, the following modifications were made to the final prototype:

- Increased options on the burger menu
- Placing the total of the account when filling the order

5. CONCLUSIONS AND FURTHER WORK

The development of El Mercadito Web allowed us to try to conceive a pertinent prototype by knowing our final users, so the process was not focus only on aesthetics, but on solving problems that arise from changes in society, such as those generated due to the Covid-19 pandemic. However, we detect that in our prototype is necessary to reinforce several deficiencies and errors pointed out by users in the evaluation stage, as well as considering the heuristics that generated problems in the usability of the system like control and freedom, help, consistency, family metaphors and language, to mention just a few.

Other recommendations that users gave us were that the colors used were not very striking for the interface that was proposed and that it was necessary to have more menus and categories, as well as help options to facilitate its navigation. We believe that the project could really help local merchants, but more interaction with the user is needed, because due to the restrictions implemented by the pandemic situation, we were not able to interact in person with more of them. In this way, we could obtain more specific ideas or observations to improve El Mercadito Web.

Regarding future proposals, we can point out that there is an opportunity for El Mercadito Web to be used, however, the tools with which the prototype was developed were limited, which did not allow users to know a real operation, nor could they interact with their own data, nor did they allow them to reach the stage of making a sale and that they knew if it was functional for their needs.

On the other hand, when the project was proposed, it was intended to be an interface that would host not only the sale of basic products, but also concentrate services and multiple products that are not essential items, such as those offered in WhatsApp chats that were opened by some neighborhood residents of Mexico City.

However, when tests were carried out on some users, they associated El Mercadito Web more with the sale of basic products, and therefore they did not consider it useful for the type of business or service they offered. As a proposal for the future, another version of El Mercadito Web could be considered that would allow for a greater offer of products and even services, so that it not only works as a sales channel, but also with a directory of consultation for citizens of a certain neighborhood of the Mexico City, this would also imply a name change.

Another concern expressed by users was that of remote delivery, since some do not have the option to hire staff to make deliveries and the radius or quadrant that El Mercadito Web would cover was not clear, so we think that a redesign in the name of the application by neighborhood where it is implemented would have results in making it attractive to local merchants in a specific area.

Finally, we consider that doing more tests on users, without restrictions such as doing it remotely, and with older people who may not even use their mobile phone, would make us obtain more observations and with it a better redesign of El Mercadito Web, in a way make it as functional as possible, inclusive for those who are not experts in the use of technologies or do not have the economic resources to consume the Internet. And perhaps it can compete against the multiple proposals and platforms that have emerged emergently during the pandemic.

REFERENCES

Arista, L. (2020). Boleadores, limpiadores, vendedores: ellos no pueden aplicar "sana distancia". *Expansión política*. Retrieved May 26, 2021, from https://politica.expansion.mx/cdmx/2020/03/23/boleadores-limpiadores-vendedores-ellos-no-pueden-aplicar-sana-distancia

CEPAL. (2020). *América Latina y el Caribe ante la pandemia del COVID-19: Efectos económicos y sociales.* Naciones Unidas. Retrieved May 26, 2021, from https://repositorio.cepal.org/bitstream/handle/11362/45337/4/S2000264_es.pdf

CONCANACO. (2020). Urgen estrategias para las micro, pequeñas y medianas empresas ante la afectación económica por el Covid 19: Concanaco Servytur. *CONCANACO.* Retrieved May 26, 2021, from https://www.concanaco.com.mx/urgen-estrategias-para-las-micro-pequenas-y-medianas-empresas-ante-la-afectacion-economica-por-el-covid-19-concanaco-servytur/

Gimenez, M. (2017). Hiberus tecnología. Obtenido de Análisis Heurísico para UX: evalúa la usabilidad de tu web. Retrieved May 26, 2021, from https://www.hiberus.com/crecemos-contigo/analisis-heuristico-para-ux-evalua-la-usabilidad-de-tu-web/

Hernández, L. (2020). Pérdidas en micro y pequeños negocios ascienden en México a 30 mmp por coronavirus: ALAMPYME. *El Financiero*. Retrieved May 26, 2021, from https://www.elfinanciero.com.mx/economia/perdidas-en-micro-y-pequenos-negocios-ascienden-en-mexico-a-30-mmp-por-coronavirus-alampyme

Infobae. (2020). El golpe del COVID-19 a la economía mexicana: se están perdiendo ocho empleos por minuto. *Infobae*. Retrieved May 26, 2021, from https://www.infobae.com/america/mexico/2020/05/24/el-golpe-del-covid-19-a-la-economia-mexicana-se-estan-perdiendo-ocho-empleos-por-minuto/

Newz, M. (2020). Las 'tienditas' buscan aliarse con Amazon y usan Whatsapp para la venta en línea. *Mex Newz*. Retrieved May 26, 2021, from https://www.mexnewz.mx/las-tienditas-buscan-aliarse-con-amazon-y-usan-whatsapp-para-la-venta-en-linea/

Saldaña, I. (2020). Cierra 65% de comercios en México por Covid-19; en riesgo miles de empleos, advierten. *El Universal*. Retrieved May 26, 2021, from https://www.eluniversal.com.mx/cartera/coronavirus-cierra-65-de-comercios-en-mexico-por-covid-19-en-riesgo-miles-de-empleos

Savoia, A. (2003). *Leader summaries*. Retrieved May 26, 2021, from https://www.leadersummaries.com/ver-resumen/pretotipar-esto

DESIGN GUIDELINES FOR MOBILE APPLICATIONS

Isaac Senga Lupanda and J.T. Janse van Rensburg
North-West University
Hendrik van Eck Boulevard, Vanderbijlpark, South Africa

ABSTRACT

With the widespread rapid development of computers and wireless communication, mobile computing is fast growing as the communication and sales platform of choice. The aim of this paper is to present design guidelines for mobile applications. The research intends to contribute to existing literature, highlighting popular HCI principles and design principles for mobile applications. A case study that portrays the development of a mobile application for trading used books at a university is discussed to demonstrate the utility of the consolidated design guidelines. The use of the design guidelines are strengthened with a supporting requirements analysis obtained from subject matter experts in the case study. The conceptual relationship between the aforementioned factors can be used as suggested design guidelines for mobile applications.

KEYWORDS

Human-Computer Interaction, Mobile Applications, Design Guidelines

1. INTRODUCTION

A Mobile applications have become ubiquitous in the existence of people around the world (Buller et al., 2015:3). As an intrinsic part of the daily routine of individuals, mobile applications have changed human beings' attitude towards their lives and is observable in various areas of people's behaviour (Cardamone, Eboli, Forciniti, & Mazzulla, 2016:52). Further, Cardamone et al. (2016:52) present different areas affected by the changes brought by mobile application technology including communication, the collection of information, the allocation of time and attention, and potentially how learning takes place.

In this study, the goal is to present design guidelines for mobile applications. Moreover, the study examines human-computer interaction (HCI) in a manner that will elucidate principles that could assist in the creation of an effective mobile application. HCI is known for its multidisciplinary applications which emphasises the interaction practices between humans with computer systems, mobile devices, and other devices. By observing user interface design principles and implementing them in the development process, it can be helpful to increase the performance and grasp the concept of the technical aspects of the designed application (Seraj & Wong, 2012:1015). An overview of popular design principles for HCI and mobile applications are presented in the related work section. This is followed by a consolidated and merged list of design guidelines for mobile applications. A case study is then presented to demonstrate the utility of the design guidelines, which is followed by a reflection and discussion on future work.

2. LITERATURE REVIEW ON HCI AND MOBILE APPLICATIONS

The brief literature review creates a mutual understanding on the concepts of human-computer interaction and mobile applications by highlighting common design principles.

2.1 Human-Computer Interaction

HCI practices are focused on designing interfaces that fulfil users' needs in their routine of everyday life, often known as user-centred design (Poole, 2013:403). HCI is the study of understanding how people interact with computers in their day-to-day activities (Froese, Iizuka, & Ikegami, 2014:6). HCI practitioners and designers who employ design rules in order to create an effective user experience (UX) for interactive systems (Dix, Finlay, Abowd, & Beale, 2004:259). These design principles are mostly derived from research in the fields of psychology, sociology, cognitive science, and computer science, and tend to be context free (Dix et al., 2004:259; Zhang, Carey, Te'eni, & Tremaine, 2004). Table 3 provides a summary of HCI principles found in literature by Norman (2013:72), Shneiderman (2005:2) , Johnson (2007:8) and Stone, Jarrett, Woodroffe, and Minocha (2005:97).

Table 1. Summary of commonly used HCI principles found in literature

HCI principles by Norman (2013:72)
Discoverability: The user must be able to determine the current state of the system as well as what the currently available actions are.
Feedback: The user must continually receive information about the results of actions and be able to easily determine the new state of the system after the actions were executed.
Affordances: Affordance is the relationship between the properties of an object and the capabilities of the agent interacting with the object.
Signifiers: Signifiers must be used effectively to ensure discoverability and that feedback is understandable to the user.
Mappings: Good mappings between controls, their actions and the results must exist. Mappings are enhanced through spatial layout and temporal contiguity.
Conceptual model: The system must provide all the information to the user to allow the user to create a good conceptual model of the system, which leads to understanding and feeling in control. A good conceptual model enhances discoverability and evaluation of results.
Constraints: Providing physical, logical, semantic and cultural constraints guides the user to available actions and eases the user's interpretation when using the system.
HCI principles (Shneiderman, 2005:2)
Strive for consistency in action sequences, layout, terminology, command use and so on
Enable frequent users to use shortcuts, such as abbreviations, special key sequences and macros, to perform regular, familiar actions more quickly.
Offer informative feedback for every user action, at a level appropriate to the magnitude of the action.
Design dialogs to yield closure so that the user knows when they have completed a task.
Offer error prevention and simple error handling so that, ideally, users are prevented from making mistakes and, if they do, they are offered clear and informative instructions to enable them to recover.
Permit easy reversals of actions in order to relieve anxiety and encourage exploration, since the user knows that he or she can always return to the previous state.
Support internal locus of control so that the user is in control of the system, which responds to his/her actions.
Reduce short term memory load by keeping displays simple, consolidating multiple page displays and providing time to learn action sequences.
HCI principles by Johnson (2007:8)
Focus on the users and their tasks, not on the technology.
Consider function first, presentation later.
Conform to the users' view of the task.
Design for the common case.
Do not complicate the user's task.
Facilitate learning
Deliver information, not just data.
Design for responsiveness.
Try it out on users; then fix it.
HCI principles by Stone et al. (2005:97)
Visibility: The first step in order to achieve the goal should be clear.
Affordance: The control should suggest how the user should use it.
Feedback: What happened or is happening should be clear.
Simplicity: As simple as possible and task-focused.
Structure: Sensible organisation of content.
Consistency: Similarity for predictability.
Tolerance: Prevent errors and aid in recovery.
Accessibility: Usable by all intended users in spite of handicap, or environmental conditions.

As can be seen from Table 1, many authors provide useful HCI principles that can be followed for general design guidance. It can also be seen that there is often overlap between HCI principles presented in different sources. The next section follows a similar approach to highlighting design principles for mobile applications.

2.2 Mobile Applications

A mobile application, commonly known as an app, is a type of application software developed to work on mobile devices, such as tablets and smartphones (Cueto-Manzano et al., 2015:119). Xiao-qing (2010) asserted that mobile application development requires a slightly different skillset, and certainly different design principles. The most essential thing to have in mind when developing a mobile application is to ensure that it is both useful and intuitive (Babich, 2016). Table 5 presents a summary of mobile application design principles found in the literature by Ramsay and Nielsen (2000), Stark (2012), and Babich (2016).

Table 2. A summary of mobile application design principles found in literature

Mobile application design principles by Babich (2016)
Cut out the clutter: User attention is a precious resource and should be allocated accordingly. Cluttering the interface overloads users with too much information: every added button, image, and line of text make the screen more complicated.
Make navigation self-evident: Good navigation should feel like an invisible hand that guides the users along their journey.
Create a seamless experience: Mobile app developers should not think of a mobile design in isolation. Creating a seamless experience across mobile applications, desktop application and tablet applications is very important for users.
Design finger-friendly tap-targets: Smaller touch targets are harder for users to hit than larger ones. When designing mobile interfaces, it is best to make targets big enough to easily tap (Babich, 2016).
Text content should be legible: When compared with desktops, smartphones have relatively small screens, which means that one of the challenges of mobile design is to fit a lot of information on a small UI. A rule of thumb for mobiles: text should be at least 11 points so it's legible at a typical viewing distance without zooming.
Make interface elements clearly visible: Choose primary, secondary, and accent colours for the application that support usability. Ensure sufficient colour contrast between elements so that users with low vision can see and use the app.
Design controls based on hand position: Hand positions and grip should influence the placement of controls on a mobile design: • It's important to place top-level menu, frequently-used controls and common actions to the center of the screen, because they are comfortably reached with one-thumb interactions. • Place negative actions (such as delete or erase) in the hard to reach zone, because designers do not want users to accidentally tap them.
Minimize need for typing: Typing on a mobile is a slow and error-prone process. It is therefore best to always try to minimize the amount of typing required to use a mobile app.
Test the design: Even the most painstakingly-considered user experience (UX) will ultimately contain some unseen flaw when released into the real world. Designers should treat your app as a continuously evolving entity, using data from analytics and user feedback to constantly improve the experience.
Mobile application design principles by Stark (2012)
Mobile mind set: Because of the differences between mobile and desktop, it is imperative to get yourself into a mobile mind set before getting started.
Mobile contexts: Designers should put themselves in the shoes of the users, one need to consider three major mobile contexts: Bored, Busy and Lost.
Global guidelines: Different apps call for different approaches, designs and techniques such as: responsiveness, polish, thumbs, targets, content and controls, avoid scrolling.
Navigation models: There are plenty of novel navigation models for mobile apps but if one chooses to use one of them, be sure to pick the one that makes the most sense for the designed app (Ramsay & Nielsen, 2000; Stark, 2012). • None: Single screen utility apps (e.g. Weather app on iPhone) • Tab bar: Three to six distinct content areas (e.g. Twitter for iPhone) • Drill down: List and detail content hierarchy (e.g. Settings app on iPhone)
User input: Typing stinks even on the best devices, so the developer should do what needs to be done to make it easier for mobile app users.
Gestures: One of the most iconic aspects of modern touch interfaces is that they support gesture-based user interaction.
Orientation: Portrait is by far the most popular orientation so optimise for this case first. If the designed app invites lots of typing, designers should implement landscape orientation so users can access the larger keyboard. When orientation changes unexpectedly, it is, well disorienting. If the app is intended to be used for long periods of time consider adding an orientation lock right in the app.
Communications: Provide feedback (Provide instant feedback for every interaction), Modal alerts (use them when something is seriously wrong. Even then, try to mitigate the intensity by keeping language reassuring and friendly), Confirmations (When you have to ask a user to confirm an action, it is acceptable to display a modal confirmation dialog).

Launching: When a user goes back into the app after having used it previously, the app should resume operations right where the user left off. This will give the illusion of speed and contribute to an overall feel of responsiveness.
First impressions: The icon has to compete for attention in a sea of other icons. Use a strong silhouette and keep text to a minimum. A polished icon suggests a polished app, so it is worth devoting serious time and money to doing it right.
Mobile application design principles by Ramsay and Nielsen (2000)
Mobility: Provide information while on the move.
Usefulness: Serving some purpose.
Relevance: Include only relevant information.
Ease of use: The degree to which a software can be used specifically.
Fluency of navigation: Most important information should be easiest to locate.
User centered: Adapt to the users' way of interaction and way of thinking.
Personalisation: Adapt to the users' needs and capability.

From Table 2 it can be seen that authors of mobile application design principles often present overlapping information as well. To this end, we propose merged guidelines for HCI and mobile applications where appropriate, which are presented in the next section.

3. COMBINED DESIGN GUIDELINES FOR MOBILE APPLICATION

In this section, the guidelines presented for HCI and mobile applications are compared for similarity, resulting in a single source of enriched guidelines for mobile design. Table 3 provides an overview of the enriched guidelines. The guidelines are numbered for later use and demonstration in this paper, by denoting mobile application principles with M, and HCI principles with H.

Table 3. Guidelines for designing mobile applications

Mobile application design principles		**Description**
M1	Cut out the clutter	User attention is a precious resource and should be allocated accordingly. Cluttering the interface overloads users with too much information: every added button, image, and line of text make the screen more complicated (Babich, 2016).
M2	Make navigation self- evident	Good navigation should feel like an invisible hand that guides the users along their journey (Babich, 2016).
M3	Create a seamless experience	Mobile app developers should not think of a mobile design in isolation. Creating a seamless experience across mobile applications, desktop application and tablet applications is very important for users (Babich, 2016).
M4	Design finger-friendly tap-targets	Smaller touch targets are harder for users to hit than larger ones. When designing mobile interfaces, it is best to make targets big enough to easily tap (Babich, 2016).
M5	Text content should be legible	When compared with desktops, smartphones have relatively small screens, which means that one of the challenges of mobile design is to fit a lot of information on a small UI. A rule of thumb for mobiles: text should be at least 11 points so it's legible at a typical viewing distance without zooming (Babich, 2016).
M6	Make interface elements clearly visible	Choose primary, secondary, and accent colours for the application that support usability. Ensure sufficient colour contrast between elements so that users with low vision can see and use the app. Make sure there is ample contrast between the font colour and the background so texts are legible (Babich, 2016).
M7	Design controls based on hand position	Hoober and Berkman (2011:231) uncovered that 49% of people rely on one thumb to get things done on their phones (Babich, 2016). • It is important to place top-level menu, frequently-used controls and common actions in the center of the screen because they are comfortably reached with one-thumb interactions. • Place negative actions (such as delete or erase) in the hard to reach zone, because you do not want users to accidentally tap them.
M8	Minimize need for typing	Typing on a mobile is a slow and error-prone process. It is therefore best to always try to minimize the amount of typing required to use a mobile app (Babich, 2016; Stark, 2012): • Keep forms as short and simple as possible by removing any unnecessary fields. • Use auto-complete and personalized data where appropriate so that users only have to enter the bare minimum of information.

M9	Test the design	Even the most painstakingly-considered user experience (UX) will ultimately contain some unseen flaw when put into the real world. Designers should treat your app as a continuously evolving entity, using data from analytics and user feedback to constantly improve the experience (Babich, 2016).
M10	Mobile mind set	Because of the differences between mobile and desktop, it is imperative to get yourself into a mobile mind set before getting started (Stark, 2012).
M11	Mobile contexts	Designers should put themselves in the shoes of the users, one need to consider three major mobile contexts: Bored, Busy and Lost (Stark, 2012).
M12	Global guidelines	Different apps call for different approaches, designs and techniques such as: responsiveness, polish, thumbs, targets, content and controls, avoid scrolling (Stark, 2012).
M13	Navigation models	There are plenty of novel navigation models for mobile apps but if one chooses to use one of them, be sure to pick the one that makes the most sense for the designed app (Ramsay & Nielsen, 2000; Stark, 2012). • None: Single screen utility apps (e.g. Weather app on iPhone) • Tab bar: Three to six distinct content areas (e.g. Twitter for iPhone) • Drill down: List and detail content hierarchy (e.g. Settings app on iPhone)
M14	Gestures	One of the most iconic aspects of modern touch interfaces is that they support gesture-based user interaction (Stark, 2012; Ramsay & Nielsen, 2000).
M15	Orientation	Portrait is by far the most popular orientation so optimise for this case first. If the designed app invites lots of typing, designers should implement landscape orientation so users can access the larger keyboard. When orientation changes unexpectedly, it is, well disorienting. If the app is intended to be used for long periods of time consider adding an orientation lock right in the app (Stark, 2012).
M16	Communications	Provide feedback (Provide instant feedback for every interaction), Modal alerts (use them when something is seriously wrong. Even then, try to mitigate the intensity by keeping language reassuring and friendly), Confirmations (When you have to ask a user to confirm an action, it is acceptable to display a modal confirmation dialog) (Stark, 2012; Ramsay & Nielsen, 2000).
M17	Launching	When a user goes back into the app after having used it previously, the app should resume operations right where the user left off. This will give the illusion of speed and contribute to an overall feel of responsiveness (Stark, 2012).
M18	Usefulness	Serving some purpose (Ramsay & Nielsen, 2000).
M19	Relevance	Include only relevant information (Ramsay & Nielsen, 2000).
M20	Ease of use	The degree to which a software can be used specifically (Ramsay & Nielsen, 2000).
HCI design principles		**Description**
H1	Strive for consistency	Sequences of actions should be required in similar situations (Shneiderman, 2005:2).
H2	Offer informative feedback	For every operator action, there should be some system feedback (Shneiderman, 2005:2).
H3	Permit easy reversal of action	This feature relieves anxiety; it thus encourages exploration of unfamiliar options (Shneiderman et al., 2009:82).
H4	Offer simple error handling	If an error is made, the system should be able to detect the error and offer simple, comprehensible mechanisms for handling the error (Shneiderman, 2005:2).
H5	Mappings	According to Norman (2013:11) good between controls, their actions and the results must exist. Mappings are enhanced through spatial layout and temporal contiguity According (Norman, 2013:11).
H6	Affordance	According to Norman (2013:11) affordance is the relationship between the properties of an object and the capabilities of the agent interacting with the object. In terms of systems, it relates to the possibilities of how users can interact with a system (Norman, 2013:18).
H7	Discoverability	The user must be able to determine the current state of the system as well as what the currently available actions are (Norman, 2013:70)
H8	Usefulness	The user needs to be able to accomplish what is required through the use of the computer (e.g. sending an email) (Dix et al., 2004:5). In other word serving some purpose
H9	Dialog	Design dialogs to yield closure so that the user knows when they have completed a task (Shneiderman, 1992:60).

Using Table 3 as a reference, the next section will present a case study of how these guidelines can be applied to the design of a real-world example.

4. DEMONSTRATION OF DESIGN GUIDELINES IN A CASE STUDY

In this section, an overview of a case study used to demonstrate the usefulness of the consolidated guidelines are presented.

4.1 Case Study Background

The research problem for this case study centred on how to develop a suitable design for a mobile application that could be used for the trading of used books at universities. Various sources indicate that expensive textbooks is one of the factors that contribute to students being unable to attend universities (Ackroyd, 2015; Lethoba, 2017; Mothibi, 2015; Nelson, 2014; Tsimong, 2016). There was a need for an electronic platform that would ease the process of purchasing and selling used books at a specific university, with the aim of distributing the application to other universities as well. It was suggested that creating a mobile application towards this end would be a suitable artefact to address the research problem. The primary objective of this case study was to design a mobile application for the trading of used books at a university by following a design science research approach. To achieve the primary objective, a number of theoretical objectives were proposed:

- To achieve an understanding of human-computer interaction and its principles.
- To achieve an understanding of mobile applications and its design principles.
- To form a conceptual link between appropriate mobile application principles and HCI principles in order to facilitate the design of the proposed artefact.

As part of the empirical work for the case study, four expert design participants were interviewed in order to highlight key elements as part of a requirements analysis. The research approach used was to map their rich feedback to the highlighted design guidelines presented in the previous section. The interviews were audio-recorded, transcribed, and analysed through interpretive content analysis to find themes in the data.

4.2 Guidelines Applied

The knowledge that was used to develop the mobile application draws from the descriptive knowledge explored in previous sections. The findings from the requirements analyses conducted with the expert participants were used as a baseline for themes that needed to be addressed in the mobile application. The applicable design principles presented in the previous section were then mapped to the themes of the requirements analysis. Table 4 presents the identified themes with their relevant corresponding mobile and HCI principles.

Based on the requirements presented in Table 4, Figure 1 provides a brief illustration of how some principles were applied. As part of the platform selection and interface design, HTML5 was selected to create a responsive web application. The interface was presented in a minimalistic manner so that only the most relevant information is provided, in order to create a useful and user-friendly experience. In terms of the colour usage, negative contrast was used where darker text is presented on lighter backgrounds, incorporating the primary corporate colour (green) of the relevant university. Generic information that was required as part of the core functionality of the application, included adding text fields for input such as the title, author, ISBN, and price of a book to be sold. With reference to visible features of the application, camera functionality was included in order to upload pictures of the cover and condition of the used book.

Table 4. Refined guidelines to design a mobile application

Themes	Mobile principles	HCI principles
Platform selection and interface design: • Use a hybrid platform to create a responsive mobile web application. • Create a pleasant user interface (useful and friendly).	M1, M2, M3, M4, M5, M6, M7, M8, M12, M19, M18, M20	H1, H2, H3, H4, H6, H8, H9
Colours: • Use negative contrast and corporate colours of the institution where the app will be used	M3, M5, M6, M10, M11, M12, M22	H5, H6, H8
Information: Include the following information: • Title of the book, author of the book, ISBN, price of the book, details of owner of the book	M1, M5,M16, M18, M19, M21	H2, H7, H8, H9

Features: • Integrate the application with the learning management system of the institution. • Include barcode, camera and calendar features	M2, M4, M7, M13, M14, M15	H3, H4, H5, H9
Test the application: • Use participants from the target audience (students) to test the application	M3, M9	H6, H8

As a brief demonstration of how the design guidelines were applied, it can be seen that consistency (H1) in the layout and colour usage was used across the design. Informative feedback was offered (H2), as can be seen in the last screen where the user receives a notification that their request has been processed. Affordances (H6) are demonstrated through the use of highlighted selected areas in the design that are presented as buttons, providing guidance to the user that it is a 'clickable area'. The web application is presented in the preferred orientation format (M15), portrait. As a last example, a tab bar navigation model (M13) is used to specify distinct content areas for finding a book, adding a book, and buying a book.

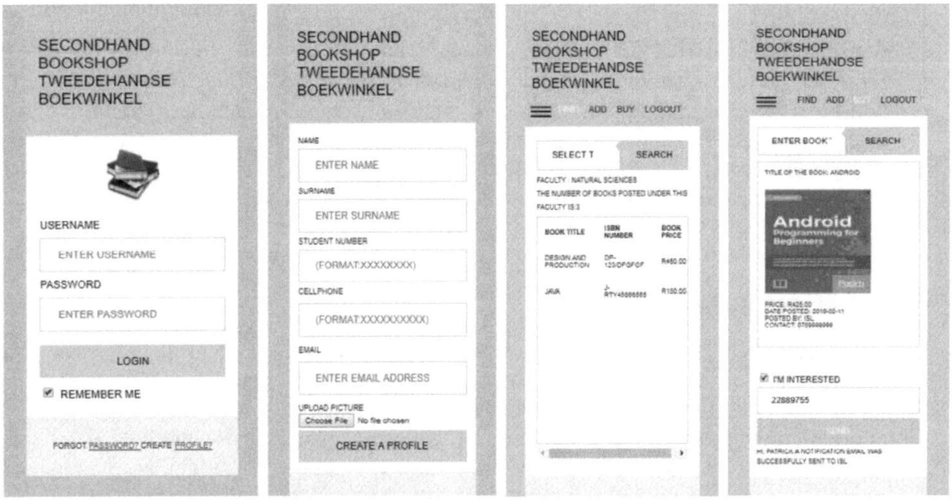

Figure 1. Screenshots demonstrating the mobile application created in the case study

5. REFLECTION AND FUTURE WORK

The objective of this paper was to present design guidelines for mobile applications. This was achieved by presenting existing literature on HCI principles and mobile application design principles. Overlapping principles offered by different sources were merged to provide a consolidated list of guidelines that can be used for mobile design. To demonstrate its utility, a case study was discussed where a mobile application for trading used books at a university was developed. The paper highlighted how a requirements analysis could possibly be mapped to the design guidelines in order to provide a clear approach to design elements that need to be considered.

A limitation of the paper was that the complete design science research (DSR) strategy followed to develop the artefact could not be presented. Therein lies additional information pertaining to the evaluation methods that were used to perform usability testing with target users, the related results, and recommendations. Future work includes reporting on the DSR strategy followed and evaluation methods of the artefact so that other researchers may benefit from the recommendations.

REFERENCES

Ackroyd, B., 2015. INFOGRAPHIC: Which SA university is the most expensive? Retrieved from https://www.enca.com/south-africa/infographic-which-sa-university-most-expensive

Babich, N., 2016. Mobile UX Design: Key Principles. Retrieved from https://uxplanet.org/mobile-ux-design-key-principles-dee1a632f9e6

Buller, D. B., Berwick, M., Lantz, K., Buller, M. K., Shane, J., Kane, I., & Liu, X., 2015. Smartphone mobile application delivering personalized, real-time sun protection advice: a randomized clinical trial. *JAMA dermatology*, 151(5), 497-504.

Cardamone, A. S., Eboli, L., Forciniti, C., & Mazzulla, G., 2016. Willingness to use mobile application for smartphone for improving road safety. *International journal of injury control and safety promotion*, 23(2), 155-169.

Cueto-Manzano, A. M., Gallardo-Rincón, H., Martínez-Ramírez, H. R., Cortés-Sanabria, L., Rojas-Campos, E., Tapia-Conyer, R., Medina, M., 2015. A pilot study of a mobile phone application to improve lifestyle and adherence of patients with kidney disease. *Journal of telemedicine and telecare*, 21(2), 119.

Dix, A., Finlay, J., Abowd, G. D., & Beale, R., 2004. Editorial Pearson Education. *Human-Computer Interaction*. Third edition. Último acceso el, 12.

Froese, T., Iizuka, H., & Ikegami, T., 2014. Using minimal human-computer interfaces for studying the interactive development of social awareness. *Frontiers in psychology*, 5, 1061.

Hoober, S., & Berkman, E., 2011. *Designing mobile interfaces: Patterns for interaction design*. O'Reilly Media, Inc.

Johnson, J., 2007. *GUI bloopers 2.0: common user interface design don'ts and dos*. Elsevier.

Lethoba, T., 2017. The Most Expensive University in South Africa. Retrieved from https://golimag.co.za/2017/06/28/the-most-expensive-university-in-south-africa/

Mothibi, M., 2015. Youth Leading Change: Views on #FeesMustFall. Retrieved from http://enke.co.za/youth-leading-change-views-on-feesmustfall-1/

Nelson, L., 2014. Three reasons college textbook prices are out of control. Retrieved from https://www.vox.com/2014/8/25/6058017/why-are-college-textbooks-so-expensive

Norman, D., 2013. *The design of everyday things*. Revised and expanded edition: Basic books.

Poole, E. S., 2013. HCI and mobile health interventions: how human–computer interaction can contribute to successful mobile health interventions. *Translational behavioral medicine*, 3(4), 402-405.

Ramsay, M., & Nielsen, J., 2000. *WAP usability deja vu: 1994 all over again*. Nielsen Norman Group, 1-90.

Seraj, M., & Wong, C. Y., 2012. A study of User Interface Design principles and requirements for developing a Mobile learning prototype. *International Conference on Computer & Information Science* (ICCIS).

Shneiderman, B., 1992. Tree visualization with tree-maps: 2-d space-filling approach. *ACM Transactions on graphics* (TOG), 11(1), 92-99.

Shneiderman, B., 2005. *Designing for Fun: Can we design user interfaces to be more fun*?

Stark, J., 2012. The 10 principles of mobile interface design. Retrieved from https://www.creativebloq.com/mobile/10-principles-mobile-interface-design-4122910

Stone, D., Jarrett, C., Woodroffe, M., & Minocha, S., 2005. *User interface design and evaluation*. Elsevier.

Tsimong, P., 2016. I support Fees Must Fall. Retrieved from https://www.news24.com/MyNews24/i-support-fees-must-fall-20161018

Xiao-qing, L., 2010. User Experience Design Based on User Mental Research. *Information Science*, 5, 763-767.

Zhang, P., Carey, J., Te'eni, D., & Tremaine, M., 2004. Integrating human-computer interaction development into SDLC: A methodology. *AMCIS 2004 Proceedings*, 574.

LEVERAGING VOICE ASSISTIVE TECHNOLOGY TO ENHANCE HEALTH MONITORING OF OLDER ADULTS

Swaraj Rath and Swati Chandna
Department of Informatics, SRH Hochschule, Heidelberg, Germany

ABSTRACT

With the growing population of older adults, the need for mHealth to address specific aging features is also increasing. However, various research and usability studies on those mHealth applications indicate that mHealth is still not planned with older adults and their needs in mind. It is critical to gain insight into aging obstacles that affect the usability of mHealth as encountered by older adults in order to improve mHealth designs targeted at this demographic.
Voice as a new interaction modality has been heavily emphasized in recent product launches such as Apple's Siri and Google's Voice Search. A user-centered design methodology was used to create a mobile health application to help independent living older adults keep track of their health and routine in this research. To help these individuals, I have designed CORE-Energy, a conceptual context-aware assistive application by integrating a language-technology-driven interface into mHealth. First, a Survey on mHealth was conducted to gather the opinion of various stakeholders. The functional design criteria used to direct the design were identified through an analysis of the data collected during this process. Integration of VUI, keeping track of Blood pressure, blood sugar, body temperature, and fitness tracking functionality was explored using a rapid prototyping method. The ease of use and perceived usefulness of the final prototype produced in this study were assessed. After conducting usability testing on 5 users, this application received a System Usability Scale (SUS) score of 75.4%, which indicates that the interface was found to be user-friendly in general. The application created during the research work can be extended to create a more diversified set of voice input to make the user experience even smoother.

KEYWORDS

mHealth for Older Adults, VUI, Elder Healthcare

1. INTRODUCTION

In recent years due to the rapid growth of digitization, health and medical organization have also increasingly begun to create digital tools supported by mobile (mHealth) technologies. Research shows that mHealth application can improve patients' quality of life, patient's health, and nutrition by providing real-time data to both patients and health care workers (Paiva, 2020). Agnihothri S. et all explored the use of mobile technology to manage chronic conditions and observed that patients who use mHealth observe improvement in their health (Agnihothri, 2020). Also, Elizabeth et all did experimental quantitative studies to support self-management for adult cancer survivors and found that mHealth interventions can improve pain and fatigue outcome among the users (Silva, 2019). Moreover, it is evident that access to timely information, assessment, and treatment are vital for patients in long-term conditions (Paiva, 2020). The quality and demand of mHealth applications have been incremented due to the high usage of mobile devices in clinical practice.

According to W3B Report from Fittkau & Maaß Consulting, around 67% of the population uses Health or Fitness applications, but among them, only 18% are older adults (Fittkau and Maaß Consulting, 2015). mHealth applications are prevalent among the younger population, but despite the technological advancement, the application developer failed to attract older adults as their end-user of the healthcare application. A usability assessment done by the University of Illinois for mHealth application for self-managing chronic health conditions states several usability issues like navigation, data entry, recovery from error, and Visualization in two of the major heart apps designated for older adults (Morey, 2017). The application users usually face a lot of issues with navigation between screens and scrolling within the application page. Besides, seniors often get confused over providing new health-related data. The existing applications designed for older adults failed to provide clear direction for recovering from errors. According to the International Journal of Medical Informatics stated that Computer Literacy, Hand-eye coordination, Visual acuity, and various other factors which causes usability issues in major mHealth application for older (Wildenbos, 2018). Also, the text available in the GUI is very smaller to be readable for them. Besides that, the swipe concept in an application doesn't seem to grasp among older adults, which results in difficulty using an application for older adults.

Due to the popularity of Voice User Interface (VUIs), it might pave the way to connect the advantage of technology to older adults while accounting for age-related changes and the challenges posed by those changes. VUI allows for more efficient, hands-free, intuitive, and rich interactions than any other type of user interface (Ziman, 2017). Voice-controlled personal assistants will be leveraged to help older adults in an easier, hands-free voice interaction, which will provide their health information. Our planned technique is to produce continuous, on-demand health information to freelance living older adults employing a voice-assistant system.

In response, we have developed CORE-Energy, a high-fidelity prototype of a mHealth application to track blood pressure, blood glucose, body temperature, and various other health-related factors using voice command. Based on the research findings from some published guidelines (Ziman, 2017) (Ma, 2017) (Chung, 2018), the design requirement for the application are drafted. When creating this mobile application, the psychological and physical characteristics of the elderly were considered. Screen, touchscreen, text, information, keypad, function label, etc. are all being taken into considerations during the design process of the CORE-Energy application.

2. RELATED WORK

Mobile monitoring and care systems (MMCs), which incorporate observing and counseling systems for essential care, are being utilized to diminish the well-being care burden on open care offices and assist families looking after more seasoned grown-ups within the domestic environment (Malwade, 2018). In hospitals or healthcare institutions, they use diverse mobile monitoring devices and care systems to care for older peoples in need. But it not possible to always keep them in healthcare institutions and older adults always need constant care. In case of older adults, they are impossible to dependably connected with or carry savvy gadgets, and the often-overlooked burden of customary charging may posture an extra utilize challenge (Malwade, 2018). As such, there are one-of-a-kind physiological and mental boundaries hindering these individual's get to and utilization of these technologies. Cognition function affects older adults by reducing the working capacity, semantic, procedural memory, and attention. Around 15% of men who aged above 65 are affected with moderate to severe cognitive impairment also, memory impairment affects 11% of women above 65 age (Wildenbos, 2018). The effect of aging is that each time, older people process fewer discrete information bits in a certain time and recall also decays faster. Also, physical impairment like arthritis, muscular dystrophy and heart disease, influence learning time, speed of performance, error rate, retention of time, and subjective satisfaction affecting technology use (Wildenbos, 2018).

3. METHODOLOGY

Various approaches were used in this research to understand the current condition of older adults better. However, activities such as literature studies, field studies, user activities, design, and development are ongoing and parallel activities that are cornerstones of this research project.

In the initial phase, a preliminary search was conducted to investigate other studies on what are the existing mHealth applications for older adults and how far it can attract them as their end-users. Requirement gathering and designing of the initial prototype of the mobile self-management software is being done in a parallel manner. Also, we have conducted a very in-depth survey to know how potential users view towards mHealth application. Most users of age above 50 participated in the Survey. For user who doesn't understand the Survey or doesn't own a smartphone, we have organized a telephonic meeting and asked the questions verbally. Participants were generally positive about the definition and script, with some suggesting that they planned to use a mHealth app that could be controlled by speech. Then we started the design process by imagining situations in which a voice-based intervention could help older adults with early-stage dementia with their self-management. Self-health management entails keeping track of blood pressure, heart rate, and blood glucose level, as well as providing information on any deadly viruses and maintaining a health record, among other things. A formative usability approach was introduced to design and build the initial prototype with an understanding of how users are supposed to communicate with the mobile application.

3.1 CORE-Energy Application

Based on the information gathered in the questionnaire study, the mobile app (CORE-Energy) was designed and developed using the best possible frameworks and database. React Native using Expo was chosen to implement this mobile app as it is a cross-platform framework allowing the app to run on mobile devices with iOS and Android. For ease of implementation and storing vital health-related information of the user, we have used Firebase because it's a great way to create cloud-based functionalities that developers can use in their mobile apps. For the most critical function i.e. to integrate Voice User Interface, we have used a library called "Alan AI." Alan allows users to have real-time human-like interactions with mobile apps and websites, which are very effective. Figure 1 represents the architecture of the application.

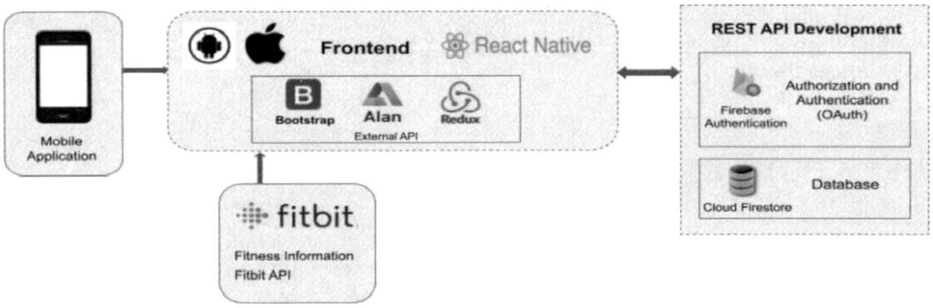

Figure 1. Architecture of the application

It is evident that the primary purpose of the application is to record information. A user can easily record their blood pressure, blood glucose, and body temperature in the application. Also, the fitness-related information like heart rate, steps, and calories comes from the Fitbit device of the user. At the start of the application, an onboarding UI will be shown to the user where all the specifications of the application will be mentioned in an interactive manner. It is essential for the first-time user to get most of the application app by giving on-boarding information at the app startup. After the Onboarding UI, the user will be navigated to the Login/Sign up screen. A user can either sign up by creating a new account or login with social media option is also available.

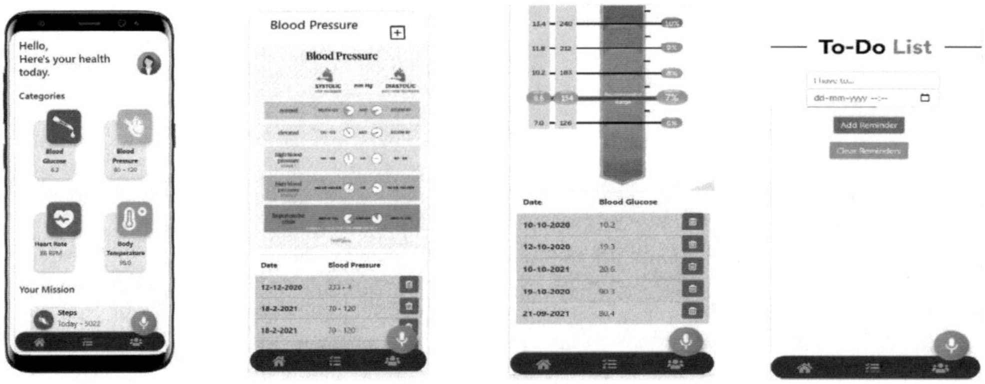

(a) Home Screen (b) Blood Pressure Monitor (c) Blood glucose Monitor (d) To-do List

Figure 2. Screenshots of CORE-Energy application

The app takes to the home screen when someone opens it. This page functions as a dashboard that summarizes the data collected during the day and also as a platform for users to enter self-measured data. As seen from the home page of the application Figure 2(a), a user could choose to either operate via VUI or graphical interface. In the bottom right part of the screen is the Voice command button. When a user presses this button, it starts listening and acts accordingly. The top section is a mini dashboard that shows the user's most recent blood glucose, blood pressure, body temperature and average heart rate. The details for blood pressure and blood glucose entity are shown in Figure 2(b) and 2(c). In contrast to command-based modalities and/or one-turn exchanges, voice interfaces are now implicitly supposed to be conversational. There are a collection of training phrases for each purpose. The training phrases are made up of all the different ways a question can be phrased with the same intent. Designing a conversational interface entails influencing user requests and modeling our voice agent's responses.

The voice request has two layers:

- Utterance: A user utterance is what the user says. In simple terms, an utterance is a way a user expresses a request.
- Intent: This is the primary goal of any user request. It represents the actual task that a user wants to do. This phase also assists in identifying the 'slots' or 'variables' that are needed to complete the request. Variables are extra pieces of information or inputs that the user must have in order to finish the task.

The voice assistant needs to know the mandatory variables in order to complete the flow of requests. If a user asks for something which is not possible, it'll be treated as an invalid request. There are numerous voice commands supported in the CORE-Energy application, however, some of the elementary commands supported are listed above in table 1.

Table 1. Some of the supported commands in the CORE-Energy application

Commands	Description
Add blood pressure for today	The system will ask for blood pressure and add for today
Add blood glucose for yesterday	The system will ask for blood glucose and add for yesterday
Add body temperature for last Friday	The system will ask for body temperature and add it for last Friday
Go to Todo page	The routine management page will be loaded
Remind me to take medication	The system will ask for the date and time on which the user wants to add the task and then *take medication* will be added to the To-do list
Show my steps	
What's my blood pressure yesterday	It'll tell yesterdays recorded blood pressure
How's my health	Gives a brief about the user's blood pressure, blood glucose, and heart rate, etc.

The act of logging and reading blood pressure, blood glucose, and temperature occur on three different screens designated for these data. Figure 2(a) and 2(b) show the blood pressure and blood glucose monitoring page respectively. When the user clicks on any of the cards presented on the home screen, they will be directed to a new screen that will allow them to log their health information. On every page at the top right corner, there exists an 'Add' button which allows an individual to log the health information with respect to date. When a user clicks on that button, a pop-up will appear, and they can easily add the data by filling up the form. On each screen, an image is present to help the user with finding out whether their condition is suitable or not. Moreover, to help the individual with the information, the table cell is colored with a different pattern so that a user can quickly identify whether his condition is healthy or not. Figure 2(c) depicts the To-do list page of the application. The aim of this To-do List was to show the user what their day-to-day routine looked like at a glance. The idea is that a user can easily input their medication and other activities along with the date and time.

4. RESULTS

The overall aim was to explore whether a VUI-based mHealth application could be a valuable tool for older adults to support them in day-to-day life in keeping track of their health and self-management. So, we conducted the Usability Testing of the CORE-Energy app with 5 participants of age above 50 because according to Jeff Sauro of MeasuringU, testing with just 5 users would turn up around 85% of the problems in an interface (Martin, 2016). Every participant understands English and owns a smartphone. Overall, all of the testing were conducted in the same way. Each test lasted about forty minutes and audio recorded for later analysis. Because none of the participants owns a Fitbit device, the Fitbit device, which is used during the development, was provided to the participants. Participants were asked to complete a total of nine scenarios by engaging with the mobile application to learn more about the testing process. These tools were then used to assess tasks and conduct a thorough review of the participants' results. The following information was evaluated for each participant: 1) task completion; 2) task completion time; 3) task error rate; 4) time to recover from an error 5) qualitative analysis notes and feedback, and 6) customer satisfaction questionnaire responses.

4.1 Measuring Usability

ISO 9241-11, a specification that includes detailed indicators on how well a consumer achieves specific goals, is one of the objective methods for determining usability which incorporates the basic concepts of user-centered design (UCD) (Georgsson, 2016). During the interactions with the user, we took feedback from them for heuristic evaluation. The resulting application may be considered to have reached an appropriate level of usability if the specified measurements of efficacy, performance, and satisfaction are met adequately. Each scenario is summarized and categorizes by user role in Table 2.

Table 2. Usability testing - User tasks and scenario

No.	Task	Scenario
S1	Sign up	After installing CORE-Energy application, create your own account in there.
S2	Record Blood Pressure Information	You want to record today's blood pressure reading. Open the app and record your blood pressure.
S3	Record blood glucose level	Your goal is to keep your Blood glucose in range. So, you'd like to record yesterday's BG level in the app.
S4	Todo Page	You want to check what are the things you have to do further. Go to the To-do page to see all the tasks.
S5	Add Task to Todo List	You want to remember taking particular medication at a specific time. Add that to todo list.
S6	Register Body Temperature	You are recovering from flu, and you forget to input yesterday's body temperature. Input BT: 98.6°F for yesterday.
S7	Review recent data	Since it's the end of the day, you want to have a look through your BP, BG, BT, Calories.
S8	Find steps	You took a walk-in street, find out how many distances you have traveled today.
S9	Upcoming Task	You want to know what's on your timetable next. Find that out.

4.1.1 Effectiveness

Task completion performance and the number of mistakes made during the interaction are two common ways to assess effectiveness. Figure 2 represents the effectiveness results of each scenario. Scenario one and two were the most difficult to complete with 50% and 18% failure rates, respectively (Here, assist is also considered as failure), but They completed the rest of the tasks flawlessly. Also, for the fifth task, some participants made similar mistakes, as it is very similar to task two. To get a better understanding of task success, the number of taps/gestures off the vital route to complete a scenario was considered. To put it another way, any participant who completed a task with more taps than required was labeled a success with errors. Figure 3 below depicts the percent of participants that completed scenarios with no problems (green), with assist (orange), and failures (red).

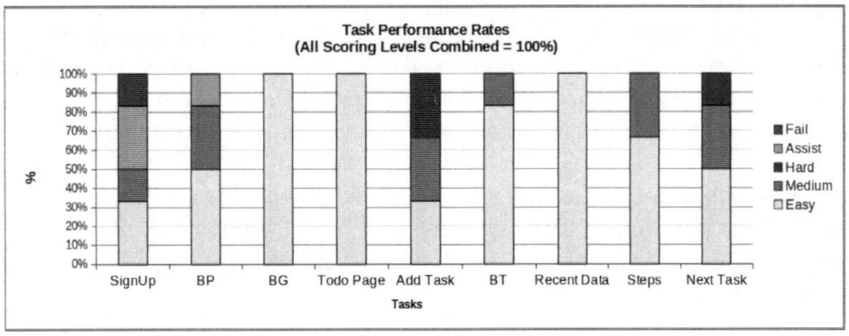

Figure 3. Different level of task performance rate

4.1.2 Efficiency

Efficiency is measured by the amount of time and resources that the user must expend in order to accomplish a task in terms of precision and completeness (Georgsson, 2016). As observed from Fig. 3 scenario 4 and scenario 7 have the least task completion time with a mean value of 7. Scenario 4 was to navigate to the To-do page using voice command, and scenario 7 was to ask for a brief about your own health. Scenario 8 was to find out how many steps traveled today, which also participants did is seamlessly (average completion time 16sec). Whereas scenario 1 and scenario 2 consumed the most extended amount of time, as might be expected given the difficulty with task success and errors mentioned above.

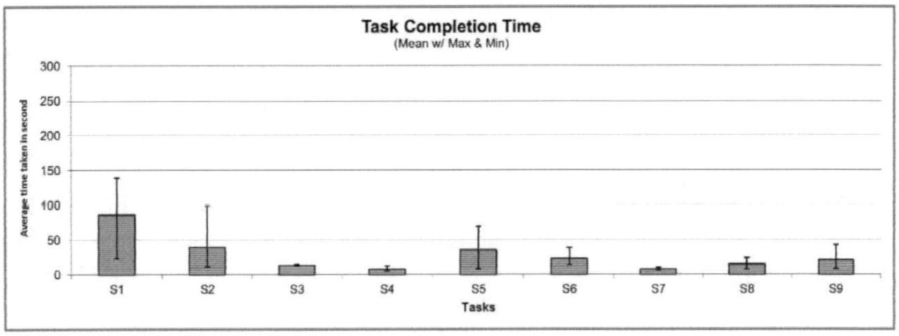

Figure 4. Average time taken to complete the scenarios

4.1.3 Satisfaction

In the sense of usability, satisfaction refers to a user's subjective satisfaction with a method or result (Georgsson, 2016). Participants were given questionnaires at the start and end of the usability testing session. The pre-test questionnaire aimed to collect background information on participant's self-management routines and their level of comfort interacting with mobile devices whereas the post-session questionnaire was focused on evaluating the design's usability. The System Usability Scale (SUS) is a reliable "quick and dirty" method for assessing usability (Brooke, 1996). The System Usability Scale (SUS) is made up of ten usability-related sentences, half of which are positive and half of which are negative (Brooke, 1996). On a 5-point Likert scale, participants were asked whether they agreed or disagreed with the scheme. On a scale of one to five, users were asked to rate how realistic each of the scenarios was to them. Participants were then asked to provide open-ended feedback. Figure 4 depicts the SUS score of 75.4%, which is "Acceptable".

5. DISCUSSION

Overall, findings suggest that the CORE-Energy application is usable, acceptable, and relevant to older adults. Results from the focus groups indicated that the initial versions of the UI and modules were broadly good and uncovered helpful directions for making improvements. Participant feedback suggested that the application features are elementary to use and required less practice to get accustomed to the application. They also appreciated the graphics, amount of text, and Voice user interface environment. Another finding shows that seniors view the GUI and VUI differently in terms of learnability, accessibility, clarity, and usefulness. More precisely, the seniors polled thought the VUI was easier to learn and use, but the GUI was simpler to understand and more functional. In the end, the VUI was favored by the participants. However, they feel frustrated sometimes when they forget the command meant for executing specific tasks, but this could be further improved by adding more simplistic controls for VUI.

A few of the participants said that *Its very simple to use, the function provided are very straight forward and It's enjoyable to use*. All the participants were already using touch screen mobile devices for essential activities. As a result, they were able to grasp the application's functionality quickly. Two of the participants liked the To-Do list functionality in the application. They added that it'd be an excellent use to input their medication into the application so that they never miss it. Blood pressure monitoring was the most helpful feature for the participants. One of them even said *I usually keep track of my blood pressure every day and write it down in a notebook. But sometimes, I lost the notebook* and commented how the application might help with that. They also wondered if it would be possible to connect their personal blood pressure machine with this application so that they don't have to input it into the application. The participants also like Body temperature monitoring. He added that *Sometimes when I have a fever, our family doctor often asks me to record body temperature three times a day*. He said using this application he can keep track of it very quickly.

Also, the feedbacks from the participants suggested that older adults were not much interested in Fitness monitoring however these features are 'nice to have' but are not crucial to developing a functional application. A better GUI is also essential to increase the popularity of mHealth among older adults. Because some of our participants raised concerned about using the VUI outside of their respective house. Developers should consider the consumers' technical ability, the type of data being collected, and the size of the mobile device display when designing the user interface. Developers could undertake design and usability studies, referring to users, in order to produce an easy-to-use application. Aside from that, our findings advise that the usage of keyboard should be limited, since it was discovered to be a time-consuming and error-prone chore for this user group. In order to improve the affordance of items, icons are used next to textual labels. From the usability testing we can conclude that older adults mostly tap on the icon.

The demography of the participants reveals no difference in terms of a task performance rate. Among the participants, one of the older adults was very acquainted with mobile devices, so he could complete every task very easily. So, it all comes to computer literacy while using the mobile application.

Throughout the project, there were several obstacles and challenging situations we have faced. The application's fitness monitoring feature was not completely developed. This was done on purpose so that experimental research into a fitness monitoring feature could be performed. Since no current smart wearable brands share their users' data due to data privacy concerns, more research is needed to incorporate that functionality into the app. Also, when it comes to usability testing also only five participants were part of the user testing of the CORE-Energy application. So, it's still not clear how older adults who have dementia or physical disability will interact with the application.

6. CONCLUSION AND FUTURE WORKS

This study is the first step in a long-term design process where we have developed a VUI integrated mHealth application based on feedback provided in a focus group study and previous literature. The applications can store blood pressure, blood glucose, body temperature and provide on-demand health information to independent living older adults. Currently, the present interaction design still stands as a simple yet effective design solution for older adults for monitoring their health. However, more thorough tests in much bigger numbers should be conducted to gain statistical proof of its effectiveness. With more research, older adults can benefit from supported self-care, equipping themselves with sufficient knowledge, skills, and the confidence to lead a relatively independent life at home.

Future research should involve a second iteration of the design that incorporates input from usability testing. Changes should be made explicitly to account for problems users encountered when communicating with the program. Fitness monitoring, VUI, and pairing with another smart wearable can all be reviewed, where the interaction mimics what it would be like to use a mHealth app in real life. Also, in recent years, hands-free, voice-activated assistants (VAAs) have gained popularity, thanks to the introduction of commercial products such as Amazon Alexa and Google Assistant. So, for further development, a voice-activated application which could provide on-demand health information to independent living older adults will make an even better option for those who don't even know the basic of a smartphone.

To conclude, there is an insatiable demand for innovative ways to assist independent-living older adults. It is hoped that this study will encourage potential researchers to come up with new and innovative ideas.

REFERENCES

Agnihothri S. et al, 2020. 'The value of mhealth for man-aging chronic conditions,' Health care management science, Vol. 23, No 2, pp. 185–202, 2020.

Brooke J., 1996. 'Sus: A "quick and dirty'usability,' Usability evaluation in industry, Vol. 189.

Chung A. and Griffin A., 2018. 'Health and fitness apps for hands-free voice-activated assistants: Content analysis,' JMIR mHealth and uHealth, Vol 6, No 9, pp. e174.

Fittkau and Maaß Consulting, Fit werden mit apps (2015, June 8). https://www.horizont.net/planung-analyse/nachrichten/Fit-werden-mit-Apps-147758, Accessed on 17-October-2020.

Georgsson M. and Staggers N., 2016. 'Quantifying usability: An evaluation of a diabetes mhealth system on effectiveness, efficiency, and satisfaction metrics with associated user characteristics,' Journal of the American Medical Informatics Association, Vol 23, No 1, pp. 5–11.

Ma M., 2017. 'Angel-echo: A personalized health careapplication,'in2017 IEEE/ACM International Conference on Connected Health: Applications, Systems andEngineering Technologies (CHASE), IEEE, pages 258–259.

Malwade S. and Abdul S., 2018. 'Mobile and wearable technologies in healthcare forthe ageing population,' Computer methods and programs in biomedicine, Vol 161, pp. 233–237.

Martin E., 2016. Why 5 is the magic number for ux usability testing, https://www.invisionapp.com/inside-design/ux-usability-research-testing/, Accessed on 17-March-2021.

Morey S., Barg-Walkow L. and Rogers W., 2017, 'Managing heart failure on the go: Usability issues with mhealth apps for older adults,'in Proceedings of the Human Factors and Ergonomics Society Annual Meeting, SAGE Publications Sage CA: Los Angeles, CA,volume61, pages 1–5.

Paiva J. et al, 2020. 'Mobile applications for elderly healthcare: A systematic mapping,' PloS one, Vol 15, No 7, pp. e0236091.

Silva E., Lawler S. and Langbecker D., 'The effectiveness of mhealth for self-management in improving pain, psychological distress, fatigue, and sleep in cancer survivors: A systematicreview,' Journal of Cancer Survivorship, Vol 13, No 1, pp. 97–107.

Wildenbos G., Peute L. and Jaspers M., 2018, 'Aging barriers influencing mobile health usability for older adults: A literature based framework (mold-us),' International journal of medical informatics, Vol 114, pp. 66–75.

Ziman R., 2017. 'Factors affecting seniors' perceptions of voice user interfaces'.

TOWARDS USABILITY INTERFACE TRUSTWORTHINESS IN E-COMMERCE SYSTEMS

Andréia Rodrigues Casare[1], Celmar Guimarães da Silva[1], Tania Basso[1] and Regina Moraes[1,2]
[1]University of Campinas (UNICAMP) – Limeira – Brazil
[2]University of Coimbra (UC) – Coimbra – Portugal

ABSTRACT

The Internet gives vendors an easy way to set up shop for electronic commerce throughout the world. However, lack of consumer trust is a critical impediment to the success of e-commerce since users avoid systems they do not trust. In this paper we present the outcome of a literature review in which we investigated personal aspects that impact the sense of trust regarding user experience when interacting with e-commerce systems. We identified and complemented a set of attributes that characterizes the perceived feeling of trust by the users and formalized a set of related trustworthiness measures. The work makes clear a process that goes from the sub attributes identification to the calculation of their values based on answers provided by the users. The goal is to help users to measure how trustworthy an e-commerce application is, toward a future benchmark.

KEYWORDS

Trust, Trustworthiness, User Experience, e-Commerce, Questionnaire, Metrics

1. INTRODUCTION

As a social being, trust is present into every aspect of human life. Without trust no business transactions take place, no new technology is adopted. Trust is a common and essential concept in different domains and even more important in e-commerce.

In computing science, *trust* can be defined as the probability that an entity demonstrates reliable behavior for specific operations under a situation with potential risks (Cho et al., 2010), while *trustworthiness* is a system characteristic that can influence the trust that a person has in the system (Mohammadi et al., 2014).

Any e-commerce application has the internet as a backdrop and a web page that allows interaction between buyer and seller. Its interface is so important that motivates a study by Bentley University Design and Usability Center, which concludes that when people first navigate to a website, businesses have about 6 seconds to create a positive impression with users (Bill 2012). Therefore, the user's perception of trust is mainly obtained from the quality of the interface. In this context, to assess how trustworthy an e-commerce application is, it is important to define a set of attributes and metrics based on user interface. The metrics can be an objective indicator to validate the trustworthiness of the system with a certain level of confidence and can drive improvements to increase trust.

In this paper we present the results of a literature review involving quality of user interface and trust in e-commerce applications. As such, we (i) identified and created a set of user interface-based attributes and sub attributes that characterizes the perceived feeling of trust by the users, and (ii) formalized a set of related trustworthiness metrics. Since the majority of the attributes are measured by subjective metrics, i.e., they depend on the user experience, we identified a set of existing questionnaires and complemented them with new ones to be used in the trustworthiness assessments under user's perception. The result is a total of 25 metrics identified and formalized and 45 questions distributed in a set of questionnaires to be used in future survey with users. In the first plan, we identified 70 questions extracted from the literature, but we were able to combine some of them to avoid that the participants on the evaluation loose attention and rush through the questionnaire.

The remainder of this work is organized as follows: Section 2 presents works related to attributes of usability, accessibility and user experience. Section 3 shows a set of user interface-based metrics. The questionnaires composition covering trustworthiness metrics are presented in Section 4. Finally, Section 5 presents the conclusions of this work.

2. BACKGROUND AND RELATED WORK

To the best of our knowledge, trustworthiness metrics from the perspective of the user experience were not extensively studied up to now. It is difficult to obtain consistent scores for trustworthiness in e-commerce because most attributes measurement are subjective and dependent on system context, users' feelings and previous experiences. Therefore, we considered works related to attributes of usability, accessibility and user experience that may not be not restricted to e-commerce interfaces but may influence them somehow.

The work presented by Jøsang, Keser and Dimitrakos (2005) examines different approaches related to online activities where trust and their potential for trust management is relevant and advocate that trust management represents a promising development for making online transactions more dependable. Their goal is to assess the potential of trust management for stimulating online activities and increasing the quality of online communities. They provided a set of definitions about trust in different context (reliability and decision trust) and disciplines (sociology and economic exchange) and a discussion about building trust in e-commerce. Despite interesting discussions came through and can be considered in the future, it differs from our purpose right now, which is to formulate measures that allow us to compare e-commerce services.

Regarding usability, Brooke (1996) proposed a set of usability metrics called SUS (System Usability Scale), which measures the efficiency, effectiveness, satisfaction in use and ease of learning attributes. SUS scores are obtained through a 10-item questionnaire applied after the respondents use the system under evaluation. Similarly, to measure the same attributes, Finstad (2010) proposed the UMUX (Usability Metric for User Experience), that uses a 4-item questionnaire. Also, based on UMUX, the UMUX-LITE (Lewis et al., 2013) uses a 2-item questionnaire. In the same direction, Seffah et al. (2006) proposed the Quality in Use Integrated Measurement (QUIM), which is a model that encompasses 10 usability attributes (with efficiency, effectiveness, satisfaction in use and ease of learning among them). These 10 factors are broken down into a total of 26 subfactors or measurable criteria that were based on 127 specific metrics.

The works of Sauro and Kindlund (2005) and Veral and Macias (2019) understand usability dimension by the composition of effectiveness, efficiency, easy of learning and satisfaction. The former work proposed a score, called SUM (Single Usability Metric), which encapsulates the majority of information in four common usability metrics: task completion rates, average number of errors, average time on task, and post-task satisfaction. The latter work proposed a usability perception assessment based on reaction cards – a popular method for obtaining subjective user satisfaction in user experience ratings. In addition, they provided a support tool based on the metric developed, presenting a structure to store historical assessments in order to obtain graphs and benchmark levels to compare the perceived usability of different artifacts. We take advantage of both, as we are proposing a single score and planning to develop a tool to support users to obtain the proposed score in order to better compare e-commerce applications regarding trust.

Standards proposed by ISO/IEC formalized some usability and accessibility attributes. ISO/IEC 25022 (ISO 2016a) defines metrics for the quality of interaction between a user and a system. Examples of measures are: satisfaction, efficiency, effectiveness, among others. Complementing the previous standard, ISO/IEC 25023 (ISO 2016b) defines a set of quality measures such as learnability, operability, user interface aesthetics, among others. A set of quality measures for each characteristic and sub-characteristic as well as an explanation of how to apply them are provided.

Concerning accessibility, Parmanto and Zeng (2005) proposed the WAB (Web Accessibility Barrier) metric that quantitatively measures the accessibility of web content. The metric is based on the Web Content Accessibility Guidelines (WCAG) 1.0 checkpoints. Also, The Unified Web Assessment Methodology (UWEM) (Nietzio et al. 2008) offers test descriptions to assess WCAG 1.0 compliance. Song et al. (2017) proposed a metric called Web Accessibility Experience Metric (WAEM), that matches the accessibility evaluation results with the user experience by pairwise comparisons between different websites. As an extension of WAEM, Song et al. (2018) proposed Reliability Aware Web Accessibility Experience Metric (RA-WAEM), which considers the user experience and reliability in assessing the severity of accessibility barriers. Vigo et al. (2007) proposed the Web Accessibility Quantitative Metric (WAQM), which generates an accessibility score from evaluation reports produced by evaluation tools (EvalAccess and LIFT).

Regarding user experience, we considered works related to questionnaires that had already been applied to assess the user's perception of trust. Lewis (1995) developed the Computer System Usability Questionnaire (CSUQ), which consists of 19 statements. User rates them on a seven-point scale of "Strongly Disagree" to "Strongly Agree", plus N/A. It evaluates attributes such as satisfaction, efficiency, usefulness, pleasure, ease of use and ease of learning. Similarly, Lund (2001) proposed the USE, which is a 7-point Likert scale questionnaire with 30 questions that evaluates usefulness, satisfaction, ease of learning and ease of use. In the same direction, Lin et al. (1997) proposed the Purdue Usability Testing Questionnaire (PUTQ), which contains 100 questions about computer interfaces, to which user rates agreement on a seven-point scale of "Bad" to "Good", plus N/A. Also, using the same scale, Hendradjaya and Praptini (2015) present a questionnaire with 9 questions that evaluates usability attributes such as navigability, ease of use, ease of learning and consistency.

Perlman (1997) proposed the Practical Heuristics for Usability Evaluation, which is a questionnaire based on Nielsen's Heuristics and Norman's principles. It consists of 13 statements to which user rates agreement on a seven-point scale of "Bad" to "Good", plus N/A. The statements are divided into learning, adapting to user, feedback and errors. Granollers (2018), in turn, proposed a new list of principles for evaluating user interfaces and also a set of questions to be answered When analyzing every principle, totaling 56 questions.

3. ELICITATION OF INTERFACE TRUSTWORTHINESS METRICS

Like any part of a software product, measuring interface quality helps to understand deficiencies and guides improvements. Based on studies of literature works (Seffah et al., 2006; ISO 2016a; ISO 2016b; W3C 2018; Nielsen 1993) it was possible to identify a set of quality attributes related to usability, accessibility and user experience, which impact user trust during interaction with e-commerce. The attributes were grouped into three main categories: usability, accessibility and user experience.

Considering the literature review presented in Section 2, a set of interface-based metrics was collected from several sources so that they could compose a single body, which was complemented by some metrics of interface components that were considered relevant, based on more recently developed evaluation techniques and guidelines (e.g. reputation seals, customers opinion, among others). In total, we formalized 25 metrics as follows (see Figure 1): Learnability (4 sub attributes), Efficiency (4), Perceivability (4), Operability (4), Safety in Use (2), Satisfaction (1), Usefulness (1), and User Experience (6). This last metric is composed by Company Information, Company Reputation, Privacy Policies, Customer Opinion, Pleasure and Padlock. It is important to note that performance is a common sub attribute between efficiency and Perceivability. The complete metric formalization document can be found in our research group website[1].

Figure 1 presents a tree model that accommodates the set of attributes and sub attributes that impacts the user perception of trust. Each one of them was formalized specifying how each one should be calculated after information has been collected at the appropriate source (e.g., automatic tool, questionnaire). It is important to highlight that the formalization structure was borrowed from ISO/IEC 25022 / 23 (ISO 2016a; ISO 2016b). This structure is composed by ID (Identification code), name, description, measurement function (formula showing how the quality measure elements are combined to produce the quality measure) and method (the source or type of method that can be used to obtain the measure). The ID of a quality measure is a code representing the quality characteristics and sub characteristics. It is a serial number of sequential order within quality sub characteristic followed by G – for generally applicable – or S – for specific needs. For example, Op-3-G means the third sub attribute generally applicable to compose Operable attribute (Op). Some notes are included for each attribute / sub attribute to complement the understanding of some specificity of the measurement function or sources to obtain the measure.

[1] https://www.ft.unicamp.br/pt-br/pessoas/docentes/regina

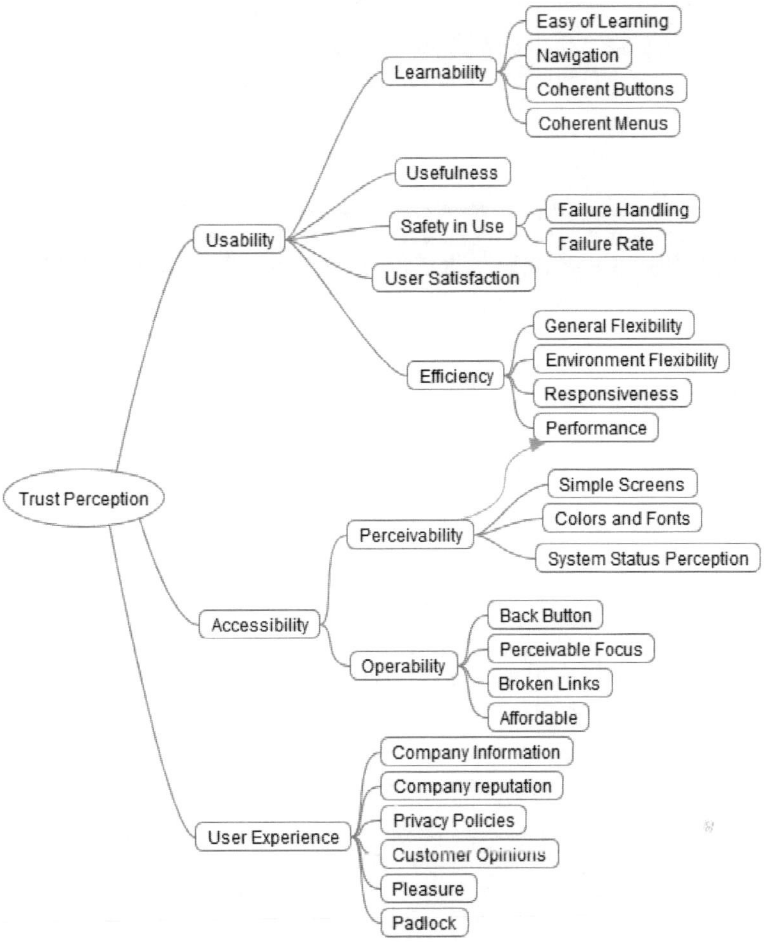

Figure 1. Trust Attributes

Figures 2 and 3 show the formalization of two of those attributes. The first one, entitled Broken Links, is a sub attribute of Operable, which in turn composes Accessibility attribute. In this case, the source in the last column, shows that it is automatically obtained by tools. In the notes, it is suggested to use at least 3 tools to obtain the total number of links inspected and the number of broken links. The measurement function is the maximum broken links rate among the used tools (then, considering the worst case).

The sub attribute in Figure 3, entitled Environment Flexibility, is a Efficiency sub attribute which in turn composes Usability attribute. This is a more subjective sub attribute and it must be obtained by applying a questionnaire that should be answered by users. The questionnaire uses a 7 point Likert scale and the measurement score is obtained by the weighted average of each question answered by all users. In the notes are highlighted that for answering the questionnaire the user must try the e-commerce application in advance and different browsers must be used.

ID	Name	Description	Measurement function	Method
Op-3-G	Broken links	The amount of website links that point out non-existent webpages.	X=Max($\sum_{i=1}^{t} S_i(B/Q)$) i = tool identifier B = the amount of broken links Q = total links of site S_i = the score of broken links provided by the tool "i"	Automatic tool
Note 1 Minimum of 3 automatic tools. For example, Dead Link Checker (https://www.deadlinkchecker.com/), Xenu's Link Sleuth (https://xenus-link-sleuth.softonic.com.br/) and Screaming Frog Seo Spider (https://www.screamingfrog.co.uk/) can be used.				
Note 2 Each tool must return the total number of links inspected and the number of defective links.				

Figure 2. Sub Attribute Formalization: Broken Links

ID	Name	Description	Measurement function	Method
Ef-2-S	Environment flexibility	The site is flexible to be used in different browsers and devices.	X=$\sum_{i=1}^{U}\sum_{j=1}^{Q} S_{ij}/(U * Q)$ i = user identifier j = question identifier U = the total number of users Q = the total number of questions S_{ij} = the score of the question "j" given by the user "i"	Questionnarie
Note 1 The questionnarie uses a Likert scale point (1 to 7) and the related questions can be found in Appendix F.				
Note 2 To answer the questionnarie, users must use the site before.				
Note 3 Minimum 31 users (to meet statistical significance in accordance to Triola(1999))				
Note 4 The site must be tested in different browsers (i.e, Firefox, Chrome, Safari) and with a minimum of 10 users in each browser				

Figure 3. Sub Attribute Formalization: Flexibility

As well as the Environment Flexibility sub attribute, several other interface attributes are dependent on the users' evaluation, since several personal factors are involved (such as cultural, professional, education level, age, among others). Therefore, the next section discusses the creation / adaptation of a set of questionnaires so that they can be applied to human users in order to obtain a survey of the users' perception regarding trust.

4. QUESTIONNARIES COMPOSITION COVERING TRUSTWORTHINESS METRICS

In addition to use the literature review to define metrics, we also use it to obtain examples of questionnaires previously used. 20 out of 25 sub attributes need to be evaluated using questionnaires, highlighting the strong subjectivity of the interface attributes. As we mentioned before, the decision is to use 7-point Likert scale questionnaires for all of them.

The total number of questions considering all questionnaires is 45, with an average of 2.25 questions per sub attribute. The minimum number of questions in one questionnaire is 1 and the maximum is 10. About 61% of the questions are borrowed or adapted from previous works and the remaining ones were defined as a complement extracted from more modern view of e-commerce systems (the ones without any citations). The whole set of questionnaires can be found in our research group website. As an example, Table 1 presents the questionnaire used to evaluate the sub attribute Environment Flexibility (as indicated in Note 1 of Figure 3 as "Appendix F"). In this case, 5 out of 10 questions came from previous works.

Table 1. Sub Attribute Questionnarie: Flexibility

Questions	Strongly disagree (1)	(2)	(3)	Neither agree nor disagree (4)	(5)	(6)	Strongly agree (7)
Can the interface elements be displayed according to the user's needs?							
Are users allowed to customize windows and commands (shortcut keys, personalization)?							
Does it provide user selection of data for display? (Lin et al., 1997)							
Does it provide zooming for display expansion? (Lin et al., 1997)							
Does the website provide function keys for track frequent inputs? (Lin et al., 1997)							
Does the website provide global search and replaceability? (Lin et al., 1997)							
Is it possible to easily perform an action previously performed?							
Does the design adapt to changes in screen resolution? (Granollers, 2018)							
The website is flexible to be used in multiple browsers?							
The website is flexible to be used in multiple devices (smartphones, tablets)?							

Once the questionnaire is applied and the answers are obtained, the weighted average must be obtained considering the Likert scale (1 to 7) and the total of responses for each of these points (n_1 – total responses as "Strongly disagree" to n_7 – total responses as "Strongly Agree"), after counting the answers of all participants. Then, the standard deviation must be evaluated allowing better analysis of the perception score.

$$AVG_j = \frac{\sum_{i=1}^{7} s_{ij} n_{ij}}{\sum_{i=1}^{7} n_{ij}} \quad (1)$$

$$SD_j = \sqrt{\frac{\sum_{i=1}^{7} (i - AVG_j)^2 \, n_{ij}}{\sum_{i=1}^{7} n_{ij}}} \quad (2)$$

Expressions (1) and (2) present the equation for calculating the weighted average and the standard deviation, respectively, where s_{ij} is the value i in the Likert Scale of the question j, n_{ij} is how many times the value i of the Likert Scale was pointed out (by the participants) for the question j, AVG_j is the weighted average score of question j, and SD_j is the standard deviation of the scores of the question j.

5. CONCLUSIONS

This paper presents the outcome of a literature review to investigate personal aspects that impact the sense of trust regarding user experience interacting with e-commerce systems.

A set of user interface-based attributes and sub attributes that characterizes the perceived feeling of trust by the users was identified and complemented. More important, for each of the 25 proposed attributes or sub attributes, the paper shows the metrics and formalized them toward the user perception trustworthiness score. Moreover, a set of existing and new proposal for questionnaires were put together to be applied to customers in a future trustworthiness survey, gathering 45 questions to deal with the subjectivity of these metrics. The complete process that starts from the definition of attributes, formalization of the respective measures, collection, calculation based on questionnaire responses and the variation of the measures was summarized.

Future works plan the application of the proposed questionnaires to validate the relation of the select attributes with trust perception, the proposed metrics and procedure to obtain the trustworthiness score and the development of a tool to support users so that they can benchmark e-commerce websites.

ACKNOWLEDGEMENT

This study was financed in part by the *Coordenacão de Aperfeiçoamento de Pessoal de Nível Superior – Brasil* (CAPES) - Finance code 001. Two research projects also partially supported this work, the ATMOSPHERE project (https://www.atmosphere-eubrazil.eu/) – Horizon 2020 grant agreement N. 777154 – MCTIC/RNP and ADVANCE project (http://acvance-rise.eu/) – Horizon 2020-MSCA-RISE grant agreement N. 2018-823788.

REFERENCES

Bill, A., 2012. How quick are we to judge? A case study of trust and web site design. Bentley University. Available in https://pt.slideshare.net/NYTechCouncil/how-quick-are-we-to-judge-a-case-study-of-trust-and-web-site-design. Last access: June 2021.

Brooke, J., 1996. SUS: a 'quick and dirty' usability. *Usability evaluation in industry*, Redhatch Consulting LTD., 189. Available in https://hell.meiert.org/core/pdf/sus.pdf. Last access: June 2021.

Cho, J.-H., Swami A., Chen I-R., 2010. A survey on trust management for mobile ad hoc networks. *IEEE Communications Surveys & Tutorials*, 13(4), pp. 562–583.

Finstad, K., 2010. The usability metric for user experience. *Interacting with Computers*, 22(5), pp. 323–327.

Granollers, T., 2018. Usability evaluation with heuristics. new proposal from integrating two trusted sources. *In: International Conf. of Design, User Experience, and Usability*, pp. 396–405. Springer.

Hendradjaya, B. and Praptini, R., 2015. A proposal for a quality model for e-government website. *In: 2015 Int. Conf. on Data and Software Engineering (ICoDSE)*, pp. 19–24.

ISO, 2016a. *Systems and software engineering - systems and Software QUality Requirements and Evaluation (SQUARE) - measurement of quality in use* (ISO/IEC).

ISO, 2016b. *Systems and software engineering - systems and Software QUality Requirements and Evaluation (SQUARE) - measurement of system and software product quality* (ISO/IEC).

Lewis, J. R., 1995. IBM computer usability satisfaction questionnaires: psychometric evaluation and instructions for use. *Int. Journal of Human-Computer Interaction*, 7(1), pp. 57–78.

Lewis, J. R. et al., 2013. UMUX-LITE: when there's no time for the SUS. *In Proc. of the SIGCHI Conf. on Human Factors in Computing Systems*, pp. 2099–2102.

Lin, H. X., Utesch, B., Maher D., 1997. A proposed index of usability: a method for comparing the relative usability of different software systems. *Behaviour & Information Technology, 16*(4-5), pp. 267–277.

Lund, A. M., 2001. Measuring usability with the USE questionnaire. *Usability Interface*, *8*(2), pp. 3–6.

Mohammadi, N. G., Paulus, S., Bishr, M., Metzger, A., Könnecke, H., Hartenstein, S., 2014. Trustworthiness Attributes and Metrics for Engineering Trusted Internet-Based Software Systems. In: Helfert M., Desprez F., Ferguson D., Leymann F. (eds) Cloud Computing and Services Science. CLOSER 2013. *Communications in Computer and Information Science*, vol. 453, pp. 19-35. Springer, Cham.

Nielsen, J., 1993. *Usability Engineering*. Morgan Kaufmann.

Nietzio, A., Strobbe, C., Velleman, E., 2008. The unified web evaluation methodology (UWEM) 1.2 for WCAG 1.0. *In Int. Conf. on Computers for Handicapped Persons*, pp. 394–401, Springer.

Parmanto, B. and Zeng, X., 2005. Metric for web accessibility evaluation. *Journal of the American Society for Information Science and Technology*, 56(13), pp. 1394–1404.

Perlman, G., 1997. *Practical heuristics for usability evaluation. Questionnaire.* Available in https://garyperlman.com/quest/quest.cgi?form=PHUE. Last access: June 2021.

Sauro, J. and Kindlund, E., 2005. A method to standardize usability metrics into a single score. In *Proc. of the SIGCHI Conf. on Human Factors in Computing Systems*, pp. 401–409.

Seffah, A., Donyaee, M., Kline, R., Padda, H., 2006. Usability measurement and metrics: a consolidated model. *Software Quality Journal*, *14*(2), pp. 159–178.

Song, S., Bu, J., Shen, C., Artmeier, A., Yu Z., Zhou Q., 2018. Reliability aware web accessibility experience metric. *In Proc. of the Reliability Aware Web Accessibility Experience Metric – W4A,* pp. 1–4, ACM.

Song, S., Wang C., Li, L., Yu, Z., Lin, X., Bu, J., 2017. WAEM: a web accessibility evaluation metric based on partial user experience order. *In Proc. of the 14th Web for All Conf. on The Future of Accessible Work*, pp. 1–4.

Veral, R. and Macias, J. A., 2019. Supporting user-perceived usability benchmarking through a developed quantitative metric. *Int. Journal of Human-Computer Studies*, 122, pp. 184–195.

Vigo, M., Arrue, M., Brajnik, G., Lomuscio, R., Abascal, J., 2007. Quantitative metrics for measuring web accessibility. *In Proc. of the 2007 Int. Cross-Disciplinary Conf. on Web Accessibility (W4A),* pp. 99–107.

World Wide Web Consortium - W3C (2018). *Web Content Accessibility Guidelines (WCAG) 2.1*. Available in https://www.w3.org/TR/WCAG21/. Last access: June 2021.

HUMAN CENTERED DESIGN PROCESS ASSESSMENT

Rüdiger Heimgärtner
Intercultural User Interface Consulting (IUIC)
Lehderstraße 71, 13086 Berlin, Germany

ABSTRACT

Process assessment is a disciplined project-oriented evaluation of an organizational unit's processes with respect to a process assessment model. In this paper, the approach according to ISO 33000 is presented of how to assess HCD processes. In detail, the standard approaches according to ISO 9241-210 and to ISO 9241-220 are considered. It is explained, how an assessment of HCD processes should be prepared, executed, and followed up.

KEYWORDS

Capability, Maturity, Process Assessment Model, Process Reference Model, ISO 9241-220, Human Centered Design Processes

1. INTRODUCTION

Experience from various fields of technology shows that it is possible for a development process recognized as mature to produce products of higher quality. Process assessments and improvement are an everyday business. Each project team member must know the current process and its optimization potential. Self-assessments can be used for continuous process improvement. Each project team member can subsequently recognize what is important for successful projects and what is also asked in assessments. Therefore, time is saved sustainably, and productivity is increased in projects. However, assessing processes is a complex endeavor and comprises those integrative parts necessary to obtain valid objective and comparable results. In this paper, the structure and content of a process assessment model (PAM) is explained and exemplified to yield an impression of how to determine the capability of the human centered design (HCD) processes.

The term "process" can be understood at three levels of abstraction. These levels of abstraction are not meant to define a strict black-or-white split, nor is it the aim to provide a scientific classification schema – the message here is to understand that, in practice, when it comes to the term "process" there are different abstraction levels, and that a PAM resides at the highest.

Capturing experience acquired during product development (i.e., at the DOING level) to share this experience with others means creating a HOW level. However, a HOW is always specific to a context such as a company, an organizational unit, or a product line. For example, the HOW of a project, organizational unit, or company A is potentially not applicable to a project, organizational unit, or company B. However, both might be expected to adhere to the principles represented by PAM indicators for process outcomes and process attribute achievements. These indicators are at the WHAT level while deciding on solutions for concrete templates, proceedings, and tooling, etc. is left to the HOW level.

2. PROCESS CAPABILITY DETERMINATION

The concept of process capability determination by using a process assessment model (PAM) is based on a two-dimensional framework. The process dimension (first dimension) is provided by processes defined in a process reference model (PRM). The capability dimension (second dimension) consists of capability levels that are further subdivided into process attributes. The process attributes provide the measurable characteristics of process capability. The PAM selects processes from a PRM and supplements it with indicators. These indicators support the collection of objective evidence which enable an assessor to assign ratings for processes according to the capability dimension.

2.1 Process Reference Model

Processes are grouped by process category and at a second level into process groups according to the type of activity they address. In general, there are at least three process categories: primary life cycle processes, organizational life cycle processes and supporting life cycle processes. Each process is described in terms of a purpose statement. The purpose statement contains the unique functional objectives of the process when performed in an environment. For each purpose statement a list of specific outcomes is mapped, as a list of expected positive results of the process performance. For the process dimension, the HCD PRM provides the set of processes in ISO 9241-220:2019-03, whereas HCP.3 is divided into further process groups according to the structured main HCD activities described in ISO 9241-210 and considered in ISO 9241-220:2019-03 as shown in Figure 1.

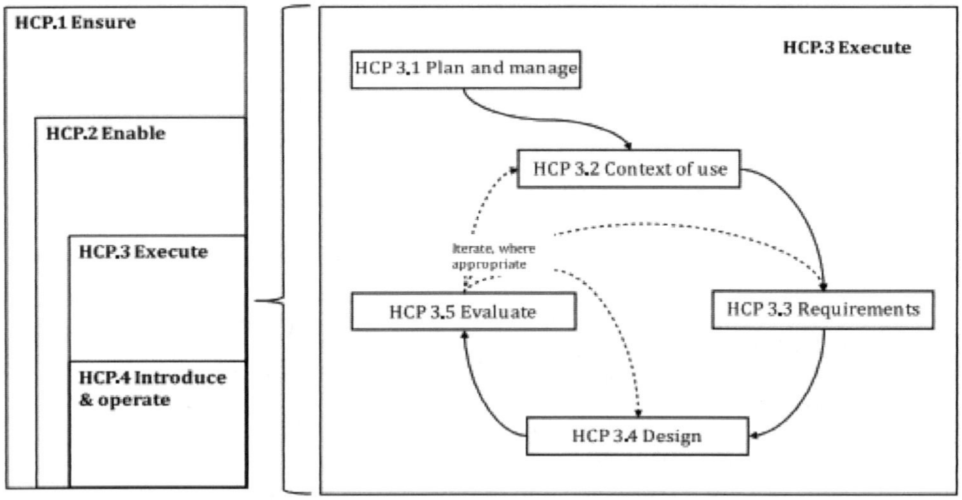

Figure 1. Relationship between the HCD processes (including the sub-processes in HCP.3) from ISO 9241-220:2019-03

2.1.1 Organizational and Supporting Life Cycle Processes Category

The organizational life cycle processes category consists of processes that develop process, product, and resource assets which, when used by projects in the organization, will help the organization achieve its business goals. The organizational life cycle processes category consists of the following groups:

- the HCD.1 ensure process group;
- the HCD.2 enable process group.

The management processes may be used by anyone who manages any type of HCD project or process within the life cycle belonging to the supporting life cycle process category.

2.1.2 Primary Life Cycle Processes Category

The primary life cycle processes category consists of processes that may be used by the customer when acquiring products from a supplier, and by the supplier when responding and delivering products to the customer including the engineering processes needed for specification, design, development, integration, and testing. The primary life cycle processes category consists of the following groups:

- the HCP.3 Execute process group;
- the HCP.4 Introduce & operate process group.

The HCP.3 Execute process group consists of processes addressing the elicitation and management of customer and internal requirements, the definition of the system architecture and the integration and testing on the system level.

3. MEASUREMENT FRAMEWORK

The measurement framework provides the necessary requirements and rules for the capability dimension. It defines a schema which enables an assessor to determine the capability level of a given process. These capability levels are defined as part of the measurement framework. To enable the rating, the measurement framework provides process attributes defining a measurable property of process capability. Each process attribute is assigned to a specific capability level. The extent of achievement of a certain process attribute is represented by means of a rating based on a defined rating scale. The rules from which an assessor can derive a final capability level for a given process are represented by a process capability level model. The HCD PAM uses the measurement framework defined in ISO/IEC 33020:2015.

3.1 Process Capability Levels

Process capability levels and process attributes are identical to those defined in ISO/IEC 33020:2015. Rough descriptions of the capability levels and the corresponding process attributes can be found in section 5 in the paper at hand. Process attributes are features of a process that can be evaluated on a scale of achievement, providing a measure of the capability of the process. They are applicable to all processes. A capability level is a set of process attribute(s) that work together to provide a major enhancement in the capability to perform a process. Each attribute addresses a specific aspect of the capability level. The levels constitute a rational way of progressing through the improvement of the capability of any process. According to ISO/IEC 33020:2015 there are six capability levels (Figure 2), incorporating nine process attributes (PA) according to the levels.

Level 0: Incomplete process	*The process is not implemented, or fails to achieve its process purpose.*
Level 1: Performed process	*The implemented process achieves its process purpose*
Level 2: Managed process	*The previously described performed process is now implemented in a managed fashion (planned, monitored and adjusted) and its work products are appropriately established, controlled and maintained.*
Level 3: Established process	*The previously described managed process is now implemented using a defined process that is capable of achieving its process outcomes.*
Level 4: Predictable process	*The previously described established process now operates predictively within defined limits to achieve its process outcomes. Quantitative management needs are identified, measurement data are collected and analyzed to identify assignable causes of variation. Corrective action is taken to address assignable causes of variation.*
Level 5: Innovating process	*The previously described predictable process is now continually improved to respond to organizational change.*

Figure 2. Process capability levels according to ISO/IEC 33020:2015

3.2 Process Attribute Rating

To support the rating of process attributes, the ISO/IEC 33020:2015 measurement framework provides a defined rating scale with an option for refinement, different rating methods and different aggregation methods depending on the class of the assessment (e.g., required for organizational maturity assessments). Within this process measurement framework, a process attribute is a measurable property of process capability. A process attribute rating is a judgement of the degree of achievement of the process attribute for the assessed process. The rating scale is defined by ISO/IEC 33020:2015 as shown in Figure 3.

N	*Not achieved*	*There is little or no evidence of achievement of the defined process attribute in the assessed process.*
P	*Partially achieved*	*There is some evidence of an approach to, and some achievement of, the defined process attribute in the assessed process. Some aspects of achievement of the process attribute may be unpredictable.*
L	*Largely achieved*	*There is evidence of a systematic approach to, and significant achievement of, the defined process attribute in the assessed process. Some weaknesses related to this process attribute may exist in the assessed process.*
F	*Fully achieved*	*There is evidence of a complete and systematic approach to, and full achievement of, the defined process attribute in the assessed process. No significant weaknesses related to this process attribute exist in the assessed process.*

Figure 3. Rating scale according to ISO/IEC 33020:2015

The rating and aggregation method in ISO/IEC 33020:2015 provides the following definitions. A process outcome is the observable result of successful achievement of the process purpose. A process attribute outcome is the observable result of achievement of a specified process attribute. Process outcomes and process attribute outcomes may be characterized as an intermediate step to providing a process attribute rating. When performing rating, the rating method employed shall be specified relevant to the class of assessment. The use of rating method may vary according to the class, scope, and context of an assessment. The lead assessor shall decide which (if any) rating method to use. The selected rating method(s) shall be specified in the assessment input and referenced in the assessment report. Further information can be taken from ISO/IEC 33020:2015.

4. PROCESS ASSESSMENT MODEL

A process assessment model (PAM) offers indicators to identify whether the process outcomes and the process attribute outcomes (achievements) are present or absent in the instantiated processes of projects and organizational units. These indicators provide guidance for assessors in accumulating the necessary objective evidence to support judgments of capability. They are not intended to be regarded as a mandatory set of checklists to be followed. To judge the presence or absence of process outcomes and process achievements an assessment delivers objective evidence. All such evidence comes from the examination of work products and the repository content of the assessed processes, and from testimony provided by the performers and managers of the assessed processes. This evidence is mapped to the PAM indicators to allow the establishment of a correspondence to the relevant process outcomes and process attribute achievements. There are two types of indicators. Process performance indicators, which apply exclusively to capability level 1, provide an indication of the extent of fulfillment of the process outcomes. Process capability indicators, which apply to capability levels 2 to 5, provide an indication of the extent of fulfillment of the process attribute achievements. Assessment indicators are used to confirm that certain practices were performed, as shown by evidence collected during an assessment. All such evidence comes either from the examination of work products of the processes assessed, or from statements made by the performers and managers of the processes. The existence of base practices and work products pro-vide evidence of the performance of the processes associated with them. Similarly, the existence of process capability indicators provides evidence of process capability. The evidence obtained should be recorded in a form that clearly relates to an associated indicator, in order that support for the assessor's judgment can be confirmed or verified as required by ISO/IEC 33002:2015.

4.1 Process Performance Indicators

Types of process performance indicators are base practices (BP) and work products (WP). Both BPs and WPs relate to one or more process outcomes. Consequently, BPs and WPs are always process-specific and not generic. BPs represent activity-oriented indicators. WPs represent result-oriented indicators. Both BP and WP are used for judging objective evidence that an assessor is to collect, and accumulate, in the performance of an assessment. In that respect BPs and WPs are alternative indicator sets the assessor can use. A PAM offers a set of work product characteristics (WPC) for each WP. These are meant to offer a good practice and state-of-the-art knowledge guide for the assessor. Therefore, WP and WPC are supposed to be a quickly accessible information source during an assessment. In that respect WPs and WPCs only represent an example structure. They are neither a "strict must" nor are they normative for organizations. Instead, the actual structure, form and content of concrete work products and documents for the implemented processes must be de-fined by the project and organization, respectively. The project and/or organization ensures that the work products are appropriate for the intended purpose and needs, and in relation to the development goals.

4.2 Process Capability Indicators

Types of process capability indicators are generic practice (GP) and generic re-source (GR). Both GPs and GRs relate to one or more PA achievements. In contrast to process performance indicators, however, they are of generic type, i.e., they apply to any process. The difference between GP and GR is that the former represents activity-oriented indicators while the latter represent infrastructure-oriented indicators for judging objective evidence. An assessor must collect and accumulate evidence supporting process capability indicators during an assessment.

5. PROCESS CAPABILITY LEVELS AND PROCESS ATTRIBUTES

Process capability indicators are the means of achieving the capabilities addressed by the considered process attributes. Evidence of process capability indicators supports the judgment of the degree of achievement of the process attributes. The capability dimension of the PAM consists of six capability levels matching the capability levels defined in ISO/IEC 33020:2015. The process capability indicators for the 9 process attributes included in the capability dimension for process capability level 1 to 5 are described in section 5.3. The generic practices address the characteristics from each process attribute. The generic resources relate to the process attribute. Process capability level 0 does not include any type of indicators, as it reflects a non-implemented process or a process which fails to partially achieve any of its outcomes.

5.1 Process Capability Level 0: Incomplete Process

The process is not implemented or fails to achieve its process purpose. At this level there is little or no evidence of any systematic achievement of the process purpose.

5.2 Process Capability Level 1: Performed Process

The implemented process achieves its process purpose. The following process at-tribute demonstrates the achievement of a performed process representing process capability level 1. The process performance process attribute for level 1 is a measure of the extent to which the process purpose is achieved. If the process achieves its defined outcomes requested by the generic practice GP 1.1.1 “Achieve the process outcomes”, then level 1 is reached. This means, i.e., that the intent of the process specific base practices is met, and the work products are produced (evidencing the process outcomes) using the generic resource “Resources are used to achieve the intent of process specific base practices”.

5.2.1 Process Reference Model and Performance Indicators (Level 1)

The processes in the process dimension can be drawn from the HCD process reference model (based on ISO 9241-220:2019-03). Each table related to one process in the process dimension contains the process reference model and the process performance indicators necessary to define the processes in the process assessment model (cf. Figure 4). The process references model describes the processes by ID, name, purpose, benefit, and outcomes. The process performance indicators consist of base practices and output work products.

Process reference model	**Process ID** **Process name** **Process purpose** **Process benefit** **Process outcomes**	The individual processes are described in terms of process name, process purpose, and process outcomes to define the human-centered process reference model. Additionally a process identifier is provided.
Process performance indicators	**Base practices**	A set of base practices for the process providing a definition of the tasks and activities needed to accomplish the process purpose and fulfill the process outcomes
	Output work products	A number of output work products associated with each process *NOTE: Refer to Annex B for the characteristics associated with each work product.*

Figure 4. Template for the process description

5.2.2 Output work Products (Level 1)

Work product characteristics (WPC) can be used when reviewing potential outputs such as work products of process implementation. The characteristics are provided as guidance for the attributes to look for, in a sample work product (WP) and to provide objective evidence supporting the assessment of a process. A documented process and assessor judgment are needed to ensure that the process context (application domain, business purpose, development methodology, size of the organization, etc.) is considered when using this information. WPs and their characteristics should be considered as a starting point for considering whether, given the context, they con-tribute to the intended purpose of the process, and not as a checklist of what every organization must have.

5.3 Process Reference Model and Performance Indicators (Level 2-5)

In contrast to level 1, the performance indicators on level 2-5, represented by generic practices and resources, relate to all process in the process reference model.

If the performed process is implemented in a managed fashion (planned, monitored, and adjusted) and its work products are appropriately established, controlled, and maintained, then it is called a "managed process". Thereby the performance management process attribute (PA 2.1) and the work product management process attribute (PA 2.2), together with the previously defined performance process attribute (PA 1.1), demonstrate the achievement of a managed process representing process capability level 2.

If the managed process is implemented using a defined process that can achieve its process outcomes, then it is called a "established process". The process definition process attribute (PA 3.1) and the process deployment process attribute (PA 3.2), together with the process attributes for the performed (PA 1.1) and the managed process (PA 2.1 and PA 2.2), demonstrate the achievement of an established process representing process capability level 3.

If the established process operates predictively within defined limits to achieve its process outcomes, then it is called a "predictive process". Quantitative management needs are identified, measurement data are collected and analyzed to identify assignable causes of variation. Corrective action is taken to address assignable causes of variation. The quantitative analysis process attribute (PA 4.1) as well as the quantitative control process attribute (PA 4.2), together with the process attributes for the performed (PA 1.1), managed (PA 2.1 and PA 2.2) and established (PA 3.1 and PA 3.2) process, demonstrate the achievement of a predictable process representing process capability level 4.

If the predictable process is continually improved to respond to change aligned with organizational goals, then it is called a "innovating process". The process innovation process attribute (PA 5.1) as well as the process innovation implementation process attribute (PA 5.2), together with the process attributes for the performed (PA 1.1), managed (PA 2.1 and PA 2.2), established (PA 3.1 and PA 3.2) and predicted (PA 4.1 and PA 4.2) process, demonstrate the achievement of an 'innovating process' representing process capability level 5.

6. RATING IN THE PROCESS ASSESSMENT

The assessment procedure contains at least the following steps:

- Explain process purpose and benefit and most important requirements of the process to the audience,
- Interview the audience regarding process life based on purpose, base practices and work products and collect documented evidence,
- Rate the evidence according to the rating scale,
- Accumulate the ratings for one process (e.g., HCP.3.4.2) to an overall rating considering:
- Achievement of process purpose,
- Achievement of all base practices,
- Achievement of work products.

As an example, the summary of the results of the rating up to level 2 could appear as presented in Figure 5. Depending on the rating, the HCD processes of the executing process group (HCP.3) are ratings up to level 2 in this figure addressing the performance process attribute (level 1) and the management process attributes (level 2). The only process that reached level 2 in this example is HCP.3.4.2 (Produce and refine user interface design solutions) indicating that all base practices are achieved and the work products of this process (such as system interface requirement, architectural design description and user interface specification) are available and reviewed, and the process is managed in a proper way. Other processes such as HCP.3.1.1 (Establish human-centered quality objectives) were not performed and managed properly, and the work products are mostly missing.

HCP.3 Execute	HCP.3.1.1	HCP.3.1.2	HCP.3.1.3	HCP.3.1.4	HCP.3.1.5	HCP.3.2.1	HCP.3.2.2	HCP.3.3.1	HCP.3.3.2	HCP.3.3.3	HCP.3.4.1	HCP.3.4.2	HCP.3.5.1	HCP.3.5.2	HCP.3.5.3
BP / GP Rating															
BP1	P	P	N	L	L	P	P	P	N	L	P	F	P	P	P
BP2	P	P	N	L	P	P	P	P	N	P	P	F	P	P	P
BP3	N	N	P	P	L	N	N	N	P	L	N	P	N	N	N
BP4	P	P	P	L	L	P	P	P	P	L	P	F	P	P	P
BP5	P	P	P	N	P	P	P	P	P	P	P	F	P	P	P
BP6	P	P	N	F	P	N	P	N	N	P	P	F	N	N	N
BP7		P	P	L			P	P	N	P	P	L	P	P	
BP8		N		P			N		P	N	N	F			
BP9		P		F			P		N	L		P			
BP10				F					N			F			
BP11				P					N			F			
BP12									P			F			
BP13									P						
BP14									N						
GP2.1.1	N	N	N	N	P	P	N	N	P	P	P	L	P	P	N
GP2.1.2	N	P	N	P	P	N	N	P	P	N	P	L	P	N	N
GP2.1.3	P	N	P	N	N	N	P	N	N	N	N	P	N	N	P
GP2.1.4	P	N	P	N	N	P	P	N	N	P	N	L	N	P	P
GP2.1.5	P	N	P	N	P	N	P	N	P	N	P	N	P	N	P
GP2.1.6	N	L	N	L	P	L	N	L	P	L	P	F	P	L	N
GP2.1.7	P	L	P	L	P	P	P	L	P	P	P	L	P	P	P
GP2.2.1	P	P	P	P	P	P	P	P	P	P	P	P	P	P	P
GP2.2.2	N	L	N	L	P	P	N	L	P	P	P	F	P	P	N
GP2.2.3	N	L	N	L	P	P	N	L	P	P	P	F	P	P	N
GP2.2.4	P	N	P	N	N	N	P	N	N	N	N	P	N	N	P
Process Attributes Rating															
PA1.1	N	P	N	P	P	N	P	P	N	L	P	F	P	N	P
PA2.1	N	N	N	N	P	P	N	N	P	N	P	L	P	P	N
PA2.2	N	P	N	P	P	P	N	P	P	P	P	L	P	P	N
Capability															
Level	0	0	0	1	0	0	0	0	0	1	0	2	0	0	0

Figure 5. Example Rating of the HCP.3 Process Group from ISO 9241-220:2019-03

7. DISCUSSION

With a seamless HCD development process, mistakes and unproductivity can be prevented and product quality rises with high quality process output contributing to a high-quality interactive product. Behind such experiences a causal relationship be-tween process and product quality is assumed, which consists in the fact that a more mature process with a lower probability of error produces higher quality products than a less mature process. Since quality cannot be achieved without a sustainable focus on user requirements, usability engineering is also referred to as a human-centric development process. Requirements for a human-centered development process are defined in DIN EN ISO 9241-210:2011-01. The aim of usability engineering is to do everything necessary in a development process to steer it towards an optimal quality of use of the final product. Following a PRM like that derived from ISO 9241-220:2019-03 ensures the involvement of users as requirement donors and as evaluators of

a) the achieved quality of use,
b) the application of suitable usability engineering methods,
c) the documentation of design decisions with relevance for the quality of use,
d) the establishment of a quality management system for the quality of use and
e) setting up process roles with suitably qualified personnel (cf. DIN SPEC 92412:2015-11).

8. CONCLUSION

The presented PAM for the development process of interactive products serves to assess the process quality in development projects based on objective indicators for process capability and thereby to achieve quality of use referring to the HCD processes defined in ISO 9241-220:2019-03. Even if the presented HCD-PAM is still in a working draft state and, hence, must be improved and worked out in detail in accordance with all other relevant standards, the principles of this HCD-PAM and the presented assessment procedure have been confirmed for years by assessments in the automotive industry regarding software engineering processes (cf. VDA QMC WG 13, 2017). The presented HCD-PAM can be applied in conjunction with the process reference model (PRM) for human centered design (HCD) processes derived from the processes in ISO 9241-220:2019-03 to a similar benefit. The refinement and application of the suggested HCD-PAM will show if it can be used to prove that the process has the capability of justifying trust in the HCD processes by all stakeholders and causes that the assessments can be productively conducted.

REFERENCES

DIN EN ISO 9241-210:2011-01, Ergonomics of human-system interaction - Part 210: Hu-man-centred design for interactive systems.

DIN SPEC 92412:2015-11, Ergonomics of human-system interaction - Auditing procedure for the development of interactive products based on DIN EN ISO 9241-210.

ISO 9241-220:2019-03, Ergonomics of human-system interaction - Part 220: Processes for enabling, executing and assessing human-centred design within organizations.

ISO/IEC 15504-5:2006, Information Technology – Process assessment – Part 5: An exem-plar Process Assessment Model.

ISO/IEC 33002:2015, Information technology -- Process assessment – Requirements for performing process assessment.

ISO/IEC 33020:2015, Information technology -- Process assessment – Process measure-ment framework for assessment of process capability.

VDA QMC Working Group 13 / Automotive SIG, 2017, Automotive SPICE Process Assessment / Reference Model, URL=http://www.automotivespice.com/fileadmin/software-download/AutomotiveSPICE_PAM_31.pdf, last access 06-30-2021.

MEASURING GAME IMMERSION AND FLOW WITH ELECTROENCEPHALOGRAPHY

Ehm Kannegieser[1] and Johannes Ratz[2]
[1]*Fraunhofer Institute of Optronics, System Technologies and Image Exploitation, Fraunhoferstraße. 1, 76131, Karlsruhe, Germany*
[2]*Karlsruhe Institute of Technology, Kaiserstraße 12, 76131, Karlsruhe, Germany*

ABSTRACT

Immersion and Flow are important parameters when it comes to an enjoyable experience of video games. To measure these mental states usually self-assessment questionnaires, answered by the subject after the experience, are used. Because of the shortcomings of this method, the ultimate goal is to establish an alternative measuring method through correlations of physiological sensor data. While there are many physiological data sources to be looked at, such as recording the heartrate or skin conductance, measuring brain activity with electroencephalography (EEG) is one of the most promising candidates towards a way of objectively measuring Immersion and Flow.
In this paper, an experiment to record EEG data during and questionnaire data after game play is presented. As a proof of concept, the experiment is tested with an initial test study on three subjects and the recorded data is used for analysis and a first correlation attempt. Although the results are not yet generalizable, they indicate that increased overall beta and frontal theta activity may be related to Flow and Immersion. This remains to be proven by conducting further studies in the future to achieve statistical significance.

KEYWORDS

Flow, Immersion, Serious Games, EEG, Measurement

1. INTRODUCTION

What makes people enjoy playing a video game and how can this enjoyment be transferred to other areas, such as learning or working? Those questions have always been central in games research and psychology and should be of particular interest for the development of serious games, as enjoyment is proven to be linked to an effective learning process (Deci and Ryan, 1985; Krapp, 2009).

Mihály Csíkszentmihályi defined "the optimal experience of an action" as Flow, which is achieved when the individual is so engrossed in the activity that nothing else seems relevant anymore. It is a deep sense of enjoyment, that occurs when a "person's body or mind is stretched to its limits in a voluntary effort to accomplish something difficult and worthwhile" (Csikzentmihaly, 1990). A similar experience in the video game domain is commonly called Immersion, describing the transfer of consciousness into a virtual world. They are both linked to an intrinsic motivation in the task or game, which means deriving enjoyment from the action itself rather than from external gains like money or a fear of punishment for not completing a task.

To improve the development and adaptation of serious games, it is therefore interesting to measure these mental states. Until now, the method of choice to measure Flow and Immersion is the usage of questionnaires, which are answered by the subject after the task. This method is however potentially inaccurate due to the delay in elicitation and the subjectiveness of the answers.

A way towards objectively measuring mental states is, to record subjects' physiological data during the experience and to find correlations between the physiological data and the subjective questionnaire data. A such found correlation could enable automatically measuring Flow and Immersion without the usage of questionnaires in future.

One of the most valuable physiological data sources for researching mental states is the subjects' brain activity, which is measured using electroencephalography (EEG). Measuring brain activity has recently become a hot topic in research and industry, especially with the development of brain-computer interfaces

(BCI) making it able to control a computer or machine by thought alone. Neuralink, a company founded by Elon Musk, plans on implanting a chip in the human brain, which can precisely detect neural activity with thousands of tiny electrodes spread across the whole brain. This, among other things, shall enable paralyzed people to control protheses and other devices only with their mind. Although EEG works on the same biological basis, namely the electrical activity of the brain, it is non-invasive as it only records brain activity from the scalp. This makes it easy to use in medicine and research and can still provide a lot of information on the mental states of subjects.

In this paper, an experiment is presented, that gathers and manages EEG and questionnaire data, which can be analyzed and evaluated afterwards to find potential correlations. Its setup as well as the underlying theoretical assumptions regarding Flow and Immersion are based on previous studies and experiences gathered in the last three years (Kannegieser et al. 2018; Kannegieser et al. 2019). While there are some previous studies on the potential correlation of EEG data and states of Flow or Immersion (e.g., Nacke et al., 2011; Plotnikov et al., 2012; Lim et al., 2019), they mostly assess these mental states based on different games or level designs (e.g., by varying difficulty levels). The experiment takes a new methodical approach by periodically gathering self-assessments, which allows us to correlate them with time-related EEG data. The results of previous studies can however be compared to the results of this experiment.

2. THEORETICAL ASSUMPTIONS AND UNDERLYING MODEL

The exact definitions of Immersion and Flow as well as their relation to one another are still an active area of research. Cairns et al. define game Immersion by dividing it into three levels: Engagement, Engrossment, and Total Immersion. These levels are used to describe the degree of involvement with the game (Brown and Cairns, 2004; Cairns et al 2006). Engagement is the first stage of Immersion and must occur before any other level. It describes the basic access to a game, that comes with the willingness to play it as well as the game controls being clearly defined and understandable for the player. Furthermore, players need to invest time to become more engaged with the game (Brown and Cairns, 2004). The second stage is Engrossment, which is achieved when the gamer's emotion is connected to and directly affected by the game. In addition, the game construction is overcome, and controls become invisible to the player (Jennett et al., 2008). Finally, Total Immersion can be achieved, which the authors equate with the term "presence". Players describe this stage as "being cut off from reality and detachment to such an extent that the game was all that mattered." It is an experience of completely transferring the own consciousness into the virtual world by empathizing with the game characters and accepting the game's atmosphere as reality (Brown and Cairns, 2004).

Flow on the other hand, as defined by Csikzentmihaly, is broken down into several conditions that must be met to be able to achieve this state. The perhaps most crucial and popular condition is the balance of challenge and skill, which was further formalized and depicted in the "Flow Model". Its core message is that different combinations of challenge and skill levels lead to different mental states. When the challenge level is too high for the existing skills it leads to anxiety, a feeling of being overwhelmed by an activity. Meanwhile skill, when met with insufficient challenge will lead to relaxation or boredom. Only high skill combined with high challenge can lead to the optimal experience of an action and subsequently Flow. Other important conditions include the loss of a sense of time and the sense of control over the task (Csikzentmihaly, 1990).

Due to the similarities of definitions and conditions for Immersion and Flow, some authors suggest on unifying and not separating both terms for further research, especially in the video game domain (Michailidis et al., 2018). The author's approach is, to combine the three-level definition of Immersion by Cairns et al. and Csikzentmihaly's Flow model. The highest Immersion states, Engrossment, and Total Immersion, share similar phenomena, such as a loss of a sense of time and a loss of spatial awareness. As such, a model is proposed, in which Immersion is a hierarchical structure and Flow is a state at the top of the hierarchy. The model is shown qualitatively in figure 1. This figure shows the relationship between increased Flow and the Immersion levels defined by Cairns et al. However, it must be noted that there is no relationship between the skill/challenge balance and Immersion (Kannegieser et al., 2018).

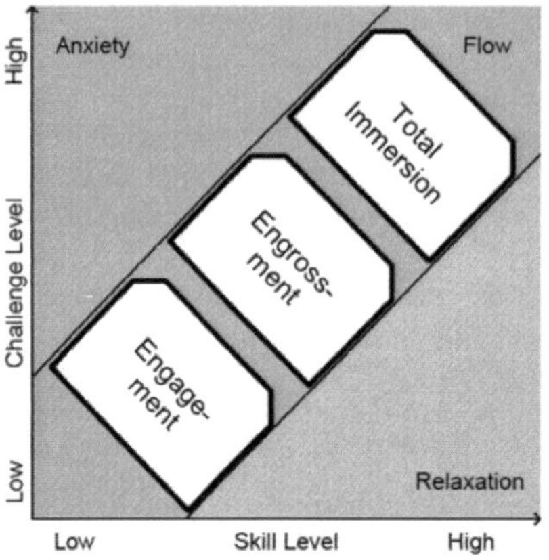

Figure 1. Proposed combined model of Flow and Immersion. The skill/challenge balance does not influence Immersion

3. EXPERIMENT

The experiment's main goal is to gather physiological data during game play that can be used to find a correlation between physiological measurements and Flow/Immersion states. It mainly consists of a measurement application, written in Java, which sets the structure of the experiment and manages different data inputs and outputs. Apart from EEG other physiological sensors such as heartrate, GSR or ECG devices can be connected to the experiment software, thereby extending the possibilities of physiological data correlations.

3.1 Structure

The experiment is split into four phases: Setup, Baseline, Gaming and Assessment. During the setup phase, the game is selected, and the sensors are placed on the participant. Game selection is free. Participants can bring their own games or use a distribution platform like Steam to install a game of their choice. Free game selection was chosen to improve the odds of players reaching higher Flow and Immersion states, at the cost of game-specific analysis options.

During the second phase of the experiment, the baseline phase, physiological data is recorded for one minute, while the subject is in a calm state of mind. This is realized by asking subjects to close their eyes and relax until they hear a given audio signal, which occurs after one minute. The physiological measurements can be monitored by the examiner of the study on a separate monitor screen showing the incoming data streams in real time. Recording a baseline is necessary as a reference for later evaluation of the mental states and can also be used as a first test of the involved sensors.

After the setup is finished, the gaming phase begins, in which the subject plays the chosen game for 30 minutes without interruption. The duration was chosen based on test runs, as 30 minutes were found to be enough to reach the Flow / Total Immersion state. While the participant is playing, the physiological data as well as the gameplay and webcam footage is recorded. When the gaming phase ends, the recorded data is stored in an output folder and the assessment phase starts.

During the assessment phase, participants watch a recording of their game session as well as web cam footage of themselves. While watching this footage, Flow and Immersion questionnaires are filled out about how immersed the participant was at the time of the recording. By making participants fill out questionnaires while watching a recording, more accurate data can be gathered without interrupting the Flow/Immersion during the game session itself to fill out questionnaires. A similar approach using video footage is used in the study by Rajava and Kivikangas (Ravaja and Kivikangas, 2008).

Three questionnaires are used in the experiment, with one of them being split into two parts. The first questionnaire used is the Immersion questionnaire presented by Cheng et al. based on their improvement upon the hierarchical model presented by Cairns et al. (Cheng et al., 2015; Cairns et al. 2006). The questionnaire was chosen, as it can be used to measure the likeliness to be in each of the individual Immersion levels, making it useful to compare Flow with Total Immersion to test the theorized model presented in 2. As the questionnaire was too long to be measured multiple times without worsening the results, it was split into an Immersive Tendency questionnaire asked at the beginning of playback and an iterative questionnaire asked every three minutes during playback. For Flow, the Flow Short Scale questionnaire by Rheinberg et al. was used (Rheinberg et al., 2003). It was originally designed for being used multiple times in a row, making it perfect for this iterative approach. During playback, it is asked every six minutes. The final questionnaire used is the Game Experience Questionnaire (IJsselsteijn, et al., 2013). It measures a more general set of questions and is asked once after playback is over.

An overview of the different phases is presented in figure 2.

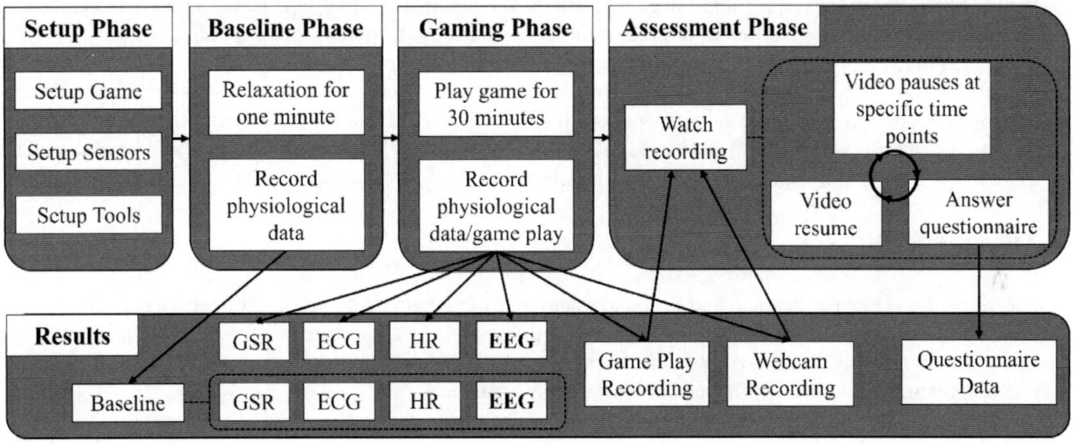

Figure 2. Phases of the experiment

3.2 EEG Measurement

EEG is a common method for measuring the electrical activity of the brain by recording voltage fluctuations between electrodes positioned on the scalp. The fluctuations are mostly generated by the firing of cortical neurons, which are located on the outer layer of the brain and range between 5 and 100µV (Hu and Zhang, 2019). They result in typical sinusoidal wave shapes which are analyzed for amplitude and frequency. In general, the waves are classified into different frequency bands: Delta (1-4 Hz), Theta (4-8 Hz), Alpha (8-13 Hz), Beta (13-30 Hz), and Gamma (30-40 Hz). The frequency bands are associated with different levels of brain activities. When the subject is awake mostly alpha and beta waves are noticed. The alpha waves are the most extensively studied rhythm of the human brain and can be usually observed while being in a relaxed awake state or having eyes closed (Teplan et al., 2002). They are associated with cortical inactivity and mental idleness as well as attentional demand (Ray and Cole, 1985). When eyes are opened during the experiment alpha waves are replaced by beta waves which is called the Berger Effect (Kirschfeld, 2005), named after its discoverer Hans Berger, who invented EEG in 1924 (Berger, 1929). Beta waves indicate a normal state of wakefulness and are usually most evident in the frontal cortex. They are connected to cognitive processes, decision making, problem solving and information processing (Ray and Cole, 1985). Delta and theta waves are most prominent during sleep (for adults). Delta waves are more present at deep sleep, more specifically during non-rapid eye movement (NREM) phases (Teplan et al., 2002). Theta waves play a greater role in REM sleep and general drowsiness (Teplan et al., 2002). They are also connected to daydreaming, creativity, intuition, memory recall, emotions, and sensations (Aftanas and Golocheikine, 2001). In some cases, gamma waves can be observed at very high concentration and flow of information. It is also seen during cross-modal sensory processing (combining two or more senses, such as sound and sight) (Kisley and Cornwell, 2006) as well as deep meditation (Vialatte et al., 2009).

There are several different types of EEG devices or systems to choose from. Most experiments and studies use closed electrode caps as they can fit multiple electrodes and offer a generally good signal quality. However, these caps usually need the head skin to be prepared with a contact gel to achieve a good conduction quality (Hu and Zhang, 2019), making it less comfortable to wear for participants. To achieve Immersion or Flow it is crucial that the subject feels well and is not distracted by the connected sensors. Therefore, the Emotiv EPOC+ was instead chosen for the experiment, which is a 14-channel EEG headset, that only requires its electrode covering felt pads to be wetted with a saline solution before attachment. It offers a sampling rate of 256 Hz and uses a wireless connection via Bluetooth, making it comfortable to wear and install during the experiment. The 14 electrodes are positioned after the International 10-20 system, which uniquely labels each electrode with letters for the brain area (F: Frontal, C: Central, P: Parietal, T: Temporal, O Occipital) and numbers for the horizontal position (odd numbers left hemisphere, even numbers right hemisphere; higher numbers are more outward than lower ones) encoding the exact position on the head. The voltage is measured between an active electrode and one of two additional reference electrodes placed on the bone behind each ear.

The EPOC+ is connected to the experiment application using the WebSocket protocol (Melnikov, 2011). It continuously sends the measured voltage values as well as current contact quality values of each electrode, indicating if an electrode needs to be repositioned or rewetted to achieve a better signal quality. The received values can be observed by the examiner, conducting the experiment, on a separate monitor screen. When the experiment is finished, the raw EEG data is automatically stored to an output file.

3.3 Test Study

Due to the Covid 19 pandemic a detailed study with many participants to achieve statistical significance could not be carried out yet. Instead, the experimental setup was tested with three different participants and trials. The participants were three male students in the age of 22-23, who had some previous experience in playing computer games and were therefore suitable for this experiment.

Before the start of the experiment, participants chose the game, they wanted to play, so that they could be installed beforehand. In this test study, three different games were played: Rocket League (multiplayer vehicular soccer game), Age of Empires 2 (real time strategy game) and The Witness (3D first person puzzle game). The whole experiment was conducted on a PC system with enough computational power to run the chosen games fluently and to simultaneously manage and record the different data streams.

At the start of each trial the EEG was prepared by wetting the felt pads with saline. After the preparation, subjects were told how they can attach it on their head. This attachment created no complications and subjects could easily handle it. The correct position and contact of the electrodes could be checked by looking at the monitor view. In some cases, one or two electrodes had to be repositioned right after attachment. During the gaming phase, it was avoided to reposition single electrodes, as this process heavily disturbs the experience. However, if multiple electrodes had been bad, an interruption would have been unavoidable to ensure a good data quality.

Once the trial was finished, participants were asked, how the EEG device felt. All participants stated that they quickly stopped noticing the attached sensors. No feel of discomfort or distraction was reported.

3.4 Analysis

The analysis of the raw EEG data consists of preprocessing the signal (i.e., filtering and artifact removal) and a spectral analysis, regarding the activation in each frequency band. There have been studies looking at the event-related potential (ERP) of certain game or task events inducing Immersion or Flow (Katahira et al., 2018). However, this does not fit to the definition of these mental states, since they are not triggered by single events but rather emerge continuously over a period of time. The whole analysis is performed using EEGLAB, an open-source MATLAB toolbox developed by Arnaud Delorme and Scott Makeig in 2004 (Delorme and Makeig, 2004).

A problem with EEG is that it is considerably affected by noise through physiological and non-physiological artifacts. The largest noise sources are muscular movements, eye blinks and movements, as well as electrical interference from the alternating mains power supply (being at 50 Hz in Europe or 60 Hz in the US). For preprocessing, the signal is first filtered with a basic IIR low-pass and high-pass filter, cutting of frequencies below 1 Hz and above 45 Hz. Secondly, bad channels with a high deviation from other channels are removed by hand.

Before further removal of data, an independent component analysis (ICA) is performed, which is used to separate independent signal sources linearly mixed in several sensors or in this case multiple electrodes. It is implemented through a machine learning algorithm, that can extract potentially artifact-related components from the multi-channel signal. Automatic labeling of the components was used, to find components, related to specific artifacts. For the study, especially eye artifacts could be mitigated by removing the respective components and thereby smoothing the original multi-channel signal.

After applying ICA, the 30-minute data is split into three-minute segments to fit to the time periods of the answered questionnaires. The signal still contains some artifacts, which could not be extracted by ICA and must be removed manually by totally rejecting the artifact-related time periods. As participants can move freely during the experiment to be able to achieve Immersion or Flow, the recorded EEG signal was relatively noisy and had a lot of artifacts. Still, most of the recorded data could be used without distorting the results too much.

The spectral analysis was performed with a MATLAB script using functions from EEGLAB to calculate the power spectra. A power spectrum contains the power contribution of each frequency over a period of time. It is calculated using the Welch's Method, which is based on the fast Fourier transform algorithm (FFT). FFT calculates the discrete Fourier transform of a discrete time signal $x[n], n = 1,2, \ldots, N$ and a discrete frequency $f = kS/N$, where S is the sampling rate and $k = 0, 1, \ldots, N - 1$ as

$$F[k] = \sum_{n=0}^{N-1} x[n] e^{-i2\pi kn/N},$$

where the number of sample points N is chosen as a power of 2 for efficiency, which can be achieved by adding a number of zeros at the end of the original time-series data. In the Welch's method, the signal is first divided into windows and then FFT is performed on each window to reduce variance (Hu and Zhang, 2019).

The created MATLAB script uses the Welch's method of EEGLAB without overlap, a window size of 256 and a FFT sample size of 256, to calculate the power spectrum of each data segment. The spectra are then averaged in power for each frequency band (Delta: 1-4 Hz, Theta: 4-8 Hz, Alpha: 8-13 Hz, Beta: 13-30 Hz, and Gamma: 30-40 Hz) in each channel. With this data, power development in each frequency band over the different time segments for each subject can be analyzed.

The gathered questionnaire data is automatically evaluated using a previously developed evaluation application, considering the different questionnaires and the analysis of the respective Likert scale. As the Immersion questionnaire by Cheng et al. is used in the experiment, Immersion is subdivided into the three levels Engagement, Engrossment, and Total Immersion, as proposed by Cairns et al. Based on the evaluation, the data segments are classified by one or more of the respective mental states as they can emerge at the same time. Additionally, the baseline data segment is analyzed and builds its own class in terms of mental states. Data segments containing the same mental state classification are then averaged over all trials.

4. RESULTS

The analysis results in the average spectral power density in the respective frequency band per channel for each of the five mental states (Baseline, Engagement, Engrossment, Total Immersion, and Flow). Figure 3 shows the results for the theta and beta band. It should be noted that channel O1 had a technical issue during the test study and therefore had to be removed from each trial.

The first frequency band regarded, is the theta band. Previous studies showed an increase of theta waves during Immersion (Nacke et al., 2011; Lim et al. 2018) and Flow (Katahira et al., 2018). In this test study, theta power appears to increase compared to baseline in the frontal areas during Engagement and especially Engrossment. Total Immersion and Flow on the other hand do not show a big difference to the baseline. Engrossment is achieved when the gamer's emotion is directly affected by the game and the game controls become invisible. As theta waves have been previously associated with emotions, intuition, and creativity (Aftanas and Golocheikine, 2001), this could therefore strengthen the proposed definition of Engrossment by (Cairns et al., 2006).

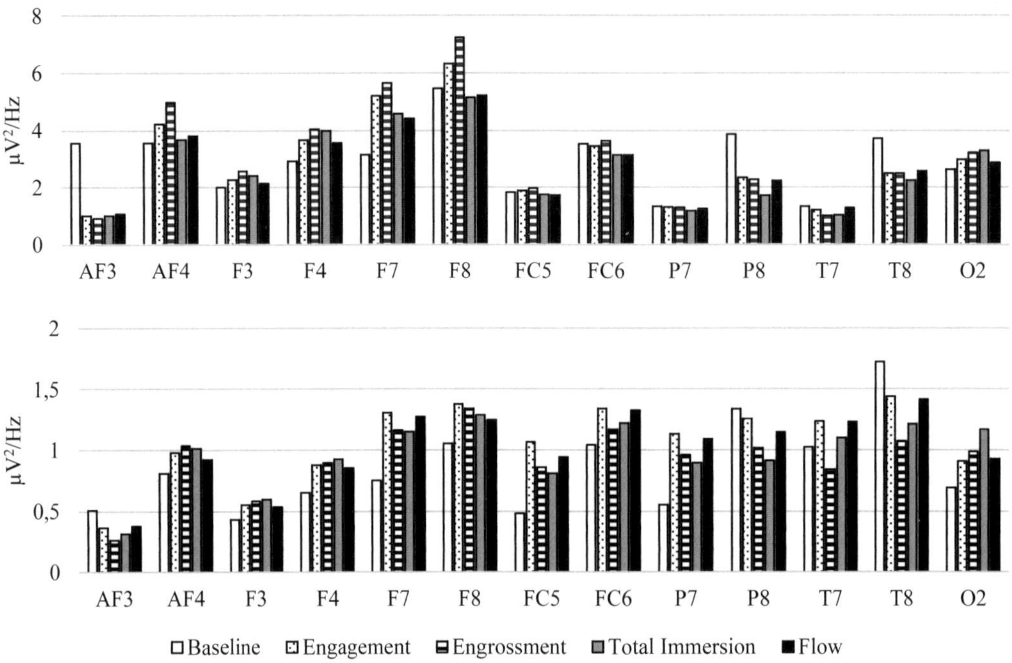

Figure 3. Results of the analysis for theta activation (above) and beta activation (below) for each channel (except O1)

Beta activity is overall higher compared to baseline during both Immersion and Flow. This was also seen in previous studies and makes sense due to the general association of beta waves with cognitive processing, decision making and problem solving (Ray and Cole, 1985). However, there are no clear differences between the individual Immersion levels or Flow.

The other frequency bands show no further relevant changes in power. Alpha activity is overall highest for the baseline. Delta waves have a contradictory power distribution across different channels. Gamma activity is only slightly higher for Immersion and Flow in frontal areas compared to baseline but is too low to be relevant. While in previous studies alpha and gamma activity were also not found to be relevant to Immersion or Flow, there is one study that found an increase in delta power during Immersion (Nacke et al., 2011).

Throughout all frequency bands, Total Immersion and Flow are very similar in their power distribution, which could indicate a close relation between total Immersion and Flow as suggested by the proposed model.

5. CONCLUSION

In this paper, a method of measuring EEG in the context of game Immersion and Flow was presented. The experiment was tested with an initial test study and the measured data could be successfully analyzed and a first correlation attempt was made. Although the results indicate a specific correlation, this remains to be proven by conducting a study with more participants to achieve statistical significance.

In addition, within future studies EEG data can be correlated to other physiological data measured during the experiment. This would not only further improve the identification of Immersion and Flow, but also enables a perhaps automated artifact removal within the EEG data. Previous studies have already shown this working, for identifying eye artifacts with eye trackers (Mannan et al., 2016) or muscle artifacts with electromyography (EMG) (Fitzgibbon et al., 2016).

Another more ambitious research goal for the future would be automatically detecting Immersion and Flow in real time. This can only work after gathering enough data and will probably require a machine learning system for pattern recognition. In terms of EEG measurement, there are many active research areas, including the BCI research, which show that this approach is possible. If proven successful, it could make the use of Immersion and Flow questionnaires redundant.

REFERENCES

Aftanas, L., & Golocheikine, S., 2001. Human anterior and frontal midline theta and lower alpha reflect emotionally positive state and internalized attention: High-resolution eeg investigation of meditation. *Neuroscience letters*, 310(1).

Berger, H., 1929. Über das Elektrenkephalogramm des Menschen. *Archiv f. Psychiatrie 87*, pp 527–570.

Brown, E., & Cairns, P., 2004. A grounded investigation of game Immersion. *CHI '04 Extended Abstracts on Human Factors in Computing Systems*, pp 1297–1300.

Cairns, P., Cox, A. L., Berthouze, N., Jennett, C., & Dhoparee, S., 2006. Quantifying the experience of Immersion in games. *CogSci 2006 Workshop: Cognitive Science of Games and Gameplay*.

Cheng, M.-T., She, H.-C., & Annetta, L. A., 2015. Game Immersion experience: Its hierarchical structure and impact on game-based science learning. *Journal of computer assisted learning*, 31(3), pp 232–253.

Csikzentmihaly, M., 1990. *Flow: The psychology of optimal experience*. Harper & Row, New York.

Delorme, A., & Makeig, S., 2004. EEGLAB: An open source toolbox for analysis of single-trial EEG dynamics including independent component analysis. *Journal of neuroscience methods*, 134(1), pp 9–21.

Fitzgibbon, S., DeLosAngeles, D., Lewis, T., Powers, D., Grummett, T., Whitham, E., Ward, L., Willoughby, J., & Pope, K., 2016. Automatic determination of emg-contaminated components and validation of independent component analysis using eeg during pharmacologic paralysis. *Clinical Neurophysiology*, 127(3), pp 1781–1793.

Hu, L., & Zhang Z., 2019. *EEG Signal Processing and Feature Extraction.* Springer, Singapore.

IJsselsteijn, W. A., de Kort, Y. A., & Poels, K., 2013. The game experience questionnaire. *Eindhoven: Technische Universiteit Eindhoven*, 46(1).

Jennett, C., Cox, A. L., Cairns, P., Dhoparee, S., Epps, A., Tijs, T., & Walton, A., 2008. Measuring and defining the experience of Immersion in games. *International journal of human-computer studies*, 66(9), pp 641–661.

Kannegieser, E., Atorf, D., & Meier, J., 2018, Surveying games with a combined model of Immersion and Flow. *IADIS International Conference Information Systems 2018,* Lisbon, Portugal.

Kannegieser, E., Atorf, D., & Meier, J., 2019, Conducting an Experiment for validating the Combined Model of Flow and Immersion, *CSEDU 2019 11th international conference on computer supported education,* Heraklion, Crete – Greece.

Katahira, K., Yamazaki, Y., Yamaoka, C., Ozaki, H., Nakagawa, S., & Nagata, N., 2018. EEG correlates of the Flow state: A combination of increased frontal theta and moderate frontocentral alpha rhythm in the mental arithmetic task. *frontiers in Psychology,* 9, pp 300-311.

Kirschfeld, K., 2005. The physical basis of alpha waves in the electroencephalogram and the origin of the "berger effect". *Biological cybernetics*, 92(3), pp 177–185.

Kisley, M. A., & Cornwell, Z. M., 2006. Gamma and beta neural activity evoked during a sensory gating paradigm: Effects of auditory, somatosensory and cross-modal stimulation. *Clinical neurophysiology*, 117(11), pp 2549–2563.

Lim, S., Yeo, M., & Yoon, G., 2019. Comparison between concentration and Immersion based on eeg analysis. *Sensors 2019*, 19(7), pp 1669-1672.

Mannan, M. M. N., Kim, S., Jeong, M. Y., & Kamran, M. A., 2016. Hybrid eeg-eye tracker: Automatic identification and removal of eye movement and blink artifacts from electroencephalographic signal. *Sensors*, 16(2), p 241.

Melnikov, A., 2011. The WebSocket Protocol. Internet Engineering Task Force, RFC6455, https://datatracker.ietf.org/doc/html/rfc6455

Michailidis, L., Balaguer-Ballester, E., & He, X., 2018. Flow and Immersion in video games: The aftermath of a conceptual challenge. *frontiers in Psychology,* 9, pp 1682-1690.

Nacke, L. E., Stellmach, S., & Lindley, C. A., 2011. Electroencephalographic assessment of player experience: A pilot study in affective ludology. *Simulation & Gaming*, 42(5), pp 632–655.

Plotnikov, A., Stakheika, N., De Gloria, A., Schatten, C., Bellotti, F., Berta, R., Fiorini, C., & Ansovini, F., 2012. Exploiting real-time eeg analysis for assessing Flow in games. *2012 IEEE 12th International Conference on Advanced Learning Technologies,* Rome, Italy.

Ravaja, Niklas, & Kivikangas, J Matias, 2008. "*Psychophysiology of digital game playing: Effects of competition versus collaboration in the laboratory and in real life.*" pp. 432–435.

Ray, W. J., & Cole, H. W., 1985. Eeg alpha activity reflects attentional demands, and beta activity reflects emotional and cognitive processes. *Science*, 228(4700), pp 750–752.

Rheinberg, F., Vollmeyer, R., & Engeser, S., 2003. Die erfassung des Flow-erlebens. *Diagnostik von Motivation und Selbstkonzept*, pp 261–279.

Teplan, M. et al., 2002. Fundamentals of eeg measurement. *Measurement science review*, 2(2), pp 1–11.

Vialatte, F. B., Bakardjian, H., Prasad, R., & Cichocki, A., 2009. Eeg paroxysmal gamma waves during bhramari pranayama: A yoga breathing technique. *Consciousness and cognition*, 18(4), pp 977–988.

RESEARCH ON THE APPLICATION OF VIRTUAL REALITY INTERGENERATIONAL GAMES TO TRADITIONAL GLOVE PUPPETRY CULTURE

Ya-Fang Chen, Wen-Huei Chou and Yi-Chun Li
National Yunlin University of Science and Technology, Taiwan

ABSTRACT

Appropriate intergenerational programs can effectively remove communication barriers between generations. The application of the latest technology can introduce traditional cultural elements, and the cultural spirit of the older generation can be passed on to the next generations. Moreover, with the help of young people, the elderly can get on track with the latest technology, while young people can pass on the cultural memory and knowledge of the elderly. In addition, with the vigorous development and advancement of science and technology, the existing traditional culture has been buried under latest technologies when undergoing changes and evolutions through different generations. Therefore, severe cultural differences and estrangements between different generations arise. In order to pass on the traditional cultures that are about to be lost, the connection and exchange of emotions and history should be emphasized. Traditional glove puppetry is taken as the pillar of the game proposed in this study, while "The Legend of the White Snake," one of the China's four major folk stories, is considered as its theme. The historical and cultural knowledge of the elderly become the guiding indicators in the game, allowing the elderly to gain sufficient self-confidence and increase their curiosity in learning modern technology through game interactions. Furthermore, young generations can acquire relevant cultural knowledge of glove puppetry. In the past, the development of virtual reality games did not consider and value the needs of intergenerational communication. If the evaluations and designs of intergenerational programs can be made based on such needs, it is believed it would benefit the elderly and young people in the evolution of generations. This research applies traditional culture to virtual reality and plan an intergenerational game that can be played by two people, promote cultural experience between generations, and make the two sides have an emotional connection with each other's cultural background.

KEYWORDS

Traditional Culture, Virtual Reality, Intergenerational Games, Intergenerational Communication, Glove Puppetry

1. INTRODUCTION

Taiwan has witnessed changes in its family structures. The research report of the National Development Council, "Family Structure Development Projection of Our Country" (National Development Council, 2017) predicted that the number of households will increase in the future, but the average family size will decrease. Family structures changes including couple family, solitaire, single parent family, or skipped-generation family will grow significantly, and the changes also decrease the intergenerational bond of the elderly and young. The prevention of mental health problems of the elderly is an important global issue; however, if the solution to the problem is developed in a mature way, it may generate great economic and health benefits (Leggett & Zarit, 2014). Well-designed digital media technology can enhance the positive psychological development of the elderly, but the problems of digital divide linger.

At time when exquisiteness is pursued in most aspects, puppets with the traditional features of glove puppetry fail to attract the attention of the present generation. In order to pass on the legacies of traditional culture, many declining traditional skills have brought the young generations closer to our country's cultural history through the application and dissemination power of the latest technology.

The technological development of virtual reality (VR) has matured in recent years, and it has now been applied to many academic disciplines such as medicine and entertainment. Through the application of sensors and multidimensional scenes as well as visual processing and control of sound distances, users can immerse themselves in a view, as if they were actually in the scene. One of the major purposes of integrating VR and the traditional cultural industries is to preserve cultural heritage. VR has long played an important role in the historical relationship between humans and images (Tseng, 2018). Ji Fang, consultant of the China Ethnic Cultural Relics Protection Association, believes that with the combination of VR technology and the protection of cultural heritage as well as large-scale display methods of cultural relics and cultural heritage that are highly precise, highly interactive, and cover wide audiences can be materialized. Such methods include digital preservation, virtual restoration, publicity and display, virtual walkthroughs, and digital museums, and they can solve the traditional problems in the protection of cultural heritage (Chan et al., 2016).

This research has the following purposes:

1. To reproduce the traditional glove puppetry (Yetai drama) from the 1940s to the 1950s through VR. The interactive game, which mainly involves puppet manipulation and performance, will encourage the young generations' exposure to the culture of glove puppetry
2. To apply intergenerational programs to game design for the elderly and young generations
3. To increase the willingness of the elderly to learn new technologies through VR interactive games.

2. LITERATURE REVIEW

In this section, the traditional culture of glove puppetry is discussed to understand the historical background and principles of traditional culture. The second part involves digital games for the elderly as well as the restrictions. By clarifying the difficulties that the elderly may encounter in the application of technology, basic rules for making interactive games are formulated. The third part involves the application of digital games to intergenerational communication. The literature review uncovers appropriate intergenerational programs and the ways to apply these programs to interaction games, so that people of different generations can interact and communicate in the process.

2.1 Traditional Culture of Glove Puppetry

Traditional glove puppetry was a smash hit in the 1940s and 1950s. Apart from setting up a stage in the temple square and performing in the form of Yetai, glove puppetry has cultural significance that involves religious ceremonies such as the birth of gods, votive offerings, the Jiao rituals, and expressing gratitude for peace (Workshop for Taiwan Folk Culture, 2000). At the time, no scripts were written for the performance of ordinary folk theater troupes. A storyteller would describe the outlines, and the performance solely relied on the actors' improvisation. The actors needed to have a wealth of stage experience to be competent in the performance of such "live dramas," but such acting methods led to loosen plots and rough performance. "Yetai drama" means "open-air theater": the performance of the drama is combined with temple ceremonies and become the sign of Taiwan's traditional culture, while watching dramas at a temple entrance is a cultural memory in the 1940s to 1950s.

The earliest form of glove puppetry in Taiwan was inherited from China. However, with the development of Taiwanese thinking toward prosperity, glove puppetry evolved into an artistic image that carried unique Taiwanese folklore style against the local social, economic, cultural, and political background. Glove puppetry was introduced from the Fujian Province, China, and was divided into three genres: Nanguan (southern pipes), Baizi (local language) Opera, and ChaoTiao (Chaozhou Tunes) (Casca, 2019).

The characteristics of glove puppetry are mainly divided into: (1) *Koubai* (spoken script): The main elements to appreciate glove puppetry are Koubai and puppet manipulation. Usually, one person dubs the Koubai of all characters in a performance (Chiang, 1996). The focuses of the main characters' Koubai include distinctive expressions of the five tones and clear enunciations, while the changes in the tones of the characters should allow the audience to understand their personal traits and distinguish between the protagonists and the antagonists. (2) Debut poetry: The debut poem highlights the personal traits of different characters, creating a unique atmosphere for the character's debut. (3) Puppet manipulation: Traditional puppet manipulation starts from putting a hand into the pocket. The index finger controls the head while the thumb controls one hand, and the middle finger, ring finger, and little finger are brought together to control the puppet's other hand. But when the puppets have to walk, the puppeteer will use the other hand to assist the movements. In addition to their physical performance, the characters' happiness, anger, sorrow, and joy are expressed through various gestures. The professional skills of the puppeteers are simultaneously reflected in such operations. (4) Music: In order to lift the atmosphere on stage, glove puppetry shows need to be set off by music. Traditional glove puppetry shows that originated in Quanzhou introduced Nanguan as background music, and when the show was brought to Taiwan, Nanguan music was also played. The main instruments of Nanguan music include pipa, *dongxiao*, *erxian*, and *sanxian*, and its performance involves singing and playing the instrument along with the use of ancient Quanzhou accents to express rich emotions (Chen, 2004).

"The Legend of the White Snake," which is the theme of the game, and is one of the four major Chinese folk stories. It is also called "Xu Xian and the White Lady." The story was set in Hangzhou, Suzhou, and relevant regions during the Song Dynasty. And mainly spread by word of mouth in the early days, which was a model of collective creation of folk tales in China; therefore, different versions and details were also derived. However, in all of the versions, classic plotlines such as "borrowing an umbrella," "stealing the miracle plant," and "Leifeng Pagoda" prevailed. After Feng Menglong's "Volume 28 of Stories to Caution the World, White Lady is Kept Forever under the Leifeng Pagoda" was published, it was recognized by scholars as a relatively complete version of "The Legend of the White Snake" as it retained the best original structure of the story (Chen, 2012).

The game developed in this research has two characteristics: Koubai and puppet manipulation. Furthermore, a debut poem is recited by a character as they first appear on stage. As the excerpt used in the game is the ending of "The Legend of the White Snake," the element of debut poetry is not included in the game content. Regarding the music, professional orchestras are crucial to the restoration of the corresponding plot music. Therefore, the game uses the basic music of glove puppetry, which is applied according to the ups and downs of the plot.

2.2 Digital Games for the Elderly as Well as the Restrictions

As VR technology matures, through proper design can allow users to have comfortable technological experiences. In contrast, VR games may also lead to problems such as dizziness, headaches, nausea, and uncomfortable feelings. Furthermore, as physiological functions deteriorate, and the lack of familiarity with technological equipment may frustrate the elderly as they fail to control the system, especially when the long-term use of VR brings about visual fatigue (such as when watching a 3D movie), they may suffer from visual discomfort or asthenopia (Aznar-Casanova et al., 2017), loss of spatial consciousness, dizziness, disorientation, epilepsy, or nausea. Ali et al. (2015) suggest that, compared with users who watch the games, VR users are more likely to have a higher heart rate and signs of dizziness and vomiting. The negative effects of VR have gradually gained public attention.

Visual decline is a common phenomenon in the elderly, and the font size and changes in the games' windows will affect their degree of comfort when playing the game. It is not appropriate to design the game with excessively complicated and difficult content; rather, the design should be easy to understand and elderly-friendly. First, in consideration of the actions' restrictions and countereffects (such as nausea), as well as the issues of sense of existence, navigation, and synchronous interaction in the immersive environment, the time of conversation should be reduced, and the intensity and agility of the actions should be changed (Paliokas et al., 2010), while the degree of comfort of visual perception should be adjusted (Iachini et al., 2009). Second , the elderly enjoy new experiences but feel more comfortable in a known or familiar environment; thus, the interface design requirements must be specially designed considering age-related cognitive changes, process of attention, working memory, and search methods (Dionisio & Gilbert, 2013; Segkouli et al., 2015). Third, the elderly do not know much about digital games and fear the complexity of installing and playing games (Mahmud et al., 2010); therefore, when no one leads them, they may struggle to play games. Fourth, 3D environmental audio effects that can stimulate immersive feelings (Silva et al., 2019) and other factors can have equal opportunities for development, in order to produce greater application benefits in ensuring the needs of the elderly, which were ignored in the previous development and application processes of VR.

2.3 Applying Digital Games to Intergenerational Communication

Intergenerational communication refers to communication between different generations. Human beings are horizontally interconnected and interdependent in the intergenerational chain. Many important emotional and historical connections have been made in the lives of our different generations (Viswanathan et al., 2000; Kaplan et al., 2017). Intergenerational communication shows the degree of interaction and dialogue between the elderly and young people. It focuses on all levels of intergenerational communication and relationships, while the quality of communication performance will also become an important social issue (Keaton & McCann, 2017).

Appropriate programs can promote intergenerational communication, eliminate mutual stereotypes, and not only allow the people of different generations to learn from each other, also to stimulate the motivation and interest in the process of learning. The application of intergenerational games is an effective way to encourage intergenerational learning among different generations. The benefits of intergenerational digital games include strengthening family relationships, strengthening mutual learning, deepening intergenerational understanding, and reducing social anxiety. When designing intergenerational digital games, both aspects of player-centered and game-centered should be considered (Cucinelli et al., 2018; De la Hera et al., 2017).

Digital games can facilitate intergenerational interaction by promoting personal happiness, prosocial behavior, and knowledge sharing; promoting common activities by enhancing social interaction between different generations; and balancing the skills and challenges of users (Costa & Veloso, 2017). By playing intergenerational games, different generations can spend time together, connect, and talk to each other, while bridging the gap between generations. It also enables the elderly to have a sense of self-identity and happiness as well as a sense of accomplishment in mastering new technologies, enhancing their mental and physical abilities, and promoting successful aging (Osmanovic & Pecchioni, 2016).

However, when designing intergenerational games, it is necessary to consider how to achieve the inheritance of traditional culture through the design of game content, so that the younger generations can be immersed in the experience and background of the older generations. It also helps younger generations to eliminate the stereotypes regarding the elderly and achieve the purposes of mutual understanding and co-creating memories. Through the booming methods in technological experiencing, mutual support and learning between different generations can be achieved, and the sustainable development of the interactive relationship between the two generations can be promoted. The main purpose of games is to stimulate the motivation to participate through the integration of elements that are echoed by different generations. Furthermore, with interactive games, they can gain a sense of accomplishment as they beat the levels and build connections by cooperation in the process of participating. The benefits of different game processes are gained as they go through the game content (Agate et al., 2018).

3. DESIGN PRACTICE

The purpose of this research is to design a VR interactive game that can enhance communication between different generations. Therefore, the design process is divided into four parts. The first part involves the function planning of glove puppetry; through the integration of puppet show and VR, suitable game functions are planned. The second part involves the game outline and features, understanding the story content and historical background of "The Legend of the White Snake," and integrate the features into the game content. The third part involves the design of intergenerational communication and game flow; through the design of interactive game flow, interaction and communication between different generations are enhanced. The fourth part involves the description of the game interface, explaining each UI and UX content in the game.

3.1 Glove Puppetry VR Function Planning

The main purpose of this research is to enable the elderly to relive the old memories of traditional culture through the application of new media and to pass on these cultural memories to the younger generations. The design plan of the interactive game is based on glove puppetry in the form of Yetai drama, while its game functions are as shown in Table 1.

Table 1. The plan for game functions

Function	Plan of function
Enter the game	1. One player needs to create a game room first and is then joined by another player.
Selections	1. Glove puppetry is mainly based on the actions of the hands, so the selections and control of the game contents are all done by hand. 2. After the elderly make their choices, corresponding feedback will be provided so that they can notice whether the operation is successful. 3. After selections are done by pressing the buttons, selections for the second time are not allowed.
Beginner's guide	1. Clear guidelines of the game should be provided to lead the elderly through clicking operations
Start the Game	1. Speed of reading the text 2. Switching between characters 3. According to different segments, switching to corresponding scenes and music 4. According to the instructions of the segment, props can be given to another player 5. At the end of the game, performance scores and feedback will be provided to the players

3.2 Game Outline and Features

"The Legend of the White Snake," a story is taken as the background of the game's story. "Kept Forever under the Leifeng Pagoda" is a highlight of the contemporary version of the story and is performed as an excerpt in many dramas and operas. In the game play, the tests play the story with words and connect with the story with which they are familiar.

"Kept Forever under the Leifeng Pagoda" is about the twists and turns of the love story between Xu Xian and White Lady. Xu Xian would like to offer incense at the Jinshan Temple with his friend. As White Lady could not stop him from going, she asked him to make three promises: (1) that he would not enter the Jinshan Temple; (2) that he would not talk to the monks; (3) that he would come home right after burning the incense and not stay any longer. However, Xu Xian forgot the demands of White Lady. Fahai, the monk, instantly noticed that Xu Xian had entered the temple. Xu Xian, who had doubts about White Lady, obeyed Fahai's words and was convinced that White Lady was a demon turned human. Too afraid to go home, Xu Xian immediately asked for Fahai's help, borrowing from him a golden bowl to subdue the demon. Fahai ignored White Lady's plea and turned her back into a little white snake. Her handmaiden, Xiaoqing (the green snake), was also subdued by Fahai. Fahai took the bowl that sealed White Lady and Xiaoqing to Jinshan Temple and built a tower to suppress it. Later, Xu Xian became a monk and build a seven-story pagoda, Leifeng Pagoda, based on the tower. He then practiced as a monk in it.

The characters in this game are mainly based on the core characters in "The Legend of the White Snake," while the historical background is based on the Song Dynasty, during which the story originated. The appearances of the puppet characters are designed according to the costumes of the Song Dynasty, and the 3D designs of the characters are as shown in Figure 1. Figure 2 shows the appearance of the theater in the game.

Xu Xian Fahai Bai Suzhen (White Lady)

Figure 1. Designs of puppets

Figure 2. Game scene

This game is based on the outdoor Yetai drama in the 1950s and the characters in the game are designed according to the prototypes of wooden puppets in traditional glove puppetry. Users can immerse themselves in the scene with a VR game and experience the setting of traditional glove puppetry.

3.3 Design of Intergenerational Communication and Game Flow

According to the literature, a good intergenerational program can effectively promote communication between different generations. In particular, the main concern of the game developed in this research is the communication and interaction between different generations; therefore, the interactivity of the game constitutes the crucial design core. Three types of connections are facilitated by this game, including the teamwork, teaching, and communication.

Figure 3 introduces the game flow and design of intergenerational communication points in the research game. Intergenerational communication points are generated in the following parts: (1) start of the game: at the beginning of the game, one party must first establish the game room and is joined by another party. **Communication** between the two parties is necessary. (2) Tutorial: when the elderly go through the tutorial, they may raise doubts about difficulties in operating the game; at this time, young people must **teach** and **communicate** to guide them through the basic operations. (3) Operation practice: it helps the players revise after consulting the guide for beginners. In this process, the two players can **discuss** and **learn from each other** and perform **teamwork** to conduct interactive exercises together. (4) Story outline: the story outline process explains the excerpts of "The Legend of the White Snake"; after reading the story, the two players can have a **discussion**. (5) Going on stage: **teamwork** is necessary for the two players to run the story to the end. Therefore, in order to coordinate switching characters, **communication** is essential. When the other party faces difficulties in operations, immediate **teaching** will allow the game to progress smoothly. (6) Counting the scores and evaluation feedback: when the game is over, the scores of the two players in the game are revealed, and feedback is given based on the performance of the two players; further, players can **discuss** their respective performance with their partners.

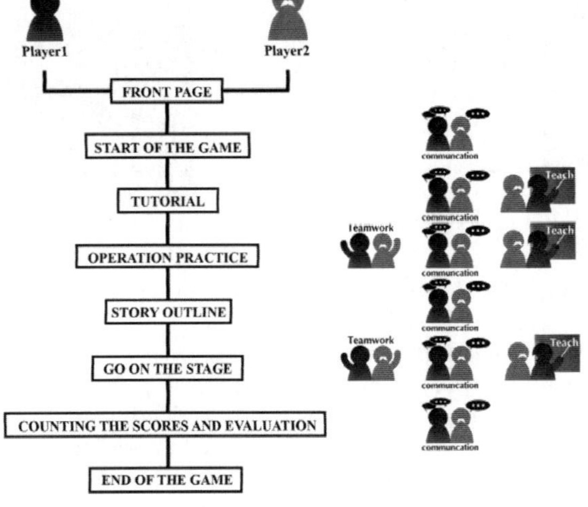

Figure 4. Game flow and the design of intergenerational communication points

3.4 Introduction to Game Scene Designs

The elderly experience physical decline as they age. Especially the changes in visual function are the most obvious. Therefore, color configuration must first be considered when designing the interface. And avoid bringing visual confusion. In the game, the main button is red, and the secondary button is black. The brightness of the color red not only attracts the attention of elderly persons but also carries a certain guiding function. Feedback is provided when the elderly click on the objects, so that they may notice whether the click was successful. The interface design of the game is explained in Table 2:

Table 2. Introduction to the game interface

Interface name	Interface	Introduction to the interface	Interfac e name	Interface	Introduction to the interface
Front Page		Strong contrasting colors are used in the buttons of this interface. The color of the main button is bright, and the button is placed in a position that can be easily reached by the dominant hand.	Story outline:		The interface should consider the respective positions of the two, and its design should: (1) avoid using small fonts in the content; (2) avoid using colors with similar chromas; (3) place the scene in the center for maximum readability.
Getting on stage		In the interface, the players are separately placed in two positions to avoid excessive overlaps of the movable ranges when they are operating.	Tutorial	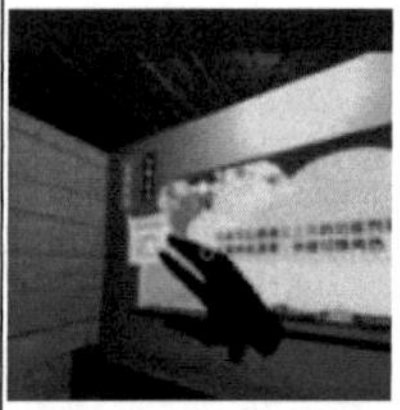	The interface after entering the game, buttons on this interface are not main buttons of the game, so they are placed on the left. When the player turns to the left to select the buttons, it is more convenient for them to use their right hands for selection.
Counting the scores		This interface displays the scores and performance of the two players. The scene is placed in the center for maximum readability.	Perform ance practice	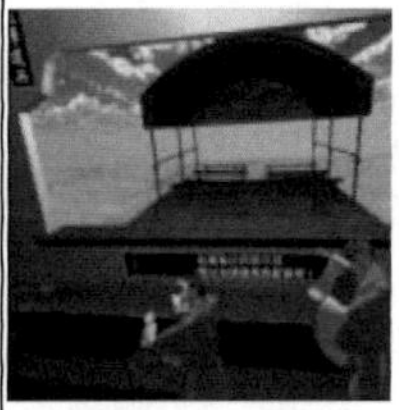	The characters will be placed directly in front of the players, reducing the hindrance of the operation. The players are able to reach out and touch the characters that they want to choose at a glance.

In the game, two players act as the characters on stage at the same time. In addition to completing the performance, corresponding scores and evaluation feedback will be provided each time they pass a level, to enhance the sense of accomplishment. It is hoped that VR interactive games that have glove puppetry as their theme will stimulate the elderly and young people's willingness to play and reduce the distance between the cultural backgrounds of different generations. In this way, the elderly may experience new technology and equipment, while young people can be exposed to traditional culture while playing games. Figure 5 shows the scene of an elderly person and a young person playing the VR game together.

Figure 5. An elderly person and a young person play the VR game together

4. RESULT

The Unity3D game engine is used in this research to complete the production of the game, while Blender and MYAY are used for the 3D modeling of the character models. The function buttons displayed are drawn with Adobe Illustrator. In addition, the VR device used in this research is the product of Oculus Quest which can translate actions into VR through the built-in sensor without the setup of base stations, while the actions are directly tracked by gestures. The functions fit the elements of puppet manipulations by hands. According to the literature, the elderly are constrained by the deterioration of their visual ability, and long-term use may cause physical discomfort. Therefore, from entering the game to the end of the game, the playing time about 15–20 minutes, and it is recommended to take 10 minutes of visual rest after a single play. This is to prevent the elderly from having unpleasant feelings while operating the VR, which would reduce their willingness to experience the latest technologies. In the future, this research will recruit test objects to examine whether the culture of traditional glove puppetry is suitable for applying to VR for the design of intergenerational games, and whether it enables people of different generations to interact and communicate more closely.

REFERENCES

Aznar-Casanova J. A. et al, 2017. Visual fatigue while watching 3D stimuli from different positions. *Journal of Optometry*, Vol. 10, No. 3, pp.149-160.

Agate J. R. et al, 2018. 'Roots and wings': an exploration of intergenerational play. *Journal of Intergenerational Relationships*, Vol. 16, No. 4, pp.395-421.

Ali, S., Vaughn, S., and Williams, J., 2015. Physiological and psychological effects of virtual reality. *Medium.* Available at https://medium.com/oculus-rift/6-physiological-and-psychological-effects-of-virtual-reality-9bc3aee94868

Casca, 2019. The tinder of Grassroots Culture in Yehai Drama. *Country Road*, August 2019 issue.

Chan, S. et al, 2018. *The Era of Revival of Glove Puppetry, Brand New Experience for Young People.*

Chen, Y., 2012. *The religion interpretation of the White Snake Legend.* Master's dissertation. Graduate Institute of Religious Studies, National Chengchi University.

Chen C., 2004. *Folklore in the Memories—The Disappearing Living Culture of Common People.*

Chiang, W., 1996. Features of puppet show *Journal of Pili*, Vol. 13, pp. 20-23.

Costa, L. V., and Veloso, A. I., 2017. *Demystifying Ageing Bias Through Learning. International Conference on Immersive Learning.* Springer, pp.201-213.

Cucinelli, G. et al, 2018. Intergenerational learning through a participatory video game design workshop. *Journal of Intergenerational Relationships*, Vol. 16, No. 1-2, pp. 146-165.

Dionisio, J. D. N., and Gilbert, R., 2013. 3D Virtual worlds and the metaverse: Current status and future possibilities. *ACM Computing Surveys (CSUR)*, Vol. 45, No. 3, 34.

Leggett, A. and Zarit, S., 2014. Prevention of mental disorders in older adults: recent innovations and future directions. *Generations*, Vol. 38, No. 3, 45-52.

Mahmud, A. A. et al, 2010. Designing social games for children and older adults: Two related case studies. *Entertainment Computing*, Vol. 1, No. 3, pp.147-156.

Iachini, I. et al, 2009. Visuospatial memory in healthy elderly, AD and MCI: A review. *Current Aging Science*, Vol. 2, No. 1, pp.43-59.

Kaplan, M., Sanchez, M., and Hoffman, J., 2017. Intergenerational strategies for establishing sustainable work environments. In *Intergenerational Pathways to a Sustainable Society.* Cham: Springer, pp. 141–162.

Keaton, S. A., McCann, R. M., and Giles, H., 2017. The role of communication perceptions in the mental health of older adults: Views from Thailand and the United States. *Health Communication*, Vol. 32, No. 1, pp. 92-102.

National Development Council, 2017. Family structure development projection of our country (2017–2026).

Osmanovic, S., and Pecchioni, L., 2016. Beyond entertainment: motivations and outcomes of video game playing by older adults and their younger family members. *Games and Culture*, Vol. 11, No. (1-2), pp. 130-149.

Paliokas, I., Buda, V., and Iancu, A. R., 2010. Archaeo Viz: A 3D explorative learning environment of reconstructed archaeological sites and cultural artefacts. *International Conference on Signal Processing and Multimedia Applications–ICETE 2010 Joint Conference*, Athens, pp.211-214.

Silva, R. S., Mol, A. M., and Ishitani, L., 2019. Virtual reality for older users: a systematic literature review. *International Journal of Virtual Reality*, Vol. 19, No. 1.

Tseng, C-Y., 2018. *Immersive experience of seamless virtual space: Virtual Reality.* University of Taipei.

Viswanathan, M., Childers, T. L., and Moore, E. S., 2000. The measurement of intergenerational communication and influence on consumption: Development, validation, and cross-cultural comparison of the IGEN scale. *Journal of the Academy of Marketing Science*, Vol. 28, No. 3, pp. 406-424.

UNDERSTANDING THE GAP BETWEEN ACADEMICS AND GAME DEVELOPERS: AN ANALYSIS OF GAMASUTRA BLOGS

Jordan Greenwood, Leigh Achterbosch, Andrew Stranieri and Grant Meredith
Federation University Australia
Mt Helen Campus, Australia

ABSTRACT

Communication between industry and academia in the fields of game development to date has been limited to the detriment of both groups. This lack of communication is more commonly known as the academia-industry divide. Blogs have been advanced as a good medium to reduce the divide because they allow academics to practice presenting their knowledge to different audiences and allows them to get suggestions and feedback from game developers. This study analyzed all blogs posted by members of Gamasutra.com in a 13-month span between March 2020 and April 2021. Forty-four of the 767 blogs were found to be referencing academic sources. Using Walton and Krabbe's dialogue types, we discovered how academia was trying to communicate their knowledge relevant to game development and report on the extent to which academia had tried to influence game design and development. Results showed that the divide is real and that access to research information for the public is still quite difficult. The results also illustrate that academia only have had a small influence on the gaming industry and that only a small amount of gaming researchers were communicating their theories of game development.

KEYWORDS

Games, Communication, Blogging, Academia-Industry Divide

1. INTRODUCTION

Communication between industry and academia in the field of game development to date has been limited (Passarelli et al., 2018). Each group has perceptions that contribute to the phenomena commonly known as the academia-industry divide (Colusso et al., 2017). Academics believe the divide arises because of conflicting interests including the perception that game industry members are focused heavily on the return on their investments (Lameman, 2010). Industry members see academics as difficult to approach and stand-offish (Norman, 2010). The divide is not just limited to academia and the game industry and has been noted between academia and industry in general (Lockett et al., 2008; Remy, 2015; Benoit et al., 2019). By having narrow views of each other, both groups can be seen at least superficially, to lose out on what they can offer each other. There have been many attempts and suggestions to bridge the divide in the Information technology industry, however the questions that arise include: Should the divide be bridged? Can academics and industry game developers interact in new ways to reduce the divide? Factors that need to be considered to answer the questions are:

1. The benefits to both groups (Remy, 2015; Benoit et al., 2019; Weststar, 2015),
2. The barriers of both groups (Lameman, 2010; Passarelli et al., 2018; Colusso et al., 2017), and.
3. Suggestions from previous attempts (Kieser & Leiner, 2012; Barroca et al., 2018; Passarelli et al., 2020).

This study will be investigating how one of the major suggestions is currently performing within the gaming industry to solve the issue of making research information more accessible to the public (Colusso et al., 2017). By making research information more accessible to the public, one of the main barriers which relate to how the public perceives academia may be improved (Norman, 2010).

Mewburn & Thomson (2013) suggested that blogs would be a good medium to make research insights more accessible because they allow academics to practice presenting their information to different audiences and to get suggestions from sources other than their academic peers.

The current study analyses posts to a popular blog in the game sector to initially identify the extent to which the academia-industry divide is present in that sector. An analysis of blogs that reference academic literature is then conducted to understand the benefits and barriers that underpin the divide.

The first section of this paper discusses the divide and then moves on to discuss the factors that need to be considered in analyzing blogs. The paper then explains the approach taken for the analysis of one popular blog, Gamastura.com, to discover the extent to which academics communicate research ideas. The third section lays out the findings of the analysis, and the fourth section discusses the impact these findings have on the progression of more accessible research. Limitations and future considerations are then presented.

2. RELATED WORK

2.1 The Academia-Industry Divide

Communication and collaboration between academia and industry in the majority of Information Technology and Science fields have been quite limited (Passarelli et al., 2018). There have been a few cases of successful attempts such as InfoLab21 (Lockett et al., 2008) and the Gaming Horizons project (Passarelli et al., 2018) but the majority either fail or result in only one-off collaborations.

Consequently, both sides suffer from not knowing what the other is doing (Colusso et al., 2017). Data gathering and knowledge acquisition are made more difficult for academics and industry practitioners. There are many theories or ideas that are overlooked by game developers such as motivational theories, monetization strategies, psychological theories, and ideas about narrative development.

The divide between the two groups has been attributed to the different cultures, beliefs, mindsets, or languages. (Gray et al., 2014; Wallin et al., 2014) Why has this divide occurred? Is it worth bridging? Many analysts have expressed beliefs about the causes of the divide and what can be gained by reducing it. However, many suggestions or ideas are not being implemented or put into practice. This could be because they are not being suggested outside the academic community.

This study examined one of the major suggestions, that academics should post to Blogs, in order to assess the extent to which this occurs and the nature of those posts that clearly reference relevant research.

2.2 Barriers

Previous research into the academic-industry divide has identified quite a few barriers. This paper will be drawing on the fields of Human-Computer Interactions (HCI) and other fields of Information Technology because, in the field of video games, research papers are rare. The barriers identified are as follows:

1. **The relatively low accessibility of research output outside of academia.** This relates to the language used (academic jargon) and the access to research being behind journal paywalls (Passarelli et al., 2018; Colusso et al., 2017).
2. **Industry's understanding of what is available from research.** This regard communication issues of research not being in forms that the public can view and current industry design processes not seeing academia as a source of information (Colusso et al., 2017).
3. **Opinions of each side.** Academics believe that industry only cares about what will make a profit (Lameman, 2010; Wallin et al., 2014). While industry groups see academics as sitting in their ivory towers (Norman, 2010; Gray et al., 2014). There are a few other opinions that refer to clique mindsets.
4. **Pace of research output vs industry output.** There is a belief that the different paces in which each field produces outcomes will hinder communication, but this depends on what is being done. For example, many game developers follow an iterative agile methodology producing outcomes and gameplay prototypes quickly, while academics must undergo multiple processes from research and analysis, to drafting results, to camera-ready publications, all of which have no solid viewable output until it is published. (Lockett et al., 2008; Passarelli et al., 2018).
5. **Intellectual property (IP) issues and trust issues.** This relates to the rights of the collaborative output when forming a partnership between academic(s) and industry. It can cause issues if not discussed and negotiated early on but is dependent on the situation at hand (Lockett et al., 2008).

6. **Motivation, incentives, and administration.** Both sides look at communication as if it is only worth doing if there is an obvious benefit. Depending on the situation, this mindset can benefit or hamper. Imagine a university investigating improvements to their gaming education courses. The industry could contribute and through a partnership, they get access to future employees with desired skills. Alternatively, they may see the cost of time and money too much of a burden on their timelines. On the administration side there are issues with managing resources, relaying communication, intellectual property issues and paperwork that slows down the process but again this depends on the situation (Kashyap & Agrawal, 2019).

2.3 Benefits of Bridging the Divide

Previous research into the academic-industry divide has not identified as many benefits as there are barriers to bridging the divide. This could be because, studies are limited, or the barriers caused more issues than are worth for bridging the divide or studies have focused more on why the divide exists and not the outcomes of successful bridge attempts. The benefits are identified below:

2.3.1 Academic

1. **Access to current industry knowledge and practices.** Researchers must be aware of the complex stages of industrial practices in which their research findings could be most beneficial and then tailor their frameworks and guidelines for the appropriate tasks. This may significantly increase the chance of academic knowledge being applied to real-world practices (Remy, 2015). Also, new research questions can be developed by knowing what is needed in practice or what has just occurred in practice, e.g., problematic gaming mechanics.
2. **Access to data.** Researchers tend to spend enormous amounts of time, and effort collecting data by conducting interviews, focus groups, experiments, and surveys. But if they had an industrial partner, they could gain access to huge quantities of unused data which could lead to valuable insights for both parties (Benoit et al., 2019). On that note, it is recommended that the academics brush up on legal frameworks and restrictions.
3. **Potential employment for students.** By working with industry, universities can enable employment options for students such as internships or graduate positions (Dalmarco et al., 2011). At this stage, this is the most common form of collaboration between academia and industry.
4. **Potential funding from governments or industry.** There might be government incentives forming collaborations or providing knowledge to industry (Swain, 2009) such as the Australian Research Council Linkage program (Australian Research Council, 2015). Also, industry could be a testbed to evaluate theories and concepts advanced by academia.

2.3.2 Industry

1. **Access to additional avenues to solve their problems**. At this point, most game developers do not consider academic research as something that could potentially solve their problems. However, academics have conducted extensive research about the motivations of players, psychological theories, theories on narrative development and game design patterns. Academia could also provide expert advice on project management or advice on specialty areas such as biomedicine which could be used to improve immersion (Nacke, 2018).
2. **Use academics to gather or analyze their data.** Academics can take time to dig deep, examine patterns, and identify structures within sales, design patterns or player data which then could lead to insights that could be used for decision making, optimization, predictions, and innovations (Benoit et al., 2019).
3. **Opportunities to work on something that could have commercial value.** Most researchers do not know or care that they have developed something which could have commercial value (Norman, 2010). This is where industry can come into play to provide commercialization services for ideas that researchers have developed (Wallin et al., 2014). On that note, both sides will have to decide on intellectual property rights and what can be written about in papers regarding the project or timeframes for when research results can be released. It has been recommended that for a collaboration of this magnitude, a contract should be put in place (Weststar, 2015).
4. **Expanding network of knowledge.** Adding additional contacts to your network even if they are not immediately useful is always beneficial. Academics could be used for advice or could analyze data (if they can write a paper on the findings). Conversely, academics with industry contacts can disseminate their results, and find people for interviews to gather data (Buie, 2013).

2.4 Suggested Solutions

Suggestions to reduce the divide can be categorized into three main groups: General suggestions, collaboration enhancement and knowledge transfer suggestions. The majority of suggestions to reduce the divide have not been implemented into practice or if they have, they have not been as successful as one would hope (Norman, 2010).

In this paper, previously proposed solutions have been summarized into key areas. Some of the solutions were disregarded because they appeared to be common courtesies or practices such as being polite and professional in dealings or having regular meetings.

2.4.1 General Suggestions

1. **Action research.** Is a form of collaborative research in which the researchers and the practitioners set out to research a problem where their interests align, and where the shared purpose is to create knowledge (Kieser & Leiner, 2012). The downside of this approach is that the scientific community regards forms of collaboration that predominantly aim at solving practical problems as less attractive (Kieser & Leiner, 2012). This reduces the chance of the researcher furthering their career but helps them build their network.
2. **Agile research network approach.** Is a model that can be used for the delivery of timely and relevant research and can be used alongside practitioners that use the agile software methodology approach. It allows the researcher/practitioner collaboration to have wider dissemination through white papers and research publications (Barroca et al., 2018). There are a few things that need to be considered when using this model such as having a full-time researcher present on-site at the games company helped with relations, trust needs to be built beforehand, contracts need to be signed, decisions made on who is funding and what happens with the outcomes. This approach is still in development and needs more tests conducted but it is a good starting point for discussions. There are a few other approaches but the two mentioned here appear to be the best suited for working with the games industry.
3. **Development of different documents for different audiences.** It has been suggested that academics need to start developing "digestible" versions of their findings to accommodate the practitioner's managerial decision making and so the practitioners can then present to stakeholders (Benoit et al., 2019). This reduces conflicts over performance and outcomes because it provides evidence that something has arisen from the collaboration.
4. **Develop trust.** If no previous relationship exists, it has been recommended that academics and industry collaborators start on smaller projects or have students placed within the game development company or have the company work on student projects (Berman, 2008; Benoit et al., 2019). This allows both sides to start building their relationship because they both start to learn what each other wants and how the other side operates.
5. **Decide early on IP and other contract obligations.** If this is left to a later date many issues will arise and will most likely result in a breakdown of communication and will hamper future communications and collaborations (Kieser & Leiner, 2012).

2.4.2 Collaboration

1. **Academics need to learn about industry practices.** It has been suggested that academics need to improve their understanding of what research means to business, and how their research will improve or support current industry practices (Berman, 2008). By doing this, academics should be able to understand and speak industry lingo, which makes it easier to present findings and have discussions.
2. **Industry need to learn about what academics are doing.** The industry needs to be aware of the requirement for academics to publish and contribute to their field, which means sharing information that companies may see as proprietary (Lameman, 2010). By understanding what both parties get from the collaboration and what can be used (e.g., data), both sides concerns should be alleviated. This step should be done regularly so both parties are content and moving in the same direction.
3. **Project management and in-between personnel.** Passarelli et al., (2020) suggested that someone needs to be explicitly put into the role of facilitating collaboration between different professionals and fragmented communities. This reduces the chances of arguments between the two parties and helps deal with issues such as IP or communication breakdowns.

2.4.3 Transferring Knowledge

1. **Consulting.** It can consist of advice and expertise provided by academics to industry, usually for personal compensation (Perkmann & Walsh, 2009). An example of how this can be used has been in the recent news concerning the game "Fortnite" using psychologists to make their game more addictive (Cuthbertson, 2019).
2. **Academics developing libraries and translational resources.** The creation of a collection of summarized work that industry can use could enhance the impact of academic research labs, by helping them find industry collaborators and new students. The downside is that many academic institutions do not reward researchers who invest in building libraries or translational resources outside of traditional academic publications (Colusso et al., 2017).
3. **Academics should blog their research.** Mewburn & Thomson, (2013) suggested that academics could learn to blog and summarize their research to help them reach a wider audience and develop their network of contacts for future research projects. This will also help academics write less obtusely. Even though this has been suggested, academics must be careful with writing online because universities are becoming more aware of the activities of their staff online. On that note, if the person is not slandering other people, or breaking IP laws, they should be safe to write up summaries of their research to get opinions from the public (Mewburn & Thomson, 2013).

The final suggested solution above concerning academic blogging will be the focus of this study. The question is how much blogging is occurring by academics in the gaming community and is it in a digestible format for game developers.

3. METHODOLOGY

All blogs posted by members of Gamasutra.com between March 2020 and April 2021 were examined. The 767 blogs included post-mortems, developer advice, reviews, and posts about indie life. Initially, each blog was assessed as invoking research if it contained a reference list, an in-line citation or links that connected to academic literature. An example of the criteria is shown in Figure 1. A list of authors or research posts was recorded.

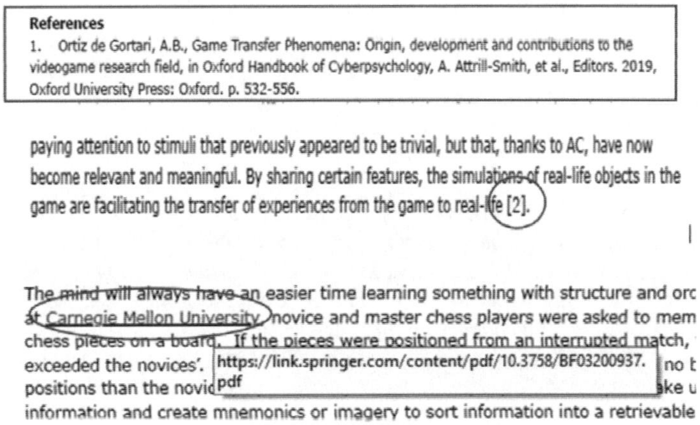
References
1. Ortiz de Gortari, A.B., Game Transfer Phenomena: Origin, development and contributions to the videogame research field, in Oxford Handbook of Cyberpsychology, A. Attrill-Smith, et al., Editors. 2019, Oxford University Press: Oxford. p. 532-556.

paying attention to stimuli that previously appeared to be trivial, but that, thanks to AC, have now become relevant and meaningful. By sharing certain features, the simulations of real-life objects in the game are facilitating the transfer of experiences from the game to real-life [2].

The mind will always have an easier time learning something with structure and orc
at Carnegie Mellon University, novice and master chess players were asked to mem
chess pieces on a board. If the pieces were positioned from an interrupted match,
exceeded the novices'. https://link.springer.com/content/pdf/10.3758/BF03200937.pdf no t
positions than the novic ke u
information and create mnemonics or imagery to sort information into a retrievable

Figure 1. Extracts of Gamasutra articles using the stage 1 criteria

The second stage of analysis was conducted to discover the roles of the authors in the gaming community and whether they had some form of higher education. Each author's profile was checked to see if they reported their education level and if they had links to LinkedIn or Twitter which provided further demographic information. Also, during the second stage of analysis, the blogs were analyzed thematically using the qualitative data analysis software tool NVivo (QSR URL) to discover emerging themes within the research blogs. This helped to understand how bloggers were presenting research concepts and their sources of information to back up their arguments.

Walton & Krabbe's (1995) Dialogue Theory was used to discover the extent to which academia was attempting to communicate their views on gaming theories and to see how much academia had influenced game design and development.

The majority of blogs did not have any outsourced links or reference to where the game was purchasable or where you could access software e.g., Gimp or GitHub. Blogs classified as not having the criteria analyzed in stage 2 were ignored in our study.

4. RESULTS AND DISCUSSION

After examining the Gamasutra blogs, only 44 of 767 blogs met the criteria of having some form of referencing in their work. These blogs were imported into NVivo to discover how the authors were using references to academic papers to justify their arguments.

There were 43 authors (one wrote two blogs), but not all of them were academics. Only five were professional academics, while nine were student academics, 18 were developers and eleven were in marketing or consulting. Also, 67% of the authors indicated in their posts that they had some form of higher education presumably because this was considered important. Half of the 14 academic bloggers wrote in a semi-academic style, (using a first-person format but with clear citations or a reference list) which suggests that these individuals were attempting a more informal style of writing for the general layperson, similar to Mewburn & Thomson's (2013) suggestions of summarizing research in blogs to reach wider audiences.

However, the other 50% were still presenting their research as if it was an academic piece of literature.

The academics' blogs were analyzed against Walton & Krabbe's (1995) Dialogue Theory to understand what they were trying to achieve with their blogs. The theory categorizes dialogues into 6 categories:

1. Persuasion - Where one party tries to persuade the other to their point of view;
2. Negotiation - A form of interest-based dialogue, in which the goal is to make a deal;
3. Inquiry - Which is a collaborative investigation aimed at proving a proposition or showing the impossibility of proving it;
4. Inform - The goal of the inform dialogue is to spread knowledge. e.g., to promote other people's ideas;
5. Deliberative - Similar to inquiry since it starts from an open problem, however, the goal of deliberation is to decide on how to attempt to answer a problem; and,
6. Eristic - Can be considered a family of dialogues characterized by verbal fighting.

After analysis, it was discovered that only three of the six dialogues were being used alongside academic sources, although most of them were using multiple dialogues throughout their blog. The most common dialogue type used by authors of the research posts was the persuasion dialogue: 12 of the 14 academic bloggers were using this type of dialogue within their blog, by attempting to convince readers that their point-of-view or theories were useful to the gaming community. The following example was categorized as a persuasion entry:

"My 100+ hours of gameplay have resulted in several encounters with Game Transfer Phenomena (a broader understanding of what some refer to as the Tetris Effect). Resemblances between virtual and real stimuli have triggered most of my experiences. Game Transfer Phenomena (GTP) comprise sensory perceptions, spontaneous mental processes, and behaviors derived from interactions with digital simulations in a video game environment. The content and the characteristics of a particular video game (e.g., the visual field, auditory effects, and realism), the hardware utilized to control the game (e.g., gamepads), and the degree of immersion, embodiment, and flow are key factors influencing how GTP will manifest [1]." (Blogger 4, Example of Persuasion)

The least common type of dialogue observed amongst the research bloggers was the deliberative dialogue. However only 2 of the 14 academic bloggers were using this type of dialogue and they were using it to answer other bloggers, developers, or researchers' questions. The following example was categorized as a deliberative entry:

"Squire's questions have certainly been answered over the last 18 years. The games that have been created since then have shown society what topics can be covered in games (even if some still reject it, shown in Figure 1 by some of the titles of articles). As the internet has grown and more mature communities have developed, high-quality papers and discussions have come from these games and created new ways of exploring how games give us tools to 'think' in a variety of different ways."

(Blogger 16, Example of Deliberative)

The second most common type of dialogue was the inform dialogue: 7 of the 14 academic bloggers used this type of dialogue largely to inform the reader about existing theories to support their persuasive dialogue arguments. The following example was categorized as an inform dialogue entry:

"The second theory that will be discussed is the idea of the Magic Circle which was created by Johan Huizinga. Unlike most theories, Huizinga designed the name of the theory-based upon the actual image that he created. He presented the idea of the Magic Circle as one of the main factors of learning as a human being. This is because he believes that we take into the Magic Circle certain beliefs and ideas that we have and come out with new ones and more confident on what we initially thought."

(Blogger 6, example of informing)

The Walton & Krabbe (1995) dialogue type lens illustrates, three key points:

1. academics were trying to persuade readers of the merits of their ideas;
2. they were trying to inform others about theories that could be used to improve game development; and
3. they were attempting to provide answers to other bloggers, developers or researchers regarding an idea or theory.

Among hundreds of blogs within the 13-month period analyzed, only a small amount of academics were blogging using a deliberative type of dialogue. This, and the prevalence of persuasion and inform dialogues leads us to suggest that the authors of research posts were attempting to entice others to accept their views to a greater extent than they were attempting to learn from others, test their ideas, or jointly solve common problems. Not only were few academics attempting to bridge the divide, those that did tried to make research more accessible to game developers were still not doing so in a manner that reflected collaborative attitudes.

5. CONCLUSION

This paper analyzed posts of a popular blog in the game development sector to identify the extent to which the academia-industry divide is present. We found that the divide does exist and that only a small number of academics were posting research related items in the popular Gamasutra blog. Further most of these were promoting research theories in one way, persuasion dialogues. This shows that the impact on the progression of more accessible research is still limited, and with so few of the blogs using the deliberative type of dialogue, the indication is that the divide is not being bridged.

Investigation of the possible solutions to the divide and analysis of their performance can provide a clearer picture of the divide and how it can be bridged. With this information, a framework to deal with collaborations or knowledge sharing between academia and the gaming industry can be developed. This framework could lead to major improvements within the game industry, such as story development, player immersion, new technologies and further gaming-related research.

The limitations of the study are as follows. By only looking at the last year of blogs, it can present a selection bias; particularly as the blogging may have been limited due to the COVID-19 pandemic. The second limitation is focusing on a singular blog platform of Gamasutra, as it is a top-rated game developer blog, with connections to the game industry. This may have also created selection bias by only targeting one output stream. Other game development blogs will need to be analyzed to confirm insights identified by this study.

REFERENCES

Australian Research Council, (2015). Linkage Program schemes. Australian Research Council. Retrieved 14th of May from https://www.arc.gov.au/grants/linkage-program

Barroca, L., Sharp, H., Salah, D., Taylor, K., & Gregory, P. (2018). Bridging the gap between research and agile practice: an evolutionary model. International Journal of System Assurance Engineering and Management, 9(2), 323-334.

Benoit, S., Klose, S., Wirtz, J., Andreassen, T. W., & Keiningham, T. L. (2019). Bridging the data divide between practitioners and academics. Journal of service management, 30(5), 524-548. https://doi.org/10.1108/JOSM-05-2019-0158

Berman, J. (2008). Connecting with industry: bridging the divide. Journal of higher education policy and management, 30(2), 165-174. https://doi.org/10.1080/13600800801938762

Buie, E., Hooper, C., & Houssian, A. (2013). Research-practice interaction: building bridges, closing the gap. In (Vol. 2013-, pp. 2493-2496).

Colusso, L., Bennett, C., Hsieh, G., & Munson, S. (2017). Translational Resources: Reducing the Gap Between Academic Research and HCI Practice. In (pp. 957-968).

Cuthbertson, A. (2019). Fortnite Lawsuit: Epic Games Hired Psychologists to Make Game Very Very Addictive. Independent. Retrieved 14th of May from https://www.independent.co.uk/life-style/gadgets-and-tech/gaming/fortnite-lawsuit-gaming-addiction-epic-games-a9146486.html

Dalmarco, G., Dewes, M. d. F., Zawislak, P. A., & Padula, A. D. (2011). Universities' intellectual property: Path for innovation or patent competition? Journal of technology management & innovation, 6(3), 159-170.

Gray, C., Stolterman, E., & Siegel, M. (2014). Reprioritizing the relationship between HCI research and practice: bubble-up and trickle-down effects. In (pp. 725-734).

Kashyap, A., & Agrawal, R. (2019). Academia a new knowledge supplier to the industry! Uncovering barriers in the process. Journal of advances in management research, 16(5), 715-733. https://doi.org/10.1108/JAMR-02-2019-0017

Kieser, A., & Leiner, L. (2012). Collaborate with Practitioners: But Beware of Collaborative Research. Journal of management inquiry, 21(1), 14-28. https://doi.org/10.1177/1056492611411923

Lameman, B., El-Nasr, M., Drachen, A., Foster, W., Moura, D., & Aghabeigi, B. (2010). User studies: a strategy towards a successful industry-academic relationship. In (pp. 134-142).

Lockett, N., Kerr, R., & Robinson, S. (2008). Multiple Perspectives on the Challenges for Knowledge Transfer between Higher Education Institutions and Industry. International small business journal, 26(6), 661-681. https://doi.org/10.1177/0266242608096088

Mewburn, I., & Thomson, P. (2013). Why do academics blog? An analysis of audiences, purposes, and challenges. Studies in higher education (Dorchester-on-Thames), 38(8), 1105-1119. https://doi.org/10.1080/03075079.2013.835624

Nacke, L. E., Mirza-Babaei, P., Spiel, K., Toups, Z. O., & Isbister, K. (2018, April). Games and Play SIG: Engaging Small Developer Communities. In Extended Abstracts of the 2018 CHI Conference on Human Factors in Computing Systems (pp. 1-4).

Norman, D. (2010). The research-practice gap: the need for translational developers. interactions, 17(4), 9-12. https://doi.org/10.1145/1806491.1806494

Passarelli, M., Earp, J., Dagnino, F. M., Manganello, F., Persico, D., Pozzi, F., Buijtenweg, T., Haggis, M., Bailey, C., & Perrotta, C. (2020). The distant Horizon: Investigating the relationship between social sciences academic research and game development. Entertainment Computing, 34. https://doi.org/10.1016/j.entcom.2020.100339

Passarelli, M., Earp, J., Dagnino, F. M., Manganello, F., Persico, D., Pozzi, F., ... & Perrotta, C. (2018, January). Library not found: The disconnect between gaming research and development. In CSEDU 2018-Proceedings of the 10th International Conference on Computer Supported Education (Vol. 2, No. 2, pp. 134-141). SCITEPRESS-Science and Technology Publications.

Perkmann, M., & Walsh, K. (2009). The two faces of collaboration: impacts of university-industry relations on public research. Industrial and Corporate Change, 18(6), 1033-1065. https://doi.org/10.1093/icc/dtp015

Remy, C., Gegenbauer, S., & Huang, E. (2015). Bridging the Theory-Practice Gap: Lessons and Challenges of Applying the Attachment Framework for Sustainable HCI Design. In (Vol. 2015-, pp. 1305-1314).

Swain, C. (2009, April). Improving academic-industry collaboration for game research and education. In Proceedings of the 4th international conference on Foundations of Digital Games (pp. 191-198).

Wallin, J., Isaksson, O., Larsson, A., & Elfström, B.-O. (2014). Bridging the Gap Between University and Industry: Three Mechanisms for Innovation Efficiency International Journal of Innovation and Technology Management, 11(1). https://doi.org/10.1142/S0219877014400057

Walton, D., & Krabbe, E. C. W. (1995). Commitment in dialogue: Basic concepts of interpersonal reasoning. SUNY Press.

Weststar, J. (2015). Understanding video game developers as an occupational community. Information, communication & society, 18(10), 1238-1252. https://doi.org/10.1080/1369118X.2015.1036094

GESTURE-BASED HEAD-MOUNTED AUGMENTED REALITY GAME DEVELOPMENT USING LEAP MOTION AND USABILITY EVALUATION

Pu-Hsuan Chien and Yang-Cheng Lin
Department of Industrial Design, National Cheng Kung University
No.1, University Road, Tainan, Taiwan

ABSTRACT

The environment of augmented reality created by head-mounted displays can provide players with an immersive gaming experience and proper gestures can enable the integration of real-world objects with the virtual environment. This study explores the usability of gesture operations applied to games and tries to find new applications using current mature gesture sensors. This study develops a head-mounted augmented reality game based on gesture recognition, and evaluates their usability and impact on the user's interaction with the virtual interface. It uses the Unity engine and open-source glasses designed by Leap Motion to develop an adventure game, and it contains elements of a first-person shooter game. There is no need for any joystick or touch screen to control the game, as the game relies only on the player's hands to operate through a controller-less interface. The results show that the system usability score is 79.4, which indicates a good usability level. This study may be of importance in clarifying problems that may be encountered in the development of interactive-gesture head-mounted display augmented reality games. Finally, this study offers suggestions for the challenges and future of head-mounted augmented reality games.

KEYWORDS

Natural User Interface, Gesture, Leap Motion, Head-Mounted Displays, Augmented Reality Game

1. INTRODUCTION

Games are a daily pastime for many people, and various ways of playing can affect the mental state of players (Shin, 2019). In the last decade, many human-computer interaction methods ranging from traditional keyboards to motion sensors have provided new methods of interaction. As this technology advances, games can bring players an immersive experience. Head-mounted displays (HMDs) can impart players with an immersive gaming experience. The technology behind head-mounted virtual reality (VR) games is very mature, with several devices based on them available in the market. However, HMD technology is not used as much in augmented reality (AR) games — currently, most augmented reality (AR) games are on mobile platforms, often requiring holding a mobile phone to play. In recent years, there has been an increasing research interest on AR (Gugenheimer et al., 2019), and most of the research on the use of HMDs in AR games has focused on either solving technical problems (Hua, 2017; Xiao & Benko, 2016) or on improving input factors (Xu et al., 2019). In this study, a set of head-mounted display AR games that can be controlled with both hands has been developed to bring players a new gaming experience.

There are many gesture recognition sensors available. Among them, Microsoft's Kinect and Leap Motion have much related research (Cabreira & Hwang, 2015, Vokorokos et al., 2016). Leap Motion allows users to use gestures to control the operation and is currently widely used in sign language recognition, rehabilitation, and interactive game development (Khademi et al., 2014, Potter et al., 2013). To realize the functions of gesture recognition and AR at the same time, we use the AR HMD developed by Leap Motion in 2018 with open-source glasses. Most of the components are 3D printed, so the price is lower than other head-mounted AR glasses. This method broke through the original form of operation and increased the application of AR, opening up more possibilities for human-computer interaction. Unlike the general Leap Motion operation method, it places the sensor on top of the head so it can effectively recognize gestures when moving.

To study the potential of this device, we developed an AR game, considering the player's operation process and the game interface. The major purpose of this study was to assess the usability of this kind of prototyping game, so participants were asked to rate its usability. Finally, we put forward some problems that may be encountered in the development of this type of game.

2. RELATED WORKS

The game development in this study involves many areas, such as the choice of gesture sensors, how the gestures are used in games, and the game interface design. We consider that the application of gestures in current gesture-based game operation has not been fully studied, so we have limited literature to consider in developing games.

2.1 Gesture Sensor

To date, there have been many studies on the application of gesture sensors. Previous studies have also compared the advantages and disadvantages of these sensors. Some researchers have used Leap Motion in various fields. For example, Cabreira and Hwang conducted experiments on three sensors and analyzed 250 applications, of which more than half were game programs. Their analysis of 15 gestures on each platform indicated that Kinect is more limited than other devices for finger and hand tracking (Cabreira & Hwang, 2015). Leap Motion recognized a wider range of gestures. The most commonly used gestures for Myo were rotation and waving, which could be used consistently in the various programs. Vokorokos et al. (2016) also conducted experiments on three sensors in their research, using pointing, waving, rotating, and fist to determine the gesture accuracy of the devices. Many tests were conducted on the sensors of the three platforms for each movement. Kinect performed well in waving, while Leap Motion performed well in pointing, rotating, and punching. It was fast and intuitive, but the sensing distance was limited. Myo was also very good in rotation, with the advantage that the user can put their hands down to feel more comfortable. Because it uses muscle detection, motion can be easily detected even if the hands are covered or the device is placed in a pocket. Based on the above research, it can be determined that Kinect is very smooth under large-scale gesture sensing such as waving hands. However, other gestures are not very accurate. Its advantages are that it can detect the skeleton of the face and the whole body and that the detection range is wider. Leap Motion's research on AR applications is far more advanced than those of other manufacturers. (Katahira & Soga, 2015; Wozniak et al., 2016). Leap Motion provides open-source AR HMD glasses, the sensor can be placed in a head-mounted device, which solves the original distance limitation of the sensing, but no current research on these glasses has yet appeared. Based on the above research and viewpoints, and because of the good accuracy of Leap Motion and the availability for purchase, this study uses Leap Motion as the sensing device for the AR glasses. Although the sensing range is somewhat limited, changing the Leap Motion device above the HMDs can effectively address this question.

2.2 Gesture Interaction Applied to Games

Existing research on the application of gestures in games, based on their recognition method, can be broadly categorized into two types: visual recognition and motion sensor recognition. Visual recognition primarily relies on Kinect, Leap Motion, and mobile phone lenses for gesture analysis (Pirker et al., 2017; Yeo et al., 2015), while motion sensor recognition uses six-axis sensors or electromyographic signals and usually requires the user to wear additional devices (Esfahlani et al., 2018; Lee et al., 2017).Regarding the research on the use of gesture interactions in games, Silpasuwanchai and Ren (2015) held that in gesture interaction games, not all operational methods are suitable for all players. Therefore, they used user feedback and user-elicitation to get a clear understanding of the actions the players felt were most intuitive and found that various people experience the game differently, and there were also differences in their actions, but there were some gestures that players agreed on. For example, the preferred gesture for shooting was the gesture of using one hand to draw a pistol.

There have been several studies that have investigated the application of Leap Motion in medical, entertainment, and educational fields, such as two-handed drone operation (Fernandez et al., 2016) and hand rehabilitation exercises (Alimanova et al., 2017). The above points out the potential of Leap Motion in the natural user interface. However, little research has been done on the development of in-game applications. Overall, we believe that it has great potential in gaming and entertainment, and we use Leap Motion with AR HMDs to design and develop a game, which will help researchers study the application of human-computer interaction in related game fields in the future.

2.3 Diegetic Interface

When only gestures are used, the interface plays a primary role in games. Previous studies have also pointed out that the design of the interface affects the player's immersion (Brown & Cairns, 2004, Qin et al., 2009). The word "diegesis" was originally a term used in movies to refer to all the stories about the character. Galloway applied this concept to the role of the game. The operation of the role of the game is regarded as diegesis, and non-diegesis refers to the game outside the narrative world. He also distinguished between the behavior of the player and the character. The behavior of the player is divided into diegetic and non-diegetic elements, so according to the corresponding interface of its behavior classification, the heads-up display (HUD) can be used. The HUD is mainly for players to see, so it is an interface superimposed on the game screen (Galloway, 2006). Later writers have voiced the same view. Peacocke et al. studied the user interface of a first-person shooter game based on Galloway's theory. They compared the player's preferences and immersion between the diegetic and non-diegetic interfaces based on the display of the remaining ammunition, using a 5-point Likert scale to evaluate their immersion. He concluded that the digital display interface works best in the diegetic interface (Peacocke et al., 2015). Fagerholt and Lorentzon's theory offered a sounder theoretical basis for interface design. They analyzed and classified first-person design game interfaces, constructed some appropriate professional terms, and provided design guidelines to increase game immersion. However, they deemed that to complete these design guidelines, it is still necessary to have a game prototype design for evaluation (Fagerholt & Lorentzon, 2009). Because this study's game is not a pure first-person shooter game, we primarily divided the interface into the diegetic interface and non- diegetic interface and applied it to our design theory.

3. GAME DESIGN AND DEVELOPMENT

Because this study uses HMDs, we think it is very suitable for first-person games. To allow players to be more integrated into the game, we have created some stories and relatable characters, so it can be regarded as an adventure game with first-person shooting elements. In this study, the player is acting as an adventurer and must help the good dinosaurs defeat the evil dinosaurs within the time allotted for the mission.

The task of the game is to defeat the subordinates of the Demon Ass Dragon King. We established three subordinates with different attributes. The player must switch to an attack with the relative attribute to damage to the target. At the same time, the player must pay attention to supplement their magic value, or they will be unable to attack. Play continues in this level until either the time expires or all monsters are defeated, at which point the game ends.

The gameplay is different from typical games. Because there is no controller, all operations must be done by hand. Operation of the game is as follows:

—Confirm/Next step: thumb up, right hand (Figure 1a).

—Shoot: make a pistol gesture with right hand (Figure 1b).

—Select: finger toggle button interface (Figure 1c).

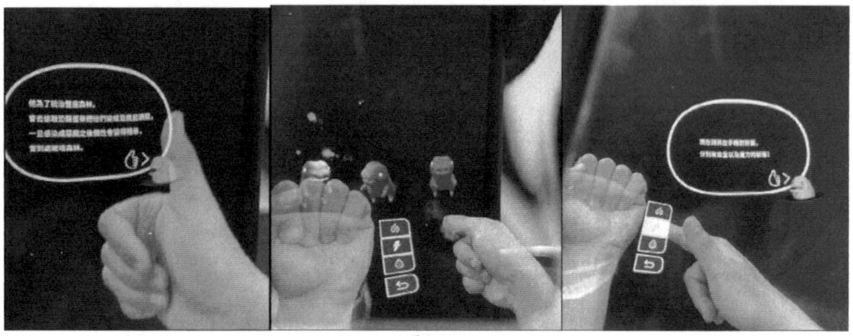

(a) (b) (c)

Figure 1. (a) Confirm, (b) Shoot, (c) Select the menu

According to Galloway's theory, interfaces can be divided into diegetic and non-diegetic interfaces for characters and players. However, there is no relevant research on the interface for first-person head-mounted AR games. Therefore, this study adopted expert interviews and semi-structured interviews. We used expert interviews to understand some professional knowledge of game interfaces to be appropriate for the player's operation.

We interviewed Associate Professor Hu Minjun, an expert in the fields of computer vision and AR/VR. The main questions that the interview was intended to clarify were (1) the current interface problems of HMD games, (2) The way in which players operate games and the priority of visual communication, and (3) the advantages and disadvantages between the diegetic and non-diegetic interfaces and the application suggestions.

After compiling the data from the interview, the following conclusions were drawn. First, we should note the detection sensitivity. It is recommended not to use the most complex gestures in AR or VR. Second, visual communication is more important than the method of operation because a good design can be used to communicate the interaction and make up for the player's lack of experience. Finally, the diegetic interface gives players higher interactivity. If it is desired that the player be a first-person character experiencing the game, the diegetic interface is very important, but the non- diegetic interface is used to assist it, and the two should be used in conjunction with the situation. Therefore, we decided to use the diegetic interface as the main interface first to minimize the HUD on the screen.

The interface plan is as follows:

—Time: diegetic interface (Figure 2).

—Health bar and mana: diegetic interface (Figure 2).

—Menu: diegetic interface (Figure 1c).

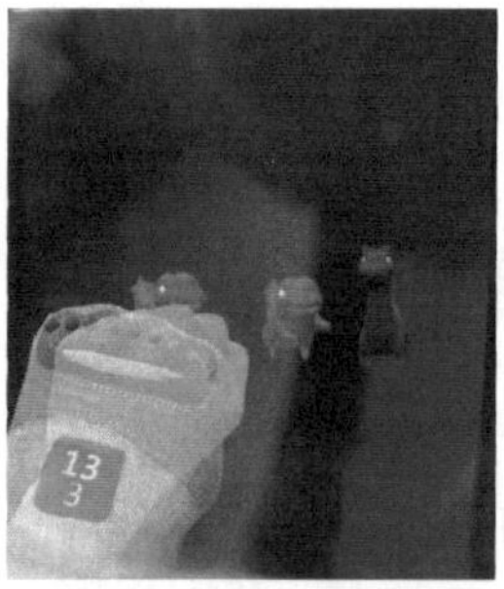

Figure 2. Health bar, mana, and time interface

Thus, the left hand is mainly to display the interface, and the right hand is used for attacking and selecting. After the game starts, a non-player character guides the player into the game, through the story of the game, and to the operation instructions. The thumb is used to attack the monster, and the designated button is used to switch the attack attribute. When the mana is exhausted, the mana must be replenished as soon as possible, or the player will be unable to attack. They need to complete the task within the allotted time, and completing the task sooner will lead to a higher score.

Because we use it with HMDs and Leap Motion, we must first import some software development kit files into Unity. We referred to Takahashi's article to build the game environment, which includes hand calibration and adjustment of the position of the glasses window. This is to allow the player to match the virtual hand in Unity with the actual hand position during the game.

The game also needs related materials such as characters and interfaces. The 3D character model, its skeleton, and animation were all created in Blender, and the material and rendering were done in Unity. The special effects were drawn using Illustrator, with post-production in Photoshop, and the particle special effects were done in Unity. Finally, after the program is created, the game detects the player's hands, with the left hand for the panel, and the right hand for attacking. We use Leap Motion to detect the skeleton of the hand; when the distance between the thumb and the tip of the index finger reaches a certain value, an attack is launched.

Figure 3. Game development screen: Thunder attribute attacks monsters

4. METHOD

This research is a relatively novel way of gaming, and Leap Motion's input method is very different from traditional operation. Most people have not used this type of input device. To understand the usability of the device in the future and how players feel about the game. We evaluated the ease of use based on the system usability score (SUS) and conducted semi-structured interviews to analyze subjective player feedback.

4.1 Participants

We recruited eight participants (four males and four females) ranging in age from 24 to 31 years old ($M = 24.8$, $SD = 1.6$). All were right-handed. Regarding their gaming experience, all participants had experience with VR games, five had experience with AR games, and all were in the habit of playing games. However, no one had ever played a game using gesture controls.

4.2 Apparatus and Material

This research used the AR HMD Project North Star kit released by Leap Motion in 2018 (Figure 4). The helmet was 3D printed and equipped with special polycarbonate lenses and two screens with a resolution of 1440 × 1600 pixels and a frame rate of 120 FPS. The screen image is reflected on the lens so the user can see the real and virtual images at the same time. In addition, we combined headphones with the HMD so players could hear sounds in the game. The game was developed using Unity rather than modifying an existing game. A new game was chosen because existing games usually required a controller to operate and could not be used on our equipment. The interface also needed to be developed by itself. The interface was designed based on the results of the interview and with reference to the videos released by Leap Motion.

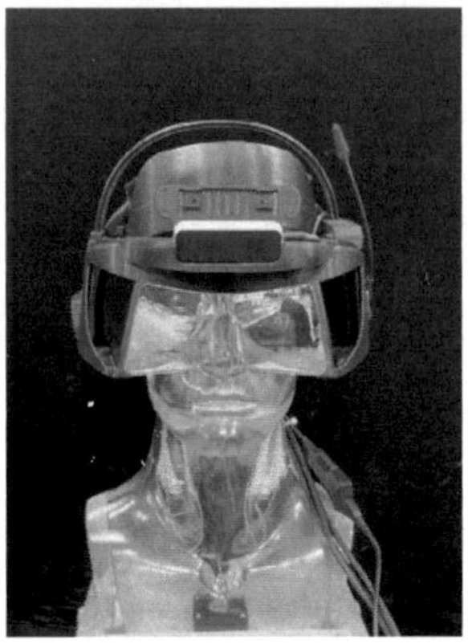

Figure 4. Leap Motion AR HMD with Project North Star kit

4.3 Procedure

The participants selected were instructed to play the game to the best of their ability. Because there were instructions in the game, we did not teach the subjects separately. This was to allow players to play the game smoothly just by watching the instructions. After the game started, NPCs explained the plot, operation methods, and tasks to the players. Monsters had different attributes, and players needed to attack them with corresponding attributes. All players had eight points of mana, and each attack consumed one point. After the mana was exhausted, the player needed to click on the interface to replenish the mana. The game was over after they killed all the monsters. After completing the task, the players filled in the SUS to evaluate the usability of the game subjectively, and we conducted semi-structured interviews to obtain more in-depth and specific suggestions.

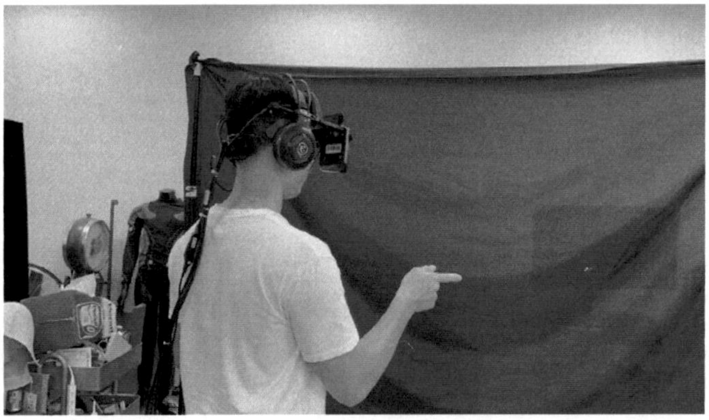

Figure 5. The process of players operating the game

5. RESULTS AND DISCUSSION

The participants were asked to fill out the SUS. The SUS score is divided into six levels: A, 90–100 points; B, 80–89 points; C, 70–79 points; D, 60–69 points; and F, 0–59 points. A qualified system should be higher than 68 points. The SUS was originally intended to evaluate system usability, but it can also be used to evaluated websites and games. Therefore, the word "system" in the questions was replaced by "game." The results show that our game SUS average score was 79.4 points, which falls in the C grade, which means that the usability qualified. The questions were as follows, of which 2, 4, 6, 8, and 10 are reverse questions:

Table 1. SUS Questions and Score

Question	Score	STDev
1. I think that I would like to play this game frequently.	**8.4**	0.52
2. I found the game unnecessarily complex.	**6.9**	0.72
3. I thought the game was easy to use.	**7.8**	0.64
4. I think that I would need the support of a technical person to be able to play this game.	**7.2**	0.83
5. I found the various functions in this game were well integrated.	**7.2**	0.64
6. I thought there was too much inconsistency in this game.	**9.1**	0.52
7. I would imagine that most people would learn to play this game very quickly.	**8.8**	0.53
8. I found the game very cumbersome to play.	**8.1**	0.89
9. I felt very confident playing the game.	**6.6**	0.74
10. I needed to learn a lot of things before I could get going with this game.	**9.4**	0.46

The weighted means of each question are presented in Figure 6. All players thought that the rules of the game were easy and they did not need to learn many things. Question 9 had the lowest score, which may be due to players sometimes being inaccurate, which would lower their self-confidence.

In the post-experiment interviews, the responses were generally positive. This study yielded the following results: Some players thought it was very interesting because they could see their hands operating the game. Four subjects said they felt immersed and felt that the characters in the game seemed to exist in the real world, and they could be even more integrated into the game than in VR games. The game instructions were simple and easy to understand, which helped players enter the game. It is worth mentioning that the sound effects played a helpful role in the game. Most players thought that the sound effects gave them significant feedback. If they lacked these sound effects, they would not be able to control the game, and the music brought about emotional changes, which were also indispensable.

However, our game is not without problems. Due to the limitation of Leap Motion's detection range, gestures may sometimes not be detected. Various angles should be attempted for detection. Regarding the interface, some players suggested that the button interface should be larger and that a gap between the buttons would make them easier to operate and reduce the chance of accidentally touching other buttons. In addition, participants noted that the mana had to be filled too frequently. I interpret this to mean that the participants probably did not like frequent operations.

Based on the information from previous interviews and the literature, we chose to use the diegetic interface. The advantage is that it allows players to become more integrated into the game, but the disadvantage is that some interfaces cannot be displayed immediately. Some players liked this interface because they thought it made the screen concise, but it also required frequent operation of the interface. Some players also pointed out that they preferred the HUD interface, that is, the non-diegetic interface, which helped them understand the required information in real time, although it occupied part of the layout. It can be seen that players have different preferences for the interface. The players' immersion and preference for the interface need additional study. Overall, we think this project is a success. Although there are some restrictions regarding sensor issues that need to be resolved, all the players had a good gaming experience. Finally, we believe that the interface should be able to successfully assist players. If players can fully master the game, their immersion will increase. Therefore, future goals should focus on these projects.

6. CONCLUSION

Previous studies on the application of Leap Motion to games mostly focus on object manipulation, but this research uses Leap Motion in the game mode of HMDs. There has thus far been relatively little research in this area. This research adds many interface aids, such as buttons and the interface attached to the hand, which can provide help for the development of gesture-related interactive games in the future. Our results show that even without operating a controller, a player can still control the game and have an interesting gaming experience. Players have indicated that this method of operation is very new. The lack of precision of the operation, if not complete control of the game, will result in the loss of the player's sense of immersion. Thus, this input method may be more suitable for the type of game that does not require precise operation rather than a competitive type of game. Although this study has its limitations, this game can serve as a basis for relevant head-mounted gesture-based game development.

We think there are two directions for development in the future: First, additional location trackers should be added to ensure that every gesture of the player can be detected. We also think that if gestures can achieve more precise operations, the game will have broader development opportunities, not limited to simple minigames but also more gesture operations can be developed. Second, we plan to do further research on the game interface and test diegetic and non-diegetic interfaces, including displaying the player's health bar, menu, time, and remaining ammo/mana, to understand the player's preference for the interface and create an interface suitable for HMD AR games.

REFERENCES

Alimanova, M. et al., 2017. Gamification of hand rehabilitation process using virtual reality tools: Using leap motion for hand rehabilitation. *In IEEE 2017 First International Conference on Robotic Computing (IRC).* Taichung, Taiwan, pp. 336-339.

Brown, E. and Cairns, P., 2004. A grounded investigation of game immersion. *In CHI'04 extended abstracts on Human factors in computing systems.* Vienna, Austria, pp. 1297-1300.

Cabreira, A. T. and Hwang, F., 2015. An analysis of mid-air gestures used across three platforms. *Proceedings of the 2015 British HCI Conference*, Lincoln Lincolnshire, United Kingdom, pp. 257-258.

Esfahlani, S. S. et al., 2018. Validity of the Kinect and Myo armband in a serious game for assessing upper limb movement. *Entertainment Computing*, 27, pp. 150-156.

Fagerholt, E. and Lorentzon, M., 2009. *Beyond the HUD-user interfaces for increased player immersion in FPS games.* Master's thesis. Chalmers University of Technology, Göteborg, Sweden.

Fernandez, R. A. S. et al., 2016. Natural user interfaces for human-drone multi-modal interaction. *In 2016 International Conference on Unmanned Aircraft Systems (ICUAS), IEEE.* Arlington, USA, pp. 1013-1022.

Galloway, A. R., 2006. *Gaming: Essays on algorithmic culture (Vol. 18).* U of Minnesota Press, Minnesota.

Gugenheimer, J. et al., 2019. Challenges using head-mounted displays in shared and social spaces. *Paper presented at the Extended Abstracts of the 2019 CHI Conference on Human Factors in Computing Systems.*

Hua, H., 2017. Enabling focus cues in head-mounted displays. *Proceedings of the IEEE, 105*(5), pp. 805-824.

Katahira, R. and Soga, M., 2015. Development and evaluation of a system for AR enabling realistic display of gripping motions using Leap Motion controller. *Procedia Computer Science, 60*, pp. 1595-1603.

Khademi, M. et al., 2014. Free-hand interaction with leap motion controller for stroke rehabilitation. *In CHI'14 Extended Abstracts on Human Factors in Computing Systems.* Toronto, Canada, pp. 1663-1668.

Lee, S. et al., 2017. User study of VR basic controller and data glove as hand gesture inputs in VR games. *Paper presented at the 2017 International Symposium on Ubiquitous Virtual Reality (ISUVR).*

Peacocke, M. et al., 2015. Evaluating the effectiveness of HUDs and diegetic ammo displays in first-person shooter games. *Paper presented at the 2015 IEEE Games Entertainment Media Conference (GEM).* Toronto, Canada, pp. 1-8.

Pirker, J. et al., 2017. Gesture-based interactions in video games with the leap motion controller. *Paper presented at the International Conference on Human-Computer Interaction.*

Potter, L. E. et al., 2013. The leap motion controller: a view on sign language. *Paper presented at the Proceedings of the 25th Australian computer-human interaction conference: augmentation, application, innovation, collaboration.* Adelaide, Australia, pp. 175-178.

Qin, H. et al., 2009. Measuring player immersion in the computer game narrative. *Intl. Journal of Human–Computer Interaction*, 25(2), pp. 107-133.

Shin, D., 2019. How does immersion work in augmented reality games? A user-centric view of immersion and engagement. *Information, Communication & Society*, 22(9), pp. 1212-1229.

Vokorokos, L. et al., 2016. Motion sensors: Gesticulation efficiency across multiple platforms. *In 2016 IEEE 20th Jubilee International Conference on Intelligent Engineering Systems (INES), IEEE.* Budapest, Hungary, pp. 293-298.

Wozniak, P. et al., 2016. Possible applications of the LEAP motion controller for more interactive simulated experiments in augmented or virtual reality. *Paper presented at the Optics Education and Outreach IV.*

Xiao, R. et al., 2016. Augmenting the field-of-view of head-mounted displays with sparse peripheral displays. *Paper presented at the Proceedings of the 2016 CHI Conference on Human Factors in Computing Systems.*

Xu, W. et al., 2019. Pointing and selection methods for text entry in augmented reality head mounted displays. *Paper presented at the 2019 IEEE International Symposium on Mixed and Augmented Reality (ISMAR).*

Yeo, H.-S. et al., 2015. Hand tracking and gesture recognition system for human-computer interaction using low-cost hardware. *Multimedia Tools and Applications, 74(8), pp.* 2687-2715.

USING INTERACTIVE MOBILE APPS FOR HEALTHCARE EDUCATION WITH A MIGRANT INDIAN POPULATION IN HONG KONG

Matthew William Fendt[1], Shelby Garner[1], Cho Lee Wong[2], Carolin George[3], Phil Young[1], Hope Koch[1], Gina Green[1] and Julia Hitchcock[1]
[1]*Baylor University, USA*
[2]*The Chinese University of Hong Kong, Hong Kong*
[3]*Bangalore Baptist Hospital, India*

ABSTRACT

Due to mobile devices' prevalence, mobile health applications can provide healthcare education to populations that might not otherwise have access to it. A mobile health app was developed to teach about the prevention and treatment of hypertension and diabetes. This app was specifically designed and tailored for an Indian population since these noncommunicable diseases are large contributors to death in Indian adults. A population of migrant Indian workers located in Hong Kong was given healthcare instruction through the app. They showed statistically significant improvement on a pre/post-test about both hypertension and diabetes after interacting with the videos and game in the app. This demonstrates the effectiveness of mobile health apps at providing targeted healthcare education.

KEYWORDS

Mobile Health, Health Care, Learning Games

1. INTRODUCTION

The World Health Organization (WHO, 2019a) describes mobile health, or mHealth, as the use of mobile or wireless technologies to improve public health outcomes and advocates for its use among vulnerable populations who may have poor access to healthcare. The evolution of cell phones from 2-way analog devices to smartphones in recent years has provided an accessible pathway for interactions between health providers and public health populations (Garner et al., 2018; Sondaal et al., 2016). mHealth applications (apps) are increasingly designed to promote a wide range of health interventions such as public health education, disease prevention, diagnosis and management (Haenssgen & Ariana, 2017). However, mHealth apps containing culturally relevant information to address health priorities among some vulnerable populations remain limited (Garner et al., 2018; Garner et al., 2021; Sondaal et al., 2016).

Noncommunicable diseases (NCD) such as hypertension and diabetes are among the top contributors of death among adults ages 30-70 in India. Asian-Indians have one of the highest mortality rates from these diseases in the South East Asia region (WHO, 2019b). These poor health outcomes extend to Asian-Indians who have migrated to Hong Kong where the migrant worker population is proliferating and make up at least 10% of the domestic workforce (Agyemang et al., 2019; Liu et al, 2013 & Lestari & Li, 2019). In a clinical trial of 760 migrants from India to China, diabetes and hypertension outcomes (glycemic control and blood pressure) were poorer than that of Chinese nationals (Department of Family Medicine, Queen Elizabeth Hospital, 2014). Health providers recognize there is a need for culturally relevant health resources for this population to improve health knowledge and health outcomes.

We sought to create a mHealth app that teaches about hypertension and diabetes in an engaging and accessible way. A combined hypertension-diabetes app that contained culturally relevant videos and also small games and other engagements was developed for a specifically Indian population. We evaluated the app's effectiveness at teaching about hypertension and diabetes through a pre/post-test evaluation and found statistically significant improvements in participants regarding both hypertension and diabetes.

2. RELATED WORK

Mobile health initiatives have shown effectiveness in improving health outcomes, particularly in low and middle income countries (LMICs) (Sondaal et al., 2016). A systematic review was conducted to assess the impact of mHealth interventions on improving maternal and neonatal care in LMICs. Authors found mHealth interventions contributed to health service utilization including increased use of birth attendants and improved vaccination rates. However, few mHealth studies have focused on improving NCD outcomes among Indian populations. In a systematic review of clinical trials to assess the health-related impacts of mHealth on NCDs in LMICs, only 2 out of 8 studies were included from India (Stephani et al., 2016). These studies focused on the use of mHealth apps to improve compliance related to diabetes (Shetty et al., 2011) and cardiovascular disease (Tian et al., 2015). Results from the systematic review indicated mHealth interventions were primarily positive in promoting health, improving health appointment follow up compliance and providing clinical decision support systems (Stephani et al., 2016).

Our multidisciplinary and international mHealth team was composed of researchers and industry professionals from Computer Science, Nursing, Medicine, Management Information Systems, Art, Animation and Information Technology from the United States and India. The team collaborated from 2017-2020 to design and test two mHealth NCD apps among participants in Bengaluru, India. In 2018, our hypertension app was designed and tested among N=346 participants living in rural villages (48.3%) and urban slums (51.7%) (Garner et al., 2021). A single arm pre/post-test design was used. Results indicated that the app was effective in improving hypertension health knowledge among participants ($p<.0001$). In 2020, a clinical trial was conducted to assess the effectiveness of our diabetes app in improving diabetes knowledge among N=291 participants in an urban slum in India. The intervention group who used the diabetes mHealth app (N=142) was compared with a control group (N=149) who received oral counseling on diabetes, the standard of care in India. While both groups yielded statistically significant improvements in knowledge after learning about diabetes ($P<.0001$) there was no statistically significant difference between post test scores between groups.

3. APP DESIGN

This study used an app that was a combination of the two health apps previously developed by the team. The first app was a 3D animated video designed to teach about hypertension. This app was not interactive, but just consisted of the instructional video. The second app was a 3D animated video that also used games and other interactions in addition to the video. It consisted of four 2-minute videos, each with a game or interaction presented afterwards designed to reinforce the video's instructional material. This app was designed to teach about diabetes. For the combined version of the app in this study, a 10 question pre and post-test was added for each of hypertension and diabetes. The overall flow of the app is shown in Figure 1.

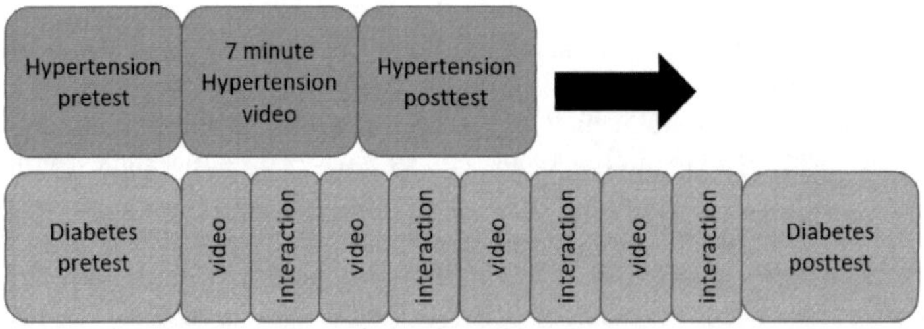

Figure 1. The structure of the combined mHealth app on hypertension and diabetes

Both apps were designed to teach about a particular disease that is especially prevalent to Indian culture. They were designed in collaboration with Indian doctors and software designers. Since the majority of the research team is American, these cultural resources were essential so we could target appropriate references to the audience. For example, we might have listed potato chips as an example of junk food, but our Indian team members suggested jalebi instead, which is a more common snack food in India. Another example of cultural advice our Indian team members provided was appropriate color and dress of the characters in our animation.

For the animation and interactions, we wanted to make sure to provide the content in an exciting and engaging manner. Another consideration is that although the material is serious, we wanted to make sure that it was not presented in a frightening fashion that would be a deterrent to the viewer and prevent them from engaging. An anthropomorphic animated monkey is the key character in both parts of the app. A narrator describes the dangers of the diseases and what can happen if it is left untreated, as well as how to prevent and treat the disease. The monkey character acts out both aliments and the treatments. The hypertension video takes place between three people as a casual interaction at a sales stand. In the diabetes video, guests at a wedding talk with a woman who has diabetes and is now successfully treating it. An example screenshot of the diabetes app is shown in Figure 2.

Figure 2. A screenshot of the instructional video portion of the app

4. GAMES AND INTERACTIONS IN THE APP

The primary author was brought on the project at the beginning of creation of the second app, the one on diabetes. He helped develop the games and interactions that are interspersed in the diabetes app. The intention is to engage the viewer so that they are not just a passive observer. The viewer watches a two-minute video, then plays through an interaction that reinforces the section's instructional content. The interaction is designed to only take a few seconds to complete as to not break the immersion of the video.

The first small video is about how diabetes can be caused. The interaction reinforces the concept of insulin acting as a key to unlock the body's cells to be able to receive blood glucose. This is a simple interaction where the viewer sees an animation of the blood glucose unable to enter the cell. They then hit a button showing a key, and the video shows the insulin acting as a key to unlock the cells.

The second video discusses the dangers of untreated diabetes. The interaction presents the viewer with a series of animated buttons illustrating possible ailments caused by the disease. After they select each correct answer, the app reinforces their correct answer.

The third video shows how to eat in a healthy way to prevent and manage diabetes. In this interaction, the viewer is presented with a number of foods and a plate split into one half and two quarters. Following the MyPlate method of one-half fruits and vegetables and one-quarter grains and proteins, the viewer selects an appropriate meal. They must avoid junk food and choose correction portions for the food. This process is repeated two more times with different foods. This activity was the longest, most game-like, and involved of all four interactions. A screenshot of the game is shown in Figure 3.

Figure 3. The plate game challenged participants to create a healthy meal and portion correctly in order to help prevent diabetes

Finally, the last video talks about healthy habits to prevent and manage diabetes. The interaction shows an animated loop of the happy monkey and his bird friend walking towards the user. Like the second interaction, the viewer is shown illustrated buttons with possible activities that one might do to combat diabetes, and after each correct selection, the viewer is given positive reinforcement.

The intention of all of these simple interactions is to engage the viewer so they are not completely passive. The interaction is meant to contribute to the learning aspect which is evaluated by the post-test.

5. EXPERIMENTAL DESIGN

Research Assistants fluent in English and Hindi recruited particpants who were participating in activities associated with a variety of ethnic minority organizations in Hong Kong. 46 Indian people, living in Hong Kong, completed the study. They were asked a number of demographics questions, including how long they have lived in Hong Kong. 10 lived there less than one year, 19 lived there 1-10 years, and 17 lived there 11 years or more. Most (25) were in the 35-59 age group, with 18-34 being the second most common. 28 were women, and 18 were men.

Among participants, 30.4% lived in urban Hong Kong and 59.6% were from rural areas. Most, 65.2%, completed the app in English while 34.8% completed it in Hindi. 8.7% had never attended school, while 91.3% had completed at least a 9th-10th grade education. The majority were employed at 73.9%. 15.2% reported a history of diabetes or hypertension, 17.4 reported the use of cigarettes or smokeless tobacco and 41.3% reported alcohol use.

A researcher explained the purpose of the student and obtained consent from the participant. They completed the demographic information survey and then went through the pretest/ instruction/post-test sequence for hypertension and then diabetes. The research also collected qualitative feedback from the participant.

Our hypothesis is as follows:

Hypothesis: Participants that engaged with the instructional videos and interactions would show a statistically significant improvement on their post-test scores compared to their pretest scores.

6. EXPERIMENTAL RESULTS

A paired t-test was run on the pretest and post-test scores for both hypertension and diabetes. In both cases, there was a statistically significant improvement on the participants' post-test scores.

For hypertension, t = 5.498, degrees of freedom = 45, and the p value was 1.725e-06. The descriptive statistics for the hypertension pretest were: mean 6.48, standard deviation 2.008, median 7 and for the post-test were: mean 7.74, standard deviation 1.357, median 8.

For diabetes, t=8.46, degrees of freedom = 45, and the p value was 7.467e-11. The descriptive statistics for the diabetes pretest were: mean 6.413, standard deviation 2.578, median 7 and for the post-test were: mean 9.5, standard deviation 1.188, median 10. A summary of these statistics is given in Table 1.

Table 1. A summary of the post-test improvement for the hypertension and diabetes sections of the app. Participants showed a statistically significant improvement in both sections

	Pretest	Posttest	Improvement	p value
Hypertension	6.48	7.74	1.26	1.725e-06
Diabetes	6.41	9.50	3.10	7.467e-11

The number of participants that got each question correct versus incorrect for the pre and post-tests was also measured. This data is shown in Table 2. Most participants got almost all of the questions correct in the post-test except for questions 6, 8, and 9 in the hypertension test. These questions were "Does high BP always cause symptoms?", "Someone having a stroke might have which happen?" and "The best way to know if I have high BP is to pay attention to abnormal feelings is:" It seems like these questions were either confusing or not taught well in the app, and account for the larger improvement in the diabetes test scores.

Table 2. Pre and post-test correct answers for hypertension and diabetes

	Q1	Q2	Q3	Q4	Q5	Q6	Q7	Q8	Q9	Q10
H pre	33	36	26	36	34	25	43	19	9	37
H post	45	42	38	44	44	20	46	28	7	42
D pre	21	32	34	15	22	19	33	40	38	41
D post	46	45	44	43	45	44	44	43	41	42

ANOVA was run on the improvement of the post-test scores and the demographic variables for both hypertension and diabetes. There was a statistically significant difference between people that had attended school versus not people that had attended school on their post-test scores (p = 0.04 for hypertension and p = 0.006 for diabetes). Figure 4 summarizes this data. Those that had not attended school showed a significant gain in knowledge in both hypertension and diabetes, compared to the more modest gain for those that had attended school. Both groups had statistically significant gains overall and ended at a similar post-test score. However, those that had not attended school had their knowledge start low and ended high, as opposed to those that had attended school whose knowledge started medium and ended high.

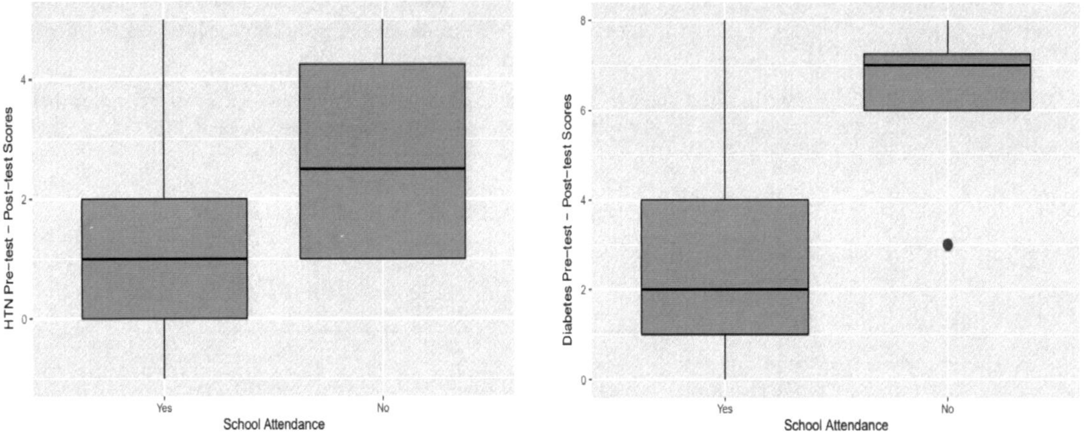

Figure 4. Those that have not attended school showed a statistically significantly larger improvement on their post-test scores, compared to those that have attended school, on both hypertension and diabetes

7. QUALITATIVE DATA

Researchers conducted 18 after-study interviews to assess the participants' perception of the app's strengths and weaknesses. The perceptions addressed the app overall and the plate game.

Overall app and interaction: Several participants said they liked the interactive nature of the app, which has a cyclic learning process of showing and evaluating understanding of the material. They appreciated that the app was not scary, with one person saying: "*even if somebody is suffering from something, it does not scare you.*" Five different people commented explicitly on the entertaining nature of the game, with one saying, "*It's not a very boring doctor speech kind of a thing.*" Many people liked the monkey and the parrot mascots. We had some feedback that the app could be shown to a younger audience so that the intervention could begin at an early age or that the app could send out reminders on people's phones to reinforce the learning content.

Plate game specifically: Many people reported that they liked the plate game, citing that it was a useful tool at teaching healthy eating and proportions. One person said that "*It's not only fun; you also learn. I didn't know that – I always thought you had to consume more protein than vegetables, but now I know through the app that I should consume more vegetables and one-fourth of protein, and one-fourth of carbohydrates.*" Some people suggested having more or different food options to choose from when constructing their plates or having fewer iterations of the game's plate composition aspect or having fewer iterations of the game's plate composition aspect.

8. DISCUSSION AND FUTURE WORK

The app produced statistically significant learning gains in healthcare education about both hypertension and diabetes, demonstrating its effectiveness as a learning tool. The app seemed disproportionately effective for those that have not attended school. Also, people found the app interesting and engaging and participants found the plate game useful at learning healthy meal composition and proportions. It could be useful in the future to evaluate long-term learning that was a result of the app as opposed to just short-term learning gains, or evaluate to see if learning from the app led to any change of behavior. Since the app was designed specifically for an Indian population, it is likely that a different population would not benefit from it as much as did the Indian population. However, a different population could also be evaluated to see how much of the learning gains would transfer over. If there is still sufficient learning gain, opening the app up to a general audience would allow for more people to benefit from it.

In addition to the app being an effective learning tool, creating and distributing a mHealth app can be easier than providing traditional medical interventions. In the traditional Indian model (Balagopal et al., 2008), healthcare workers go out to the people and teach about health care individually to the population. This direct intervention requires time, training, and expense. In contrast, delivering medical education with an app only requires publish the app in an available location and publicizing it to the target audience. A future study could evaluate to see if there is a difference for the participants in learning between this app and a healthcare worker. To increase its accessibility, the app is in the process of being published on the Google Play store as "I Feel Great India." The prevalence of mobile devices greatly increases the accessibility of healthcare education.

9. CONCLUSION

A mobile health app was designed to teach about hypertension and diabetes, specifically targeting an Indian population. This app was evaluated for effectiveness in healthcare education among a migrant Indian population in Hong Kong. The research found statistically significant improvement in post-test scores about both hypertension and diabetes after interacting with the videos and games in the app. The app's efficacy, combined with the reach that mobile apps provide, shows a promising route for providing targeted healthcare education, especially to vulnerable populations.

REFERENCES

Agyemang C, van den Born B-J, 2019. Noncommunicable diseases in migrants: an expert review. J Travel Med. 26(2). doi:10.1093/jtm/tay107

Balagopal P. et al, 2008. A community-based diabetes prevention and management education program in a rural village in India.By: Diabetes Care, 31(6), 1935-5548,

Department of Family Medicine and GOPC, Queen Elizabeth Hospital, 30 Gascoigne Road, Kowloon, Hong Kong, Chen CX, Chan K. Type 2 diabetes management in Hong Kong ethnic minorities: what primary care physicians need to know. Hong Kong Med J. Published online January 30, 2014. doi:10.12809/hkmj134035

Garner, S. et al, 2021. Effectiveness of an mHealth application to improve hypertension health literacy in India. International Nursing Review. 67(4), 476-483. doi:10.1111/INR.12616

Garner, S.L. et al, 2018. Smart phone accessibility and mHealth use in a limited resource setting. International Journal of Nursing Practice, 24, e12609. https://doi.org/10.1111/ijn.12609

Haenssgen, M. J., & Ariana, P, 2017. The social implications of technology diffusion: Uncovering the unintended consequences of people's health-related mobile phone use in rural India and China. World Development, 94, 286-304. http://dx.doi.org/10.1016/j.worlddev.2017.01.014

Lestari E, Li P, 2019. Fighting for Migrant Workers in Hong Kong. Mon Rev. Published online February 1, 2019 56-63. doi:10.14452/MR-070-09-2019-02_4

Liu S. et al, 2013. Comparison of Health Status and Health Care Services Utilization between Migrants and Natives of the Same Ethnic Origin—The Case of Hong Kong. Int J Environ Res Public Health. 10(2):606-622. doi:10.3390/ijerph10020606

Shetty AS. et al, 2011. Reinforcement of adherence to prescription recommendations in Asian Indian diabetes patients using short message service (SMS)–a pilot study. J Assoc Physicians India. 59(7)11–4.

Sondaal, S. F. et al, 2016. Assessing the effect of mHealth interventions in improving maternal and neonatal care in low and middle income countries: a systematic review. PLoS One, 1–26. https://doi.org/10.1371/journal.pone.0154664

Stephani, V. et al, 2016. A systematic review of randomized controlled trials of mHealth interventions against noncommunicable diseases in developing countries. BMC Public Health, 16, 572. doi:10.1186/s12889-016-3226-3

Tian M. et al., 2015. A cluster-randomized controlled trial of a simplified multifaceted management program for individuals at high cardiovascular risk (SimCard Trial) in Rural Tibet, China, and Haryana, India. Circulation. 132(9):815–24.

World Health Organization, 2019a. WHO guideline: Recommendations on Digital Interventions for Health System Strengthening. https://www.who.int/publications-detail/who-guideline-recommendations-ondigital-interventions-for-health-system-strengthening accessed 1 June 2019 .

World Health Organization, 2019b. Monitoring Health for the SDGs Sustainable Development Goals. https://www.who.int/publications/i/item/world-health-statistics-2019-monitoring-health-for-the-sdgs-sustainable-development-goals Accessed 1 December 2020.

INTRICATE COLLABORATION AND TECHNICAL INTEGRATION

Tobias Karlsson
Division of Game Development
University of Skövde, Sweden

ABSTRACT

This article presents a literature review of game research that focuses on the interdisciplinary, collaborative, practical and social aspects of game development. It investigates recurring research questions, topics and suggested purpose of current research in order to generate a coherent summary of the state of research and future possibilities. Due to the interdisciplinary, technical and creative nature of game development, it constitutes a broad and complex research field. However, as researchers often approach game development from a specific research field, the interdisciplinary aspects and complexities are set aside. This has created a substantial gap between academia and the game industry. Thus, it has been suggested that an overarching understanding of each element of game development, as well as their interconnectivity is essential to reduce the gap between academia and game industry, and generate research that is beneficial to both sides. The presented literature review focus on research that applies a more overarching approach, in an effort to explore and distinguish key factors and propose future research areas. Based on the gathered data, it is clear that the investigated field is still in an exploratory stage. However, comparison of recurring topics generated indications towards research areas that could potentially be of importance to both industry and academia.

KEYWORDS

Game Development, Game Production, Game Industry, Interdisciplinary

1. INTRODUCTION

With a predicted market worth of $256.97 billion and approximately 2.5 billion players world-wide by the year 2025 (Dobrilova, 2019), video games is a continuously growing focal point for society as well as researchers. Although a number of studies have been conducted regarding societal and cultural aspects of video games from a player-centric perspective, until recently, there has been lacking focus on development side of games. However, as the game industry grows, it is not only important to focus on the outcomes of playing games, but also on game development as well as the people creating the games (McDaniel, 2015; Panourgias et al., 2014; Weststar, 2015, 2015; Whitson, 2020). Previous studies regarding game development have mainly encompassed narrow areas of development, especially from a software engineering perspective, albeit some articles focus on creative or managerial aspects of game development (Engström et al., 2018; Whitson, 2020). As game developers utilize a highly collaborative and interdisciplinary work process, narrow research might not be applicable for practitioners, as it only engages a small part of the production, whilst everything and everyone needs to work together in game development (Engström et al., 2018). Looking at game research as a whole; there has been a lack of holistic research focusing on the intricate collaboration between creative disciplines, such as artists or composers, and technical disciplines, such as engineers (Engström et al., 2018; McDaniel, 2015; McDaniel and Daer, 2016; Panourgias et al., 2014; Weststar, 2015; Whitson, 2020).

Engineering culture certainly intersects with the work of game development, but it is precisely the intersection of engineering worlds with art, design and business perspectives that makes the study of game development distinct. (O'Donnell, 2014, p. 7)

Research regarding the complex interdisciplinary practice of game development might not only provide new research opportunities and expand the research field, but may also be used to improve work practices within the industry and game education (McDaniel and Daer, 2016; Passarelli et al., 2020; Whitson, 2020). By observing and interviewing game developers in their daily work routine, researchers strive to reduce a knowledge gap in game research. This gap constitutes a lack of knowledge in everyday realities for game developers and the sociotechnical aspects of game development, as those subjects have heretofore been sparsely researched (McDaniel, 2015; Panourgias et al., 2014; Weststar, 2015; Whitson, 2020).

This paper presents a systematic literature review of game research that covers the everyday realities for game developers and the interdisciplinary, collaborative, practical and social aspects of game development. Recurring aspects and discrepancies are analyzed and discussed to elucidate key points in current research.

2. REVIEW METHODOLOGY

2.1 Search Process and Exclusion Criteria

Just like game development, research focusing on game development transcends disciplines, which subsequently results in a varied terminology. Thus, instead constructing a general search query, a three phase search method was used, to expand queries as the process progressed:

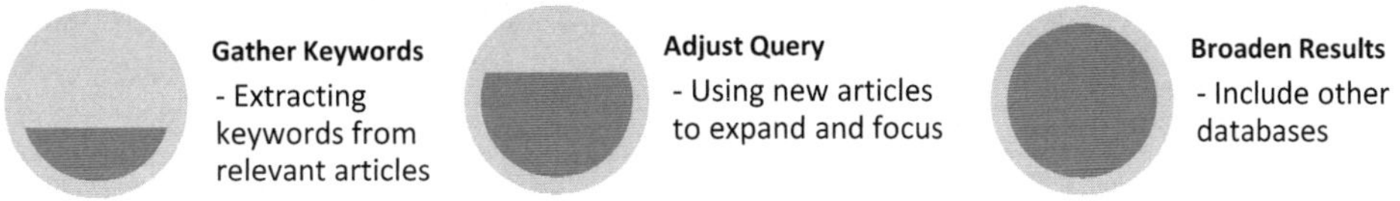

Figure 1. Search phases

A screening process, using abstract analysis, was also set up to exclude articles that were deemed irrelevant to the subject matter. Criteria for exclusion was;

- articles focusing on serious games or student projects (as the primary focus of this paper was commercial/entertainment games);
- articles focusing on playing games, rather than developing games;
- non-English articles. Due to the language barrier for the researcher.

Criteria for inclusion was:

- articles focusing on development of commercial/entertainment games;
- articles focusing on game companies and/or the game industry;
- articles focusing on game developers;

The literature search process began by locating recurring keywords and terminology in a set of relevant articles from different venues on the subject of interdisciplinary game research; (Berg Marklund et al., 2019; Jørgensen, 2019; McDaniel and Daer, 2016; Whitson, 2020). The initial title, abstract and keyword search was conducted on Scopus using the query; *(game* W/1 (develop* OR produc*)) AND (game* W/1 (studio* OR firm* OR compan*)*), resulting in 212 records (2020-09-23). After the abstract review, applying exclusion and inclusion criteria, only 10 articles remained. Thus, the search algorithm was adjusted, using keywords from some of the newly acquired articles. The second search, also on Scopus, used the query; *(game* W/2 (develop* OR design* OR produc*)) AND (artist* OR designer* OR programming OR engineer* OR musician* OR composer* OR writer* OR author*) AND studio**, resulting in 112 records (2020-09-23) and 14 more articles after abstract review. In an attempt to broaden the results, searches were conducted with more inclusive queries, such as; *(game* W/2 (develop* OR design* OR produc*)) AND interdisc**, resulting in more records (312 records, 2020-09-24), but generating no new articles after abstract review. Finally, as an inclusive measure, searches were conducted in two other databases using some of the most prominent keywords. IEEE Xplore was searched using; *(game* NEAR/2 (develop* OR design* OR produc*)) AND "Full Text .AND. Metadata":studio**, generating 425 records (2020-09-24) and 2 new articles after abstract analysis. Web of Science was searched using; *((game* NEAR/2 (develop* OR produc*)) AND "game industry" AND ("case stud*"))*, generating 27 records (2020-09-24) and 4 new articles after abstract analysis.

2.2 Content Coding

The content of the selected articles was analyzed and coded using MaxQDA (*MaxQDA2018*, 2018). Two general research questions were created to facilitate the coding process and elucidate the purpose of the review:

- RQ1. What is the most prominent research focus within the gathered literature?
- RQ2. How does the gathered literature cover everyday realities for game developers and the interdisciplinary, collaborative, practical and social aspects of game development?

A coding scheme was produced, alongside the research questions, to facilitate the literature review and give an overview of the most prominent research topics. The first coding pass categorized each article, based on its primary topic or focus area, to distinguish key elements in the gathered literature. This generated four primary topics. The second coding pass categorized specific paragraphs in each article as an effort to facilitate cross-referencing and comparing subtopics in the gathered literature.

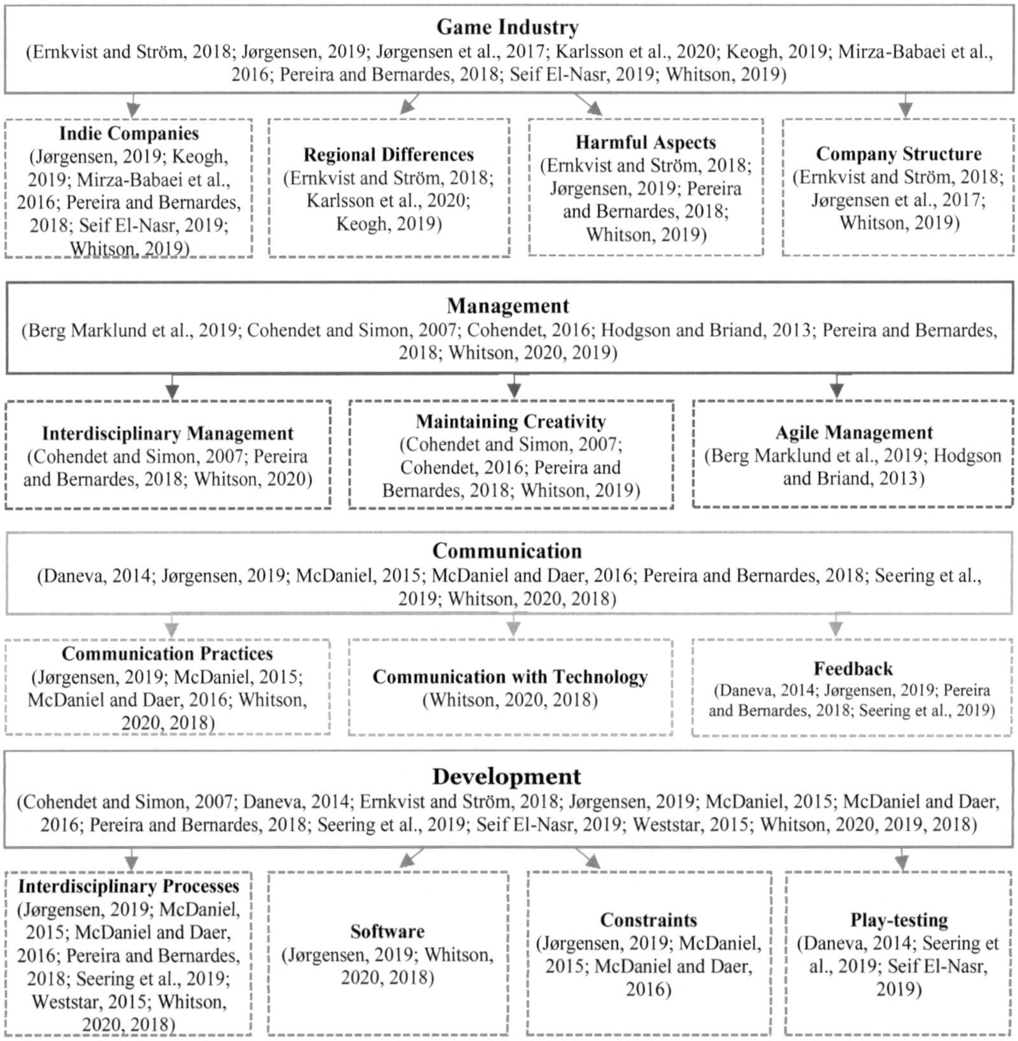

Figure 2. Research topics and sub-topics

3. LITERATURE REVIEW

Based on the primary topics derived from the content coding, the literature review was divided into four sections to make the structure more coherent. Thus, the following sections will account for research regarding *Game Industry, Management, Communication* and *Development,* and specify recurring sub-topics and aspects in each.

3.1 Game Industry

Research focusing on the evolution of the industry usually describes the history and impact of the game industry in specific regions, but also includes technical or cultural advancements or issues that have evolved in the industry over time (Chung and Kwon, 2020; Ernkvist and Ström, 2018; Jørgensen, 2019; Jørgensen et al., 2017; Keogh, 2019; Whitson, 2019). Literature discussing regional aspects of the game industry often aim to distinguish and elucidate critical factors regarding the evolution of the game industry in a specific region. For instance; studies describing the evolution of the game industry in Australia (Keogh, 2019) and Japan (Ernkvist and Ström, 2018; Karlsson et al., 2020) reveals, not only regionally specific backstories, but also presents different issues affecting each region. The following paragraphs will present examples of issues concerning the game industry in Australia and Japan.

Australia. As the Australian game industry lacks any large blockbuster game companies, both the economic and societal situation is affected for the game industry as a whole. Since the industry consists of solely of small indie game companies, influx of money and generation of reputation is halted. One reason for the situation depends on the global financial crisis 2008. However, due to the shared hardships facing the Australian game companies, a strong identity and community has evolved amongst the developers (Keogh, 2019).

Japan. As Japan is a strong player in the game industry, with several large blockbuster game companies, they do not face the same issues as Australia. Instead one of the primary issues in the Japanese game industry is related to company structure (Karlsson et al., 2020). Progressing from the manufacturing industry, via arcade games, to being one of the forerunners of modern video games, the history of the Japanese game industry has greatly affected its company structure. Japanese game companies were effectively structured to produce games at high speed with minimal resources. This meant applying a strict vertical company structure, as opposed to the more flexible horizontal structure common in western game companies. This modus operandi was very successful for creating level based arcade games, but has proven less optimal as technology has quickly progressed and games today allow extreme levels of detail, vast open game worlds, enormous amounts of content, and intricate storytelling (Ernkvist and Ström, 2018; Karlsson et al., 2020). Thus, some Japanese game companies have begun to scale up and restructure their game development teams (Karlsson et al., 2020).

Another evolutionary aspect of the game industry relates to technical or social evolution. An example of this is the field of data-driven game design (Seif El-Nasr, 2019; Whitson, 2019). While the technology that allows game designers to gather data from players has evolved, so has the social repercussions alongside of it. From a strictly technical point of view, there are many applications for data gathered from players (Schertler et al., 2019; Seif El-Nasr, 2019), however, the social repercussions that come with them might be problematic. When companies have a continuous influx of data that allows them to perfect everything from level design to business plans, the result tends to be a significant increase in workload rather than alleviation (Whitson, 2019).

3.2 Management

The managerial focus includes, but is not limited to, topics such as company structure, planning, or balancing creative and technical development aspects (Berg Marklund et al., 2019; Cohendet and Simon, 2007; Cohendet, 2016; Hodgson and Briand, 2013; Pereira and Bernardes, 2018). One recurring aspect in articles with managerial and structural elements is the term *Agile*, which is used to define an unstructured and flexible work method. Researchers explore Agile project management philosophy, because of its unstructured and flexible nature, to describe or evaluate management in game development (Berg Marklund et al., 2019; Hodgson and Briand, 2013; Jørgensen, 2019; Pereira and Bernardes, 2018). Research results however indicate that Agile might not be an optimal method, or at least not a sufficiently descriptive term, for game development. For instance; creative disciplines sometimes impugn the Agile method, believing the collegial democratized planning involved complicates their individual process (Hodgson and Briand, 2013). Consequently, balancing creativity with technical aspects, or simply maintaining creativity in game companies, are topics that recur in research surrounding managerial aspects of game development (Cohendet and Simon, 2007; Cohendet, 2016; Kultima and Alha, 2017; Whitson, 2019). While large companies might struggle with maintaining creativity while focusing on efficiency and organizational stability (Cohendet and Simon, 2007; Cohendet, 2016), smaller game companies tend to cherish their creative freedom resulting in a struggle to maintain efficiency and organizational stability instead (Whitson, 2019). Smaller game companies usually describe creativity, or rather creative freedom, as one of the cornerstones in indie development while claiming that large scale game production tend to prioritize profit and popularity (Jørgensen, 2019; Pereira and Bernardes, 2018). However, the creative freedom at indie companies tend to become somewhat compromised by matters of economic struggles, organizational, administrative and business related matters (Pereira and Bernardes, 2018). This generates a similar issue, as the one facing larger game companies, namely how to maintain a creative atmosphere. In regards to this, many indie companies strive for a flat company structure with flexible or no specific work methodology, to avoid infringing on creative freedom. Some indie companies also avoid collaboration with publishers, to minimize outer influence on creative decisions, consequently sacrificing financial stability for creative freedom (Pereira and Bernardes, 2018). Many companies, however, adapt and are willing to compromise some of the creative freedom to generate financial and organizational stability (Jørgensen, 2019). Thus, the problem of balancing creativity seems to affect game companies, disregarding differences in size or structure.

3.3 Communication

Communication is a significant topic in the gathered literature, as interdisciplinary, collaborative, and social aspects of game development constitutes a core focus of several articles (McDaniel, 2015; McDaniel and Daer, 2016; Politowski, 2018; Seering et al., 2019; Whitson, 2018). The sociological approaches maintained in the gathered literature includes observation, interviewing and otherwise gathering data directly from game developers. Consequently, interaction between developers is often studied and although research has located communicatory issues in game development, the general purpose of current research is not to suggest solutions but rather to investigate and gain understanding (McDaniel, 2015; McDaniel and Daer, 2016; Seering et al., 2019; Whitson, 2020). Investigating communication between different disciplines reveals chasms between them as their specializations tend to influence, not only their knowledge base, but also their language (Whitson, 2018). When conversing on an interdisciplinary level it is therefore common to use an inclusive jargon that is influenced by something that each discipline have in common, namely games (O'Donnell, 2014; Whitson, 2018). However, during interdisciplinary collaboration, the specialized language amongst disciplines can be problematic.

By researching interactions like this, conflicts between artists and engineers have been noticed on several accounts (McDaniel, 2015; McDaniel and Daer, 2016; Whitson, 2018). One recurring conflict surrounds resource management, as artists ask engineers to create tools to facilitate art production. According to interviews, this aspect can be frustrating as the engineers have to use their time to alleviate time from artists, thus not saving time for the project overall (McDaniel and Daer, 2016; O'Donnell, 2014; Whitson, 2018). Another common communicatory issue arises with new employees, both due to insecurity, but also that they have not yet been introduced to the company culture and jargon. Without proper introduction or communication practices, new employees can overstep boundaries, consequently disrupting workflow (McDaniel, 2015). Insecurity, especially with new employees, can negatively affect feedback, as the new employee tends to misunderstand or ignore feedback, or sometimes taking it too literal in fear of underperforming.

"I've seen a lot of people who are junior often have problems with either ignoring all of it or listening to all of it too much." (Seering et al., 2019, p. 434)

3.4 Development

Intricate software plays an integral part in game development, adding to the technical complexity surrounding the development process. Game engines, such as Unity or Unreal, are commonly central for collaboration, consequently unifying the team. However, the game engine often constitutes a primary source of breakdown, as bugs tend to arise frequently, and conflict, as constant multidisciplinary input is prone to mishaps (Whitson, 2020). Each discipline usually has its own discipline specific software as well, such as 3D-software, code-software or sound editing-software. This further complicates the work process, as each software needs to communicate properly with the game engine, but also as the developers need to communicate correctly with the technology (McDaniel, 2015; McDaniel and Daer, 2016; Whitson, 2018). This sociotechnical challenge is expanded even more when including version control software and bug reporting systems into the mix. Despite their purpose of minimizing risk factors, version control software and bug reporting systems also increases the amount of software that could possibly cause complications. By observing the sociotechnical interactions arising from this intricate setup of software and developers, help researchers better understand game development and gain insights into possible improvement areas for future research (Whitson, 2020, 2018).

Technical constrains is one of several constraints pinpointed in game development research. Interviews and observations suggest common constraints to be:

- Constraints of internal resources (e.g. time, personnel or technology) (McDaniel, 2015; Whitson, 2018)
- Constraints of interdisciplinary work practices (e.g. communication and collaboration) (McDaniel, 2015; Whitson, 2020)
- Game design constraints (e.g. limitations in game mechanics and rules) (McDaniel and Daer, 2016)
- External constraints (e.g. management and budget) (Jørgensen, 2019; McDaniel, 2015; Pereira and Bernardes, 2018)

To effectively cope with this type of challenging circumstances, game developers usually maintain a flexible approach to production and create strategies (McDaniel, 2015; McDaniel and Daer, 2016). As such constraints are usually present throughout production, from the ideation stage to (and sometimes after) release, coping strategies are usually organic and evolve with each project (Whitson, 2020).

To improve and finalize games, large game companies apply quality assurance (QA) teams to perform playtests to make sure everything works as intended and to raise the chances of a well-received game at release (Liu et al., 2019; Seering et al., 2019; Seif El-Nasr, 2019). QA teams, external or advanced playtests can however be either expensive or time consuming. Thus, many indie game developers are unable to perform them, while some simply do not see the value to begin with (Jónasdóttir and Müller, 2020; Mirza-Babaei et al., 2016). For indie developers this often means that playtesting is limited to internal tests, making actual game release more risky.

4. DISCUSSION AND CONCLUSION

RQ1 investigated prominent focus and topics within the gathered literature. The results of this literature review suggests a broad focus area with four recurring topics; *Game Industry, Management, Communication* and *Development*. RQ2 investigated how the gathered literature cover both the subject of game developers and game development. Due to the recent emergence of research that covers the interdisciplinary, collaborative, practical and social aspects of game development, most of the gathered literature apply an exploratory approach. The exploratory approach primarily aims to provide insight and understanding regarding the complexities of game development and the everyday realities of game developers. Trough observation, interviews, workplace surveys and analysis of post mortems, researchers hope to reduce the gap between academia and the game industry, subsequently facilitating higher industry relevance in future game research. Thus, the current state of research has not only brought forth a promising interdisciplinary approach to game research, but also begun gathering sought after data directly from the game industry. This will contribute to a more accurate depiction of game development in research, and might improve future collaboration between industry and academia as well.

An observation that was made when analyzing literature containing case studies from individual game companies (e.g. (Cohendet, 2016; Jørgensen, 2019; McDaniel and Daer, 2016; Whitson, 2020)), was that the same issues often recur, sometimes regardless of company size. That in itself is not very surprising, as they share similar goals and development pipelines. What is interesting, however, is that each company always seem to struggle with solutions to those issues by themselves, even though other companies might have already solved the same issue in a successful manner. This internal struggle seems like it could be reduced if more information was shared among game developers. However, sharing information might be restricted, just as researchers often experience limited access game companies “due to the secrecy of the game industry and concerns about inadvertent leaking of trade secrets” (Whitson, 2020, p. 271).

Looking at each recurring topic in this paper; *Game Industry, Management, Communication* and *Development,* recurring issues can also be acknowledged:

- balancing creativity and efficiency at game companies (Cohendet and Simon, 2007; Cohendet, 2016; Jørgensen, 2019; Pereira and Bernardes, 2018),
- regional challenges for the game industry (Ernkvist and Ström, 2018; Keogh, 2019),
- communicatory issues in interdisciplinary collaboration (McDaniel, 2015; McDaniel and Daer, 2016; Seering et al., 2019; Whitson, 2020),
- sociotechnical complications (Whitson, 2020, 2018).

Analyzing these types of potential problematic areas when producing research questions might eventually generate potential solutions that can be shared in the game development community, thus allowing research to play a larger part in the evolution of game development.

This literature review initially aimed towards providing key points for future research. However, it proved difficult to draw generalized conclusions due to the exploratory nature, and limited amount, of research literature on the subject. Thus, the ultimate outcome instead provides an overview of an emerging research field and suggests areas in need of further research.

REFERENCES

Berg Marklund, B., Engström, H., Hellkvist, M., Backlund, P., 2019. What Empirically Based Research Tells Us About Game Development. Comput Game J 8, 179–198. https://doi.org/10.1007/s40869-019-00085-1

Chung, S.W., Kwon, H., 2020. Tackling the crunch mode: the rise of an enterprise union in South Korea's game industry. ER 42, 1327–1352. https://doi.org/10.1108/ER-10-2019-0382

Cohendet, P., Simon, L., 2007. Playing across the playground: paradoxes of knowledge creation in the videogame firm. J. Organiz. Behav. 28, 587–605. https://doi.org/10.1002/job.460

Cohendet, P.S., 2016. Always Playable: Recombining Routines for Creative Efficiency at Ubisoft Montreal's Video Game Studio 20.

Dobrilova, T., 2019. How Much Is the Gaming Industry Worth in 2020? TechJury. URL https://techjury.net/blog/gaming-industry-worth/ (accessed 9.30.20).

Engström, H., Berg Marklund, B., Backlund, P., Toftedahl, M., 2018. Game development from a software and creative product perspective: A quantitative literature review approach. Entertainment Computing 27, 10–22. https://doi.org/10.1016/j.entcom.2018.02.008

Ernkvist, M., Ström, P., 2018. Differentiation in digital creative industry cluster dynamics: the growth and decline of the Japanese video game software industry. Geografiska Annaler: Series B, Human Geography 100, 263–286. https://doi.org/10.1080/04353684.2017.1423506

Hodgson, D., Briand, L., 2013. Controlling the uncontrollable: 'Agile' teams and illusions of autonomy in creative work. Work, Employment and Society 27, 308–325. https://doi.org/10.1177/0950017012460315

Jónasdóttir, H., Müller, S.D., 2020. Theorizing Affordance Actualization in Digital Innovation from a Socio- Technical Perspective. 35.

Jørgensen, K., 2019. Newcomers in a Global Industry: Challenges of a Norwegian Game Company. Games and Culture 14, 660–679. https://doi.org/10.1177/1555412017723265

Jørgensen, K., Sandqvist, U., Sotamaa, O., 2017. From hobbyists to entrepreneurs: On the formation of the Nordic game industry. Convergence 23, 457–476. https://doi.org/10.1177/1354856515617853

Karlsson, T., Sato, Y., Kurabayashi, S., 2020. Investigating the Elusive Role of Level Design, in: 2020 IEEE Conference on Games (CoG). Presented at the 2020 IEEE Conference on Games (CoG), pp. 584–587. https://doi.org/10.1109/CoG47356.2020.9231624

Keogh, B., 2019. The Cultural Field of Video Game Production in Australia. Games and Culture 155541201987374. https://doi.org/10.1177/1555412019873746

Kultima, A., Alha, K., 2017. The intertwined role of play at game studios: an examination of office play strategies, in: Proceedings of the 21st International Academic Mindtrek Conference on - AcademicMindtrek '17. Presented at the the 21st International Academic Mindtrek Conference, ACM Press, Tampere, Finland, pp. 45–53. https://doi.org/10.1145/3131085.3131115

Liu, J.-W., Wang, Y.-H., Tsai, J.C.A., Chang, J.Y.T., 2019. Ambidextrous Innovation and Game Market Fit Performance: Feedback from Game Testers. Journal of Computer Information Systems 59, 233–242. https://doi.org/10.1080/08874417.2017.1330127

MaxQDA2018, 2018. . VERBI Software, Berlin.

McDaniel, R., 2015. Communication and knowledge management strategies in video game design and development: A case study highlighting key organizational narratives, in: 2015 IEEE International Professional Communication Conference (IPCC). Presented at the 2015 IEEE International Professional Communication Conference (ProComm), IEEE, Limerick, pp. 1–8. https://doi.org/10.1109/IPCC.2015.7235773

McDaniel, R., Daer, A., 2016. Developer Discourse: Exploring Technical Communication Practices within Video Game Development. Technical Communication Quarterly 25, 155–166. https://doi.org/10.1080/10572252.2016.1180430

Mirza-Babaei, P., Moosajee, N., Drenikow, B., 2016. Playtesting for indie studios, in: Proceedings of the 20th International Academic Mindtrek Conference on - AcademicMindtrek '16. Presented at the the 20th International Academic Mindtrek Conference, ACM Press, Tampere, Finland, pp. 366–374. https://doi.org/10.1145/2994310.2994364

O'Donnell, C., 2014. Developer's dilemma: the secret world of videogame creators, Inside technology. The MIT Press, Cambridge, Massachusetts.

Panourgias, N.S., Nandhakumar, J., Scarbrough, H., 2014. Entanglements of creative agency and digital technology: A sociomaterial study of computer game development. Technological Forecasting and Social Change 83, 111–126. https://doi.org/10.1016/j.techfore.2013.03.010

Passarelli, M., Earp, J., Dagnino, F.M., Manganello, F., Persico, D., Pozzi, F., Buijtenweg, T., Haggis, M., Bailey, C., Perrotta, C., 2020. The distant Horizon: Investigating the relationship between social sciences academic research and game development. Entertainment Computing 34, 100339. https://doi.org/10.1016/j.entcom.2020.100339

Pereira, L.S., Bernardes, M.M.S., 2018. Aspects of Independent Game Production: An Exploratory Study. Computers in Entertainment 16, 16.

Politowski, C., 2018. Learning from the past_ A process recommendation system for video game projects using postmortems experiences. Information and Software Technology 16.

Schertler, R., Kriglstein, S., Wallner, G., 2019. User Guided Movement Analysis in Games using Semantic Trajectories, in: Proceedings of the Annual Symposium on Computer-Human Interaction in Play. Presented at the CHI PLAY '19: The Annual Symposium on Computer-Human Interaction in Play, ACM, Barcelona Spain, pp. 613–623. https://doi.org/10.1145/3311350.3347156

Seering, J., Mayol, R., Harpstead, E., Chen, T., Cook, A., Hammer, J., 2019. Peer Feedback Processes in the Game Industry, in: Proceedings of the Annual Symposium on Computer-Human Interaction in Play. Presented at the CHI PLAY '19: The Annual Symposium on Computer-Human Interaction in Play, ACM, Barcelona Spain, pp. 427–438. https://doi.org/10.1145/3311350.3347176

Seif El-Nasr, M., 2019. Developing Games That Capture and Engage Users, in: 2019 IEEE/ACM 41st International Conference on Software Engineering: Companion Proceedings (ICSE-Companion). Presented at the 2019 IEEE/ACM 41st International Conference on Software Engineering: Companion Proceedings (ICSE-Companion), IEEE, Montreal, QC, Canada, pp. 9–10. https://doi.org/10.1109/ICSE-Companion.2019.00025

Weststar, J., 2015. Understanding video game developers as an occupational community. Information, Communication & Society 18, 1238–1252. https://doi.org/10.1080/1369118X.2015.1036094

Whitson, J.R., 2020. What Can We Learn From Studio Studies Ethnographies?: A "Messy" Account of Game Development Materiality, Learning, and Expertise. Games and Culture 15, 266–288. https://doi.org/10.1177/1555412018783320

Whitson, J.R., 2019. The New Spirit of Capitalism in the Game Industry. Television & New Media 20, 789–801. https://doi.org/10.1177/1527476419851086

Whitson, J.R., 2018. Voodoo software and boundary objects in game development: How developers collaborate and conflict with game engines and art tools. New Media & Society 20, 2315–2332. https://doi.org/10.1177/1461444817715020

PROTOTYPE DESIGN OF ALLEVIATING CHILDREN'S NIGHTTIME FEARS USING DIGITAL GAME

Ching-Chih Hsu and Wen-Huei Chou
National Yunlin University of Science and Technology
Graduate School in Digital Media Design, Taiwan

ABSTRACT

Nighttime fears are a type of childhood fear, which, under normal circumstances, reduce as children grow older. However, in instances where nighttime fears persist, there may be negative physical and psychological effects on the child. In addition to serving as an entertainment medium, researchers have used digital games as a method for training children to handle and alleviate their fears. This study aimed to investigate nighttime fears among children in Taiwan and to use the collected data to design a conceptual digital game for mobile devices that may assist children to face and alleviate their nighttime fears. A focus group with seven parents was organized to collect data on children's nighttime fears. The Koala Fear Questionnaire (KFQ) was subsequently used as a survey instrument, conducted among 35 children, aged between 7 and 10 years old. Finally, a conceptual digital game design was proposed based on the analysis results of the focus group and survey.

KEYWORDS

Nighttime Fears, Childhood Fears, Digital Game Design, Adventure Game

1. INTRODUCTION

Fear comes in many forms, and the loci of that fear for children vary with changes in cognitive ability during each phase of growth (Gordon et al., 2007). According to a study conducted among children aged between 4 and 12 years old, 73.3% had nighttime fears. It was thus concluded that nighttime fears are common among children (Muris et al., 2001). The most common features of nighttime fears include the inability to fall asleep alone and reduced sleep quality. As a result, affected children may be unable to concentrate during the day and face an increase in their anxiety (Kushnir & Sadeh, 2011; Lewis et al., 2015). Hence, although nighttime fears are quite common among children, chronic nighttime fears are likely to have a long-term negative impact on children. In response to many current issues, there has been a focus on digital games. With improved technology, the game media have increased. It has been demonstrated that playing games is a valid method of alleviating negative emotions in children (Mandryk et al., 2017). Researchers in Taiwan have demonstrated this by using digital games to help alleviate children's fears of medical care (Lin et al., 2017). On that basis, the present study intended to explore how digital games can be designed to alleviate the anxiety and uneasiness children face when suffering nighttime fears.

The game proposed in this study aims to alleviate children's negative emotions, promote self-confidence, and provide training in mechanisms for dealing with fear. The purposes of this research are as follows:

1) to develop a study of the methods used to alleviate childhood fears.
2) to collect and compile relevant data on nighttime fears as references for in-depth investigation in future studies.
3) to design digital game that assists children in alleviating their fears.

2. BACKGROUND STUDY

2.1 Nighttime Fears among Children

Studies have suggested that childhood fears are affected by external information, where fears are generated due to receiving negative information (Muris et al., 2011; Ooi et al., 2016). The causes of childhood fears are correlated to the stages of cognitive development as well as the negative information to which they are exposed (Gordon et al., 2007; Muris et al., 2001).

In terms of the association between age group and children's nighttime fears, the survey conducted by Gordon et al., (2007) among children and adolescents aged between 8 and 16 years showed that 79.4% of the investigated children had nighttime fears, while only 48.8% of the adolescents reported nighttime fears. Stewart and Gordon (2014) revealed that children aged from 6 to 10 years had the most severe cases of nighttime fears. Hence, when compared to adolescents, younger children are more prone to nighttime fears.

In terms of specific fears that may be encountered, Gordon et al. (2007) conducted a study to investigate what children and adolescents (aged from 8 to 16) feared, using the nighttime fear categories proposed by Mooney (1985) and Muris et al. (2001). The results showed that the fears of children aged between 8 and 12 years were related mostly to personal security, followed by an environmental threat. It can thus be deduced that children have varied nighttime fears, which differ across age groups. Things that children fear have been demonstrated to include intruders/home invasions (such as thieves and kidnappers), imaginary creatures (such as ghosts, monsters, and witches), frightening dreams (nightmares), environmental threats (such as darkness, storms, and strange sounds), insects and animals (such as spiders), and frightening thoughts (such as threats to one's life or a threat of the death of a parent) (Gorden et al., 2007; Mooney et al., 1985; Muris et al., 2001; Rafihi-Ferreira et al., 2018).

In addition to emotional instability, confidence may be lost, and behaviors may manifest that affect the quality of children's lives (such as inability to go to the bathroom alone at night or the need for the company from a family member to fall asleep). Nighttime fears may also lead to a reduction in sleep quality, which may indirectly affect their quality of life (Ducasse & Denis, 2015; Kushnir & Sadeh, 2011).

Some researchers have used methods such as bibliotherapy alongside communication aids, such as toys, to alleviate children's night fears (Rafihi-Ferreira et al., 2018). Specifically, story books and a kangaroo stuffed toy have been introduced to train children to sleep alone. The research demonstrated that, among children aged from 4 to 8 years, such techniques may reduce insomnia and co-sleeping time. The method adopted in the present study attempts an approach by indirectly assisting children to face their fears. The story-telling method adopted allows for children to immerse themselves in a situation so as to avoid excessive fear.

2.2 The Impact of Digital Games on Children's Emotion

Although the emotion of fear is a kind of defense mechanism (Tzeng, 2000). Excessive fear may cause negative influence on the quality of life or mental health (Friedl, 2003). In addition to the medical care of children or cases of children's nighttime fear mentioned in the introduction and background review, some game elements were more or less added to divert children's attention. Therefore, this chapter will organize the impact on association of games on children.

Children are able to develop and gain experience and learn life skills, through games without special training. Hence, playing games is an innate ability that all children have, and doing so may help to teach them how to effectively control their emotions and behaviors (Kao & Chen, 2011). Chiu et al. (2010) pointed out that, when playing games, children tend to rely on their own natural logic to uncover the most beneficial behaviors of the game world. In other words, games stimulate critical thinking and the ability to adapt to new environments. Therefore, the influence of digital games on children are not necessarily sweepingly negative; in some contexts, digital games can provide children with a medium for learning and interaction. On the other hand, Martins et al. (2014) found that the touchscreen functionality is easier to understand than using a mouse. Correspondingly, Couse and Chen (2010) discovered that, by using tablet computers and digital pens, it was easier for children to communicate and to share creative ideas with peers. In addition, tablet computers increase the probability of diverse interactions between children. For those reasons, digital games for mobile devices (such as tablet computers and cellular phones) are a viable media for alleviating children's fears.

2.3 Section Summary

Nighttime fears are common in childhood and occur in many children and adolescents. When the fears worsen or become chronic, there may be adverse physical and psychological effects on children as well as those surrounding the children, impacting life quality. According to the findings of the Background study, structured guidance in handling fear can help children to face and handle their fears independently. The adoption of a reward mechanism facilitates children's participation in the process; story-telling and role-playing encourage children to approach their fears from an alternative angle; and auxiliary instruments divert their attention from their negative emotions. The development and property of digital games have subsequently been found to have positive effects on children. Given the plasticity and attractiveness of digital games, they can be designed for various media and devices. If games can transform children's fears into other emotions or help them approach their sources of fear from a different perspective, digital games can be useful tools for nighttime fear interventions.

3. RESEARCH DESIGN

The goal of this study was to design a digital game that alleviates children's nighttime fears. In order to achieve this goal, questions such as "Do Taiwanese children aged between 7 to 10 years have nighttime fears?" and "What are the things that they fear the most?" were firstly investigated. The study was thus conducted in two stages. In the first stage, a focus group and the Koala Fear Questionnaire (KFQ) were used to collect information related to nighttime fears among children. The collected data were compiled and analyzed. In the second stage, a game was planned and designed based on the information acquired during the first stage.

3.1 Focus Group

The focus group targeted parents with children aged between 7 and 10 years. A preliminary request was sent through social media to explore willingness to participate. Next, detailed information of the focus group and an outline of the topics to be discussed were provided to the parents who were willing to participate. Eventually, seven parents (with children aged between 6 to 10 years) were recruited, among which, one was male and six were female.

Gordon et al. (2007) adopted the interview questions used by Muris et al. (1997, 2001) to investigate the frequency of nighttime fears, severity of anxiety, and things that children fear the most. The questions developed to be used in the focus group, with parent participation, were based on the aforementioned research and the studies of Mooney (1985) and Pincus et al. (2012).

The purpose of the focus group was to collect information related to children's nighttime fears. Therefore, the questions were divided into five dimensions, including children's sleeping habits, the frequency of nighttime fears, the most prominent loci of fear, their anxiety levels, and how parents handle such nighttime fears. A verbatim transcription of the focus group was used for data categorization and analysis.

3.2 The Koala Fear Questionnaire (KFQ)

The Koala Fear Questionnaire (KFQ) is an instrument used to assess fears among children aged between 4 and 12 years old. By visualizing different types of fears and the severity of the fear, through corresponding images, the KFQ is a more appropriate aid for young children, when compared to surveys that only contain text, such as the Fear Survey Schedule for Children (FSSC-R) (Muris et al., 2003). Many studies have used the KFQ to investigate children's nighttime fears (Lewis et al., 2015; Kushnir et al., 2014; Zisenwine et al., 2012). Therefore, in addition to the focus group, the present author adopted the KFQ to further investigate nighttime fears, such as the specific loci of fear.

The participants of the KFQ were 44 lower and middle-grade primary school students (aged approximately between 8 to 10 years). Specifically, the questionnaires were distributed in Chongwen Elementary School, Chiayi City, and 28 students participated in the survey on the day of distribution. Thereafter, with the assistance of the schoolteachers, more students were included in the survey.

The items used in the KFQ were designed based on the fear categories proposed in past studies and the results of Hung's (2011) survey among lower-grade primary school students in Beichen Elementary School. Each item was presented as an image and the children were asked to rate how they feel toward each item. In addition, an example was included at the beginning of the questionnaire to facilitate children's understanding of how to answer the questions.

To understand the fears of the participants, the following categories were included in the questionnaire: intruders/home invasion, imaginary creatures, frightening dreams, environmental threats, insects and animals, and other frightening thoughts. In order to ensure that the items included in the survey were familiar to the primary school students in Taiwan, additional items were included such as cockroaches, dogs (insects and animals), zombies, vampires, and human skeletons (imaginary creatures). The fear level was rated on a 3-point scale using a koala face (happy face = no fear, face with a little fear = some fear, and face with a lot of fear = a lot of fear). The participants' age and gender were also collected. The last item of the questionnaire was an open-ended question, which aimed to investigate any loci of fear that was not already covered in the questionnaire, the reasons for their fear, and how they handle the fear.

3.3 Analysis Results

The KFQ survey yielded 35 valid responses; 13 of the respondents were male and 22 were female. Moreover, one child was seven years old, 4 children were eight years old, 22 children were nine years old, and 8 were ten years old. The analysis results of the focus group and the KFQ survey are presented in the following paragraphs.

In terms of sleeping habits, some parents reported that their children required specific external environment stimuli (such as a night light or the company of a family member) to fall asleep. These findings were in line with the findings of Kushnir and Sadeh (2011) on the sleeping patterns of children with nighttime fears and parents respond to such fears. It was found that not all of the children of the participating parents had nighttime fears. Nevertheless, the two parents who had not encountered nighttime fears among their children still provided suggestions in terms of how to handle such fears. Given that they lacked corresponding experience, they did not answer the question related to the frequency of occurrence.

According to the participants, nighttime fears made the children feel uneasy. This reduced their ability to sleep by themselves and increased the requirement of an accompanying family member or pet. The children generally openly expressed their fears with an expectation of a calming and reassuring response. Sometimes, the children were unable to complete tasks that they were able to usually accomplish independently (such as going to the toilet in the evening). Requests, such as the company of a family member or a stuffed toy and a talk before sleep, generated a sense of security and distracted them from their feelings of fear. In terms of handling methods, the participating parents reported that accompanying their children to sleep was most effective, while other methods were less commonly utilized. Particularly, if the parents were with their children, they were unlikely to adopt other methods (such as attempting to create a safer feeling in the environment). In addition, comparisons between peers were found to be beneficial to improving sleep habits.

In terms of the frequency of nighttime fears, some participants claimed that due to their efforts to avoid the occurrence of nighttime fears, there was limited incidences; two participants reported that they occurred once per day, and one participant reported that they occurred once every two to three days. The differences in the frequencies may be due to the children's personality (such as timidity). According to the parents, the loci that generated the most fear included imaginary creatures such as the "tiger aunt" and possessed toys (*Tukta Phee*), and environmental threats such as stressful events and external stimuli. The participants believed that the reasons behind the fear could be age and incomplete information absorption.

The total ratings provided by the participants for each item were used to identify the items that were the most feared by the children. Differences in the feared items by gender and age were also examined. The results showed that the participants feared kidnappers the most (84%), followed by death and zombies (82%), and burglars (81%), which covered the fear categories of intruders/home invasion, frightening thoughts, and imaginary creatures. These findings echo the survey results of Gordon et al. (2007), in which fear of intruders/home invasion ranked as the second fear of children and adolescents.

Moreover, the differences in fears by gender and age were also similar to the results of the study of Muris, et al. (2001) among children aged between 4 and 12 years old. Specifically, the top two categories of fears were intruders/home invasion and imaginary creatures. Additionally, the fear of imaginary creatures tended to reduce as they grew older, while the fear of intruders/home invasion tended to increase with age. It can be concluded that, concurrent with literature, cognitive development may affect both the type and loci of children's fear.

In terms of the sources of fear, dead people, ghosts, and earthquakes were the most mentioned items in addition to those listed in the questionnaire. Fearing dead people and demons belonged to the category of imaginary creatures, which likely originate from imagination, perceptive associations, and negative information received from their social environments. Fearing earthquakes belonged to the category of environmental threats, which could originate from uneasiness due to past experiences of sudden environmental changes.

The findings from the focus group and questionnaire survey shed light on nighttime fears among Taiwanese children and facilitate understanding of the current situation and the specific foci of fear. The results of the focus group and the survey were similar; the majority of nighttime fears originated from children's imagination and associations, negative information stimuli, and natural disasters. In addition, due to differences in cognitive development stages, children from different age groups tended to have different fears. The majority of the children were found to cope with fears by seeking the company of a family member. It is worth noting that both parents and children preferred the combination of an enhanced sense of security and a distraction from the fear (Table 1.).

Table 1. Coping solutions of nighttime fears reported by children

Coping solutions	Total (n =35) (percentage)
1. Distract attention from doing things	3 (8.6%)
2. Seeking the company of a family member	13 (37.1%)
3. Hide	9 (25.7%)
4. Dependent items	2 (5.7%)
5. Escape from fear	1 (2.9%)
6. Scream	3 (8.6%)
7. Sleep	2 (5.7%)
8. Hit people	1 (2.9%)
9. Do nothing	1 (2.9%)

4. DESIGN PRACTICE

Based on the findings from the focus group and questionnaire survey, the second stage of this research focused on the game design. First, the design principles were defined, and the overall plan was drafted prior to execution. The following sub-sections introduce the game design process.

4.1 Design Principles

4.1.1 Defining the Story and Plots

According to the findings of the background study, bibliotherapy and picture book stories can be used to alleviate fear by immersing the children in the stories and using that immersion to alter their perceptions. Hence, a similar approach should be adopted in the game design. In addition, the KFQ demonstrates that visually illustrated information is easier for children to understand than written information; hence, the storyline and plots of the game should be presented through images. Therefore, the foci of fear, collected from the focus group and survey, should be introduced at the beginning of the game and the story should be developed accordingly to focus the theme of the game and to help the player explore the cause-and-effect relationships through gameplay.

4.1.2 Defining the Characters

According to the findings of the focus group and survey, the majority of parents and children relied on the company of a family member as a coping mechanism. However, training children to go to bed and cope with their fears independently is more conducive to their overall sleep quality and quality of life. In order for children to learn to cope with their nighttime fears through playing the game, the main character (operated by the player) should have a similar age and background to the player (in this case, the survey participants).

4.1.3 Defining the Challenges and Obstacles

In order to alleviate their nighttime fears, the challenge faced by the players should be the loci of fear (in this case, the loci defined by the focus group and survey). According to research and investigations, it was determined that the fear children experience at night involves, most commonly, separation from parents, death, and the fear of intruders and fictional creatures. The game aims to extend the emotional reaction to such loci from anxiety and negative thoughts to more positive outcomes by allowing the player to examine these fears from a different perspective, using positive mindset behaviors to alter the child's negative thoughts. The idea is that, through overcoming the challenges within the game, when encountering fears in real life, they will have developed new coping mechanisms from the gameplay.

4.1.4 Defining the Gameplay

The results of the focus group and survey showed that parents and children applied a range of methods to cope with nighttime fears, and such methods were generally helpful in eliminating the fears. Therefore, when designing the gameplay processes, the previously collected coping mechanisms should be introduced so that players are able to indirectly learn new mechanisms, and subsequently apply the methods from the game in real life. For example, in the gameplay, player can try using the method of hiding and distracting the enemies in the game (Figure 1).

Figure 1. Obstacles and solutions in the game

4.2 Game Design

Similar to the other game elements, the storyline of the game was developed based on the findings of the focus group and survey. To promote a sense of connection between the player and the character, the main character in the game was a child that was of a similar age as the participants in the survey. The storyline was as follows: After reading a scary story book, the protagonist (a 9-year-old girl) found that many monsters in the story had suddenly appeared in her house and abducted her family members. In order to save her family, she embarked on an adventure, fighting against the monsters. The plots of the story were presented through images (Figure 2), and children's feelings were considered when designing the overall style of the images so as to avoid creating a frightening experience.

Figure 2. One of the images for game story

The game was a horizontal-scrolling action adventure composed of three levels. Each level had obstacles and a "boss," each of which represented a locus of fear. The bosses for levels one to three were arranged based on the ratings of the KFQ survey (from less feared to most feared) (Figure 3). At each level, the player is expected to obtain a key that unlocks the next level and then defeat the "boss" of that level. Successfully obtaining all the keys and defeating all the bosses, the player could find their parents and claim victory. However, if the enemies and bosses touched the protagonist, her "energy level" would decrease. When the "energy level" reaches 0 or the protagonist falls into a "trap," the game ends and the player has to restart from the beginning of the corresponding level.

Figure 3. Levels in the game

Regarding gameplay, the protagonist has limited abilities when fighting enemies and removing obstacles; as such, they need to use the tools provided in level. Specific tools can be acquired by exploring the map. Given that nighttime fears may originate from distorted perceptions and negative thoughts, the game encourages the player to assess the loci of fear from an alternative perspective, revealing their true appearance by applying positive fear coping solutions to avoid attacks and remove obstacles. For example, in the game design, enemies will disappear happily from the map, as soon as the player find the item enemies wanted.

The interface of the game was designed in a way that facilitated rapid mastery gameplay. In addition to incorporating a brief introduction to the gameplay requirements, the design of the interface was designed to be intuitive and clear on what is expected of the player. For example, referring to the method used in the KFQ to indicate the level of fear, in the game, smiling, neutral, and sad faces were used to indicate the player's remaining energy level (Figure 4).

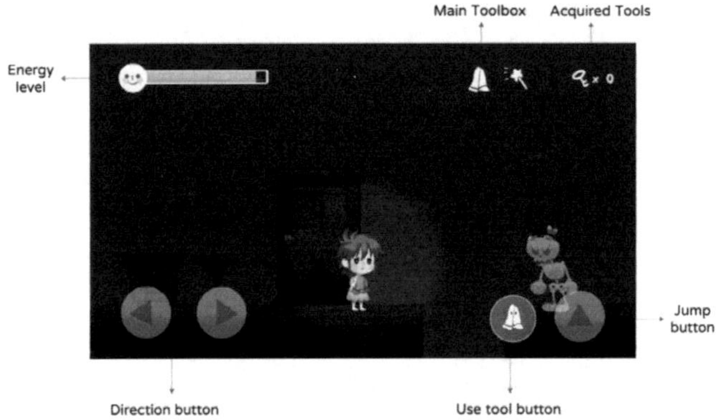

Figure 4. The interface of the game

In order to reward the player for overcoming the obstacles, in addition to finding their parents at the end of the game, a medal is given to the player as they pass each level, to indicate that the protagonist has overcome the fears presented in the corresponding level. It is expected that, by overcoming the fears alongside the protagonist, the player is able to actively engage with and overcome their fears. The final game purpose is to alleviate children's nighttime fears. Thus, in addition to enhanced motivation to play the game, the player is able to gain a sense of personal accomplishment.

5. CONCLUSIONS

Based on the background study and follow-up research, it was found that children's nighttime fears are common in the daily lives of children and adolescents, regardless of location. Given that Taiwanese studies on the subject were limited when compared to the range of diverse research conducted around the world, it was deemed necessary to conduct an in-depth exploration of the nighttime fears experienced by Taiwanese children. Using the information collected from the background study and research, the present author designed a game to help children alleviate their nighttime fears, from the perspectives of plot, character, level development, and gameplay interface. The game embedded children's nighttime fears into the story so that players may learn to overcome them through gameplay. It should be noted that, although the conceptual design of the game was developed for the present study, the game itself is yet to be developed. When the game is developed, a further study will be conducted to test its fear-alleviating effects. It is expected that the findings of this study could serve as a useful source of information for future investigations on children's nighttime fears.

REFERENCES

Couse, L. J. and Chen, D. W., 2010. A Tablet Computer for Young Children? Exploring its Viability for Early Childhood Education. *Journal of Research on Technology in Education, 43*(1), pp. 75-96.

Ducasse, D. and Denis, H., 2015. Peurs nocturnes pathologiques de l'enfant: particularités cliniques et thérapeutiques efficaces. *L'Encéphale, 41*(4), pp. 323-331.

Gordon, J. et al, 2007. Nighttime fears of children and adolescents: Frequency, content, severity, harm expectations, disclosure, and coping behaviours. *Behaviour Research and Therapy, 45*(10), pp. 2464-2472.

Gordon, J. et al, 2007. Treatment of children's nighttime fears: The need for a modern randomised controlled trial. *Clinical Psychology Review, 27*(1), pp. 98-113.

Huoy-Jia Tzeng, 2000. A Study of Fear. *Journal of National Taipei Teachers College*, 13, pp. 265-292.

Johanna Friedl and Doris Rübel, 2003. *Spielerisch mit Angst umgehen. Spiele und Übungen für den positiven Umgang mit Ängsten*. Ravensburger Buchverlag, Ravensburg.

Kushnir, J. and Sadeh, A., 2011. Sleep of preschool children with night-time fears. *Sleep Medicine, 12*(9), pp. 870-874.

Kushnir, J. et al, 2014. Nighttime fears of preschool children: A potential disposition marker for anxiety? *Comprehensive Psychiatry, 55*(2), pp. 336-341.

Lewis, K. M. et al, 2015. Treating nighttime fears in young children with bibliotherapy: Evaluating anxiety symptoms and monitoring behavior change. *Journal of Anxiety Disorders, 30*, 103-112.

Mandryk, et al, 2017. Games for the Assessment and Treatment of Mental Health. *CHI PLAY '17: The annual symposium on Computer-Human Interaction in Play*, United States: Association for Computing Machinery, pp. 673–678.

Martins, S. et al, 2014. Mobile Games for Children Cham: Springer International Publishing, pp. 455-464.

Mooney, K. C., 1985. Children's nighttime fears: Ratings of content and coping behaviors. Cognitive *Therapy and Research, 9*(3), 309-319.

Muris, P. et al, 1997. Common childhood fears and their origins. *Behaviour Research and Therapy, 35*(10), pp. 929-937.

Muris, P. et al, 2001. Children's nighttime fears: parent–child ratings of frequency, content, origins, coping behaviors and severity. *Behaviour Research and Therapy, 39*(1), pp. 13-28.

Muris, P. et al, 2003. The Koala Fear Questionnaire: A standardized self-report scale for assessing fears and fearfulness in pre-school and primary school children. *Behaviour Research and Therapy, 41*, pp. 597-617.

Muris, P. et al, 2011. Reduction of verbally learned fear in children: A comparison between positive information, imagery, and a control condition. *Journal of Behavior Therapy and Experimental Psychiatry, 42*(2), pp. 139-144.

Ooi, J. et al, 2016. Do you think I should be scared? The effect of peer discussion on children's fears. *Behaviour Research and Therapy, 87*, 23-33.

Peng-Chia Kao and Yu-Ling Chen, 2011. Exploring the Relationship between Play and Children Development-Theory and Practice. (113), pp. 15-21.

Pincus, D. et al, 2012. Differential Efficacy of Home Monitoring and Cognitive-Behavioral Treatment for Decreasing Children's Maladaptive Nighttime Fears. *Child & Family Behavior Therapy - CHILD FAM BEHAV THER, 34*, pp. 1-19.

Rafihi-Ferreira, R. E. et al, 2018. Brief treatment for nighttime fears and co-sleeping problems: A randomized clinical trial. *Journal of Anxiety Disorders, 58*, pp. 51-60.

Shu-Hui Chiu et al, 2010. What Did They Do Playing MapleStory? Examining Children's Behaviors and Attitudes. (94), pp. 25-39.

Stewart, S. E. and Gordon, J. E., 2014. Parent-Assisted Cognitive-Behavioural Therapy for Children's Nighttime Fear. *Behaviour Change, 31*(4), pp. 243-257.

Tzu-min Hung, 2011. The Research of Fear Images in Picture Books—An Example from Illustrators' And Low-grade Students' Sensation. Department of Visual Arts and Design Master Thesis. Data from: https://hdl.handle.net/11296/vfkjkq

Yen-Miao Lin et al, 2017. Experiences of Nursing Care a Child after Surgical Removal of Lung Abscess and his Caregiver by Therapeutic Play Interactions.*Chang Gung Nursing, 28*(1), pp. 163-174.

Zisenwine, T. et al, 2012. Nighttime Fears and Fantasy–Reality Differentiation in Preschool Children. *Child psychiatry and human development, 44*.

THE PAC-PAC AUTHORING ENVIRONMENT FOR GAME DESIGN TEACHING: TWO LEARNING EXPERIENCES COMPARED

Raffaele Argiolas[1], Sara Cuccu[1] and Andrea Piano[2]
[1]*DICAAR – University of Cagliari, Facoltà di Architettura, Italy*
[2]*University of Cagliari, Facoltà di Studi Umanistici, Italy*

ABSTRACT

Video games are part of ordinary life for many people, with a noticeable effect on the way of thinking, acting, and learning. In addition, it appears that video games have a great potential to communicate and teach specific knowledge, by designing experiences that could lead to desired learning outcomes. This was proved also in communicating the values of cultural heritage, both material and immaterial, and in increasing the interest in physical places where videogames are set. The representation of reality and real places in video games is a topical theme. In fact, the accuracy in the representation of a real place is not a supplementary value, but it can make the difference in the choice of a video game.

The contribution proposes a digression on the use of a new unreleased tool in two learning events related to heritage. The tool and the events are parts of a research, aiming to explore the potential of first-person cinematographic video games as support for cultural and environmental heritage promotion. Analysed events differ in many aspects, including learner categories, spatial and temporal organization, and finally the social condition in which the events were held. The first one was held in attendance, before the Covid-19 pandemic, and the other in a period of strong mobility restrictions, as an online experience.

KEYWORDS

Cultural Heritage, Game Authoring Tool, Learning

1. INTRODUCTION

Some Italian territories seem to lack the ability to produce innovative touristic imaginaries, which are no longer scholastic-oriented, but leaning towards integrated, narrative, and experiential uses. One of these territories is Sardinia, which despite its recognized cultural and landscape values, is penalized by the obsolescence of communication and promotional practices.

From these premises, the Pac-Pac top-down cluster research project was born, acronym of "*Point-And-Click per la promozione del Patrimonio Ambientale e Culturale*", developed and coordinated by the University of Cagliari and funded by Sardegna Ricerche. The main goal of Pac-Pac is the proposal of an alternative model for the promotion of cultural and environmental heritage (henceforth, for brevity, only heritage) for touristic-cultural purposes, to trigger contamination mechanisms between new technologies and multimedia content production practices, especially for territories that are not part of traditional tourist circuits, and with a particular focus on Sardinia.

The proposed model consists of digital games and interactive storytelling, created through a web-based platform "designed and developed to allow end-users without development skills to create point-and-click games, exploiting different media and in particular 360-degrees videos." (Blečić et al., 2021).

Parallel to the platform, the Pac-Pac project aimed at defining a production methodology, in order to create a complete package designed for cultural associations, public administrations or generic stakeholders who have similar interests. A feature that often unites the persons identified as users of the platform is the partial or total lack of previous coding and/or game design skills and experiences. It was therefore necessary for the platform to be user friendly and easy to learn. For this reason, the project has envisaged a series of events with the dual objective of testing the ease of learning in the use of the platform and, at the same time, offering basic training on game design mechanics, oriented towards the awareness of heritage.

The events therefore had two constraints: the use of the platform as a development tool and having as case study the heritage of the places where they took place.

The events were organized with the intention of exploiting and highlighting the bivalent potential of game design as a teaching tool (Kiili & Tuomi, 2019) and as a means of promoting heritage, trying to combine both aspects in a single didactic program. Two of these events were analysed, the qualitative results of which are presented in this paper, in order to verify the effectiveness of learners' learning (Robertson & Howells, 2008).

2. VIDEO GAMES AND LEARNING

Video games are nowadays a largely diffused medium on a worldwide scale. They have become part of ordinary life for many people, often with no constraints of gender, age, or cultural origins. Alongside a huge impact on the economy and on pop culture, there is also a noticeable effect on the way video games are now part of the way we think, act, and learn.

It has been observed before (De Kerckhove, 1991) how every medium eventually has both positive and negative outcomes in influencing behaviours and abilities of its users: when the user approaches the medium, something can be gained, and something can be lost. It may vary from case to case, from individual to individual. Yet, when it comes to video games, this process appears to be clear, as the player is required to internalize behaviours and schemes in order to acquire the problem-solving skills necessary to traverse the game-text itself. Interactive properties, or ergodic abilities (Aarseth, 1997), are in fact required to progress through any given game.

However, the structure of many games reinforces or creates new behaviours in players by design. This peculiarity has been defined as procedural rhetoric (Bogost, 2007): through repetition of mechanics and dynamics, a process of internalization of behaviours becomes possible (Fauconnier & Turner, 2010). Based on this assumption, it appears that exists a great potential for using video games to communicate, or even teach, specific knowledge (Squire, 2006), by designing experiences that could lead to desired learning outcomes.

It appears possible to design ludic experiences that could lead to a positive outcome in changing people's behaviours towards cultural heritage. Specifically, using games to communicate a given heritage could influence many aspects of culture, from shared knowledge to tourism.

Based on the previously mentioned assumptions, video games can therefore be considered as designed experiences, which eventually lead to positive outcomes when it comes to teaching and learning. From this perspective, it appears important that the professional figures entitled to designing said interactive experiences are properly formed and trained.

3. VIDEO GAMES AND CULTURAL HERITAGE

Using a metaphor related to space, video games can be understood as an "experiential route" through the game world (Grodal, 2003), unfolding their potential of spatial engagement, which is the core and distinctive trait of the medium (Calleja, 2011).

This particular connection with space can create an affective relation with represented places, enhancing the awareness of cultural values (Calabrese & Ragone, 2016). The involvement might also increase when a video game is set in real places or inspired by those.

The representation of reality and physical places in video games is a topical theme, which is gaining more and more attention not only from game designers but also architects and urbanists (Gerber & Götz, 2019). In fact, the accuracy in the representation of a real place can make the difference in the choice of a video game and provoke delusion when it falls short of expectations (Aarseth, 2019).

The accurate representation of real places is particularly important when it involves cultural heritage, in its wider sense, from constructive cultures to customs. Video games proved their potential in communicating the values of cultural heritage, both material and immaterial (Anderson et al., 2010), and increasing the interest in places, attracting visitors, and inducing tourism (Dubois and Gibbs, 2018). The use of digital games in the communication and promotion of cultural and environmental heritage is well-known and it involves companies and associations that work with heritage, museums, and institutions (Mortara et al., 2014; Paliokas and Sylaiou, 2016).

Moreover, when speaking about video games and cultural heritage we can distinguish between those realized mainly with educational purposes, serious games for cultural heritage, and commercial ones, with an entertainment purpose. In serious games for cultural heritage, the focus is the information and transmission of the values of the heritage represented, trying to go through all its stratifications and complexities. In commercial games, real places and cultural heritage are usually used for thematizing or creating certain atmospheres, and its accuracy could be biased by game mechanics or the plot's necessity (Balela & Mundy, 2015). However, the effort put into the realistic representation of heritage is noteworthy, and since video games are a fundamental component of pop culture, they act as a driver for the transmission of cultural values and are therefore an important way to increase heritage awareness. Having a wide range of examples in which heritage can be narrated and represented, from the didactic to the entertaining, in the experiences discussed in the next section we sought to convey these assumptions to learners.

4. THE PAC-PAC AUTHORING ENVIRONMENT

In the didactical experiences reported in the contribution, the Pac-Pac Authoring Environment was used.

The tool presents a user-friendly interface, designed to recall widely used common tools like PowerPoint, in which users can add traditional or panoramic (360°) video or images to create the game scenes. The interface is composed by a toolbar in the upper side, where the game objects are located, a main preview of the current scene is in the centre of the screen, with a list of thumbnails of the scenes on the left and object properties on the right; under the main preview the table of the rules can be found (Figure 1).

Figure 1. The interface of the Pac-Pac Authoring Environment

In each scene is possible to add interaction objects, classified on the type of interaction offered to the player. Some examples are "transitions" that allow the player to move between the scenes, "switch" and "buttons" used to trigger events, "points of interest" that can be used to script some camera movements, and so on. In addition to these local objects, specific to every scene, the tool offers some global features, including counters for scores and player life points, and a timer for the total in-game time.

All the mechanics of the games are controlled by the rules associated with the game objects, local or global. The rules follow an Event Condition Action (ECA) logic, written in natural Italian language according to a fixed pattern (Fanni et al., 2019):

When <subject> <action> <object/value>
If <condition>
then <subject> <action> <object/value>

Event and action sentences, introduced mean the identify words "when" and "then" respectively, are mandatory; condition sentences introduced by the word "if" are optional (Figure 2). A single rule can involve multiple sentences for both condition and action types.

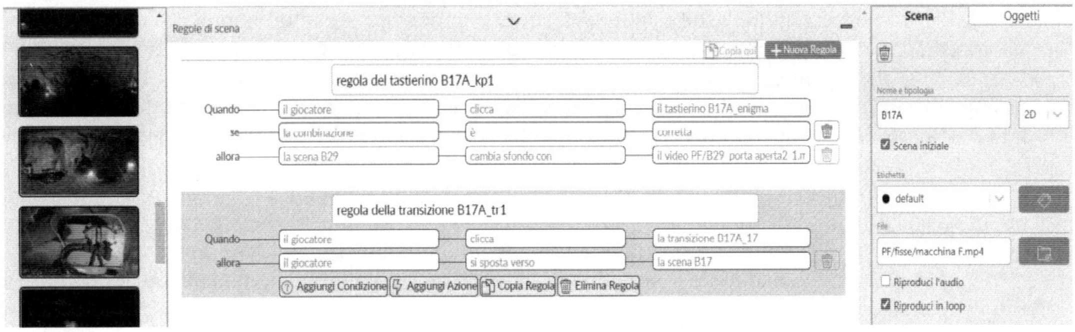

Figure 2. Some examples of rules used in the software

In parallel with the tool development, an exploratory research phase was conducted to establish a methodology for optimising the design and creation processes of the games. In fact, multidisciplinary knowledge is needed, involving cinema, music, audio, storytelling, and game design professionals. Furthermore, to test and analyse the features of the tool, some prototypes and games were designed and developed (Piano & Cuccu, 2020). Part of these prototypes are the results of two didactical events held during the project, the "Scientific School" and the "Video Game Design and Production Workshop", analysed in next chapters.

5. THE PAC-PAC TOOL FOR EDUCATIONAL PURPOSES

The Pac-Pac project supposed to include educational and communication events, on the one hand to test the intuitiveness of using the development environment and on the other to explore what possible new ways of using it could arise from users not involved in the project itself.

The contribution proposes a comparison between two of these events, chosen for their differences in terms of users and teachers categories involved, spatial and temporal organization, and learning activities management. The chosen experiences are a scientific school, involving undergraduates and professionals, and a workshop, involving exclusively high school students.

5.1 The Scientific School

The first analysed event is the "Scientific School", held in Pula (Italy) in the research structures of Sardegna Ricerche, in September 2019. The scientific school was designed as a hybrid of game jam and educational laboratory, during which the learners could learn multiple aspects related game design and the use of the authoring environment, and at the same time develop games located in the research structures or in the surrounding spaces.

In order to teach the multidisciplinary approach required for the game design activity, professionals from each sector involved were chosen for teaching; professional skills included experts in game studies, storytelling, multimedia production, social studies, up to informatic sciences. As learners, 38 applicants were selected in order to form six groups of six to seven members, including different skills; in this way a minimum level of competences in required skills was achieved in each group. This was possible thanks to the presence of candidates with very diverse professional and academic backgrounds.

The whole science school lasted six days of full immersion activities, organized in alternating lectures in the mornings, and material production and game development sessions in the afternoons; except for the multimedia production, all the activities took place in a common space, to induce and facilitate dialogue and cross fertilization of ideas between the various groups. In the production and development phases, each group was supported by two teachers and two tutors, selected for their different skills.

After a brief introduction to the structure of the "Scientific School", morning lectures involved an overview of video game design principles (specifically aiming to explain "point-and-click" games language), prototyping, approaches to a game jam, and teamworking. Storytelling and cultural heritage communication through digital media were the main topics, tackled from various perspectives in order to meet the scope of the workshop. Lecturers included professors from different Universities, professionals in game design and video making, and entrepreneurs.

With the willingness to create colloquial moments, lunch times and coffee breaks were organized in dedicated locals next to the classrooms; these were essential opportunities to create links between people who did not know each other before the school, both within and between the groups.

The school also planned a final event with a public presentation of the six developed prototypes including comments and debates between guests, learners, teachers, and professionals. The presentation highlighted the extreme variety of mechanics used in the games, with some attempts to rework the genre set by the development platform; in some cases, the very concept of first person was questioned, providing interesting hints on possible new viewpoints to be used. Another important aspect is that, although in some cases in a more or less veiled way, all the prototypes respected the requirement to represent the spaces provided for the school, offering quite a few original points of view. In addition, questionnaires were distributed and filled in during the final event, the data from which could be used as a basis for future quantitative analyses of learners' results and expectations.

5.1.1 Resulting Prototypes

The emphasis on storytelling and communication of heritage during the lectures set the conditions for a series of resulting video game prototypes that aimed to involve the players with a compelling narrative. All the projects were in fact distinguished by a story strongly connected to the environment - mostly the rural area surrounding Sardegna Ricerche's structures.

As the class involved a good number of established professionals, the prototypes also included high quality artworks or audio-visual hybrid productions. The limitations imposed by technologies and scope apparently led the participants to search for a strong visual identity for their video games, with some interesting results that integrated mechanics and aesthetics into effective design.

The prototype *Polaris Inc.* (Figure 3a) is a good example of this trend: the students combined a simple grayscale artstyle with pictures, obtaining an interesting effect that merged perfectly with the ironic narrative of the game. In this project, the player was asked to help a sassy spy in stealing the secret of eternal life from fictional laboratories set in Sardegna Ricerche's structures, while interacting with the security system.

5.2 Video Game Design and Production Workshop

The second example is a workshop held from February to March 2021 with the collaboration of the Institute "Enrico Fermi" of Ozieri, Italy. Ozieri is a small town located in a rural context on the Sardinian mountains. The "Enrico Fermi" Institute focuses on teaching tech and includes software programming in its formative offer.

Expected outcomes and formative objectives focused on the application of game design for communicating cultural and environmental heritage, while giving the students the instruments for becoming self-sufficient in the workflow process of creating video games.

The workshop involved 16 participants, all students from 13 to 15 years old, selected as volunteers from two different classes. Given the number of participants, it was decided to split them into four teams of four people each.

With regards to teachers, three of them were involved from the "Enrico Fermi" Institute, while the team of tutors was selected to cover as much as possible the multidisciplinary fields of knowledge required for the workshop. Alongside a coordinator and game designer, there was a storytelling consultant, two architects, one of which was also an expert of the Pac-Pac platform, and a technician who was entitled to solve any given bug that could emerge during the course.

The workshop was structured to overcome the difficulties related to the Covid-19 pandemic, and therefore all communication, including lectures, was migrated on an online platform. In order to not interfere with the regular curricular activities, the schedule of the workshop involved five weekly lectures of two hours each. All the remaining activity was handled through Microsoft Teams, with constant communication by chat and file exchange between the tutors and the students.

Lectures involved a brief introduction to video game design and teamwork, notions of storytelling, and environmental narrative. A tutorial for properly using the Pac-Pac platform was also part of the didactic program. Given the scope of the workshop, and the age of participants, every topic was simplified in order to not overburden the students with too many technical notions.

This approach allowed students to be extremely free on their workflow while assuring continuous monitoring by all the tutors at once. Although the local teachers noted a lack of commitment by the participants in the first phase of the workshop, as time passed students showed more and more interest in what they were doing and in the video game prototypes they were producing.

The resulting four prototypes showed that the involved students were able to properly produce a playable version of their original concept idea in the given time. They also could implement an interesting variety of mechanics, although the themes that emerged from the prototypes showed that a shared cultural background influenced them all.

5.2.1 Resulting Prototypes

Interestingly enough, the students tended to focus on dark and gloomy narratives for their games, while trying to involve the urban environment as much as possible. They mostly did not have much previous knowledge of audio-visual production, therefore a consistent intervention by tutors has been necessary through the whole creative process.

The lack of a cinematic-production skillset has been reflected on the amount of effort all students put into their respective projects, as they tried very hard to make appealing video games despite such technical shortcomings. Simple puzzles and mechanics were at the core of almost every project, with a certain inclination to re-using familiar or popular video game elements.

A prototype by the title of *The Unknown Priest* (Figure 3b) perfectly shows how the students aimed to replicate previous ludic experiences: inspired by *Dark Souls III* (From Software, 2016) they tried to mock the fighting mechanics of a third-person adventure game in the Pac-Pac system, which is optimized for point-and-click games only. The result was an interesting mix between the dynamics of *Dark Souls* and environmental storytelling, a trial-and-error experimental project.

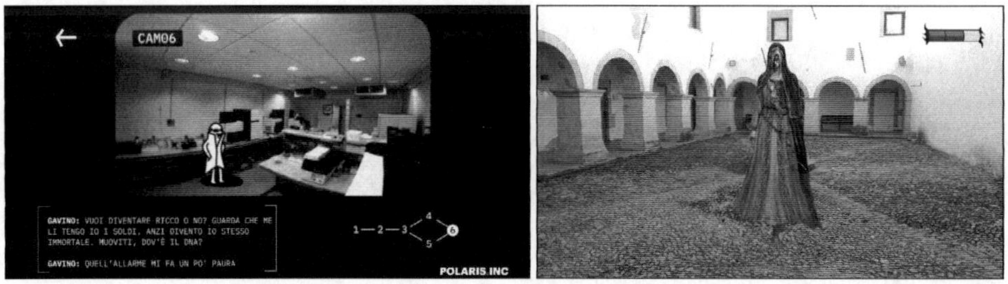

Figure 3. Screenshots from two prototypes produced; (a) on the left, *Polaris Inc.* from scientific school, and (b) on the right, *The Unknown Priest* from the workshop

6. CONCLUSIONS

Two learning events were analysed in order to test the potentials offered by Pac-Pac Authoring Environment, a still unreleased tool, designed as support for communication and teaching of cultural heritage. The events, chosen for their differences (Table 1), have offered the opportunity to compare the outcomes achieved by learners with different skills and backgrounds, when dealing with an unknown tool.

Table 1. Comparison of the main features of the two events analyse

Main features	Scientific School	Workshop
N. of students	38	16
Categories of learners	Undergraduates and professionals	High school students
Categories of teachers	Academics and professionals	Academics
Fruition mode	In attendance	Online
Time schedule	One week	Six weeks
Expected outcomes	Full playable demos	Full playable demos
Formative objectives	Use of game design for heritage	Use of game design for heritage

Despite these differences, in both cases full-working prototypes were obtained; this seems to prove a minimum level of knowledge of the software was reached by the participants. Furthermore, even if the tool was designed for a very specific genre of video games, a wide amount of mechanics declinations have been used in all the demos produced.

This is particularly interesting if it is considered that in the case of the workshop, all the learners belong to a group with a shared cultural and social background; moreover, the members of this group had many more opportunities and time to share their ideas with each other, since they live in the same town and attend lessons in the same two classrooms. In spite of this, the variety of the final products is quite comparable to that obtained by the learners' groups of the scientific school, which was composed of extremely heterogeneous learners who, to a large extent, did not even know each other before the school.

In conclusion, the Pac-Pac Authoring Environment showed to be an intuitive user-friendly tool that allows inexperienced users to design and develop digital games. The easy-to-learn nature of the software allows users to focus on other aspects of game creation, such as media production or story writing.

The next stage of the research will involve the organisation and investigation of further case studies to carry out quantitative analyses as well as extending the qualitative ones.

REFERENCES

Aarseth, E. J. (1997). Cybertext: Perspectives on ergodic literature. Baltimore, MD, US: Johns Hopkins University Press.

Aarseth, E. J. (2019). Ludoforming. Changing Actual, Historical or Fictional Topographies into Ludic Topologies. In *Ludotopia: Spaces, places and territories in computer games* (pagg. 127–140). Transcript Verlag.

Anderson, E. F., McLoughlin, L., Liarokapis, F., Peters, C., Petridis, P., & de Freitas, S. (2010). Developing serious games for cultural heritage: A state-of-the-art review. *Virtual Reality*, *14*(4), 255–275. https://doi.org/10.1007/s10055-010-0177-3

Balela, M., & Mundy, D. (2015). Analysing Cultural Heritage and its Representation in Video Games. *DiGRA '15 - Proceedings of the 2015 DiGRA International Conference*, *12*.

Blečić, I., Cuccu, S., Fanni, F. A., Frau, V., Macis, R., Saiu, V., Senis, M., Spano, L. D., & Tola, A. (2021). First-person Cinematographic Videogames: Game Model, Authoring Environment, and Potential for Creating Affection for Places. *Journal on Computing and Cultural Heritage*, *14*(2), 18:1-18:29. https://doi.org/10.1145/3446977

Bogost, I. (2007). Procedural rhetoric. In Persuasive games: The expressive power of videogames, 1-64. Cambridge, MA, US: MIT Press.

Calabrese, S., & Ragone, G. (A c. Di). (2016). *Transluoghi: Storytelling, beni culturali, turismo esperienziale*. Liguori.

Calleja, G. (2011). *In-game: From immersion to incorporation*. MIT Press.

Ceccherelli A. (2012), Videogiochi e apprendimento tra medium e messaggio. Considerazioni sull'uso didattico dei videogiochi, Rivista Scuola IaD, n.6. http://rivista.scuolaiad.it/n06-2012/videogiochi-e-apprendimento-tra-medium-e-messaggio-considerazioni-sull'uso-didattico-dei-videogiochi

De Kerckhove, D. (1991). Brainframes. Technology, mind and business. Utrecht, Netherlands: BSO/Origin.

Dubois, L.-E., & Gibbs, C. (2018). Video game–induced tourism: A new frontier for destination marketers. *Tourism Review*, *73*(2), 186–198. https://doi.org/10.1108/TR-07-2017-0115

Fanni, F. A., Senis, M., Tola, A., Murru, F., Romoli, M., Spano, L. D., Blečić, I., & Trunfio, G. A. (2019). *Pac-pac: End user development of immersive point and click games*. Paper presented at the International Symposium on End User Development. https://doi.org/10.1007/978-3-030-24781-2_20

Fauconnier, G., & Turner, M. (2010). The way we think: Conceptual blending and the mind's hidden complexities. New York, US: Basic Books.

Gerber, A., & Götz, U. (2020). *Architectonics of Game Spaces: The Spatial Logic of the Virtual and Its Meaning for the Real*. https://nbn-resolving.org/urn:nbn:de:101:1-2020042811581292795306

Grodal, T. (2003). Stories for Eye, Ear, and Muscles: Video Games, Media, and Embodied Experiences. In *The Video Game Theory Reader* (pagg. 129–155). Routledge.

Kiili, K., & Tuomi, P. (2019). Teaching Educational Game Design: Expanding the Game Design Mindset with Instructional Aspects. In A. Liapis, G. N. Yannakakis, M. Gentile, & M. Ninaus (A c. Di), *Games and Learning Alliance* (pagg. 103–113). Springer International Publishing. https://doi.org/10.1007/978-3-030-34350-7_11

Mortara, M., Catalano, C. E., Bellotti, F., Fiucci, G., Houry-Panchetti, M., & Petridis, P. (2014). Learning cultural heritage by serious games. *Journal of Cultural Heritage*, *15*(3), 318–325. https://doi.org/10.1016/j.culher.2013.04.004

Paliokas, I., & Sylaiou, S. (2016). The Use of Serious Games in Museum Visits and Exhibitions: A Systematic Mapping Study. *2016 8th International Conference on Games and Virtual Worlds for Serious Applications (VS-GAMES)*, 1–8. https://doi.org/10.1109/VS-GAMES.2016.7590371

Piano, A., & Cuccu, S. (2020). *Cultural Heritage and Environmental Communication Through Digital Games*. Paper presented at the DiGRA '20 - Proceedings of the 2020 DiGRA International Conference: Play Everywhere. http://www.digra.org/wp-content/uploads/digital-library/DiGRA_2020_paper_380.pdf

Robertson, J., & Howells, C. (2008). Computer game design: Opportunities for successful learning. *Computers & Education*, *50*(2), 559–578. https://doi.org/10.1016/j.compedu.2007.09.020

Squire, K. (2006). From Content to Context: Videogames as Designed Experience. Educational Researcher, 35(8), 19–29. https://doi.org/10.3102/0013189X035008019

MATH IN THE EARLY YEARS: IMMERSIVE VIRTUAL ENVIRONMENT

Gabriel Santana Fleury[1], Ana Carolina Gondim Inocêncio[1], Ana Paula Freitas Vilela Boa Ventura[1], Eliane Raimann[2] and Marcos Wagner de Souza Ribeiro[1]
[1]Universidade Federal de Jataí
Rodovia BR 364 – km19, 3800, Jataí-Goiás-Brazil
[2]Instituto Federal de Educação, Ciência e Tecnologia de Goiás – Campus Jataí
Rua Maria Vieira Cunha, 775, Residencial Flamboyant, Jataí-Goiás-Brazil

ABSTRACT

This paper presents an Immersive Virtual Environment to assist in the teaching-learning process of the basic math operations of the early years. From a problem established in the learning difficulties and the bad results verified in the formal evaluations in the area of mathematics, it is proposed an environment that is established on some presuppositions (abstraction, contextualization, motivation, and cognition) and seeks to be an ally in the construction of this mathematical knowledge. The results obtained through evaluations (SUS and GQM) allowed demonstrating the validation of the built tool and its effectiveness in achieving the proposed objectives.

KEYWORDS

Early Years, Education, Learning Difficulties, Mathematics, Virtual Reality

1. INTRODUCTION

Studies mention how essential Math is, both for the daily life of the humans and construction of knowledge in other areas (KEITEL, 1989), (KUBO, 2001). However, the reality Brazil has been facing for years is a scenario in which, it was not possible to reach an ideal level of learning in the aforementioned area. According to national and international evaluations as, for example, the National System for the Assessment of Basic Education (SAEB) and the International Education Program Student Assessment (PISA), based on the indicators of the latest exams. According to (NACARATO, 2017), recent reports presented in the SAEB, PISA, and National High School Exam (ENEM) on non-math skills enough, as they are not enough to meet the demands of contemporary society.

Occasionally, the learner is haunted by impressions and negative beliefs that “Math is difficult”. Because of this, in the first contacts with mathematical concepts an aversion to content is created, which can cause even more learning difficulties and can accompany you throughout your whole life. In addition, such difficulties can also come from the lack of family assistance, the inappropriate methodology used by teachers, or even internal conflicts of the student, such as cognitive issues, unwillingness to study, not understanding the subjects, and among others reasons (DE OLIVEIRA, 2019), (SANTOS, 2010). Research indicates that students with continuously low performance in mathematics could lose interest and refuse to learn more (BAUGIS, 2016), (SILVA, 2018).

The early grades educator, on the other hand, has a great responsibility for seeking solutions to the problems mentioned, because it is the phase when the base for posterior contents is built. However, teachers are also under the influence of some factors. Making it difficult to create a ludically conducive environment to facilitate learning, build a relationship with their students will enable them to make their classes more motivating, effective, and efficient when working with mathematical concepts. Moreover, it is very important to consider the initial instruction of the educators and the school environment they work, which most of the time do not provide an appropriate context to promote teaching (NACARATO, 2017), (BRANDT, 2016), (SANTOS, 2010).

According to other researches, (LEE, 2013), (FALCÃO, 2010), (GOMES, 2015), this is strongly linked to traditional methods of teaching that expose children with different cognitive profiles to the same method. The variation between individuals in the same classroom creates an opportunity to propose alternative methods of cognitive stimulation for the purpose of promoting cognitive development and increase the ability to learn for students that still have some persistent difficulties in the early years. Additionally, stimulating cognition in children in the early years may be more efficient due to the typical neuroplasticity characteristics of this period in which occurs the development of the nervous system (MUNDKUR, 2005), (RUEDA, 2005).

This author (SILVA, 2018) affirms the importance of learning Maths as a pleasant knowledge, which goes beyond the board, chalk, pencils, and paper, in order to further favor your actions of everyday life that need reasoning related to what has been learned.

From this problem and the probable paths to take below, four points need to be taken into consideration in this didactic proposal, from the previous notes:

- Use of the concrete confronting the abstract;
- Contextualization by means of some metaphor;
- The search for motivational appeal and;
- Focus on understanding and not automatism (something rhythmic).

Searching for a solution that adheres to these four assumed, computation presents effective and adequate means to the current public of this teaching phase. Flashing back to history is clear that in the beginning humans used visual means to record and recall information, such as cave paintings. These means have undergone significant changes over the temporal evolution, reaching today's Society Knowledge and/or Information, or Society of Media or even Virtual Society. Among the technologies inserted in these societies, Virtual Reality (VR) has been shown as an extremely useful tool in specific areas, such as medicine, training, history, Maths, tourism, among others, as a means of improving the ability to remember and retain information (KROKOS, 2019).

And, allied to the fact that VR has stimulating characteristics (immersion), propositional (contextualization) and adequate to teaching (cognition), technological advancement has favored access to a type of Virtual Reality, Immersive, which was not possible before, thanks to the use of common and everyday devices (Smartphones) with a lens coupling in a simple and low-cost structure, 3D glasses.

When performing exercises combined with VR using these devices (Smartphone 3D glasses), the degree of immersion provided efficiently stimulates the main human senses all together as a whole experience (KROKOS, 2019). Because (BARSALOU, 2008) states that the way the mind moves through how we interact and perceive. Therefore, they proved that through this gadget there are greater chances of success when looking for ways of retaining and remembering information.

Thus, The Immersive Virtual Reality (RVI) and the method chosen to achieve the purpose of the four assumptions previously presented, explaining:

- The definition of "concrete" will be implemented by the possibility of the creation of simulated or imaginary environments (creation metaphors).
- Contextualization will accompany the metaphor and bring math, specifically the operations of addition and subtraction, in the environment scenario.
- Motivation will be by the insertion of playfulness in the environment, gameplay concepts.
- And, finally, the process of understanding will be practiced by the set of previous items plus an incentive to understand the results of actions within the environment.

Therefore, this work has as main objective to build an Immersive Virtual Environment (IVE) with the characteristic game with a focus on learning the operations of Addiction and Subtraction. Some premises are part of this objective:

- Attractiveness, because the player will have the opportunity to manipulate the environment in which it is inserted, plus the fact that this is still new to most of the population
- Interactivity, enabling the user to receive instant feedback through experimentation and exploration that together provide curiosity and learning by discovering;
- Immersion, allowing directing human senses to the virtual environment, suppressing distractions from the external world.

  In order to achieve the general objective, some specific objectives were defined:
- Develop metaphors that allow the user to have contact with the concrete and the abstract.
- Build attractive and motivating contexts that fit into a Virtual Environment.
- Establish the method of building knowledge (understanding the content).

- Implement an Immersive Virtual Environment.
- Test and validate the system, as well as the impacts generated in learning.

2. RELATED WORKS

The following works have a greater relationship with the objectives of this work, which is to work with mathematical concepts using playful, computational means or not, as a form to facilitate the understanding and generate meaningful learning, proven in the literature according to (DE OLIVEIRA, 2019), (DE BARROS, 2018) (FLEURI, 2015), (DA SILVA, 2016), (SOUZA, 2018), (BAUGIS, 2016) that presents reports and solutions to the difficulties of mathematical learning, including in the early years of elementary school.

3. METHODOLOGY

This section will introduce you to the entire methodological process behind the research describing how the Systematic Revision, the Research Classification and the Procedures and Methods used specifically to achieve the objectives.

3.1 Systematic Revision

3.1.1 Research Questions

During the survey of related works, questions were defined to be answered after the analysis of the surveyed articles. The following questions were defined: a) Virtual Reality is useful in math learning? b) What are the difficulties found in understanding mathematical concepts in the early years? c) What are the advantages of using the playfulness to learn math in the early years? d) What are the advantages of using virtual reality to learn math in the early years?

3.1.2 Selection Criteria for Articles and Procedures

Kitchenham (2004) says that inclusion and exclusion criteria must be followed for articles that are returned by the search string. Therefore, the following criteria were defined: a) Inclusion of Articles (Research which deals with the use of virtual reality to teach mathematics; Research which deals with cognition in virtual reality in the context of adequate teaching; Research which deals with immersion in virtual reality in the context of stimulating learning); b) Exclusion of Articles (Researches that do not meet any inclusion criteria will not be selected; The research did not present the form used to collect data; The research did not use statistical models to analyze the obtained data; The research did not use models or questionnaires to assess whether students have difficulties learning; It was not possible to have access to complete research.

3.1.3 Classification of the Research

Aiming at a better understanding of this work, it was divided into the following categories. As for nature of it, the research was methodological; regarding the objectives it was exploratory; regarding the object of study it was ; about the approach it was quantitative as for the procedures to be researched those were from a documentary source and the following procedures were contemplated to achieve the objectives proposed in this job:

Present difficulties related to the process of teaching-learning of mathematics in the early years - present, through works related to the main learning difficulties in mathematics in the early years, in which they propose ludic means as a way to overcome any difficulties. This project will have as a product an immersive virtual environment created from solutions generated by studies in computer graphics, in order to promote logical methods assisting students in the early years;

Elaborate a set of exercises - elaborate exercises based on thematic units and objects of knowledge proposed by the National Common Curricular Base (BNCC), as well as literacy exercises that have the same focus as this work, and then the adaptations them to the virtual environment (AV) in a contextualized way, dynamic and interactive promoting playfulness in order to facilitate understanding of concepts.

Develop an action plan - together with those involved (advisor/ (who will use this product) classes)) in this project to elaborate how the activities will happen, how many times per month, how long should each action take, what content is being addressed by the teacher to adapt it to the IVE, among others important aspects for the execution phase;

Develop the immersive and interactive virtual environment - use protocols to avoid the product here originated to lose the main focus, in order to generate better learning through contextualized exercises. These exercises will be present in the IVE as challenges similar to daily problems, using techniques and concepts of immersive virtual reality. The components for displaying the IVE will be: Google Cardboards and smartphones;

Create a roadmap and define rules - elaborate good metaphors and rules of each challenge so that they fit each class respecting its specificity.

4. DEVELOPMENT

4.1 System Architecture and Tools Used

IVE requires two components, a smartphone with an Android/IOS operating system and a Google Cardboard. This work is being used as a generic device and the second version of Google Cardboard that uses a mechanical button eliminating the need for images to interact with the environment. The IVE was developed using the game engine Unity3D (2D and 3D game development tool) using the programming language C#. In search of efficient and cost-effective ways to reach our objectives, we agree with the choice of authors (FLEURI, 2015) use the Unity3D tool and resources from the Google-like, the glasses Google Cardboard in which your own development kit(Software Development Kit (SDK)) for creating applications for your use.

Besides that, Unity providing a large number of models 3D for free, other factors are mentioned by the author as relevant to the choice of this tool, such 1 - Portability; 2 - Low cost; 3 - Integration.

4.2 User Interaction and Experience

IVE uses natural human interaction through screening of the head for the user to be located in the three-dimensional space and clicks on the cardboard trigger to navigate the environment, selection of options, and interactions with objects. Thus to move around in the environment the user must aim where he wants to go and pull the trigger. The IVE interface is composed mostly of low polygon objects so that that execution is faster with no user delays move your head or interact with the environment. This delay may mainly imply problems such sensations feeling sick and losing the sense of presence, both imply a bad user experience.

4.3 Metaphors and Gameplay

This author (SILVA, 2018) define metaphors as "cognitive operations, in which we employ a more concrete experiential domain, closely linked to the experience with our own body and the world in which we live to understand a more abstract domain, whose nature of human experience does not allow a direct representation ". Thus, the use of metaphors becomes fundamental for the realization of this logical method of learning mathematical concepts. The metaphors present in this work are based on the story of Little Red Riding Hood, with the student being his own character and protagonist of the story.

4.4 History

An allusion to the traditional history of Little Red Riding Hood is created here. So now the wolf has learned his lesson from the hunter (now a lumberjack), ceasing to be the villain and starting to help Little Red Riding Hood (student) on the way to Grandma. The story starts when the little hat has to go to Grandma's house to deliver some food. In order to fulfill its objective, the little hat must solve the challenges found in the forest path. However, you need to return home before nightfall (limit time for the execution of the challenges). For at dusk the woodcutter and the wolf go away and they can no longer have a little hat.

4.5 The Environment

The environment is a representation of the countryside in which it has two farms, that of Little Red Riding Hood and that of the grandmother. When the little hat is close to either one and a melody that refers to the field is reproduced. When she reaches the forest, the melody becomes an instrumental of the original music of the story and sounds characteristic of the environment. The scenario is filled with numbers ranging from 0 to 9 spread all over the field. To make it easier to understand the order, size, and of the numbers, they were created in different sizes, as shown in Figures 1 and 2.

The lighting in the environment will darken over time, if the player reaches the border of the scenery it partially will darken and the "It didn't happen this time" screen is shown, restarting the scenery. The forest path that leads to Grandma is composed of several challenges of addition, subtraction, comparison, among others. Each completed challenge counts 10 points for the player. Each wrong answer will cost one life. If you use a hint the challenge it will cost 5 points. Following are some examples of how challenges may arise, since the numbers of certain challenges must be chosen by the player, aiming at autonomy. That is, the student must set up the operation according to the proposed signal. If it was wrong: the next challenge will address the same concept; if got it right: next concept (See Figures 1 and 2).

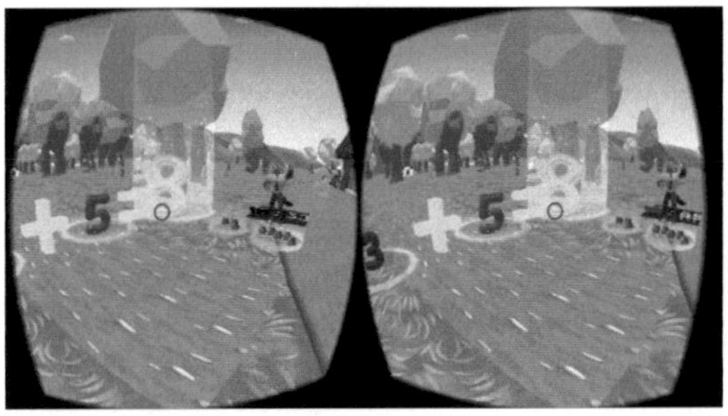

Figure 1. Numbers in sequence

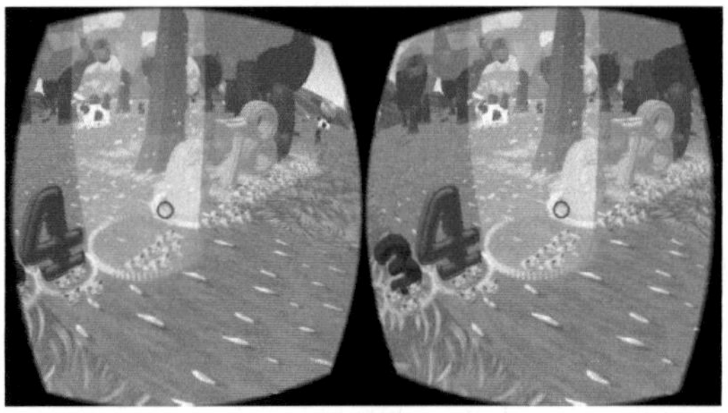

Figure 2. Numbers' Addition

There's no victory based on the number of points. The important thing is the experience because the error is the path of learning. Returning before the time is over is a motivational appeal generating competitiveness among the participants.

The "It didn't happen this time" can happen in two ways: missing 3 challenges or the environment darkening indicating that time is over.

5. EVALUATIONS

To carry out the evaluation of this AVI, one of the most known and simplest methods of investigating the level of usability of a system was used, it is called: System Usability Scale (SUS), proposed by Brooke et al., 1996. SUS can be used to evaluate applications, software, websites, services, hardware any other type of interface. SUS allows the evaluation of the following criteria: a) Effectiveness (can users complete their objectives?) B) Efficiency (how much effort and resources are needed for this?) C) Satisfaction (was the experience satisfactory?)

SUS is summarized in 10 questions, and for each of them the user can answer on a scale ranging from 1 to 5, where 1 means "Completely Disagree" and 5, means "Completely Agree". This same scale was also used to answer other questions in the category "knowledge" and "correctness" that will be presented below. In conjunction with the model proposed by Brooke et al., 1996, the Goal / Question / Metric (GQM) paradigm (; ROMBACH, 1994) was used, which consists of an objective-oriented approach to measuring products and ˜ software processes

According to Caldiera and Rombach (1994) the GQM is divided into three parts, which are: a) Conceptual level(objectives): at this level, one must define which goals it is intended to achieve; b) Operational level (questions): At this level, a set of quantifiable questions is elaborated that specify the appropriate measures for its evaluation; And c) Quantitative level (metrics): a set of data is associated with each question so that it can be answered in a quantitative way. In addition to the 10 basic questions of the SUS method, 6 other questions were asked regarding the categories "acquired knowledge" and "correctness" of the concepts applied to the system.

Based on the SUS model and the GQM approach, the evaluation model of the system proposed in this work consists of the following objectives: a) Analyze the system with the purpose of verifying usability. b) Analyze the system with the purpose of verifying its usefulness in the teaching/learning process of basic mathematical operations. c) Analyze the system with the purpose of verifying if the mathematical concepts were addressed correctly.

To collect the metrics of this evaluation model, three different groups of evaluators were considered (G1 Professionals - Mathematics teachers, G2 Academics of the Mathematics Course and G3 Academics of the Computer Science Course), according to Nielsen (1994), groups of evaluators should be formed by at least three individuals and, at most, by five individuals.

Based on metrics of the GQM model, an average result was reached, as can be seen in Figure 3. The average obtained by the SUS method was 76.66 points, with the result that the metrics MEDIAOK (one of the metrics used) was achieved, proving the ease of use by professionals and academics.

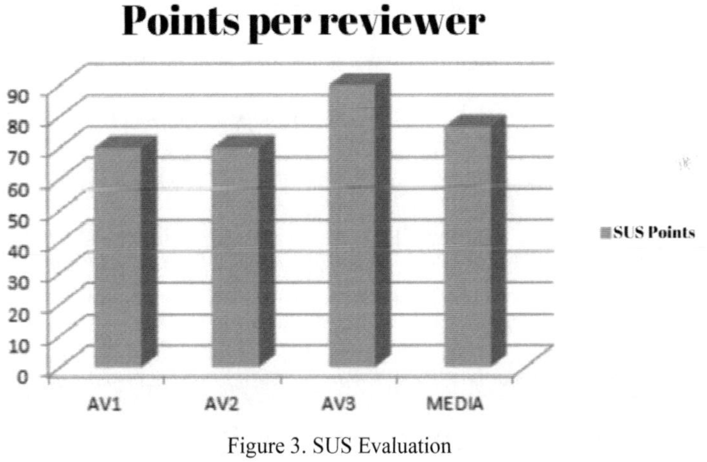

Figure 3. SUS Evaluation

6. CONCLUSION

The purpose of this research (final product) was to present an auxiliary tool in the teaching-learning process of maths in the early years, especially in basic operations. With this intention, the first step was the validation of the proposal, which despite being presented briefly in the previous section (Analysis and Tests) was achieved, based on an exhaustive analysis. The learning process itself is more complex and has many variables to consider, mainly consider wider metrics to reach conclusions, something that is being implemented in the current time.

REFERENCES

Barsalou, L. W. (2008). *Grounded cognition.Annu.* Rev. Psychol., 59:617–645.

Baugis, A. R. P. and Soares, W. B. (2016). *The use of technology as a teaching methodology: application geof geogebra in the study of analytical geometry.*

Brandt, C. F. and Moretti, M. T. (2016). *Teaching and learning math: possibilities for educational practice.* Editora UEPG.

da Silva Marinho, A., Melo, A. V. C., Poggi, G. H., Kosiur, M. B., Marrane, W. R., & Boghi, C. (2016). *Mobile application of mathematics in basic education for elementary school children from first to third grade. Research, Society and Development*, 3(1), 69-90.

de Barros, A. C. M., Cristina, A., de Medeiros, A. N. S., Andrye, C., Madeira, G., de Souza Rabelo, D. S., & Burlamaqui, A. M. F. (2018). *Tobomatics: developing learning skills with basic mathematical operations through the educational digital game.*

de Oliveira Pastana, C., da Rocha, A. P., Pereira, L. F., & Rocha, Q. H. P. (2019). *Learning Difficulties in Addiction, Subtraction, Multiplication and Division: A Case Study using CONTIG 60 with students in the 6th year of Fundamental Education.* MADRE CIÊNCIA-EDUCAÇÃO, 1(2).

Falcão, T. P., & Price, S. (2010). *Informing design for tangible interaction: a case for children with learning difficulties.* In Proceedings of the 9th International Conference on Interaction Design and Children (pp. 190-193). ACM.

Fleuri, G. S. B. and de Souza Ribeiro, M. W. (2015). Project of an immersive serious game, of low cost and high portability, aimed at learning people with ediscalculia dyslexia. Sociedade Brasileira de Computacao (SBC), 6:193–195

Gomes, N. V., & Santos, W. L. S. (2015). The Process of Teaching and Learning in Mathematics: linking theory with practice in the school space. Maiêutica-Matemática.

Keitel, C., Damerow, P., Bishop, A., Gerdes, P. (1989). Mathematics, education, and society. Science and Technology Education, Document Series.

Krokos, E., Plaisant, C., Varshney, A. (2019). *Virtual memory palaces: immersion aids recall.* Virtual Reality, 23(1), 1-15.

Kubo, O. M., & Botomé, S. P. (2001). Teaching-learning: an interaction between two behavioral processes. Interaction in Psychology, 5(1).

Lee, I., & Jones, C. J. (2013). In full bloom: A brain education guide for successful aging. SCB Distributors.

Mundkur, N. (2005). Neuroplasticidade em crianças. The Indian Journal of Pediatrics , 72 (10), 855-857.

Nacarato, A. M., da Silva Mengali, B. L., & Passos, C. L. B. (2017). Mathematics in the early years of elementary school-Weaving threads of teaching and learning. Authentic.

P. L. C. Lima, R. Gibbis Júnior, e E. Françozo, (2011). *Emergence and nature of the primary metaphor to wish is to be hungry*, Cad. Est. Ling., vol. 40, p. 107-140.

Rueda, M. R., Rothbart, M. K., McCandliss, B. D., Saccomanno, L., & Posner, M. I. (2005). *Training, maturation, and genetic influences on the development of executive attention.* Proceedings of the National Academy of Sciences, 102(41), 14931-14936.

Santos, W., & Santos, D. (2010). Mathematical Education and Playful Activities: Building Productive Spaces for Thought in the Elementary Schools.

Silva, L. G., da Silva Ribeiro, J. L., & Teixeira, A. L. (2018). *Math Learning in the First Phase of Fundamental Education.* Ciclo Revista, 3(1).

Souza, F., Barreto, F., Rodrigues, A., Barboza, B., & Silva, M. (2018, October). *Development Process of a Serious Game for Teaching the Four Mathematical Operations.* In Proceedings of the Workshops of the Brazilian Congress on Informatics in Education. (Vol. 7, No. 1, p. 1147).

HOLOGRAPHIC INTERACTION: FROM DESIGN TO CONSTRUCTION OF A HOLOGRAPHIC DISPLAY ANIMATED BY REAL-TIME MOTION CAPTURE

Gabriel Antonio Corso Anciuti and Mônica Stein
Universidade Federal de Santa Catarina, Brazil

ABSTRACT

In this paper, a method for designing a 3D hologram controlled by motion capture and visualized through a holographic pyramid is presented. The paper covers the prototyping of the equipment with a view applied to the use of an interactive display with the public. This prototype can be used so that, for example, in a superhero exhibition, the visitor will be able to choose a character and, by using a motion capture suit, control that character in a way that he or she wishes. Since the holographic pyramid allows more than a single person to make part of the scene and the others around also watch the interaction, its advantage is that it is not an individual experience, as is the case with other current technologies.

KEYWORDS

Motion Capture, Real-time Animation, Hologram, Interactivity, Display

1. INTRODUCTION

Holography, a technique for projecting three-dimensional images through the use of light, was presented and popularized as we know in the film Star Wars: Episode IV – A New Hope (1977). In that instance, the practice consisted in projecting a light beam in the space during playback of an audio recording. Spectators, thus, would be able to, in addition to hearing the message, see the person speaking.

With the rise of computer graphics, creating entirely digital content became possible, through the process known as computer-generated imagery (CGI). An interesting aspect of producing 3D CGI is that by making use of 4 cameras around the same object and the position of the camera in the display it is possible to project an object that truly appears to be three-dimensional inside the pyramid as, when looking at it from different sides of the pyramid, it will be possible to see the object in different perspectives.

It is possible to bring that object to life using different animation techniques. In traditional 3D animation, predefined movements are generated, and, with the aid of programming tools, movement flows may be created in response to actions or commands assigned through specific programs. Another solution for animating an object is motion capture, also known as mocap. Commonly used for animation of humanoid beings. After capture, there is a refinement process to improve movement quality. In both forms, the procedure is conducted in steps and results are determined after the rendering process is concluded.

Few softwares in the market can generate results in real time. Among them is the game engine called Unreal Engine 4 (UE4). With this software it is possible to create in real-time high-end quality animation.

Considering that, the aim of this prototype is to create, for commercial purposes, a holographic display integrated with motion capture and real-time rendering to allow interactions with the public, transforming the spectator from a receiver of information into an active agent, able to move around and interact with the content presented inside the display.

2. APPLICATIONS

Before showing how to integrate motion capture into a character and project it onto a holographic pyramid, this section presents some solutions that use motion capture as a means of interaction with the audience or users, these being The Void park, the VRChat application, and a new wave of vloggers, the VTubers.

The VOID: When we talk about entertainment, we have advanced interaction technologies such as the one employed by the company THE VOID, which merges a virtual scenario into a real structure and is presented in more detail in a video on youtube, accessed through the link: https://www.youtube.com/watch?v=cML814JD09g.

VRChat: It is a chat and social interaction app that the user can use from the basics of the virtual reality system, as well as augment it with full body trackers for an even more immersive experience. You can see in this video from ChrisQuitsReality channel, the use of full body trackers and how the result is seen within the platform. Access the video through the link: https://www.youtube.com/watch?v=2OROYh0KXss.

VTubers: With the high demand for content on the Internet stemming from the social isolation caused by the coronavirus pandemic, content producers for stream platforms have been reinventing themselves to create content that is unique and differentiated from the market. One such example is the use of full body motion capture to build a virtual vloguer by using motion capture to transmit the actor's every move to his avatar. You can see this technique at work directly on CodeMiko's channel on Twitch.tv, available at: https://www.twitch.tv/codemiko/.

3. OVERVIEW

From this point on, the structuring of the project begins, bringing a summary of all the topics that will be covered during the work - operation of the holographic pyramid; motion capture; real-time integration.

3.1 Pyramid Functioning

A holographic pyramid is a construction that reflects the image projected by a light source back into itself. In this prototype we use an image projector and a pyramid composed of 3 sides with a 45 degree angle.

3.2 Concepts of Motion Capture

The motion capture system used in this prototype was inertial, which consists of trackers positioned at the main points of articulation of the human body that send the information of the movement of these points in space. Using specialized software that reads the information and triangulates the movement captured by the trackers and transferring to the character the actor's real movement.

3.3 Real-Time Integration

Today, there are graphics engines capable of interpreting and reproducing the information captured from motion sensors and applying it to a character in real time. This allows new types of interaction to be made with the information received from the mocap as presented in the Black Mirror episode "Rachel, Jack and Ashley Too".

During the research and development phase of the prototype, there were two applications of this interaction that drew attention.

One of them, the Bebylon project by the company Kite & Lightning, winner of Siggraph's Real-Time Live category in 2018, in which Xsense clothing and the iPhone's 3D camera are used to control the character in the project presentation - presentation available at https://www.youtube.com/watch?v=lXZhgkNFGfM.

The other was the Corridor Digital channel showed the steps on how to create a video entirely through 3D animation, without the need to have people present, available at https://www.youtube.com/watch?v=iHaEJ7Qslds. For this, they used the same system as the Bebylon project presentation, but not in real time.

3.4 Interaction with the Public

The interaction with the audience for the prototype in question, was born from the analysis of the Bebylon project presentation along with the success that the dances in the game Fortnite had, considering that in a first moment, how-to videos teaching the dances featured in the game reached the top of Youtube views and now, EPIC has been working to implement famous dances within the game. Still, when we proposed this prototype, the idea was for the spectator to be able to interact with the characters he likes, not only imitating the character's gestures, but also making the character move the way the spectator wants.

4. METHOD

The execution of the prototype had two fronts, the physical and the digital. Both could be executed in parallel until the camera system stage, because to obtain a good result, it was important that this camera system was tested with the physical part finalized.

4.1 Building the Pyramid

The construction of the pyramid was divided into 3 phases - the adaptation of the model to optimize the projection space, scaling and fabrication.

Adaptation: In order to maximize the space available for use, a three-sided pyramid was chosen, so that the application area would be bigger, as shown in Figure 1.

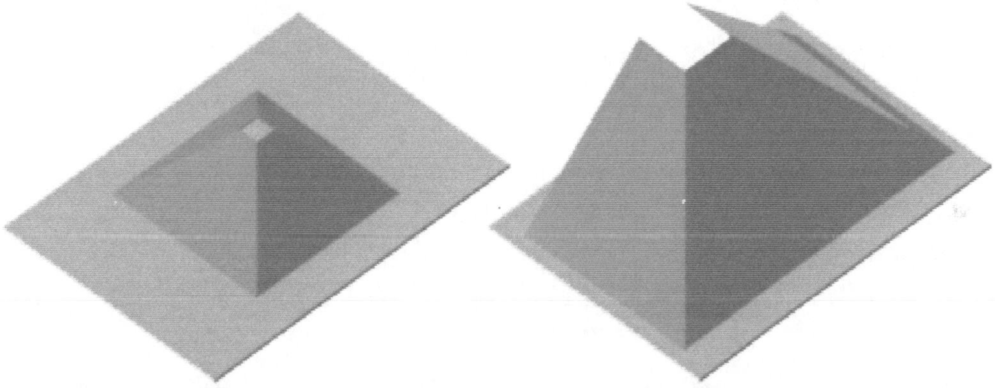

Figure 1. Comparison of space utilization of a four-sided pyramid versus a three-sided pyramid

Scaling: From this, we scaled the pyramid presented by Schivani (2018) that had trapezoids with dimensions 24 cm base, 14 cm height and 4 cm top by increasing its size by 1.35 times, thus, the trapezoids became 32.4 cm base, 18.9 cm height and 5.4 cm top, so that the total size of the pyramid does not exceed the usable area of the chosen screen.

Fabrication: In the tests conducted by Schivani (2018), he pointed out that the use of acrylic in making the pyramid generates internal reflection. From the calculations and schematics shown in his article, it was noted that the thicker acrylic results in less perceptible reflection. Therefore, the thickness of the acrylic used in the prototype was 2mm.

4.2 Equipment Installation and Configuration

During the execution of this prototype, the company's inertial mocap system Noitom, Perception Neurom, the company's own data interpretation system called Axis Neuron, and UE4 were used. To perform the configuration of streaming data between from Axis Neuron to Unreal Engine, you need to follow the AXIS NEURON + Unreal Configuration (2019) guide to the end.

Briefly, the procedure was:

a. Configure the *Broadcasting system* and *data output format* within Axis Neuron;

b. Create a project in UE4 with the name "NEURONDEMO";

c. Insert the plugin files into the "Plugins" folder of the project and restart the EU;

d. Import the character with the *Skeletal Mesh* option activated;

e. Create an *animation blueprint* on the *skeleton* with a node of type *NewPoseCalc* and linked to *FinalAnimationPose*;

f. Create an *actor* and add the *PerceptionNeuron* and *SkeletalMesh* components, linking the animation and the previously imported character;

g. Insert the actor in the scene and check in the *PerceptionNeuron* component if the *Avatar Name* corresponds to the character name in Axis Neuron;

h. Add the *Perception Neuron Manager* in the scene, and configure so that the settings are coherent with the ones placed in step a.

4.3 Motion Capture Suit

With the system properly setup, the actor was dressed and the system was calibrated.

The calibration of this system was done in the Steady, A and T poses, ensuring that the system interpreted the information generated by the markers correctly.

4.4 Creating a Scene for Hologram Composition

To create the scene composition for the hologram required a character model, the camera setup, and the video output configuration so that the projected image would match the desired one.

4.4.1 3D Character

To adapt the 3D model so that the skin and skeleton of the character were compatible with the information received from the trackers, we used Adobe's Mixamo platform.

4.4.2 Camera Settings

To project the hologram on this pyramid, it was necessary to capture the object through 3 cameras at the same time and arrange them so that each one presents its content in a specific part of the screen. For this, the user interface system was used, so it was possible to better control where each camera projected the captured image.

In the following, the entire step-by-step description of how to create this interface to reproduce the hologram will be described.

a. Create a third-person project in Unreal Engine to have the basis of a character followed by a camera;

b. Remove all the components of the scene, keeping only the ground;

c. Open the *ThirdPersonCharacter* component editor;

d. Apply the *Skeletal Mesh* of the character that was previously configured to receive the motion capture data;

e. Create 3 *Spring Arm Components* and add 1 camera of type *2D Scene Capture Component* as a child of each of them, this way we will have the hierarchy as shown in Figure 2;

f. To make the images from the side cameras fit correctly in the interface we add to the *Springs Arms Components* an x-axis rotation of +90 degrees and -90 degrees for the left and right sides of the object, respectively;

g. The distance between the cameras and the object is at the discretion of whoever is doing this configuration, as it depends on the size of the object to be projected and how the scene will be displayed. Ideally it should be configured at the end of the process so that it is possible to see the result with the interface already configured.

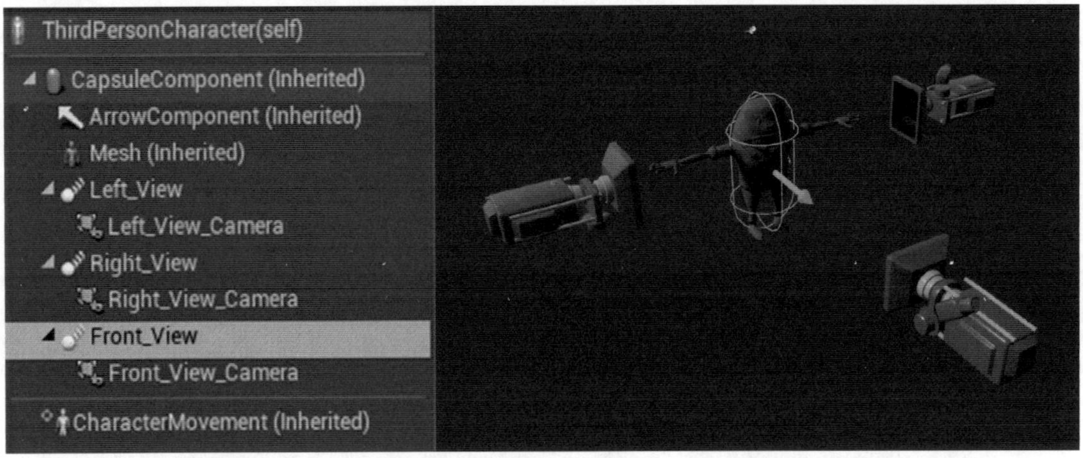

Figure 2. Hierarchy of basic components for output image creation and Third-person character view with all the componentes configured

4.4.3 Video Output Configuration

With the 3 cameras pointed at the character, it was necessary to turn them into part of the User Interface.

The following procedure should be performed three times, once per camera.

a. To set up a *User Interface element*, we need to create a *Material* and change its properties from *Material Domain* to *User Interface* and from *Blend Mode* to *Translucent*. This way it is possible to use an opacity mask to not overlap one camera with another, as shown in Figure 3;

Figure 3. Image of the three masks used in display creation. For the right, center and left camera, respectively

b. You need to add two *Texture Samples* to the *material blueprint*, one will receive the image from the *2D camera* that was created in the *ThirdPersonCharacter* and the other the *mask* relative to that camera.

c. To finish creating the *User Interface element*, you must adjust the size parameters of the X and Y axis of the *2D camera* so that they are the same size as the *mask* that will be applied.

d. With the 3 *User Interface elements* created, it is time to create the *User Interface* through the *Widget Blueprint*.

e. Within this *blueprint*, it is necessary to define the size to be compatible with the scale of the monitor or projector that will be used.

f. Afterwards, you must import the interface elements. To do this, simply select them and drag them into the *Widget Blueprint*.

g. At the end of the process, the resulting image will be close to the one shown in Figure 4.

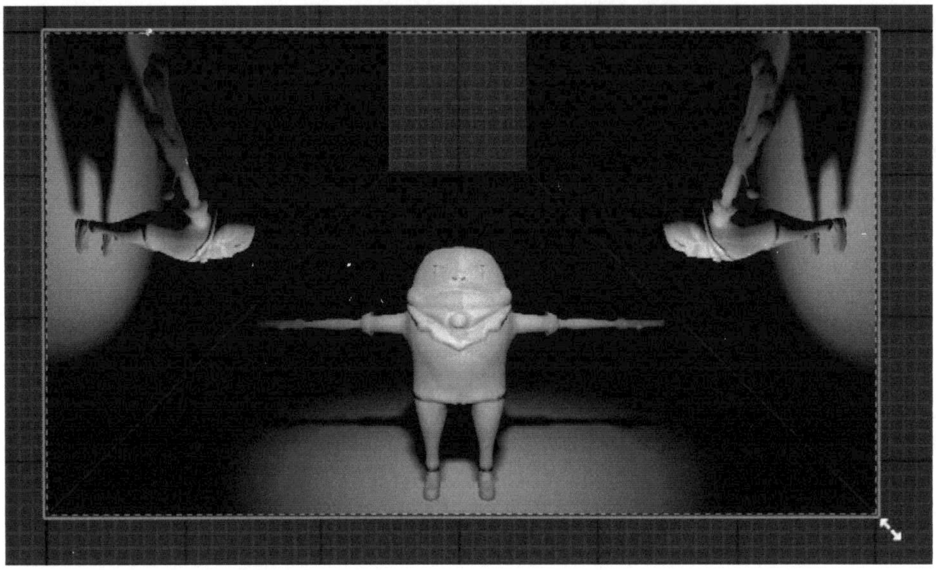

Figure 4. Output image compatible with the pyramid display

4.5 Presentation of Results

When running the project, the pyramid will present the image as seen in the video below:

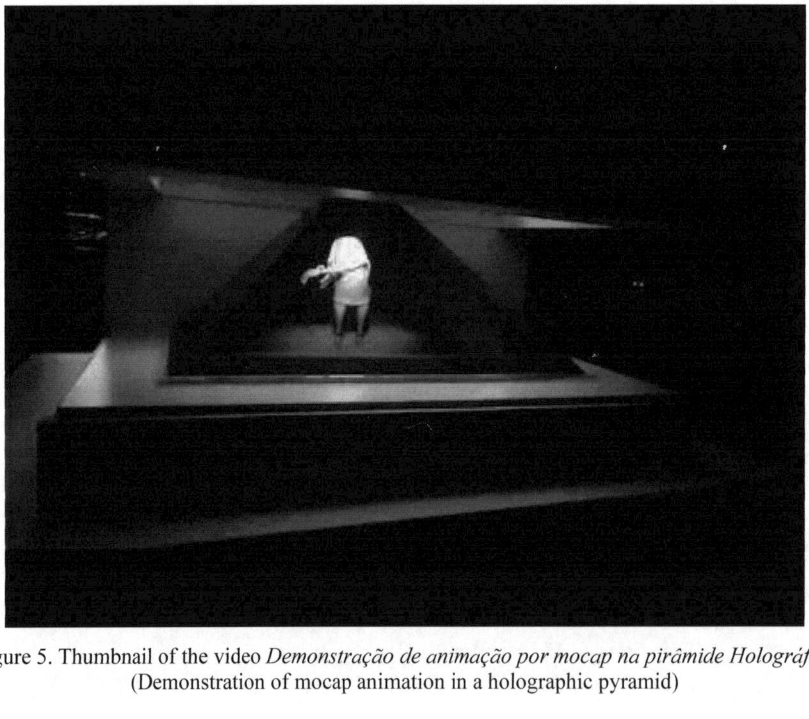

Figure 5. Thumbnail of the video *Demonstração de animação por mocap na pirâmide Holográfica* (Demonstration of mocap animation in a holographic pyramid)

5. IMPROVEMENTS AND IMPLEMENTATION

Since it is a prototype, the system has several points for improvement and we foresee cases where there may be problems that we could not test during the production of this prototype.

Improvements: Among the improvements foreseen for the prototype we have the shape tests, varying angulation of the sides and shape of the pyramid to be able to generate larger projections in reduced spaces and the amplification of the motion capture system, using full body trackers, facial recognition, and the addition of other actors to the scene, being able to use cameras fixed on the scenery and not on the actors, creating an interaction space instead of an individual projection. The application of this display can also be thought with the actor located inside the pyramid, producing around himself, a projection of the character, as if it were an aura, effects already reproduced in miniatures as can be seen in this video from ZW Design, on YouTube (available at: https://www.youtube.com/watch?v=22hp-WBoTTc), aiming for a result close to the one represented in the image compilation of figure 6.

Figuras 6. Compilation of images taken from the internet that illustrate the Jinchūriki forms in Naruto, Razor's elemental burst in Genshin Impact and ZW Design's holographic display for comparison

Implementation: There are some problems that we have already foreseen for the final implementation phase, among them the possibility of external lighting interfering with the pyramid's reflection, making it difficult to see the effects in brightly lit spaces or under an open sky, we also know that to recreate a hologram in larger sizes, a considerable amount of space and other display formats will be required, and also, in this prototype, we do not pay attention to the hologram's performance issues, requiring an optimization by programming in the game engine in order to generate a result with higher image quality and more elements.

6. CONCLUSIONS

The development of this holagram aiming at the commercial market of a project opens ways to explore new applications of the holographic pyramid, showing that this technology can still be explored in other ways. With the project model created during this project, it is possible for any animator to create their 3D content for display inside a holographic pyramid, making the necessary adaptations for each case.

Considering these results, we see that the use of holographic pyramids in fairs and exhibitions can stop being a passive environment, where the spectators just watch the animations, and become an active environment, allowing the public to interact with the content inside. Besides entertainment, other branches can take advantage of this technology, such as engineering, where it can be used for the same purpose as Virtual Reality prototypes.

REFERENCES

Araújo, E. P., (2018). *Pirâmide" holográfica": uma introdução ao estudo da óptica no ensino fundamental*. MS thesis, Universidade Federal do Rio Grande do Norte. [Viewed 12 may 2021]. Available from: https://repositorio.ufrn.br/handle/123456789/26475

Black Mirror, Series 5, Chapter Three, Rachel, Jack and Ashley Too., (2016). [Online]. Directed by Anne Sewitsky. Scotts Valley, C.A.: Netflix. Available from: Netflix.

ChrisQuitsReality., (2020). Full Body Trolling in VRChat! (Index + Trackers) [online]. *YouTube*. [Viewed Viewed 12 may 2021]. Available from: https://youtu.be/2OROYh0KXss

Corridor Crew., (2020). How I Made a Movie WITHOUT Actors, Sets, or Cameras [online]. *YouTube*. [Viewed Viewed 12 may 2021]. Available from: https://youtu.be/iHaEJ7Qslds

Deepak Tulsyan., (2019). How to Do The Backpack Kid Dance (THE FLOSS) | Deepak Tulsyan Dance Tutorial [online]. *YouTube*. [Viewed Viewed 12 may 2021]. Available from: https://youtu.be/0Kj3wWKjMSQ

Faber, T., (2021). VTubers and the women behind the masks. *Financial Times* [online]. 2021. [Viewed 12 may 2021]. Available from: https://www.ft.com/content/9d8ec8be-1329-4840-8428-e787058169ff

Helm 361° Marketing., (2014). Dreamoc Scandinavia 360 XXL Champagne Case [online]. *YouTube*. [Viewed Viewed 12 may 2021]. Available from: https://youtu.be/6wIAfvbaeRU

Park, G., (2015). Fortnite was the biggest pop culture phenomenon of 2018. *Washington Post* [online]. 2018. [Viewed 12 may 2021]. Available from: https://www.washingtonpost.com/technology/2018/12/27/fortnite-was-biggest-pop-culture-phenomenon/

Schivani, M. et al. (2017). Pirâmide "holográfica": erros conceituais e potencial didático. *Revista Brasileira de Ensino de Física* [online]. **40**(1). [Viewed 12 may 2021]. Available from: doi: 10.1590/1806-9126-RBEF-2017-0186

The VOID., (2015). First look at THE VOID [online]. *YouTube*. [Viewed Viewed 12 may 2021]. Available from: https://youtu.be/cML814JD09g

uniSheffieldLib., (2016). The benefits of Open Access: researchers' perspectives [online]. *YouTube*. [Viewed 17 August 2016]. Available from: https://youtu.be/Tcc-SwhDlD4

xanadu., (2018). Bebylon Wins 1st Siggraph Real-Time Live 2018! [online]. *YouTube*. [Viewed Viewed 12 may 2021]. Available from: https://youtu.be/lXZhgkNFGfM

ZW Design., (2015). ZW Design - Holografia Goku - Dragon Ball Z [online]. *YouTube*. [Viewed Viewed 12 may 2021]. Available from: https://youtu.be/22hp-WBoTTc

TELEWORK OF INTERIOR ENVIRONMENT IN JAPANESE STUDENT

Takeshi Sato[1], Mizuki Nakajima[1], Ryota Murano[2], Macky Kato[2] and Yousuke Takeishi[3]
[1]*Jissen Woment's University, 4-1-1, Osakaue Hino, Tokyo Japan*
[2]*Waseda University, 3-579-15, Tokorozawa, Saitama Japan*
[3]*Kyushu Institute of Information Science , 6-3-1, Dazaifu, Fukuoka Japan*

ABSTRACT

Due to the pandemic of the COVID-19 infection, almost Japanese university were to move the classes online. Heretofore, there were canceled as a face-to-face gave the guidance for entrance ceremony, registering for the course and lectures except for special skill trainings. Almost university student had to join the classes from their room of the residence. Under in ordinary circumstances, it was free utilization of campus equipment as open space PC and library for their own learning. For the experienced student, it was prepared high performance computer in each laboratory. However there were expected up to about 90 minutes in a day by 5 frames, approximately totally 8 hours at the longest, and additional assignments of these lessons will be handled by telework in their room. Originally, it was hard to say that all university students were able to get telework in an appropriate environment, because of conditions precedent using campus equipment as schooling. Moreover, prolonged VDT work in improper posture cause to increase the frequency of ergonomic injuries and illnesses. The purpose of this study was to investigate the individual student environment of working for ICT in the rooms. The individual data from photo was classification desk, chair, chair with armrest or not, desk light, cushion for ergonomic evaluation as a guideline of Ministry of Health, Labour and Welfare. The Data were collected over 300 students via cloud e-Learning system from May to December in 2020.There were 30% student who has no chair, using low table and sitting the floor. There were 23% student has used Japanese style low table called Chabudai for the attend their classes. The major findings out of this study, it was not enough the equipment for the long hours study in a day about 23% student from their room. There was significant difference population proportion teszt between male and female, using desk or low table. It was conducted an online questionnaire to over 300 university students in their 20s to investigate whether an appropriate working environment was established. Compare and evaluate with the ideal working environment and report the current situation.

KEYWORDS

Telework, Household Goods, Room Interior

1. INTRODUCTION

In 7th April 2020, the Government of Japan had first issued a state of emergency. It was performed time leg for staggered school attendance at least, almost university classes were to change the online mode as same as e-Learning in Tokyo. Generally, Japanese university has a few computer rooms for free to use every student to study activity as same as library. That's why, the student has to study their own room and interior equipment.

It was well known subjective discomfort, work posture and muscle activity of PC users were quantitatively evaluated. Risk assessment and prevention of musculoskeletal disorders (MSDs) or physical discomfort of personal computer (PC) users have been a frequent topic in previous research from prevalence PCs the 1980s. These studies have described biomechanical and epidemiological evidence that supports the association between prolonged use of computer displays and data entry devices as keyboard and mouse in awkward postures and the development of MSDs or discomfort of the neck, shoulder, wrist and hand of PC users of various ages (Jaschinski et al. 1998, Gerr et al. 2004). However, it was focused on between office workers and exclusive use for prevention of human error, using alternative data entry devices or displays, such as touchscreens. Therefore, there was not enough data about telework environment of individuals, about desk and chair. It is not known how users would determine the most preferred position of the screen when they are required to operate what they see in the display and how the preferred position of the posture in home would influence user discomfort and other biomechanical risk factors, such as the activity of upper extremity and neck muscles. Many companies were to permit bring back to home the monitor and chair in office. In the Tokyo metropolitan area of universities were to assist communication of first Internet connection for video conference as the Zooming classes.

In the current study, the sitting position, shoulder and neck muscle activities, subjective ratings of visual discomfort and the movement of participants' elbows were quantified during an individual computer use task in home (typing using keyboard, mouse operations) of their own ICT environment. It was hypothesized that the use of PCs would be associated with home goods and subjective depended on desk and chair in home equipment more frequent fatiguing postures for long hours learning by PC using.

2. METHODS

There were 388 university students from 19 to 23 years old participated in this study. It was collected the telework environment as their room photo of taken the room by themselves. It was performed analysis procedure, with or without chair, kind of chair, with chair high adjustment function or without, seating face environment, chair elbow holder or not, kind of desk shape, kind of chair type, lighting, overall working environment. The analysis was done manually. There was a few student no desk and no chair. During the process of the analysis, there was a few student having multiple study room, then items that did not correspond to the items were excluded. Therefore, the total for each item was different. After classification from photos, it was calculated the popular proportion each sort items while sexuality and universities.

3. RESULT

There were 91 % students using the laptop PCs in their room (Figure 1). There were about 20 % without chair (Figure 2). In case of own the chair, not adjustable chair high was 43 % (Figure 3). It was 17 % chair with arm rest (Figure 4), 32% sheeting face with something of cushion (Figure 5). There was 14% using Japanese low table called "Chabudai" (Figure 7). It was illustrated Japanese low table on the PC, called Chabudai. There was significant difference population proportion test between male and female in desk or low table, also arm rest or not in chair. It was preferred to choose the room interior in women's university student as low table than normal desk. Then, it was a lot of population proportion in statically, male student has sitting the chair with arm rest.

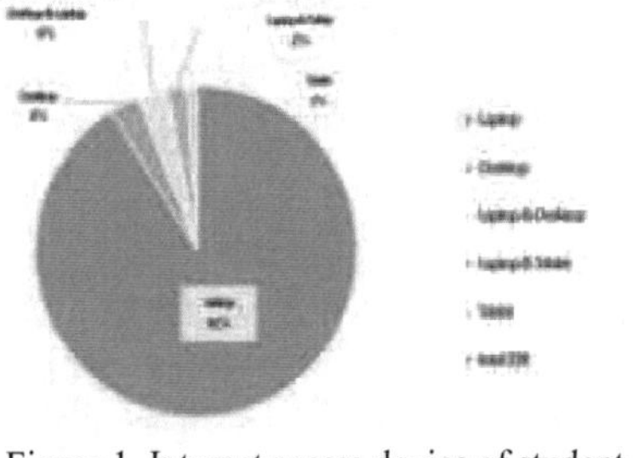

Figure 1. Internet access device of student

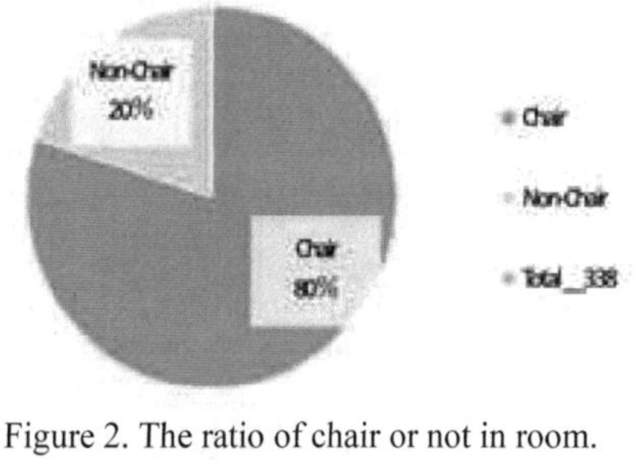

Figure 2. The ratio of chair or not in room.

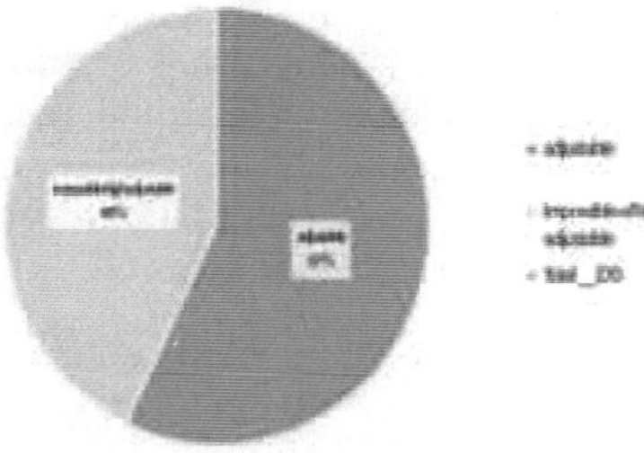

Figure 3. The ratio of high adjustable chair or not

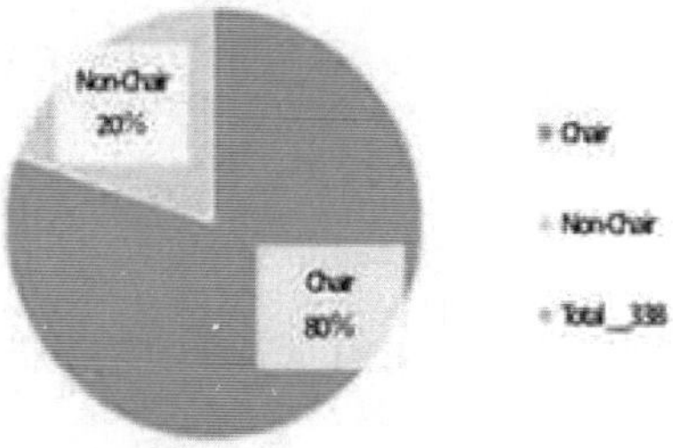

Figure 4. The ratio of arm rest with chair or not

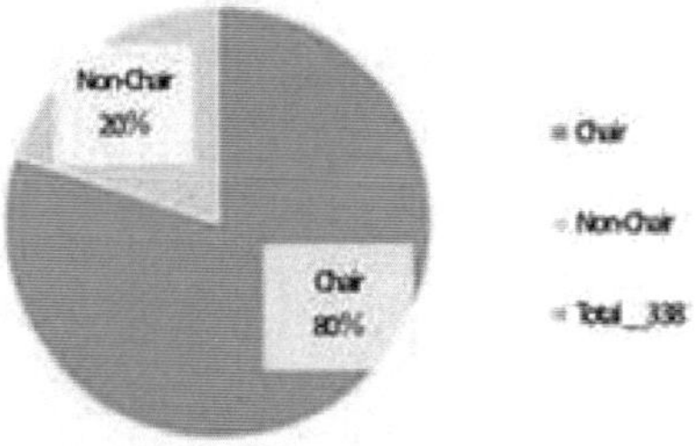

Figure 5. The ratio of cushion using with bearing surface of chair or not

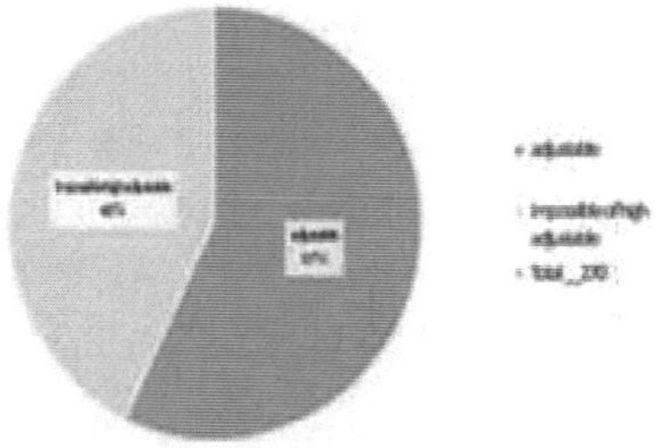

Figure 6. The ratio of type of table as a desk

Figure 7. Japanese low table, called Chabudai on PC

Figure 8. Typical recommendation home goods in room

4. DISCUSSION

About 80% of university students use chairs in their work environment. Although it occupies, the ratio of proper maintenance as a VDT work environment is less than 30% as a whole. Traditional Japanese-style rooms have floors of tatami mats (Figure 7). The mats are made of straw and rush and consist of a thick base and a soft, smooth surface that covers the base. There was not suitable to put on computer chair in traditional Japanese room, because of soft material for floors in Japanese houses. It is not unsuitable for teleworking, but it is clear that most students are working in an environment that is inadequate for several hours of continuous work. If you continue to work in this environment, you will be more likely to suffer health problems such as VDT syndrome, which is a concern. It was considered that there was a low awareness and awareness of the recommended work environment, and there was a limit to the improvement of the work environment for students living alone or not having their own room. Therefore, it may be possible to raise awareness and promote improvement of the working environment by knowing the current state of the teleworking environment of university students through this survey. In addition, it is expected that it will contribute to the development of a fulfilling learning environment that matches the learning content.

5. CONCLUSION

A reasonable accommodation is required as any change in the telework environment to help a student with a better performance apply for their student life, or enjoy the benefits for health conditions. Then sitting behind a desk for hours at a time, it was possibility of a career of neck and back pain or sore wrists and fingers. It was considered proper home ergonomics, including correct chair height, adequate equipment spacing and good desk posture, for student stay comfortable at their room.

ACKNOWLEDGEMENT

We wish to thank the timely help given by Miss. Mei Takiguchi in analyzing the large number of photos.

REFERENCES

Gerr, F., Marcus, M., and Monteilh, C., 2004. Epidemiology of musculoskeletal disorders among computer users: lesson learned from the role of posture and keyboard use. Journal of Electromyography and Kinesiology, 14 (1), 25–31.

Jaschinski, W., Heuer, H., and Kylian, H., 1998. Preferred position of visual displays relative to the eyes: a field study of visual strain and individual differences. Ergonomics, 41 (7), 1034–1049.

INVOLVING DIVERSE USERS FOR INCLUSIVE TECHNOLOGY DEVELOPMENT

Kristin Skeide Fuglerud[1], Till Halbach[1] and Mikael Snaprud[2]
[1]*Norsk Regnesentral, Postboks 114 Blindern, NO-0314 Oslo, Norway*
[2]*Tingtun AS, Lillesand, Norway*

ABSTRACT

This work discusses recommendations for including diverse users in universal and inclusive design of ICT and discusses some challenges and possibilities of remote user involvement. Related research recommends a user-centered design process, the involvement of individuals with a wide range of abilities and disabilities, and to have user participation in all development stages, such as needs assessment, co-creation sessions and trials. However, there is little guidance in the literature regarding tools and techniques for inclusive co-creation on equal means for all, especially when it comes to remote participation. The paper discusses various methods and techniques for inclusive design that can be performed remotely, including focus groups, workshops, personas, and scenarios. Our analysis suggests that, with the proper tools and techniques, performing such activities remotely can have other advantages than traditional approaches, such as reduced time and costs for both participants and researchers, as well as the potential for greater diversity since one can recruit from a greater geographic area. Finally, we present ongoing work to make use of remote feedback as a valuable tool for user involvement in inclusive design.

KEYWORDS

Accessibility, Universal Design, Inclusive Design, Remote, Disabilities, Impairments

1. INTRODUCTION

The Norwegian government wants to put the user's needs in the center during the digitalization and development of public services (KMD, 2021). Their strategy underscores that, as the EU Web Accessibility Directive (EU-WAD, 26 October 2016) will be incorporated into Norwegian law, public entities are to follow the requirements for universal design of ICT solutions, and that this also applies to public procurement.

Besides the political regulations, research has found good reasons why users should be involved during the development of new technology. Simple conformance to accessibility guidelines is a common strategy on the road towards more accessible products and services. However, following accessibility guidelines do not necessarily uncover all barriers that people experience when using ICT solutions (Power *et al.*, 2012). Moreover, there is no clear relationship between the priority levels provided in the guidelines and how severe usability and accessibility problems were rated by accessibility experts and users with disabilities (Harrison and Petrie, 2007).

It is, however, not clear what user involvement implies in order to assure the inclusiveness of the final product or service. This work tries to answer some aspects related to this question, in particular in light of the need for remote participation, as we have seen since the beginning of the Covid-19 pandemic.

In the following, we review and discuss related research with the objective to compile some recommendations for the inclusive development of an accessible and usable user feedback channel for websites, as required by EU's WAD. The conclusion summarizes our discussions and gives a brief outlook of future work.

2. RELATED WORK

For a better overview, we have categorized related work according to six broader topics and dedicate each topic to a section of its own.

2.1 Human-Centered Design and Continuous Focus on Diversity

Researchers and practitioners recommend any effort for the universal design of ICT to be based on a human-centred and participatory design process, involving a broad range of stakeholders throughout the design process, including people from vulnerable populations (Stephanidis *et al.*, 2019). The development should be iterative and include empirical evaluations with diverse users throughout the design process (Horton and Sloan, 2014).

Several standards include guidance on how users can be involved in design processes in order to implement accessible ICT systems. The international standard ISO/IEC 30071-1:2019 takes a holistic approach by combining guidance both at an organizational and a system development level (ISO/IEC, 2019). The standard also details how to conduct user testing with diverse users. The international standard ISO 9241-210:2019 provides general and broad guidance regarding human-centered design principles and activities throughout the life cycle of computer-based interactive systems (ISO 9241-210, 2010). Also, NS 11040:2013 is a Norwegian standard with recommendations for how to involve diverse users when developing ICT products and services (NS 11040, 2013).

In many current development projects, user involvement is not prioritized because of various constraints, such as lack of awareness, priority, time, and costs (Hussein *et al.*, 2019). Involving users with disabilities is often viewed to be extra challenging, for example due to a limited availability of users, and lack of training and costs (Power and Petrie, 2019). While the success of user involvement depends on how it is conducted and managed, researchers have found that user involvement can make an important and positive difference, particularly when it comes to ease of use for various user groups involved (Borch and Strandbakken, 2019; Fischer, Peine and Östlund, 2020).

2.2 Inclusive Co-Creation

Some authors make a distinction between traditional user-centered design (UCD) on the one side, and participatory design (PD) and co-creation on the other side, where UCD is about designing *for* the users while PD and co-creation is about designing *with* the users (Andrews, 2014). Universal design emphasizes the latter, and depending on context and project phase, a variety of methods and techniques can be used. In this paper, a method is considered to be a class of specific operating procedures, while a technique refers to a single procedure or heuristic, that is, a specific implementation of a method.

There are a plethora of methods and techniques from UCD, PD, user experience and design thinking that could be relevant for inclusive co-creation. Examples include Paper Prototyping, Personas, Card sorting, Storytelling, Dot voting, Empathy map, Inspiration cards, etc. See e.g. (*How To & Tools*, 2020). However, it is often necessary to adapt or to develop new and more accessible techniques because current techniques are not accessible to a wide diversity of users. For example, many techniques depend upon participants being able to use and draw on visual materials (Andrews, 2014). Such techniques should therefore be adapted or changed to engage and include visually or motor impaired participants.

Including people with disabilities in research and development projects requires extra awareness of various needs such as accessibility of tools and materials, transportation, mobility, health, communication, conflicts of values, professionals' attitudes, and interpreting data from diverse populations (Wattenberg, 2005). In the following we discuss the inclusivity of a few common methods for user involvement that can be conducted remotely.

2.3 Online Focus Groups

Online focus groups have been used to study consumer attitudes since the early 1990s (Reisner *et al.*, 2018). In the early days, they were conducted mainly through text-based chat. An important advantage of online focus groups is that traveling and getting to a suitable and accessible physical setting are not necessary. This can reduce complexity, costs and time for both research participants and researchers. Also, conducting focus groups online allows for participants from a greater geographic area, making it easier to reach participants from small subgroups of the population, and provide potential for greater diversity among participants.

A disadvantage of online settings is the limited possibility to pick up nonverbal signals. This may lead participants to misunderstand one another or researchers to miss nuances conveyed through body language. The more impersonal nature of online environments may also negatively affect the group dynamic and engagement among the participants (Reisner *et al.*, 2018).

Although online and in-person focus groups may differ, research has found that the content generated by the two forms is notably similar (Woodyatt, Finneran and Stephenson, 2016). Reisner et al. (2018) provides recommendations to counteract potentially negative aspects of online focus groups. While the recommendations are mainly related to text-based focus groups, they may be worth considering for video-based arrangements as well. To facilitate group cohesion, it is recommended to encourage participants to interact and share information about themselves in the beginning. They also found that encouraging storytelling among the participants can further promote rich data sharing.

2.4 Co-Creation Workshops

Various types of workshops are common in co-creation (Akoglu and Dankl, 2019). Usually, co-creators are gathered in one physical room, giving the participants the possibility of getting to know each other and to participate in exercises and discussions to explore a subject or a design. Common aspects of methods are roleplay, prototyping and sharing of ideas to foster joint solutions based on empathy and mutual learning.

Various digital design tools for co-creation are also emerging, see e.g., Miro.com, Mural.com and Hoylu.com. However, such tools may also have challenges when it comes to accessibility for various user groups. While there are guidelines and standards for accessible meetings and conferences, there is little knowledge on accessible digital tools for inclusive co-creation.

2.5 Co-Creation of Personas and Scenarios

Fuglerud et al. (2020) review both benefits and critiques of personas, which is a method to develop fictional characters that can be used in design. Some of the claimed benefits of personas are that they can prevent designers from referring to themselves as users, support empathy with users, help designers understand users and aid designers in prioritizing product requirements. It is recommended that personas be generated from aggregated user research, combining input from many users into a narrative form, but the creation process may vary from project to project.

A common critique of personas is the danger of creating stereotypical pictures of users which again can create an illusion of understanding them. Personas has also been criticized for lack of representativity (Fuglerud *et al.*, 2020). However, striving for representativity may lead to personas that are unlikely and not coherent, with the consequence that the method may lose some of its potentially strongest properties, such as its ability to create a deeper understanding, empathy, and focus.

Fuglerud et al. (2020) assert that co-creation personas together with people with disabilities will reduce the risk of stereotyping while generating rich data about user needs. They used co-creation of personas for the development of a novel digital health tool. Along with the persona description, a persona scenario was created, consisting of a narrative of events in the life of the persona together with contextual information explaining the needs of the persona in relation to the aforementioned health tool. This provided valuable insight about the lived experiences of people with particular disabilities and health conditions. The participants found the method to be engaging, and the persona approach made it possible to talk about events and experiences without disclosing one's or others' personal information. It was hence easier to discuss potentially difficult and vulnerable issues (Fuglerud *et al.*, 2020).

2.6 Remote Usability Evaluation

Recent work has investigated the use of video conferencing systems in remote evaluations of usability and accessibility of web applications (Simon-Liedtke *et al.*, 2021). Because of the Covid-19 pandemic, many people with and without impairments who had previously not used video conferences, have gained experience with these collaboration tools. In addition, manufacturers of such systems claim that their tools are inclusive and has built in accessibility features. The researchers developed a protocol for online user evaluation with diverse users and piloted this protocol with a few users, including an individual with visual impairment, using a screen reader. The protocol included an option for synchronous and asynchronous evaluation. In the synchronous version the user and the researcher were separated by space alone and used an online video conference system. In the asynchronous version, the user was provided with instructions about how to conduct the evaluation and how to report the results. Here, the user could then perform the evaluation on their own, while the use of a video conferencing system made it possible to follow facial expressions and non-verbal cues and also opened up for screen sharing. The researchers found no clear favorite method or system, which highlights the need to be flexible in order to accommodate diverse users. They conclude that conducting remote evaluations of the usability and accessibility of web applications can be feasible for participants with different impairments including people using assistive devices such as screen readers, provided that the tools and materials used are accessible and known to the users in question (Simon-Liedtke *et al.*, 2021).

3. CONCLUSION AND FUTURE WORK

In this work, we have reviewed and discussed related work for universal and inclusive design of ICT in remote settings. We found little guidance on tools and techniques for digital inclusive co-creation. The general recommendation, however, is to involve diverse users – individuals with a wide range of abilities and disabilities – throughout the entire user-centered design process. This implies that user involvement should start as early as possible and be a part not only during the assessment of expectations, needs, and other requirements, but also in trials and evaluations, and during development iterations with co-creation. User involvement can for instance be implemented as online focus groups and workshops, persona- and scenario-creating sessions, and combinations thereof. Special attention should be given to accessible tools and techniques, both of which should support the needs of each participant and enable their full participation equally to others.

In our current research project, we plan to employ a combination of digital questionnaires, interviews, focus groups and co-creation workshops for the development of a user feedback channel for websites. We have an ongoing collaboration with a wide variety of interest- and user organizations, which facilitates user involvement. Because of the Covid-19 pandemic, most of these activities must be performed remotely through video conferencing tools. We have found that some of the aforementioned techniques can be performed remotely with the aid of common video conferencing tools with results similar to approaches with face-to-face activities. Our contact with user organizations indicates that the population's access to, skills in and use of digital video conferencing platforms is now quite good, and increasing in Norway, also among people with disabilities.

A user feedback mechanism can in itself be a valuable add-on to any technology development project to make it easy for users to voice their opinion on the design. In our research project, we will explore further how to make digital co-creation both inclusive and effective. In particular, we will explore the use of the accessible feedback channel as a tool for inclusive co-creation in an agile development process.

ACKNOWLEDGEMENT

This work is supported by the Norwegian Labour and Welfare Administration.

REFERENCES

Akoglu, C. and Dankl, K. (2019) 'Co-creation for empathy and mutual learning: a framework for design in health and social care', *CoDesign*, pp. 1–17.

Andrews, C. (2014) 'Accessible Participatory Design: Engaging and Including Visually Impaired Participants', in Langdon, P. M. et al. (eds) *Inclusive Designing*. Springer International Publishing, pp. 201–210.

Borch, A. and Strandbakken, P. (2019) 'User Involvement of People with Mild Disabilities in Technology Innovations: Does It Make a Difference?', *Social Inclusion*, 7(1), p. 136.

EU-WAD (26 october 2016) 'Directive (EU) 2016/2102 of the European Parliament and of the Council of 26 October 2016 on the Accessibility of the Websites and Mobile Applications of Public Sector Bodies', *eur-lex.europa.eu*. (OJ L 327), pp. 1–15. Available at: https://eur-lex.europa.eu/legal-content/EN/TXT/HTML/?uri=CELEX:32016L2102&from=EN (Accessed: 9 February 2021).

Fischer, B., Peine, A. and Östlund, B. (2020) 'The Importance of User Involvement: A Systematic Review of Involving Older Users in Technology Design', *The Gerontologist*, 60(7), pp. e513–e523.

Fuglerud, K. S. *et al.* (2020) 'Co-creating Persona Scenarios with Diverse Users Enriching Inclusive Design', in *Universal Access in Human-Computer Interaction. Design Approaches and Supporting Technologies*. Springer International Publishing, pp. 48–59.

Harrison, C. and Petrie, H. (2007) 'Severity of Usability and Accessibility Problems in eCommerce and eGovernment Websites', in Bryan-Kinns, N. et al. (eds) *People and Computers XX --- Engage: Proceedings of HCI 2006*. London: Springer London, pp. 255–262.

Horton, S. and Sloan, D. (2014) 'Accessibility in Practice: A Process-Driven Approach to Accessibility', in *Inclusive Designing*. Cham: Springer International Publishing, pp. 105–115.

How To & Tools (2020) *Usability.gov: Improving the user experience*. Available at: https://www.usability.gov/how-to-and-tools/index.html (Accessed: 27 June 2021).

Hussein, I. *et al.* (2019) 'The user centred design (UCD) and user experience design (UXD) practice in industry: Performance methods and practice constraints', *International Journal of Recent Technology and Engineering (IJRTE)*, 8(2S2), pp. 175–182.

ISO 9241-210 (2010) 'Ergonomics of Human System Interaction: Human-centred design for interactive systems'. Geneva, Switzerland: International Organization for Standardization, p. 32.

ISO/IEC (2019) *Information technology — Development of user interface accessibility — Part 1: Code of practice for creating accessible ICT products and services*. 30071-1:2019. Available at: https://www.iso.org/standard/70913.html.

KMD (2019) *Én digital offentlig sektor: Digitaliseringsstrategi for offentlig sektor 2019–2025*. H-2448 B. Kommunal- og Moderniseringsdepartementet. Available at: https://www.regjeringen.no/no/dokumenter/en-digital-offentlig-sektor/id2653874/.

KMD (2021) 'Digitaliseringsrundskrivet'. regjeringen.no (Rundskriv). Available at: https://www.regjeringen.no/no/dokumenter/digitaliseringsrundskrivet/id2826781/ (Accessed: 11 February 2021).

NS 11040 (2013) 'Universell utforming – Brukermedvirkning og IKT'. Oslo, Norway: Standard Norge, p. 24. Available at: http://www.standard.no/no/Sok-og-kjop/produktkatalogen/Produktpresentasjon/?ProductID=669903.

Power, C. *et al.* (2012) 'Guidelines are only half of the story', in *Proceedings of the 2012 ACM annual conference on Human Factors in Computing Systems - CHI '12*. New York, New York, USA: ACM Press, pp. 433–442.

Power, C. and Petrie, H. (2019) 'Working with Participants', in Yesilada, Y. and Harper, S. (eds) *Web Accessibility: A Foundation for Research*. London: Springer London, pp. 153–168.

Reisner, S. L. *et al.* (2018) 'Sensitive Health Topics with Underserved Patient Populations: Methodological Considerations for Online Focus Group Discussions', *Qualitative health research*, 28(10), pp. 1658–1673.

Simon-Liedtke, J. T. *et al.* (2021) 'Remote Evaluation in Universal Design Using Video Conferencing Systems During the COVID-19 Pandemic', in *Lecture Notes in Computer Science (LNCS)*. SpringerLink Digital Library.

Stephanidis, C. *et al.* (2019) 'Seven HCI Grand Challenges', *International Journal of Human–Computer Interaction*, 35(14), pp. 1229–1269.

Wattenberg, T. L. (2005) 'Online focus groups used as an accessible participatory research method', *Proceedings of the 7th international ACM SIGACCESS conference on Computers and accessibility*. Baltimore, MD, USA: ACM Press. doi: 10.1145/1090785.1090819.

Woodyatt, C. R., Finneran, C. A. and Stephenson, R. (2016) 'In-Person Versus Online Focus Group Discussions: A Comparative Analysis of Data Quality', *Qualitative health research*, 26(6), pp. 741–749.

TWEAKING MORAL COMPLEXITY IN VIDEOGAMES? OPTIMISING PLAYER EXPERIENCES ON BASIS OF MORAL COMPETENCE

Benjamin Hanussek[1], Tom Frank Reuscher[2] and Tom Tucek[1]
[1]*University of Klagenfurt, Austria*
[2]*Institute of Experimental Psychology, Heinrich-Heine-Universität, Germany*

ABSTRACT

The gaming industry has been, compared to social media platforms, rather slow in developing its effective methods of game analytics. Considering the difficulty of interpreting player behaviour, this might be no surprise, yet the possibility of modelling player ethics might bring more reliable user metrics. Modelling ethics is the creation of user profiles based on their ethical decisions in-game. Recent publications in that field show an increasing interest in this practice and consider the outcome of succeeding in creating profiles containing data on applied player ethics as highly valuable. Modelling ethics is still not a well-studied practice, but its implications in perspective to cases of data abuse by Big Tech companies seem troubling. It is important to consider, interrogate and discuss the possibilities of this emerging practice critically. How can ethical profiles be rendered? How does inconsistent player behaviour affect the ethical metric? Who owns this kind of data, and for which purpose is its utilisation admitted? These and many more questions must be addressed immediately before unethical practices take place, and policies lag behind. Therefore, we intend to present the work of Pereira Santos to define the modelling of ethics as a new method of Game Analytics, how it can be applied, which data it can extract and how it can be interpreted. Further, we propose a new experimental design for how the modelling of ethics may be approached. For that, we want to shift the attention from trying to create full-fledged ethical profiles of players to their measurable moral competence as a more reliable metric. Moreover, we discuss the prospects of modelling ethics and the moral implications for the industry and move towards a conclusion that urges immediate policies to address the method.

KEYWORDS

Moral Competence, Moral Complexity, Player Modelling, Game Analytics, Game Studies,Videogame Ethics

1. INTRODUCTION

The production of videogames has been, from a historical standpoint, not data-driven (El-Nasr et al. 2016: 3). This has changed in the last decade, and game analytics have become increasingly important in the industry's decision-making processes. "Game analytics is the application of analytics that should provide B[usiness]I[ntelligence] for game development. Game analytics consist of telemetry data, which are raw data collected outside organisational boundaries, and game metrics, which provide visualisation and quantitive measures of this raw data" (Lassila et al. 2019: 2149).

Applying Game Analytics to develop and optimise videogames is connected to the more substantial emergence of free-to-play business models around 2010 (cf. Livermore 2016: 35-36; Mäntymäki et al. 2019: 1164) and is hence "heavily inspired by web- and mobile analytics [that] relies on analysis of comprehensive user behaviour data to drive revenue." (El Nasr et al. 2013: 4). While game analytics seems to be an aspiring methodology for the industry to optimise development procedures and in-game performance, player metrics remain challenging to analyse and interpret (Santos Pereira 2020: 104).

While player metrics can assess player behaviour as fact, players' motivations or emotional states that endorse particular behaviour is a black box to the data analyst. S/he cannot know why a player chose to design an avatar in a certain way or why a player applied specific behaviour based on that singular metric (Zagal 2013: 80-81). This black box causes a considerable problem to the reliability and value of user data from players' in-game behaviour. So, the question is not if or how player metrics should be rendered but rather which data applies for a faithful rendition.

In 2013, the game designer Sylvester described videogames to be engines of experiences that are fundamentally concerned with engaging players on an emotional basis. Emotional triggers are used in games to engage players, create attachment, anticipation and an overall desirable experience (Sylvester 2013: 11). Emotional triggers cause intimate emotional reactions by players which can be representative of the players' self-esteem, mental state, beliefs, socio-cultural background and ethical understanding (Sylvester 2013: 12-13; Pereira Santos 2019: 32-33).

However, the question remains: which design decision within a game causes which emotion, thus making a game a desirable experience to the player? I argue that moral encounters in videogames may be an effective opportunity to extract, analyse and interpret player experiences and preferences.

This approach of modelling ethics can be considered as a sub branch of Player Modelling. "Player Modelling [...] is applied directly to games and explores the detection, modelling, prediction and expression of human player characteristics which are manifested through cognitive, affective and behavioural patterns." (Pereira Santos 2019: 4). In regards to modelling ethics, this is a method that brings at this early stage three main concerns with it. (1) The inconsistency of applied in-game ethics by players. (2) Useful and valid methods of rendering applied in-game ethics by players (3) The ethical and respectful use of such data by game developers.

Therefore, we intend to present Pereira Santos's work on "Profiling Ethics Orientation through play" (2019) to define the modelling of ethics as a new method of Game Analytics; how it can be applied, which data it can extract and how it can be interpreted. Further, we propose an experimental design that refrains from trying to assess clearly defined ethical profiles on basis of player behaviour. Instead, moral competence (Lind 2015) shall be used as a metric to assess players' interest in degrees of moral complexity in order to capture player preferences, thus subsequently being able to tweak moral encounters in videogames according to the individual moral competence of a player. At the end, we will discuss remaining problems but also prospects of this approach to data rendition. Also, the moral implications for (both) the industry and players will be addressed.

2. MODELLING ETHICS

Profiling players based on their reaction towards moral encounters has been barely tested, but may offer a valuable understanding of how players perceive these encounters as either constitutive or distracting in terms of their desired in-game experience. This approach draws on the tools of Game Analytics to look at Game U[ser][E]X[perience]. Game UX deals with "how [players] will perceive the game and interact with it, and the emotions and engagement elicited from this interaction, relative to the design intentions" (Hodent 2020: 28). Games such as Papers Please (Pope 2013) or Frostpunk (11bit Studios 2017) are wrapped in moral dilemmas. Complex predicaments that let players decide over the fate of their or other in-game characters. The dilemmas are presented to players through powerful rhetoric devices and strategies to engage them emotionally (Zagal 2013: 71). Therefore, ethical decisions by players (i.e., saving character A but causing character B to suffer consequences) may hold representative data to their actual moral competence through the intimate emotional engagement. These moral dilemmas in games are often designed to be experienced in a limited or rather pressing time frame which can cause affective responses by the player (Hodent 2018: 77).

However, how should one approach the assessment and interpretation of player ethics? Pereira Santos has proposed two crucial research questions in that regard. "Is players' moral judgment related to their in-game behaviour?" and "How can an interactive narrative be designed to allow implicit profiling of players' ethical orientation?" (Pereira Santos 2019: 63). These questions indicate that it is not sufficient to have singular moral dilemmas or give players the possibility to apply ethics in-game, but the game design must include a carefully implemented and scientifically backed evaluation plan. Alternatively, subsequent moral dilemmas in a game must follow a scheme of a scientific test that can profile player ethics.

Pereira Santos implemented the Multi-Dimensional Ethics Scale (Reidenbach & Robin 1990) into a prototype of an interactive narrative game in his research. The MES can measure the ethical orientation of a participant within five dimensions. (a) Moral Equity (ethics based on concepts such as fairness or justice); (b) Contractualism/Deontology (ethics based on principles such as Kant's categorical imperative); (c) Utilitarianism (ethics oriented towards the greater good of society); (d) Ethical Relativism (ethics based individual on culture, feelings or religion; and (e) Egoism/Consequentialism (ethics based on one's [long-term] interest) (Pereira Santos 2019: 63-66).

The MES was implemented as a sci-fi adaptation into an interactive story using a branching narrative that suggested different plot outcomes. 80 participants were paid to participate and needed, on average, 30 minutes to complete the game (Pereira Santos 2019: 68-69). Participants had to complete a raw MES questionnaire before they played the game, and the results were then compared. The outcomes showed no statistically significant correlation at first. (Pereira Santos 2019: 71-72).

However, based on these data sets, a genetic machine learning algorithm was applied to create weights for the individual decisions within branching narrative. A new test group with similar age and gender participants like the original group were invited to do the test again (Pereira Santos 2019: 72). This time, the results correlated in a statistically significant way. Pereira Santos concluded "identifying one's ethical inclinations through the choices they make in interactive stories is a promising direction as an alternative to questionnaires." (Pereira Santos 2019: 76). However, how could developers make use of this kind of data? His conclusion suggests that the development and optimisation of video games (i.e., improving applied rhetoric and design of moral dilemmas or ethical encounters) and the commercialisation of player profiles could result from harvesting data sets on player ethics on a large scale (Pereira Santos 2019: 75).

Nevertheless, no matter how innovative Pereira Santos research may be, his research design includes an aspect that already causes friction in the collected data. Players are given the MES test before playing the interactive narrative with the adapted test. This implies that the MES test already biases players before attempting the game (Hodent 2016: 92). Players may recognise patterns within the narrative and remain faithful to their decisions of the questionnaire as a reaction and not by situational decision making. That may have led to a misrepresented correlation of ethical behaviour in between the decisions of the MES questionnaire and the narrative game.

However, Pereira Santos pioneering work on profiling player ethics has provided substantial perspectives and has proven the significant role of machine learning techniques in assessing patterns in telemetric user ethics to predict moral decision making in simulated experiences. The experiment shows also how game design choices could be affected by basing gameplay on the ethical evaluation of the player. Regarding videogames as procedural artefacts one needs to consider "how software functions and thereby directs its use and users" (Sotamaa 2016: 5). Should optimised modelling possibilities be prioritised in game design? Or should it remain a side feature for the developer?

3. MORAL COMPLEXITY & MORAL COMPETENCE

In the previously described experiment, the MES was used to create complex ethics-based profiles of players. This approach seems problematic due to (1) the inconsistency of applied in-game ethics by players. In facing the black box problem of unidentifiable player motivations for certain ethical behaviour, such a complex rendering method seems unreliable. Only on the basis of a plethora of data, machine learning could possibly conclude a tendency of players to act on behalf of, for example, deontology or consequentialism.

Therefore, we decided to use a simpler but more reliable method, namely Lind's Moral Competence Test (2014). While moral competence can be described as "not only how people think about moral dilemmas and their solution, but also their moral conduct and prosocial behaviour" (Park & Peterson 2006: 892), for Lind, it was essential to include within this definition "the ability to solve conflicts between opposing moral concerns by discussion with opponents." (Lind 2019: 52).

The MCT can test the moral competence of a participant by presenting fictional moral dilemmas and how a person resolved them. On a scale from -3 to +3, participants are asked to rate the decision made by a third party. Furthermore, "after each story, the participants are confronted with six arguments for and six arguments against the third party's decision – and, therewith, also for and against their opinion on this decision [...]. They must mark their answers on a scale from -4 (completely reject) to +4 (completely agree)" (Lind 2019: 56). Based on the test results, a score (0-100) will be assigned that represents the degree of moral competence (low/high) of the participant (Lind 2019: 62).

Using this test enforces a shift in focus from players' distinct ethical preferences to players' moral competence or rather their interest in moral complexity. For now, we define moral complexity in videogames as an indicator for the presence of conflicts that can be solved non-violently or as the depth in which a critical commentary on violent solutions of conflicts is presented. This allows us to formulate the working hypothesis that players with a higher moral competence would be more satisfied with a game that provides a higher degree of moral complexity (i.e., Papers Please, Frostpunk) than players with a lower moral competence, who would be rather satisfied with a game that provides a lower degree of moral complexity (i.e., GTA 5, Call of Duty: Modern Warfare). Based on this assumption, we have conceptualised an experimental design which is divided into three parts.

The first part encompasses the pre-test based on the MCT in which the participants receive their moral competence score. The second part is the randomised assignment of one of two versions of the same self-developed videogame. Moreover, the third part entails the assessment of the *subjective satisfaction* with the game experience which is operationalised by the three basic needs in social-determination theory: (a) competence, (b) autonomy and (c) relatedness (Adams et al. 2017: 49).

(a) The need for competence entails the "desire to effectively master [one's] environment and experience a sense of competence in it" (Adams et al. 2017: 49)

(b) The need for autonomy encompasses an experience of "choice and volition in [one's] action", and the feeling "to be the origin of [one's] actions (Adams et al. 2017: 49)

(c) The need for relatedness is constituted by "a sense of connectedness with others; to care and be cared by others" (Adams et al. 2017: 49)

While the first part concerning the MCT has been already previously explained, the second part needs further clarification. To provide valid results, both of the randomly assigned games would need to be identical in terms of their core aesthetics (graphics, mechanics, gameplay, etc.). The only difference allowed would be the distinct forms of behavior that would be permitted in each game.

Therefore, we have conceptualised a game with two versions (A & B) that sets out players on a quest to get medicine for their sick mother from another town. On their way (traversing from their mother's home to the doctor and back), they encounter three distinct situations in which the player is forced to take action. In game A, all options involve socially appropriate forms of dialogue (i.e., convincing, bargaining, asking) while in game B, all options involve forms of socially inappropriate or violent behavior (i.e., fighting, threatening, stealing). In both cases the player is always allowed to proceed to the next stage and besides the modes of interactions in these distinct situations game A and game B are identical. Once players finish the game, which should take them no longer than 3-5 minutes, they are asked to fill out a questionnaire that assesses their *subjective satisfaction* with the game itself. Our hypothesis is that the *subjective satisfaction* with the game can be predicted by the compatibility of the persons MCT score and the given version of the game. Thus players with a higher MCT score should show higher ratings of satisfaction when given version A, while players with a lower MCT score should show higher ratings of satisfaction when given version B.

If the results will back the hypothesis, this means that a diametrically opposed playership could be reached and satisfied within the same game. Being able to not just adjust difficulty but also moral complexity within games according to players' moral competence, could prove as an innovative game design method to foster the optimisation of individual player experience while pushing the boundaries of inclusion further.

4. CONCLUSION: TOWARDS ETHICAL MODELLING

Game analytics will become more critical to the industry in the upcoming years (Pereira Santos 2019; Mäntymäki et al. 2019; Lassila et al. 2019). Therefore, it is not unlikely to expect an increased interest in further developing effective methods such as the modelling of applied player ethics or, as shown here, measuring moral competence and adjusting moral complexity. Certainly, there are many issues that arise from this approach, including the specific game design choices for the experiment, as for how interactivity is established can already distort what is being measured. Also, participants' reactivity must be considered, however as the final questionnaire does not measure the ethical preferences of players but the satisfaction with the game, we are able to control this factor. In addition, what moral complexity and the players' interest in resolving moral conflicts constitutes must be clearly defined before the experiment and effectively implemented into both versions of the game to ensure a clean acquisition and analysis of data. Also, we admit that what we have termed *subjective satisfaction* must be defined with care. Whether we are asking the player to assess something such as replay value of the game or if we remain faithful to the social-determination theory and its understanding of satisfying "basic psychological needs" (Adams et al. 2017: 49) remains under discussion, for now.

However, we see in the eyes of the data-driven turn of the industry and the increased use of automated, personalized and procedurally generated content a high chance that this method might provide an innovative way to consider the modelling of player ethics as useful for game development to optimize the individual player experience and addressing diametrically opposed player demographics with one game.

Yet, if further substantial research in this field will be pursued, it must be stated that new forms of data abuse might emerge with the advent of new ways to extract and render data. Hence, we propose not the mere modelling of ethics but instead Ethical Modelling as a progressive practice in Game Analytics that can help create and optimise novel virtual experiences while respecting and protecting payers' privacy. After all, "as game scholars, we are often called upon to illuminate power relations and networks of production to interrogate ideological systems that may or may not be in the best interest of the people involved" (Conway & deWinter 2017: 3). And while the ability to model ethics in videogames remains at an early stage, it seems best to address these issues far before unregulated practices take place.

REFERENCES

Adams, N. et al, 2017. Self-Determination Theory. In: Wehmeyer M., Sogren K., Little T., Lopez S. (eds), *Development of Self-Determination Through the Life-Course* (pp. 47-54). Springer, Dordrecht.

Conway, S. and Jennifer deWinter, (eds.), 2017. *Video Game Policy.* Routledge, Oxon.

El-Nasr, M. et al, 2013. *Game Analytics: Maximizing the Value of Player Data.* Springer-Verlag, London.

Hodent, C., 2018. *The Gamer's Brain: How Neuroscience and UX can Impact Video Game Design.* CRC Press, Boca Raton.

Hodent, C., 2021. *The Psychology of Video Games.* Routledge, Oxon.

Infinity Ward, 2019. *Call of Duty: Modern Warfare*. Activision.

Lassila, E. et al, 2019. Visualising a "good game": analytics as a calculative engine in a digital environment. *Accounting, Auditing & Accountability Journal, 32*(7), pp. 2142-2166.

Lind, G., 2019. *How to teach moral competence.* Logos Verlag, Berlin.

Livermore, O., 2016. Digital Locks, Labor, and Play in Canada's Copyright Policy: Filtering Power through Configurations of Game Development. In S. Conway, & J. deWinter (Eds.), *Video Game Policy: Production, Distribution, and Consumption* (pp. 27-41). Routledge, Oxon.

Mäntymäki, M. et al, 2019. How Do Small and Medium-Sized Game Companies Use Analytics? An Attention-Based View of Game Analytics. *Information Systems Frontiers, 22*, pp. 1163-1178.

Pope, L., 2014. *Papers, Please.* 3909 LLC.

Park, N. and Christopher Peterson, 2006. "Moral competence and character strenghts among adolescents: The development and validation of the Values in Action Inventory of Strengthss for Youth. *Journal of adolescence*, *29(6)*, pp. 891-909.

Rockstar North, 2013. *Grand Theft Auto V.* Rockstar Games

Santos, C., 2019. *Understanding people through games.* Eindhoven, Technische Universiteit Eindhoven.

Sotamaa, O., 2016. Artifact. In M. Wolf, & B. Perron (eds.), *The Routledge Companion to Video Game Studies* (pp. 3-9). Oxon, Routledge.

Sylvester, T., 2013. *Designing Games: A Guide to Engineering Experiences.* Sebastopol: O'Reilly.

Zagal, J. P., 2013. Encouraging Ethical Reflection with Videogames. In J. P. Zagal (ed.), *The Videogame Ethics Reader* (pp. 67-82). San Diego, Cognella.

11 bit studios, *2018. Frostpunk.* 11 bit studios.

DEVOPS METHODOLOGY IN GAME DEVELOPMENT WITH UNITY3D

Gabriel Barroso da Silva Lima, Cristina Souza de Araújo, Luis Cuevas Rodriguez,
Clairon Lima Pinheiro and Jucimar Maia da Silva Junior
Escola Superior de Tecnologia – Universidade do Estado do Amazonas (UEA), Brazil

ABSTRACT

The DevOps methodology comes to facilitate the interaction between developers and operations, automating many of the steps necessary to generate the final version of a software application. It is a current trend in software development. However, today, many game projects are developed using procedures that cause delays and crunches. The games industry could benefit from incorporating these models, and their associated tools, into the complex process of developing a game. In this article, a study of the application of integration models in the game development process and a software-tools evaluation available in the market for this purpose is introduced. In addition, an initial DevOps methodology experience is presented, serving as a reference to other similar projects, thereby demonstrating the real possibilities of using DevOps in game development.

KEYWORDS

DevOps, Games, Game Development

1. INTRODUCTION

Every software project in its life cycle goes through different analysis, design, implementation and testing processes. It is common for a project to guarantee its quality by having to perform hundreds of different tests. In a game, a failure can not only be caused by an error in the code, but also by a corrupt audio file or a 2D / 3D model. In the game creation process, in addition to quality controls and normal UX tests, play testing is required: checking if the game is fun, if has a fair difficulty, if has a good progression.

At the moment, AAA games have hundreds of people helping on the development, advanced logistics and dozens (or even hundreds) of millions of dollars of production costs. With scopes getting astronomical scales, even some AAA studios cannot handle it. Even before the pandemic, big games are already getting delayed [Jones 2020]. One of the areas game development still lack of infrastructure. Much of the time on a game production is wasted on motion, task switching, waiting, defected files or even unnecessary processes and features. All this done in detrimental to the integrity and reliability of the process, with high costs and, most of the time, manually. These problems can be avoided by using the DevOps methodology.

The DevOps tools and philosophies combine practices capable of increasing the capacity of an organization to deliver applications faster than traditional software development processes. DevOps can be applied in more areas, one of them is game development and, using Unity in the development, the process can be drastically optimized and problems that causes time lost, useless tasks and crunches.

The article presents the following structure: after this first Introduction section, a general review of the DevOps methodology, its phases and its application in software development is presented, including a summary of the main existing tools for each phase. Some of the main features of game development are detailed in section 2.3, particularly using the Unity game engine. Finally, the considerations made by the authors about the possibilities of using DevOps methodology for the development of games is presented in session 3, where a discussion of the possible tools to be used in each phase is carried out and is described the experience of a development team, using these tools.

2. DEVOPS IN GAME DEVELOPMENT

Emerged in the context of agile methodologies, DevOps responds to the need experienced by the technology sector to provide a faster response to the implementation and operation of applications.

DevOps is a work methodology that, based on code development through the use of new tools and practices, reduces the traditional distance between programming and systems technicians. This new collaboration approach that is DevOps allows teams to work more closely, bringing greater agility to the business and notable increases in productivity. It is also, therefore, a cultural change that allows companies to accelerate the life cycle of their applications.

2.1 Software Development using DevOps

The main purpose of the DevOps is to create a continuous development and improvement environment with small upgrades. This is achieved through a series of processes that extends from the base development until post production updates [Virmani 2015]. The DevOps lifecycle can be divided in phases: continuous planning, continuous integration continuous deployment, continuous testing and continuous monitoring. These phases are necessary to have an operational environment with continuous integration and delivery.

The continuous planning allows teams to quickly change and adapt plans or business strategies based on the market responses. Continuous integration means all the changes have to be early implemented, validated, and shared with the development team. Continuous Deployment depends on a hardware infrastructure that allows a quickly test provider anywhere and anytime. The principle of continuous testing is to automate every test. The continuous monitoring provides early details about the product operations and how to response to them. The Table 1 shows some of the tools used in each phase.

Table 1. DevOps tools

Phase	Tool	Language	License	Advantages
Continuous Planning	Trello	Cloud based	Commercial	Kanban based project management
Continuous Planning	Jira	Java	Commercial	User stories and issues tracking
Continuous Integration	Jenking	Java	MIT	Large active community and limitless integrations
Continuous Integration	TeamCity	Java	Commercial	.NET support and built-in features
Continuous Integration	Bamboo	Java	Commercial	Multiple notification methods and good integration with other Attlasian tools
Continuous Deployment	Puppet	Java	Apache	Focus on desired end state infrastructure
Continuous Deployment	Chef	Ruby	Apache	Client-server tool that can be used as an isolated installation;
Continuous Deployment	Ansible	Python	GPL	Open source, do not require installing agents
Continuous Testing	Selenium		Apache	Multiple browser platforms testing and highly flexible operations
Continuous Testing	Appium	C#	Apache	Focus on mobile applications
Continuous Monitoring	Nagios	C	Open source, GPL	End-user stations, IT services and active network components
Continuous Monitoring	New Relic		Commercial	Web and mobile applications
Continuous Monitoring	Cacti	PHP	GPL	High customizations and a template-base configuration

The DevOps cycle tries to automate all the repetitive processes and bring all the changes to the final product as fast as possible while obtain feedback from your costumes to future improvement. With this, the software can receive small but constant improvements that quickly respond to the consumer feedback. The DevOps often complements the agile cycle because the agile methodologies focus on the gap between developers and software requirements and the DevOps between developers and operations [Lwakatare, Kuvaja, Oivo 2016]. The Figure 1a shows a diagram of the DevOps cycle.

2.2 Game Development

A game development is similar to every other software development, with analysis, design, development, testing, implementation and maintenance. The difference when developing a game is doing these stages while creating a game that is fun and enjoyable to play, making the player want to play more. These elements are what make game creation one of the most challenging software development process on the digital industry.

The beginning of the game development generally starts with an idea. It is from this idea that the 'High Concept' is made. Providing the fundamental bases of the game design. With the High Concept, it is possible to elaborate the core concepts of the game: game design, level design, mechanics, story, art, music; even marketing aspects like target audience and divulgation strategies. These concepts, ultimately, become what is known as Game Design Document (GDD) [Bethke 2003], which is the primary font of description of a game.

With all defined, the development team can use the GDD to create a prototype of the game with the predefined concepts implemented. When the prototype is approved, the team creates a direction of what have to be done. From this point, the development continues until the eventual release of the game. After that, the focus point becomes the maintenance, bug fixes and additional content. The development cycle shown in Figure 1b projects the process flow, with the analysis and the High Concept in Initiation, prototype in Pre-Production, core development in Production, testing in Testing and Maintenance in Beta and Release.

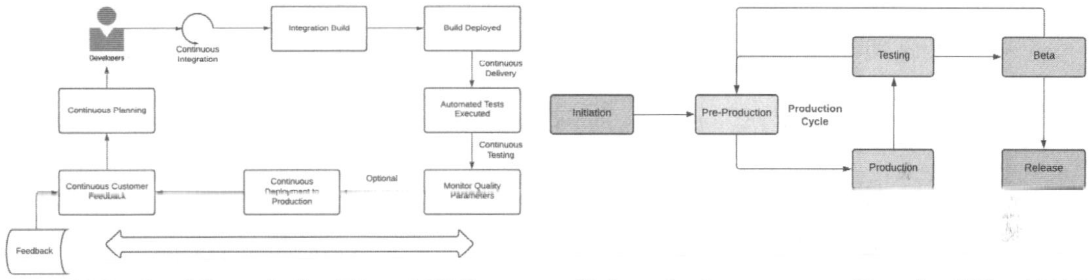

(a) DevOps delivery pipeline [Virmani 2015] (b) Game development process [Ramadan, Widyani 2013]

Figure 1. Processes used as base to create an electronic game using DevOps

The tools required for developing a game is determined by the necessities of the team: art, music, prototype software; all of them are very important, but the most important is the game engine. The game engine is a game IDE that combines all the assets in a build. One of the biggest is Unity [Goldstone 2009]. Unity is a free and powerful game engine (with paid licenses) that works with C# language and an object-oriented architecture, capable to help create a lot of genres of games. Unity also works with external tools.

3. PROPOSAL FOR THE USE OF DEVOPS METHODOLOGY IN THE DEVELOPMENT OF GAMES WITH UNITY3D

On a team, the development planning has to be very clear with the tasks of the team. With continuous planning, the team keeps tracking of the feature workflow. One of the best continuous planning tools is Trello. In an unorganized team, with a big assets transit, problems like long waits, manual transit and defect files can occur. With continuous integration practices, every change is tested in the source and fast sent using a system like GitHub, making team members focus on their work and less on waiting and task switching.

The deployment with continuous deployment has to be made constantly with small changes each, making easier to track bugs and avoiding bug propagation. Using an automatic build-creator that can be trigged when detecting changes can avoid hours of manual creation of builds. Depending on the size of the project, even small changes can cause bugs, and the QA team have to detect them before they cause others. Automatic testing allows testing a one or more features, multiple times in various platforms with minimum efforts.

The development team have to be aware about eventual bugs. The continuous monitoring ensures that by allowing the team to fix a bug before that cause more serious problems. This not only help monitoring the build but automating the QA feedback. Trello for Unity is a tool that allows to create a Trello card directly from Unity. These processes allow the team to create more content without crunching. The Unity engine have its own tools, such as the Unity Cloud Build for continuous integrations and Unity Test Framework for continuous testing. Other external tools can help more, such as Trello integration or automatic build creator.

These game development processes with DevOps methodology and practices can be combined in a diagram with focus on production and automation (Figure 2). The initiation gives the game concepts. Pre-production involves the creation and the revision of game design and prototype, the continuous planning application allows quickly changes based on players and market feedback. The production involves the creation of assets and the integrations of these elements, with continuous integration, every change is committed directly in the source.

With the game on Beta or even on Release, customers can create their own feedbacks, which motion is also automatized, making the team respond quickly to the customers and release fast updates passing through the same processes of pre-production, production and testing.

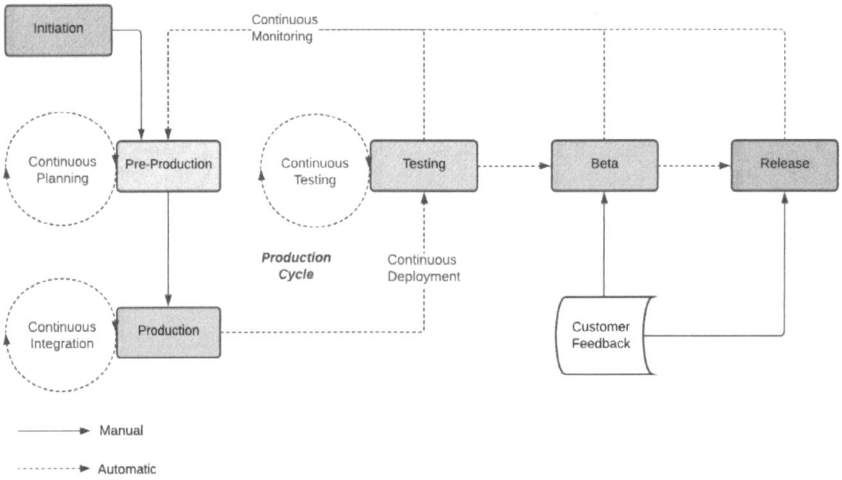

Figure 2. Game development process with DevOps integration

The authors of this paper, participating in an R&D project that includes game development, have used some of the phases of the DevOps methodology in the project. The DevOps phases implemented in the project were continuous integration, continuous deployment and continuous testing. Before, the development of the project had some difficulties, but after applied the DevOps methodology, the team had notice drastic reduction of severe or unnoticed bugs, a greater control of the functionalities in the project and a fast integration of changes.

Daily builds of the project were created to test and monitor each of the changes in detail. This versioning makes it possible to find bugs much faster, identify their origin more easily and monitor the changes and documentation of the team's progress, guaranteeing the quality of the product and its versioning.

4. CONCLUSION

This research has the purpose of studying and proposing the use of DevOps methodology in a game development environment such as continuous planning, continuous integration, continuous deployment, continuous testing and continuous monitoring. To facilitate the incorporation in the game development process, a workflow was proposed. The incorporation of these methods and tools in game development will allow obtaining higher quality products at a lower efforts and time cost.

In addition, some tools were proposed for each phase, particularly if the game is being developed using Unity. During the research, it was found that it is not yet fully formalized in the scientific community how to use DevOps for game development, although there are several tools that can be used for this purpose.

Also, the experience with DevOps in an R&D project, including the game development, was described. The use of this practice significantly improved the quality of the product, reducing the number of bugs and favouring the control of the implemented functionalities with creation of the different versions of the product. The use of these methodologies also had an impact on people. A greater commitment to the results was noted, since they were constantly receiving feedback on the work results. During the investigation, the feasibility of using the DevOps methodology in the development of games was evidenced.

ACKNOWLEDGEMENT

The authors would like to thank LUDUS Lab and the Amazonas State University (UEA) for the help in the making of this article. The results of this work were published by the R&D activities of the ARKADE Project, financed by TRANSIRE FABRICAÇÃO DE COMPONENTES ELETRÔNICOS LTDA, with the support of SUFRAMA on the terms of the Brazilian Federal Law Nº 8.387/1991".

REFERENCES

Abiteboul, S. et al, 2000. *Data on the Web: From Relations to Semistructured Data and XML*. Morgan Kaufmann Publishers, San Francisco, USA.

Beck, K. and Ralph, J., 1994. Patterns Generates Architectures. *Proceedings of European Conference of Object Oriented Programming*. Bologna, Italy, pp. 139-149.

Bethke, E. (2003). *Game development and production*. Wordware Publishing, Inc.

Bodorik P. et al, 1991. Deciding to Correct Distributed Query Processing. *In IEEE Transactions on Data and Knowledge Engineering*, Vol. 4, No. 3, pp 253-265.

Goldstone, W. (2009). *Unity game development essentials*. Packt Publishing Ltd.

Jones, C. 2020. *Every 2020 Game Release Date That's Been Delayed*. March, 26 of 2021. http://bit.ly/2020Delays

Lwakatare, L. E., Kuvaja, P., & Oivo, M. (2016, November). Relationship of DevOps to agile, lean and continuous deployment. In *International conference on product-focused software process improvement* (pp. 399-415). Springer, Cham.

Ramadan, R., & Widyani, Y. (2013, September). Game development life cycle guidelines. In *2013 International Conference on Advanced Computer Science and Information Systems (ICACSIS)* (pp. 95-100). IEEE.

Virmani, M. (2015, May). Understanding DevOps & bridging the gap from continuous integration to continuous delivery. In *Fifth international conference on the innovative computing technology (intech 2015)* (pp. 78-82). IEEE.

EXPLORING DATA ANALYSIS METHODS TO FIND CORRELATIONS BETWEEN PHYSIOLOGICAL DATA AND FLOW

Ehm Kannegieser and Anita Hensler
[1]*Fraunhofer Institute of Optronics, System Technologies and Image Exploitation*
Fraunhoferstraße. 1, 76131, Karlsruhe, Germany
[2]*Hochschule Karlsruhe – University of Applied Sciences, Moltkestraße 30, 76133, Karlsruhe, Germany*

ABSTRACT

In learning situations, achieving Flow, the state of ideal experience of an activity, can greatly support the learning efficacy. Utilizing this connection by detecting and measuring Flow during the learning activity could potentially help to improve the learning rate in Serious Games. In a prior study aimed towards developing a tool to link Flow to physiological measurements, no meaningful correlations were found. However, this does not rule out the existence of such a correlation and different analysis methods might deliver results that are more favorable. In this work in progress paper, the previously collected data is revisited and an approach is outlined to explore the use of a multitude of machine learning methods, based on multiple physiological measurements, to detect Flow and to investigate, whether it provides adequate tools to gain further insight into the link between physiological data and Flow states.

KEYWORDS

Flow, Serious Games, Physiological, Heart Rate Variability, Galvanic Skin Response, Machine Learning

1. INTRODUCTION

With the use of Serious Games becoming more and more prevalent, improving the learning outcome raises an important challenge. Previous studies have found that perceived fun and learning effect are connected (Deci and Ryan, 1985; Schiefele et al., 1993). As Flow, the state of ideal experience of an activity, largely coincides with player enjoyment, measuring it poses an interesting approach for analyzing the fun perceived and thus the effect on the learning rate in Serious Games. Flow is currently measured by questionnaires, although this kind of assessment faces a multitude of challenges (i.e. imprecise due to Δt between effect and measurement, subjectiveness). A solution to avoid these shortcomings might be to derive Flow from physiological signals, which are recorded during the activity under test.

In a prior study (Kannegieser et al., 2019), first steps had been taken towards developing such a method, yet based on the recorded data, no correlations between physiological signals and Flow were found. Nevertheless, this does not yet prove that no such correlation exists and better data quality and analysis methods might lead to different results. As opposed to the previously used statistical methods for finding correlations between Flow and physiological signals, machine learning is capable of establishing connections based on higher-level abstraction thus providing a promising method to augment data analysis. After briefly delineating the fundamentals of Flow, reviewing related research and depicting the previous study, this work in progress paper outlines the implementation of an approach to explore the use of machine learning to analyze previously recorded data and to investigate, whether it provides adequate tools to gain further insight into the link between physiological signals and Flow.

2. BACKGROUND AND RELATED WORK

Flow was first described by Csikszentmihalyi as the state of the optimal experience of an activity (Csikszentmihalyi, 1990). When entering a state of Flow, even taxing activities like work no longer feel taxing, but rather enjoyable. However, Flow state cannot be achieved for every activity, only for intrinsically motivated actions. Flow is reachable when the challenge presented by such an intrinsically motivated action is balanced with the skill of the person performing the task. All this makes Flow an interesting point of research concerning games, as playing games is usually intrinsically motivated.

The mentioned study of Kannegieser et al. (Kannegieser et al., 2019) was designed to gather data to link physiological measurements with Flow. About forty participants were asked to play a video game of their choice while their physiological data was recorded. The used measurements were galvanic skin response (GSR), electrocardiogram (ECG), gaze tracking and video footage. After the gaming phase, Flow states were assessed with questionnaires (Immersion Q. (Cheng et al., 2015), Flow short scale (Rheinberg et al., 2003), Game experience questionnaire (IJsselsteijn et al., 2013)). Direct correlation between physiological data and answers of the Flow questionnaires showed no meaningful correlations. A detailed depiction of the conducted experiment as well as the used analytical methods and results can be found in Kannegieser et al., 2019.

Few studies have investigated the use of machine learning to link physiological measurements and Flow in the context of gaming. While Rissler et al. (Rissler et al., 2018) only analyzed ECG data, Maier et al. applied EDA and HRV (Maier et al., 2019) and Berta et al. and Sinha EDA, ECG and EEG (Berta et al., 2013; Sinha, 2016). All studies used different machine learning methods, yet except for Rissler et al., who applied both Random Forest and SVM, all previous studies relied exclusively on one machine learning method, rather than exploring all possibilities.

3. BACKGROUND AND RELATED WORK

Ongoing work focuses on improving the previous study setup and extending the data analysis methods to get better understanding of the recorded data as well as its connection to Flow. In the following section, we present an approach to explore the use of a multitude of machine learning methods based on multiple physiological measurements to detect Flow and to investigate, whether it provides adequate tools to gain further insight into the link between physiological data and Flow states.

3.1 Physiological Data

The data obtained in the preceding study by Kannegieser et al. includes GSR, ECG, gaze tracking and video footage. From the available recordings, ECG and GSR were selected for further analysis.

Flow has been linked to the activity of the autonomic nervous system (de Manzano et al., 2010; Keller et al., 2011). As the autonomic nervous system has a substantial impact on the rhythm of the heart (Malik, 1996), it is conversely possible to gain information and draw conclusions about it from ECG recordings. The impact of the autonomic nervous system on the heart causes the time between two heartbeats, that is represented by the distance between to R peaks on the ECG recording, to fluctuate. The heart rate variability (HRV) is used to measure and characterize these fluctuations. Current studies examining the relationship between HRV and Flow (Bian et al., 2016; Tozman et al., 2015) have favorable results, indicating that the use of HRV is a promising direction towards further investigation of the relationship between physiological data and Flow.

GSR measures the electrical variations of the human skin. These variations are affected by sweat gland activity. Similarly to heart rhythm, sweat gland activity is also largely regulated by the autonomic nervous system (Sharma et al., 2016), thus creating a probable connection between GSR and Flow. Previous research on this connection suggests that GSR might be a substantial predictor of autonomic nervous system activation (Betti et al., 2018) as well as Flow states (Tian et al., 2017).

3.2 Preprocessing

As both the ECG and GSR signals were recorded with a non-uniform sample rate and were both resampled at 200 Hz. This frequency was chosen because it provides an adequate sampling rate for both signals (Mahdiani et al., 2015; Nourbakhsh et al., 2017). Both GSR and ECG signals were synchronized and divided into intervals of 300 seconds to fit the Flow data elicited by questionnaires. Duplicate timestamps with different values were handled by using the first occurrence and deleting the subsequent ones. The interval length of 300 seconds was chosen in the preceding study by Kannegieser *et al.* as a reasonable tradeoff between the need for data and subject disturbance.

The baseline wander in the ECG data was removed using a Butterworth high-pass filter with the cutoff frequency of 0.5 Hz (Lenis et al., 2017). Because the ECG signal was very heterogeneous and many recordings were missing the typical QRS complexes, faulty recordings were discarded and R-R-peak detection was performed only for 27 of the 39 available recordings. This was done manually (visual inspection of the data) due to the overall poor signal quality.

The quantization noise in the GSR signal was removed by using a low-pass filter with a cutoff frequency of 1 Hz (Betti et al., 2018). Because absolute GSR values differ greatly from subject to subject but the required physiological information is derived from the relative changes, the filtered signal was scaled individually for every subject in a range from 0 to 1.

3.3 Feature Extraction

62 features were calculated for every 300-second interval. The HRV features were extracted by calculating the duration of the RR-intervals based on the previously detected RR-peaks (Malik, 1996). This was done using the python toolkit hrv-analysis (Champseix, 2021). A summary of the 26 HRV extracted features is listed in Table 1.

Table 1. HRV Features

Domain	Feature
Time	Mean NNi, SDNN, SDSD, NN50, pNN50, NN20, pNN20
Geometrical	Triangular_index
Frequency	LF, HF, VLF, LF/HF ratio, LFnu, HFnu, Total_Power
Non-linear	CSI, CVI, Modified_CSI

The GSR signal was divided up into its tonic and phasic components. The tonic component represents the slower, long-term changes and the phasic component the rapid, short-term changes (Betti et al., 2018). The tonic component was extracted by using a low-pass filter with a cutoff frequency of 0.05 Hz. The phasic component was calculated by subtracting the tonic component from the original signal. An overall of 36 features were extracted, 18 for both GSR components, which are listed in Table 2. The 18 features listed in Table 2 were extracted for each the tonic and phasic components, yielding a total of 36 features.

Table 2. GSR Features

Component	Feature
Tonic/Phasic	Kurtosis, Skewness, No. of Peaks, RMS, Mean of Amplitudes, STD of Amplitudes, Sum of Rise Times, Sum of Fall Times, Mean of Rise Times, STD of Rise Times, Mean of Fall Times, STD of Fall Times, Mean of Peaks, STD of Peaks, Mean of Amplitude RMS, STD of Amplitudes RMS

3.4 Machine Learning and Results

A total of 265 intervals with each 300 seconds were used in the experiment. The Flow measurement was used as target variable. Flow is hard to quantify. An interval is used to order the answers of the questionnaires on a numeric scale between [0..1]. More positive answers to the questionnaires result in a higher interval values (>0.5), more negative answers to the questionnaires result in lower interval values (<0.5). As Flow is the ideal state of intrinsic motivation, our assumption is that the majority of criteria asked for, have to be answered true, resulting in a higher interval value. A threshold was chosen empirically to assign labels, considering all intervals with Flow values equal to or higher as 0.8, to contain Flow states.

The resulting dataset with 145 Flow and 120 no-Flow instances was divided in train and test sets with 75% being used for training and 25% for testing. Both the train and test sets were split randomly but with the same ratio of Flow and no-Flow instances. Using the train set, nine different machine-learning classifiers were trained. If applicable, initial results were further improved by hyper parameter optimization and feature reduction. Accuracy, precision, recall and F1-score were chosen to compare classifier performance. Table 3 shows the performance results of all trained classifiers including hyper parameter optimization and feature reduction.

Table 3. Classifier performance results

Classifier	Accuracy	Precision	Recall	F1-Score
Decision Tree	0.6269	0.6970	0.6053	0.6479
Random Forest	0.7463	0.7442	0.8421	0.7901
Logistic Regression	0.7015	0.7045	0.8158	0.7561
SVM	0.6716	0.6818	0.7895	0.7317
KNN	0.8209	0.8250	0.8684	0.8462
Naïve Bayes	0.6119	0.6304	0.7632	0.6905
Bagging	0.7612	0.7727	0.8947	0.8293
AdaBoost	0.7015	0.8056	0.7632	0.7838
Gradient Boosting	0.7910	0.7727	0.8947	0.8293

4. DISCUSSION AND CONCLUSION

The results indicate that detection of Flow using ECG, respectively HRV, and GSR signals might be possible with adequate accuracy and precision. Despite the promising outcome, the presented findings should be viewed with caution because of the small sample size and the poor data quality. Datasets with high dimensionality and small sample size re prone to overfitting, thus making the results unreliable (Vabalas et al., 2019).

On the other hand, the poor quality of the ECG signal and the subsequent manual R-R-peak detection might have skewed the values of the HRV features. The lack of both data quality and quantity can be traced back to issues within the data recording stage. So in order to confirm or disprove the current outcome, the data recording process should be augmented and optimized. Visual review of the ECG signals led to the conclusion that the error is presumably due to improper electrode placement. To avoid this, a change in study design is proposed: in future iterations, a trained experiment supervisor should place the electrodes (instead of the participant), to ensure proper placement. The same supervisor should check the signal regularly during the recording phase, to be able to react to error in time. Afterwards, the recorded ECG signal should be preprocessed with evidence-based tools to warrant reliable HRV features.

To battle small small sample size and overfitting, longer overall recording times per subject are proposed. With the implementation of the proposed improvements, adequate data quality and quantity can be ensured so the investigation of the promising use of machine learning in Flow detection can be pursued safely.

The next logical step upon resuming research with sufficient ECG data is to revisit classifier optimization, hyper parameter tuning and dimensionality reduction.

Incorporating the remaining collected physiological recordings, such as eye tracking and video footage, thus creating a combined model with all data available, seems like a path worth exploring.

Future research will be aimed towards further analyzing the connection between physiological measurements and Flow: On the one hand, by enhancing data quality and density by improving the study setup, examining new analysis methods and deeper exploring the use of machine learning. On the other hand by investigating additional approaches, for instance the link between Flow and the concept of Arousal and Valence.

REFERENCES

Berta, R., Bellotti, F., De Gloria, A., Pranantha, D., Schatten, C., 2013. Electroencephalogram and Physiological Signal Analysis for Assessing Flow in Games. Comput. Intell. AI Games IEEE Trans. On 5, 164–175.

Betti, S., Lova, R.M., Rovini, E., Acerbi, G., Santarelli, L., Cabiati, M., Ry, S.D., Cavallo, F., 2018. Evaluation of an Integrated System of Wearable Physiological Sensors for Stress Monitoring in Working Environments by Using Biological Markers. IEEE Trans. Biomed. Eng. 65, 1748–1758.

Bian, Y., Yang, C., Gao, F., Li, Huiyu, Zhou, S., Li, Hanchao, Sun, X., Meng, X., 2016. A framework for physiological indicators of flow in VR games: construction & preliminary evaluation. Pers. Ubiquitous Comput. 20, 821–832.

Champseix, R., 2021. Aura-healthcare/hrv-analysis. https://github.com/Aura-healthcare/hrv-analysis, Association AURA.

Cheng, M.-T., She, H.-C., Annetta, L.A., 2015. Game immersion experience: its hierarchical structure and impact on game-based science learning. J. Comput. Assist. Learn. 31, 232–253. https://doi.org/10.1111/jcal.12066

Csikszentmihalyi, M., 1990. Flow: the psychology of optimal experience. Harper & Row, New York.

de Manzano, O., Theorell, T., Harmat, L., Ullén, F., 2010. The psychophysiology of flow during piano playing. Emot. Wash. DC 10, 301–311. https://doi.org/10.1037/a0018432

Deci, E., Ryan, R.M., 1985. Intrinsic Motivation and Self-Determination in Human Behavior, Perspectives in Social Psychology. Springer US. https://doi.org/10.1007/978-1-4899-2271-7

IJsselsteijn, W.A., Kort, Y.A.W. de, Poels, K., 2013. The Game Experience Questionnaire.

Kannegieser, E., Atorf, D., Meier, J., 2019. A Study to forther understand the Link beween Immersion and Flow. pp. 373–376. https://doi.org/10.33965/g2019_201906C051

Keller, J., Bless, H., Blomann, F., Kleinböhl, D., 2011. Physiological aspects of flow experiences: Skills-demand-compatibility effects on heart rate variability and salivary cortisol. J. Exp. Soc. Psychol. 47, 849–852.

Lenis, G., Pilia, N., Loewe, A., Schulze, W.H.W., Dössel, O., 2017. Comparison of Baseline Wander Removal Techniques considering the Preservation of ST Changes in the Ischemic ECG: A Simulation Study. Comput. Math. Methods Med. https://doi.org/10.1155/2017/9295029

Mahdiani, S., Jeyhani, V., Peltokangas, M., Vehkaoja, A., 2015. Is 50 Hz high enough ECG sampling frequency for accurate HRV analysis? IEEE Eng. Med. Biol. Soc. Annu. Conf. 2015, 5948–5951.

Maier, M., Elsner, D., Marouane, C., Zehnle, M., Fuchs, C., 2019. DeepFlow: Detecting Optimal User Experience from Physiological Data Using Deep Neural Networks 1415–1421.

Malik, M., 1996. Heart rate variability: Standards of measurement, physiological interpretation, and clinical use. Circulation 93, 1043–1065.

Nourbakhsh, N., Chen, F., Wang, Y., Calvo, R.A., 2017. Detecting Users' Cognitive Load by Galvanic Skin Response with Affective Interference.

Rheinberg, F., Vollmeyer, R., Engeser, S., 2003. Die Erfassung des Flow-Erlebens.

Rissler, R., Nadj, M., Li, M.X., Knierim, M.T., Maedche, A., 2018. Got Flow?: Using Machine Learning on Physiological Data to Classify Flow, in: Extended Abstracts of the 2018 CHI Conference on Human Factors in Computing Systems, ACM, Montreal QC Canada.

Schiefele, U., Krapp, A., Schreyer, I., 1993. Metaanalyse des Zusammenhangs von Interesse und schulischer Leistung. Z. Für Entwicklungspsychologie Pädagog. Psychol. 25, 120–148.

Sharma, Mahima, Kacker, S., Sharma, Mohit, 2016. A Brief Introduction and Review on Galvanic Skin Response. Int. J. Med. Res. Prof. 2. https://doi.org/10.21276/ijmrp.2016.2.6.003

Sinha, M., 2016. A Probabilistic Approach for Detection and Analysis of Cognitive Flow.

Tian, Y., Bian, Y., Han, P., Wang, P., Gao, F., Chen, Y., 2017. Physiological Signal Analysis for Evaluating Flow during Playing of Computer Games of Varying Difficulty. Front. Psychol. 8. https://doi.org/10.3389/fpsyg.2017.01121

Tozman, T., Magdas, E.S., MacDougall, H.G., Vollmeyer, R., 2015. Understanding the psychophysiology of flow: A driving simulator experiment to investigate the relationship between flow and heart rate variability. Comput. Hum. Behav. 52, 408–418. https://doi.org/10.1016/j.chb.2015.06.023

Vabalas, A., Gowen, E., Poliakoff, E., Casson, A.J., 2019. Machine learning algorithm validation with a limited sample size. PLOS ONE 14, e0224365. https://doi.org/10.1371/journal.pone.0224365

A STUDY ON FOLK LITERATURE RESOURCES TO VIDEO GAME

Cheng Meng
National Research Center of Cultural Industries, Central China Normal University
Wuhan, China

ABSTRACT

This paper analyzes the transformation of folk literature resources to a video game. It first outlines the significance of folk literature to video games and then discusses how folk literature adapts to them. Finally, regarding the existing problems in the transformation practices, three proposals are presented.1) Player shall be prioritized to resources. 2) To counter the exploitation from playing mode, a well-done design should basically provide a possibility for players to improve life and a free expression of human nature, which also helps realize a sustainable development of video games; and moreover, by enriching folk literature genres, anonymous authority's manipulation is expected to be offset, thus more game playing modes would be shaped. 3) The absorption of folk literature into video games helps break the magic circle of the misleading ethics in video games.

KEYWORDS

Video Games, Folk Literature Resources, Transformation

1. WHY VIDEO GAMES CHOOSES FOLK LITERATURE

Folk literature is a kind of language art collectively created by folks of a nation, which is not only a means for people to spontaneously express their feelings and understandings about daily life, but also the quintessence of history, science, religion and other life knowledge. It includes folk epics, myths, legends, folk tales, proverbs, and other oral traditions, typically featured by orality, collective creation, inheritance and variability, which mirrors a nation's collective memories. Folk literature like a treasure house provides rich cultural resources to the construction of video game materially and spiritually.

Chinese video games sprouted in the late 1980s when Korean and Japanese video games overwhelmingly flooded to the Chinese market. To resist cultural colonization, Chinese game makers sought helps from traditions to unite players as a national community. Many impressive video games were published with "the image of China" from folk literature, such as *Journey to the West-Monkey King*, *King Gesar*, *The Legend of Sword Man* (Deng,2020).

In modern days, the game industry has become a new economic growth point and a novel platform to carry forward traditional culture and strengthen cultural sovereignty, Chinese government thus launched two supporting projects: National Video Game Publishing Project (2004-2016)and Original Video Game with Competitiveness Publishing Project (2016-2020), which help the game industry yield a rapid growth in revenue from ¥2.47 billion in 2004 to ¥280 billion ($43 billion) in 2020, and games adapted from folk literature of myths and legends contribute to 12.30% by revenue among the top 100 video games (China Gaming Industry Report 2020). Folk literature obviously works for video game production worldwide, for instance, the cultural archetype of Japanese Yokai leads to the popularity and financial success of *Yo-kai Watch* and *Pokemon GO* (Park,2016); Mexican traditional concept of Day of the Dead and the post-mortem worldview in Aztec mythology help *Grim Fandango* transmit a positive Mexican image to counter the denigration of Mexican culture (최명호,2016).

Moreover, folk literature meets people's spiritual and cultural needs. For example, due to covid-19, the lockdown stopped people from celebrating new year in a regular way, *Fight the Beast Nian Together* creatively transformed traditional celebration ritual and amassed players to beat this evil beast Nian in Chinese mythology by clicks in the festive atmosphere of folk music in virtual game, which in a sense acts as an spiritual alternative for traditional celebration practices, like setting off firecrackers and pasting spring poems to fight against Nian during lunar new year. Moreover, to satisfy people's increasing cultural desire in the context of globalization, we could see Chinese video game actively absorbs folk literature both at home and abroad, like folk tales behind Chinese traditional festivals and Celtic mythology in *Honor of Kings*, Japanese Yokai in *Onmyoji*, and the medieval magical world in *AFK Arena*. In addition, game makers would alter the features of the characters in mythological allusions to video game if players express such a wish directly or implicitly in the community's folklore (Ефимова,2018). Video game also creates lots of online and offline game communities, like cos-play activities, platforms for fan art and game culture derivatives for players to get involved in the construction of game culture.

2. HOW FOLK LITERATURE ADAPTS TO VIDEO GAMES

The booming momentum of transforming folk literature resources to video games benefits from their similar structure in narration, and the same development process in a hero's adventure and a player's gaming journey. Furthermore, it also ascribes to folk literature's role to realize player's recognition to the virtual and factual world.

2.1 Structure Adaption

Regardless of genre differences and complex technology, video games show four decisive factors: goals, rules, feedback, and voluntary participation (McGonigal,2012), which construct what and how player is playing. The structure by these four factors to some extent tallies with the fundamental structure of a tale Vladimir Propp proposed in *Morphology of the Folktale* that all fairy tales are narrated by different combinations of several "functions" and "scope of action". The names of the dramatis personae change, but neither their actions nor functions change (Vladimir,1968). Similarly, video games are also narrated by different combinations of goals, rules, and feedback systems under player's voluntary participation. That's why mythic Irish hero Cuchulain and Medea in Greek mythology coexist in Japanese game *fate/stay night* to find the holy grail, Chinese ancient creator god Pan Gu is fighting with the legendary heroine Hua Mulan for glory in *Honor of Kings*. Therefore, it's common to find folk literature resources in different civilizations and periods have met in one game story.

Moreover, player's exploration structure interprets the "monomyth" formula: departure→initiation→return (Campbell,2008) that mythologist Joseph Campbell proposed in his work *The Hero with A Thousand Faces*, which display the same development process. Many video games often build an awesome and mysterious virtual world inviting players to explore, like the mysterious world intertwined with human and evil spirits in *Onmyoji*, the gorgeous realm structured by human, the spirits, and the immortals in *Let him to be an immortal*, the open-world brimmed with ancient beasts and scenes in *Delusion in the Classic of Mountains and Sea*s. Akin to a heroic protagonist setting out from the known world to the unknown by undergoing transformative adventures and finally returning home, player leaves the earthly cares in real life to the game where he would overcome various obstacles to gain feedback rewards, to upgrade his level or equipment performance, and finally feels satisfied and pleased with transparent and immediately improvement and achievement. American psychologist Mihaly Csikszentmihalyi states by the hard work in the highly structured video games, players are self-motivated and regularly achieve the highest level of human happiness: nervously and optimistically get involved in the world around them (McGonigal,2012).

2.2 Realization of Recognition

Inheritance, variability, and collective values of folk literature is conducive to the realization of recognition to virtual and factual world. Recognition to game space is the prerequisite to forge group identity and a sense of belonging, which further enables players to achieve recognition to the real life.

The inheritance nature ensures a series of stable factors in folk literature to pass on in game. Taking fan art activity which could maintain and enhance player's group identity and a sense of belonging as an example, when *Honor of Kings* launched hero skin design activity for game character Chang'e, it clarified Chang'e is characterized by streamers symbolizing flying and a jade rabbit. Since these features align with the typical and stable features in the tale *The Goddess Chang's fly to the moon* (Figure 1), who steals the elixir her archer-husband asked from Queen Mother of the West and flied to the moon alone only with a fairy rabbit accompanied, they are easily recognized and accepted by players. Furthermore, the variability nature of folk literature largely reflected in language, plot, theme, image, and structure necessarily allow these features to mutate in game context where she is as a "Mage" hero, which empowers players to do creation based on their own understandings and aesthetic taste. Finally, the work "拒霜思" (Figure 2) won for transmitting a sense of loneliness and natural beauty, recognized and supported by 43.26 million players. Countless players are going to feel and imagine the beauty of Chang'e in folk mythology through the pure, ethereal, and alienated connotation of the new skin, and recall her lonely and bitter story in the moon.

Figure 1. Tale of *The Goddess Chang's fly to the moon*

Figure 2. The Best Creative Award "拒霜思"

Nowadays, entertainment technology is influencing player's game experience, like VR greatly extending players' ability in vision, auditory, and central nervous system. However, it also has aroused concerns due to its high immersion and verisimilitude, where players akin to "brain in a vat" may fail to distinguish the virtual from the real, and what's worse, if fragmented distorted information and concepts are reconstructed into our cognition, we will fall into the dilemmas of perceptual illusion, inversion of virtual world and reality, virtual "addiction" (Qian &Song,2018).

Folk literature shows potential to solve these dilemmas for it helps players recall collective memories and values, which bridge their ego with the real life as a continuum. Korean scholar Dong-Il Oh (2011) from the perspective of Japan's inherent animism culture discovered Japanese video games have a strong tendency to repeatedly remind players of the whole theme and story aimed at kami rather than making the ego of a player as a leading figure immersed in and identified with the game characters. He believes the reminder from game as well as player's familiarity to their animistic culture lead players to maintain their realistic ego rather than totally get immersed in game. However, his finding seems not justified from the perspective of folk literature, instead it would be the nature worship behind kami as collective memories on coexistence with nature, humans, and super nature handed down from generation to generation that maintains player's realistic ego and help them not lost in the virtual world. Individuals recall and represent the past based on specific collective environment (Halbwachs,2002). When participating in specific game interactions with animism culture and other players, player recalls memories of nature worship behind kami, which keeps their recognition of the real ego in virtual world.

Specifically, in two sought-after Chinese video games *Onmyoji* and *Tale of Immortal*, the collective memories of predestination manifested by "unknown dangers" in unknown world is vividly presented to players and realizes their recognition. When logging in to *Onmyoji*, the player will get an oracle (Figure 3) with an interpretation (Figure 4), and when exploring in *Tale of Immortal*, the player will meet a diviner (Figure 5) in the way to forecast his future. If player gets an inauspicious oracle, but no worries, the interpretation will assure the player of some suggestion to avoid bad luck, and the diviner will provide a solution if the player pays some virtual game asset in exchange. However, an inauspicious oracle would frighten some players to follow these suggestions to behave carefully, or to "buy" safety. These two games, by creating a mysterious unknown world for players, would remind them that unknown dangers are awaiting them. This design in turn mirrors that even in a scientific and civilized society, ancient folk belief can still exert an impact on individuals when stepping into the unknown even for young digital Natives. This is because, in old days, traveling is difficult and dangerous due to poor transportation and long journey in the vast territory in China, the fear of the unknown world is gradually engraved in our memory and shaped in oral literature. The fact that dangers are also ubiquitous in modern society makes the motif of predestination works for young digital Natives in video games, which finally helps them realize their recognition to real world.

Figure 3. Oracle

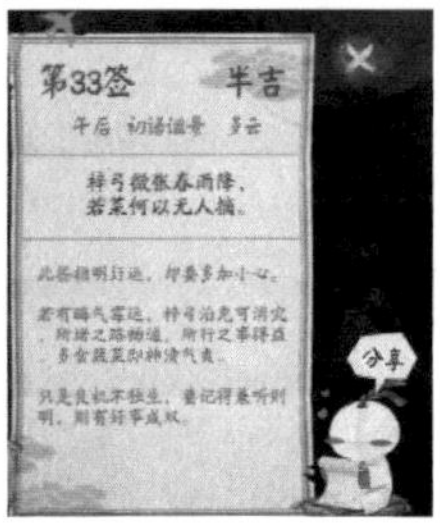

Figure 4. Interpretation

Figure 5. Diviner

3. WHAT TO REFLECT ON TRANSFORMATION PRACTICE OF FOLK LITERATURE TO VIDEO GAMES

There exist many problems in transformation practice. The first is the negligence of players' role as the subject. For instance, even *Shadow Play: Nezha* is successful in presenting shadow puppets and the folk tale *Prince Nezha's Triumph Against Dragon King* for it does help some players think of the old days when watching shadow puppets, data from Apple store, Tap Tap community and other player rating platforms shows the market doesn't buy it as player fails to get the initiative when operating but manipulated to watch the game telling folk tale mostly in a way of animated movie, which deprives the player of the right to respond in game. When video game ignores player, it will inevitably force player to be the disadvantaged party, just as what French postmodern theorist Jean Baudrillard proposed in the power relationship between the media and the audience: if the audience fails to respond to the media, then the media would be granted with authoritative power (Shan,2017). Therefore, when transforming folk literature, players shall be prioritized to resources. Enabling players to respond to game is expected to be one of an effective and feasible ways to eliminate this problem. As long as players gain the right to respond, this kind of imbalance would be counteracted. After all, lots of video games have to rely on a sufficient number of players to create interesting, emergent play, so that their players do not get bored. On a practical level, if enough players start voting with their time, attention, and wallets, and choose to play something else instead, they would turn into a force able to push the game (possibly also the game company) out of existence (Harviainen et al,2020).

Secondly, playing mode in many video games featured by exploration of the unknown is repetitive, time-consuming and labor-intensive, which imposes an exploitation and an anonymous authority on players. The playing mode that players must finish enough repetitive work to unlock new journey exhausts them at a cost of a large amount of time. Consequently, players who refuse to top up money or are misled to pay by the underlying pay-to-win mechanics to offset time cost gradually leave. Harviainen et al (2020) found even a large company, like Zynga can suffer from drastic customer attrition, if its business practices are seen as exploitative. But Zynga's ethical, rational egoism, manifested in well-done design and fair trade finally enabled the once thoroughly hated company to survive and prosper again. To realize a sustainable development of video game, a well-done design should basically provide a possibility for players to improve life and a free expression of human nature, which in turn counters the exploitation of players. In addition, this kind of playing mode is imposing "anonymous authority" (Fromm,2002) on players. Fromm of the Frankfurt School states anonymous authority is invisible, which doesn't give orders to people, nor does it make people stressful, but they are captured and manipulated by the invisible enemy. When players are motivated to unlock something new, they would feel obliged to finish that repetitive game labor because other player also will follow this practice. Therefore, to deal with this manipulation by anonymous authority, game makers could enrich the genres of folk literature to diversify the playing experience. Folk ballads, proverbs, sayings, local plays, folk rituals, folk poems, local knowledge and other oral traditions featured by different forms are potential to creatively produce different playing modes, which would also create a diverse folk aesthetic culture to answer different kinds of spiritual and cultural demands in virtual world.

Thirdly, many orthodox ethics in video games violate social ethics and mislead players. Huizinga (1971) termed the orthodox in video games as magic circle within which the normal rules of social interaction are suspended, but a new and usually temporary social contract is formed. It is common to find aggressive behaviors are accepted, unreasonable behaviors are rewarded, like violence, fraud, theft, and some disruptive behaviors, all receive additional rewards. As folk literature centers its narration on the daily life of people, thus the integration of folk literature can break the magic circle for it allows players to immerse themselves in realistic ethical practices, that means game makers don't even need to design ethics on purpose. Just as what Engels wrote in *The Books of German Folk Tales* that it cultivates his sense of morality like the Bible, so that he recognizes his power, his rights, and his freedom, and his courage, his love to his motherland are aroused. An in-depth exploration of the ethical value of folk literature to video games is expected to replace the disputed ethics and then provide a right ethical guidance for players. If the ethical values on heaven and man, on good and evil in folk literature are absorbed, it would be beneficial to a long-run and healthy development of video games, and to provide a right moral guidance for players in moral dilemmas.

4. CONCLUSION

This paper is a initial try to combine video games with folk literature resources, which on one hand aims to point out the huge potential and feasibility of folk literature resources to the construction of video games; and on the other hand, intends to highly recommend video game makers to pay attention to folk literature since the breakneck advancement of technology largely hit the growth of this kind of oral tradition in an information age, actually, whether in oral or written forms, most folk literature are instantaneous, some are even near extinction, and also reminds the professionals of folk literature research to seek new possibilities to vitalize folk literature resources in this novel field.

The key limitation of this paper is that it's mainly from the viewpoint of players, many findings may need further discussions from the perspective of game makers or the marketing side.

REFERENCES

Campbell, J., 2008. *The Hero with A Thousand Faces*. Joseph Campbell Foundation, California, USA.

Deng, J., 2020. A Study on the Development of Contemporary Chinese Game Culture. *Shanghai Culture*, Vol. 12, pp. 42-51.

Dong-Il Oh, 2011. *A* Research on the Characteristics of Japan's Video Games Focused on the Connection of Japan's Traditional Play Culture. *International Journal of Contents,* Vol.7, No.3, pp 29-37.

Engels, F., Marx K.1996. *Marx and Engels on Art.* Volume IV. People's Literature Publishing House, Beijing, China.

Ефимова, Наталья Игоревна, Efimova, NI, 2018. Folklore Sources of Computer Game Characters: from Transformation to Origins. *Traditional culture*, Vol. 19, No. 3, pp 48-55.

Fromm, E., 2002. *Escape from Freedom*. Int'l Culture Publishing House, Beijing, China.

Halbwachs, M., 2002. *On Collective Memory*. Shanghai People's Publishing House, Shanghai, China.

Harviainen, J. T. et.al, 2020. Ayn Rand's Objectivist Ethics Applied to Video Game Business. *Journal of Business Ethics* Vol. 167, No. 3, pp 761–774.

Huizinga, J. 1971. *A Study of the Play-Element in Culture*. Beacon Press, Boston, USA.

McGonigal, J., 2012. *Reality is Broken:Why Games Make Us Better and How They Can Change the World*. Zhejiang people's publishing house, Hangzhou, China.

Park, H, 2016.The Cultural Archetype of the Japanese Yokai and Its Modern Value and Utilization.*The Journal of Foreign Studies*, Vol.38, pp 211-226.

Qian Zh, Song Zl., 2018. Analysis of the Cognitive Dilemma of Virtual Reality Technology.*Journal of University of Science and Technology Beijing (Social Sciences Edition)*, Vol. 4, pp 74-80.

Shan, S. L., 2017. Cultural *Transformation: Criticism and Interpretation——Theoretical Research on Western Cultural Industry*. China Social Sciences Press, Beijing, China.

Vladimir, P.,1968. *Morphology of the Folktale*. University of Texas Press, Austin, USA.

최명호, 2016. Images of Latin America and Mexico through the Video Game.*Asian Journal of Latinamerican Studies*, Vol. 29, No. 1, pp 133-159.

China Gaming Industry Report 2020

DESIGNING EDUCATION APPLICATIONS FOR GENERATION Z

Alice Ashcroft
School of Computing and Communications, Lancaster University, UK

ABSTRACT

This paper discusses how generational differences impact on innovation processes and application design in Higher Education institutions. With both pedagogies and technologies varyingly according to generational divides, the existing literature is examined to uncover what this means for gathering requirements and designing and building educational software. The Covid-19 pandemic has made the limitations of current teaching practices through technology ever more apparent, and this paper recommends that to provide the best learning experience for students, generational research and horizon scanning for upcoming technologies should both be applied to the innovation process carried out by universities.

KEYWORDS

User Experience, Design, Generations, Gen-Z, Higher Education, Pedagogies

1. INTRODUCTION

There has been limited discussion on how UX and UI design must adapt to the needs of the current generation in the Higher Education (HE) sector; 'Generation Z', which includes most people born between 1990 and 2010 (Talmon, 2019). But what literature there is, is in strong agreement - the education sector as it stands will not serve Gen-Z in the most appropriate way (Rickes, 2016). "As many professors may attest, the attention span of Gen Z is short. Furthermore, for Gen Zers to focus on a single task for any length of time can seem arduous" (Giunta, 2017). Educators must focus their efforts on teaching students how to analyse and interpret whatever they are given, as what they are being given is changing far too rapidly (Dillon, 2007), which suggests that if the teaching model does not change, anything they are taught on entry to HE may be outdated by the time they leave. Furthermore, the Covid-19 pandemic has led to the majority of HE teaching happening online, which has raised more awareness of how pedagogies must be reflected upon and perhaps changed (Bonk et al., 2020).

Generation Z's current use of technology has led to a rise in the use of applications such as TikTok and Snapchat (Coa & Setiawan, 2017), which focus on ephemeral messaging (Dillet, 2017), which is to say messages or content that are only available for a short amount of time, or content provided to users in short bursts. There is also the argument that the way in which social media content has been connection based for so long, and is now being tailored more to interests, is something which cannot be ignored. For example; most applications focus on content being consumed by showing users content that has been created by those that they have subscribed to; such as Twitter, Facebook and LinkedIn. On these platforms, of course, posts can be shared wider than this, but on the whole creators are 'blasting' content to their followers. When it comes to newer applications such as TikTok, content is shown mainly on the 'For You' page, where their algorithm very accurately targets short videos they think the user will like. There is the option to see content purely from those accounts that are followed, but this is not the main focus of the app (Shutsko, 2020). Examining trends such as this, and applying these to education, could be an innovative way of introducing new pedagogies in HE, by designing for the generation who make up the majority of the student population.

The topic of discussion in this reflective paper is; how must the user experience be tailored to make digital tools support students from different generations in their studies and how has the Covid-19 affected this, or pushed it more into the limelight? It should also be pointed out, that when we talk about 'Generation Z' as the current target audience of students, that there are, of course, students who fall outside this range, and while they should not be ignored (arguably they may be excluded by this research), this paper will focus on 'Generation Z'.

2. GENERATION Z

When it comes to psychology, there has been much research pertaining to generational differences and divides, and how they approach different experiences. It is widely acknowledged that members of Generation Z are "fully awakened by the social responsibilities towards society, knowledge of laws, rules and regulation, they are extremely technology savvy" (Singh, 2014). Despite all this, Generation Z, as well as millennials, are often seen as selfish, being described consistently as the "me" or "we" generations almost interchangeably (Hope, 2016). However, despite the seemingly negative skew of attributes associated with this generation, there has been research carried out into how the typical traits of the generation affect education and technology independently.

2.1 Generation Z and Education

Generation Z's learning preferences lean towards; "learning that's practical, facilitated learning, independent work, solo work that leads to group work, setting their own pace, self-reflection" and they do not prefer "an information dump" and "group work only", instead they are very solution oriented (Hope, 2016), which seems to be the consistent theme throughout all literature on Generation Z. This idea of social good being a motivating factor (Hope, 2016; Singh, 2014) could surely be used as a teaching tool to encourage students to participate.

"Experience with technology and in the online world has affected Gen Z's preferences" (Talmon, 2019). This ability to find any information at a moment's notice has led students of this generation to "expect on-demand, low barrier access to all information" (McDermott et al., 2019; Talmon, 2019). This is a very clear example of where technology itself has shaped a characteristic that perhaps it must now also have to solve within the education sector. Furthermore, the idea that this information must be taught in "bite-sized" pieces (Hughes, 2018; Talmon, 2019) ties into the growth of applications that thrive on this, such as TikTok (Shutsko, 2020). Although the idea of lecturers and professors making TikTok videos might first seem quite unusual, if a convincing case was made, perhaps this would be a way of using technology trends to improve education. Talmon (2019) also states that "having grown up in the era of user reviews, they expect the ability to provide and receive real-time feedback, as well as having access to that provided by their peers" (McDermott et al., 2019; Stillman & Stillman, 2017). The idea of real time feedback and how this could apply to education is also one that perhaps should be carefully considered. If feedback on assignments, for example, is provided instantly the students are more likely to look at it and learn from it, having just completed it the (Hattie & Timperley, 2007). Could a digital tool be built so that this can be done on longer form assignments, as opposed to multiple choice quizzes?

2.2 Generation Z and Technology

Upwards of 75% of Generation Z access smart devices multiple times per hour (Beall, 2016). This could be seen as addictive behavior, or alternatively as an opportunity to use this consistent use of technology as a means of education. If an application was developed that was as 'addictive' as these other social media platforms, or existing social platforms were used as a means of education, and Generation Z ended up learning content multiple times every hour, that could surely only be seen as a good thing. Most of Generation Z spend "at least 9 hours interacting" with digital content each day, with videos being the preferred information source, with 95% watching YouTube every day and on average, a member of Generation Z watches around 70 videos a day (BARKLEY, 2017; Talmon, 2019). This constant need to consume video content can surely also be seen as an opportunity for teaching and education; and if innovation is to look for upcoming trends, this is one that is definitely already in full swing.

2.3 Pedagogies and the Covid-19 Pandemic

With all of these statistics pointing towards the idea that video content and consumption may be the best way for Generation Z to learn, it seems somewhat ironic, that since the Covid-19 pandemic began (Clements & Lewis, 2020), and most UK University tuition moving to be online (BBC, 2021b), that this has had an extremely negative reaction from students (BBC, 2021a). Of course this is purely academic, as most of the frustrations are around value for money and false expectations being set (BBC, 2021a). Perhaps as remote learning has become a necessity as opposed to simply an option people choose, maybe the way in which content is being delivered has simply moved mediums, as opposed to considering what the best way to deliver teaching content online is. It could be argued that carrying on teaching in the exact same way that worked well when face to face but doing this remotely is simply not in Generation Z's best interests. Bonk et al. (2020) frame the pandemic, in their paper 'Pedagogy in the Time of Pandemic: From Localisation to Glocalisation', as an opportunity; "Rather than be defined by the pandemic, let us seize this offered opportunity to transform HE from a paradigm that has been to the paradigm of what might be". Perhaps, this opportunity can be used as the motivation for refreshed innovation practices when it comes to designing technology for students in HE.

3. DESIGNING EDUCATION TECHNOLOGY FOR A GENERATION

With this understanding of Generation Z's educational needs and preferences, as well as an understanding of their technology habits, it seems clear that video is the way forward (BARKLEY, 2017; Talmon, 2019). But how this is delivered, and how this affects the user experience still requires exploration. Perhaps asynchronous content is the most appropriate way of doing this. Perhaps simply moving traditional teaching structures online is not the best experience for students as users. "Asynchronous content may be best received if it is video-based and personalized" (Talmon, 2019). This supports research carried out before the pandemic, that focused on "understanding learning as multisensory and contingent within everyday place-events, this framework analytically describes how people establish themselves as "situated learners"" (Fors et al., 2013). This paper showed a novel approach to redesigning learning and pedagogies based on environment; and it could be argued that the world in a pandemic is certainly a change of environment. If technology is being built for students by HE institutions, especially to cater to learning needs during a time where remote teaching is essential for safety (BBC, 2021b), then designing this technology with Generation Z in mind cannot be understated. Using innovation and participatory design practices where users are involved throughout the entirety of the project, including planning and design, can no longer be seen as simply good design practice but essential.

4. CONCLUSION

With an understanding of the educational needs of Generation Z, and their use of technology, it seems only logical that these should be combined to enable a restructure and redesign of the educational technologies used in HE. Online learning environments, mobile applications and the teaching itself must all be tailored to the generation they are aiming to provide learning to. If not just to improve the learning experience for the students, but to stay ahead of the game when it comes to development. As these technologies are created and predicted (Conole et al., 2008), beginning with the gathering of requirements through workshops and focus groups with students (Ashcroft, 2020), Generation Z's pedagogical needs must be reassessed in order to be catered for. For example, innovation workshops that are often used to work with students to gather requirements for technologies (Ashcroft, 2020; *Kickbox Foundation*, 2021) must take this into account; but they must also adapt to reflect the changing generations and environment. Furthermore, the importance of how these requirements are then designed and implemented, cannot be understated. The increased video consumption and use of ephemeral messaging by Generation Z (Dillet, 2017; Talmon, 2019), for example, perhaps should not be ignored, and these trends should be incorporated into the design process. A deeper understanding of the user base of an application could simply be seen as good design practice, however, generational differences between the designers and the users may often be overlooked in HE institutions. Therefore, this paper poses one simple recommendation to improve the innovation design process of HE digital services. Looking **at upcoming trends as part of an innovation process**, especially when it comes to forward planning for the **generations** about to enter the sector is vital. When using any well-established innovation or design process, this may be stifled by what the users and designers think is possible (Silverstein et al., 2013). However, true innovation design should look beyond what is possible, and look at what would be best for the users; in this case, Generation Z in HE, and even the generations below this.

REFERENCES

Ashcroft, A. (2020). Gender Differences in Innovation Design. *OzCHI '20, December 02–04, 2020, Sydney, Australia.*

BARKLEY. (2017). *Getting to Know Gen Z: How The Pivotal Generation is Different from Millennials.*

BBC. (2021a). *Coronavirus lockdown: "I'm not paying £9,250 for Zoom university" - BBC News.* BBC. https://www.bbc.co.uk/news/uk-england-bristol-55572694

BBC. (2021b, January 5). *Covid: West Midlands universities plan lockdown lectures - BBC News.* BBC. https://www.bbc.co.uk/news/uk-england-stoke-staffordshire-55549956

Beall, G. (2016). *8 Key Differences between Gen Z and Millennials | HuffPost.* https://www.huffpost.com/entry/8-key-differences-between_b_12814200

Bonk, R., Kefalaki, M., Rudolph, J., Diamantidaki, F., Rekar Munro, C., Karanicolas, S., Kontoleon, P., & Pogner, K.-H. (2020). Pedagogy in the Time of Pandemic:From Localisation to Glocalisation. *Journal of Education, Innovation, and Communication, Special Is*, 17–64. https://doi.org/10.34097/jeicom_sp_june2020_1

Clements, L., & Lewis, T. (2020, April 12). *Coronavirus: Students "staying put" during pandemic - BBC News.* BBC. https://www.bbc.co.uk/news/uk-wales-52256384

Coa, V. V., & Setiawan, J. (2017). Analyzing Factors Influencing Behavior Intention to Use Snapchat and Instagram Stories. *International Journal of New Media Technology.* https://doi.org/10.31937/ijnmt.v4i2.783

Conole, G., de Laat, M., Dillon, T., & Darby, J. (2008). "Disruptive technologies", "pedagogical innovation": What's new? Findings from an in-depth study of students' use and perception of technology. *Computers and Education.* https://doi.org/10.1016/j.compedu.2007.09.009

Dillet, R. (2017). *Facebook launches Stories in the main Facebook app | TechCrunch.* https://techcrunch.com/2017/03/28/facebook-launches-stories-in-the-main-facebook-app/?guccounter=1&guce_referrer=aHR0cHM6Ly93d3cuZ29vZ2xlLmNvbS8&guce_referrer_sig=AQAAAJbbAlkwytb6HJ5lQmdsoZHeBVy1F_25KVnyG3uj-gX28aeA3eV0Xv-YNSaT5M51pcHsL33AGmGJH29EJwUVigXg

Dillon, N. (2007). Educating Generation Z: What will the graduate of 2020 look like? Take a virtual peek into the future. *American School Board Journal, 194*(9), 34.

Fors, V., Bäckström, Å., & Pink, S. (2013). Multisensory emplaced learning: Resituating situated learning in a moving world. *Mind, Culture, and Activity.* https://doi.org/10.1080/10749039.2012.719991

Giunta, C. (2017). An Emerging Awareness of Generation Z Students for Higher Education Professors. *Archives of Business Research.* https://doi.org/10.14738/abr.54.2962

Hattie, J., & Timperley, H. (2007). The power of feedback. In *Review of Educational Research.* https://doi.org/10.3102/003465430298487

Hope, J. (2016). Get your campus ready for Generation Z. *The Successful Registrar.* https://doi.org/10.1002/tsr.30216

Hughes, J. (2018). *Communicating with Generation Z: Everything You Need to Know.* https://www.keystoneacademic.com/news/communicating-with-generation-z-everything-you-need-to-know

Kickbox Foundation. (2021). https://www.kickbox.org/

McDermott, P., Lucchi, M., Lope, N., & Fong, J. (2019). *An Insider's Guide to Generation Z and Higher Education 2019 4 th Edition.*

Rickes, P. (2016). Generations in Flux: How Gen Z Will Continue to Transform Higher Education Space. *Planning for Higher Education.*

Shutsko, A. (2020). User-generated short video content in social media: a case study of tiktok. *Lecture Notes in Computer Science (Including Subseries Lecture Notes in Artificial Intelligence and Lecture Notes in Bioinformatics).* https://doi.org/10.1007/978-3-030-49576-3_8

Silverstein, D., Samuel, P., & Decarlo, N. (2013). The Innovator's Toolkit. In *The Innovator's Toolkit* (2nd ed.). Hoboken, N.J.: Wiley. https://doi.org/10.1002/9781118258316

Singh, A. (2014). Challenges and Issues of Generation Z. *IOSR Journal of Business and Management.* https://doi.org/10.9790/487x-16715963

Stillman, D., & Stillman, J. (2017). *Gen Z @ Work.* Harper Collins Publishers Inc.

Talmon, G. A. (2019). Generation Z: What's Next? In *Medical Science Educator.* https://doi.org/10.1007/s40670-019-00796-0

FAMILIAR HOUSEHOLD ITEMS AS PROGRAM OBJECTS

Andrew Cyrus Smith
Council for Scientific and Industrial Research (CSIR)
PO Box 395, Pretoria, South Africa

ABSTRACT

The English language is but one of many languages globally in use, yet it seems to dominate the world of automation in its application to computer programming. Our research considers a programming environment in which the written word is not relevant; instead of text, we consider the use of physical objects to represent simple computer programs. This paper presents a reality in which artefacts, based on culturally significant objects, are chosen and arranged by the layperson in order to control the behaviour of light bulbs in a domestic environment. This work incorporates aspects of Gestalt theory and visual perception theory. We give an overview of prior work and conclude with an example.

KEYWORDS

Human Centered Design, Gestalt, Tangible Program, Perception, Human Computer Interaction

1. INTRODUCTION

Humans communicate with each other using symbols (Lull 2002). They also use symbols to communicate with computers by combining symbols in a specific manner and in a way that the computer can interpret. Unfortunately, the dominant method used to program a computer requires knowledge of technocratic programming languages, with these most often based on the English language. This requirement only serves to increase the digital divide that already exists between the group of people who can use programming to control their environment, and the layperson who is not proficient in the English language, or lacks the dexterity to operate a computer keyboard.

The science of "traditional" computer programming is founded in mathematics, and logic in particular. Here, "traditional" refers to the common description of computer programming as taught to computer science and engineering students at university. Computer programming languages that adhere to the "traditional" programming metaphor include the C, Java, and Fortran programming languages. These languages are expressed as alphanumeric characters with the latter typically instantiated using a computer keyboard and made visible to the programmer by means of an electronic display. In addition, the program constructed using the keyboard is retained in computer memory, even when the display is turned off. However, the program is vulnerable to electrical power failure, unless it is stored using a non-volatile medium such as a computer hard drive or, now obsolete, paper punch cards.

Our research considers tangible programming systems with which the layperson is able to control their environment without the need to master a traditional programming language, does not require fine motor skills to operate a keyboard, does away with an electronic display, and in which the tangible program itself is integrated in the user's general living space. To this end, we consider an environment in which the computer program logic is expressed as a static arrangement of personally meaningful tangible objects and does not have to be stored.

In this paper, we do not refer to the person who constructs a computer program as a "programmer"; instead, we use the word "user". Our explicit distinction made between a programmer and user is justified if one considers who the targeted audience is; our work aims to provide the layperson, who does not have computer programming experience, nor is inclined to master this science, with a uncomplicated environment with which simple programs can be constructed. Hence, the person who constructs a simple program using the environment presented here is referred to a "user" and not a "programmer".

The balance of this paper is structured as follows: The theoretical foundation for our work is discussed in Section 2, while Section 3 provides an overview of prior work related to that described in this paper. Section 4 covers the main contribution of this paper. Finally, Section 5 concludes.

2. THEORETICAL FOUNDATIONS

The work described in this paper has its theoretical foundations in two phycology research domains, with these being semiotics and visual perception, respectively. Semiotics is the study of how humans associate meaning with objects they encounter, while visual perception explores how we perceive the visual stimulation that results when light falls on the retina of the eye. Of specific interest to the work discussed here are the two perceptions called the Gestalt (Chandler 2007, Bergman 2009, Kimchi et al. 2003) principle of grouping, and the Gestalt principle of good continuation, respectively. These two principles are discussed next, followed by a brief description of semiotics.

2.1 Gestalt Principles of Good Continuation and of Grouping by Proximity

Grouping by proximity is one of many principles of perception that the Gestalt school of thought has identified. According to this principle, when objects are placed in close proximity to others, we tend to perceive these objects as belonging together and distinct from other objects not in the immediate vicinity. In other words, if some objects are near each other, they are perceived as a group. We therefore consider the spatial relationship between objects.

In addition to the Gestalt principle of grouping by proximity, the Gestalt school of thought identified the principle of good continuation. This principle describes the tendency for human vision to continue to follow a curve in preference to veering off at an abrupt intersection with another curve. Our research relies on this principle to determine the sequence in which clusters of physical objects should be interpreted.

2.3 Semiotics

Semiotic theory (Peirce 1935, Chandler 2007) describes the association the human mind makes when encountering an object. For example, a seashell might remind its owner of a pleasant seaside holiday, and a stack of textbooks reminds the observer of academic study at university. Of particular interest in the current study is the individual's interpretation of an object, most often distinct from another person's interpretation of the same object. Using this approach, we consider the user as being central to the choice of an object to represent a programming concept. For example, what tangible object might a layperson choose to represent the concept of an "IF" statement in the C programming language?

3. PRIOR WORK

Environments in which tangible objects are used to describe a computer program have been published since the early 2000's. For example, Horn and Jacob's (2007) Tern incorporates two-dimensional wooden blocks. Using this system, the user "translates" her problem into a combination of these wooden blocks. The blocks are pre-determined by Horn and Jacob and the user must familiarize herself with the function of each block. By combining the Tern blocks, the user constructs a small computer program to address the user's problem. Horn and Jacob mark each block using an optical code they developed for this purpose, called TopView. Blocks are available to perform various logic operations, and examples include repeating a section of program code, and the "IF" decision statement.

In 2016, Smith and Gelderblom published another programming environment. This environment also uses the static placement of physical objects to describe the computer program logic. They call this programming environment "T-Logo", with "T" representing the tangibility of their environment, and "Logo" associating the environment with the Logo programming language since the program logic of T-Logo and Logo are similar.

Whereas Horn and Jacob predetermined the objects used in their programming environment, Smith and Gelderblom's paper describes a programming environment in which the user is free to choose the physical objects that will be used to represent the program logic. They explain that the user is thus empowered to use personally meaningful objects with which to construct their small computer program.

A simple program comprised of two-dimensional Tern elements can be composed using three dimensional objects elements. In addition, the user may incorporate into a simple program toys and objects constructed using soft clay (Smith and Gelderblom 2016). These items are then used to construct a tangible program and demonstrate that this program, when executed, has the same result as Horn and Jacob's program constructed using two-dimensional Tern blocks.

The user of programming objects and the designer of the programming objects may be the same person (Smith and Gelderblom 2016). This is in contrast to the approach followed in the design of professional programming languages. In the latter, a small group of people with specialized knowledge of programming, designs the language structure as well as the textual objects that are to be used in constructing a program. Examples of textual objects are the words `for`, `while`, and assigning values to a variable using the character "=". Whereas the design of the programming language is done by the program language architect, the objects used in constructing a program can be determined by the user (Smith and Gelderblom 2016). Their paper then explains the process of how the user-selected object is associated with "traditional" text-based code snippets. Finally, their programming environment identifies the tangible object and puts together a text-based program based on this information.

4. FLOWERS AND GLOBES

We extend the examples given in Smith and Gelderblom (2016) by adding plants and manmade objects. In particular, we consider how the concept of time may be incorporated in a tangible program, which is a dimension not addressed in their paper.

As already stated, a model of the T-logo programming environment is described in the literature (Smith and Gelderblom 2016). Relevant to the current paper, the model includes the option for the user to select personally meaningful objects with which program logic can be represented. We now provide an example incorporating living objects (plants) and manmade objects (electric light bulbs) to demonstrate how the concept of time can be represented in a tangible program.

4.1 Time to Switch the Lights

In our example, the user installed outdoor lights to deter criminals during the period between dusk and dawn. To do so using a programming environment as described in the literature (Smith and Gelderblom 2016), the user has the option to select personally meaningful objects to represent the time when the lights should be turned on, and when these should be turned off. The logic of this program can be described using the C programming language as follows: `if (dusk){light=on;}if (dawn){light=off;}`

The user decides which objects will represent "dusk" and "dawn", respectively. In addition, the user selects items to represent a light that is lit, and a light that is turned off. Once selected, the user "enrolls" the four objects into the programming environment as described in the literature.

An example is now given to illustrate the object selection process. First, an Oenothera biennis, also known as the common evening-primrose (Steckel et al. 2019), represents dusk and therefore the time when the lights should be turned on. Conversely, the user decides to use a sunflower (Kutschera and Briggs 2016) to represent dawn and thus the time when the lights should be turned off. These two physical objects can next be used in a tangible program to describe two events, with these being dusk and dawn respectively.

To complete the associations and in order to construct a simple program, the user has to associate two additional objects to represent lights when these are lit (on), and when they are extinguished (off). To this end, the user again chooses personally meaningful objects, with these being a clear incandescent globe, and a blue globe. Respectively, these represent the states of lights turned on and off.

Next, the user associates each of the four objects with each of the four states, and these are dusk, dawn, lights switched on, and lights switched off. Then, she applies the Gestalt principle of grouping by proximity to construct two tangible computer program code snippets. When a light bulb is placed in close proximity to a pot plant, this grouping will be interpreted as a logic statement. Finally, the user places the two tangible program snippets in a predetermined area where they will be interpreted as a computer program (Figure 1).

```
if (dusk){
   light = on;
}

if (dawn){
   light = off;
}
```

≡

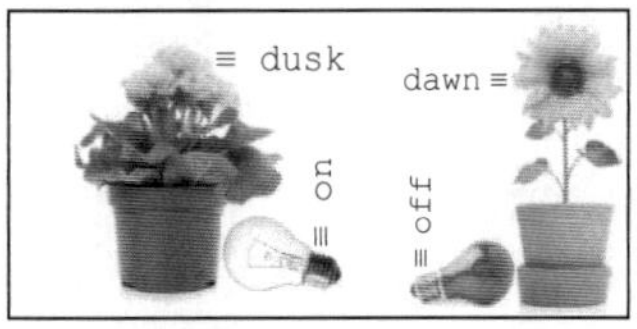

Figure 1. The text (left) and the arranged objects (right) represent the same program logic

5. CONCLUSION

Published research indicate that it is possible to arrange personally meaningful objects in such a way that their relative positions define a computer program. Personally meaningful objects are chosen by the user according to the association the user makes with events or objects; this relationship is the subject matter of research related to human perception, that is, how humans perceive their environment. Gestalt theory describes that humans tend to view items in close proximity to each other as belonging together. Although this paper did not discuss the underlying technology required to detect the objects, group them, and finally generate executable C code, it did explore the use of common garden plants and two household items to define a simple computer program. Finally, we combined two flowering plants with two light bulbs to create a program that, when executed, will turn a light on at sunset and off at dawn.

REFERENCES

Bergman, M., 2009. *Peirce's philosophy of communication: The rhetorical underpinnings of the theory of signs*. Continuum studies in American philosophy. London: Continuum International Publishing Group.

Chandler, D., 2007. *Semiotics- the basics* (second.). Abingdon, Oxon: Routledge.

Horn, M. S., and Jacob, R. J. K., 2007. Tangible programming in the classroom with Tern. *CHI '07 extended abstracts on human factors in computing systems*. San Jose, CA, USA: ACM Press, pp. 1965–1970 doi:http://doi.acm.org/10.1145/1240866.1240933

Kimchi, R., Behrmann, M., and Olson, C. R. (Eds.), 2003. *Perceptual organization in vision- behavioral and neural perspectives*. Lawrence Erlbaum Associates, Inc.

Kutschera, U. and Briggs, W.R., 2016. Phototropic solar tracking in sunflower plants: an integrative perspective. *Annals of botany*, 117(1), pp.1-8.

Lull, J. ed., 2002. *Culture in the communication age*. Routledge.

Peirce, C. S., 1935. *The collected papers of Charles Sanders Peirce*. (C. Hartshorne, P. Weiss, & A. W. Burks, Eds.) (Vol. 1–8). Cambridge: Harvard University Press.

Smith, A.C. and Gelderblom, H., 2016. End user programming with personally meaningful objects. *Psychology of Programming Interest Group (PPIG)* 27th Annual Workshop, 7 - 10 September 2016, University of Cambridge, United Kingdom.

Steckel, L., Sosnoskie, L., & Steckel, S., 2019. Common evening-primrose (Oenothera biennis L.). *Weed Technology*, 33(5), pp. 757-760. doi:10.1017/wet.2019.53

HEARING (WITH) THE BODY: ENACTIVE CONCEPTION OF BODY IN AUDITORY SENSEMAKING IN GAMES

Oskari Koskela and Kai Tuuri
University of Jyväskylä
Jyväskylä, Finland

ABSTRACT

This paper discusses the contrast between the embodied and the representative accounts of bodily presence in the sound and music of videogames. The latter highlights the aspects of experience that are of representations instead of direct presence, such as when the pain of the avatar is interpreted from the audial cues rather than felt as such. The contemporary view of embodied cognition has questioned it as an overly mechanistic and dualistic conception of mind that neglects the bodily and active aspects of lived experience. The view of embodied cognition considers the experience of game as an inherently bodily and world-involving activity, replacing the fundamental role of mental representations with that of direct interaction between the player and the game. In this paper, we aim to provide an outline of an enactive approach to auditory experience of games focusing especially on the role of the body in experiencing and making sense of the gameworld. We relate our discussion to ideas such as player involvement in terms of immersion, the acoustic ecology of videogames and the bodily basis of sensemaking in sensorimotor contingencies between sound and action.

KEYWORDS

Embodied Cognition, Enaction, Game Sound, Immersion

1. INTRODUCTION

How is the body present in the sound and music of videogames? A common sense view might begin by assuming a *subjective* gameplay experience as something being affected by the *objective* appearance of the game. The body, in this view, is easily seen as a representation of body instead of direct bodily presence. In other words, the body is present through references (e.g., iconic, indexical or symbolic) to the body that need to be interpreted from the visual and audial cues during the course of the gameplay. While this line of thought has been the conventional one within both semiotic and cognitive research of music, the contemporary views of human cognition suggest it to be not that "common sense" after all. Rather, it appears as a remnant of mechanistic and dualistic views that neglect how we actually experience the world.

Of the different views aiming to overcome the dichotomies of subject/object and body/mind, one of the most comprehensive is the enactive theory of cognition (Varela et al., 1993). In the enactive approach, cognition is considered as inherently bodily sensemaking that is grounded on the fundamental sensorimotor interactions between an organism and its environment. Within this view, sensemaking is not about inner processing of information from the world outside but about creating, or bringing forth, the world as a phenomenologically meaningful space for the organism. Simply stated, the enactive view considers our experience of the world as something that we constantly do, based on our bodily capabilities for interaction with it. Importantly, the enactive approach does not propose an additional level of cognition or something added to cognitive processing. Instead, it aims to reformulate the whole idea of cognition as an ongoing interactive process related to the dynamics of life itself.

In this paper, we consider enactive ideas by discussing the bodily involvement of the player in the game. We strive to articulate the embodiment of the player by relying on enactive notions about bodily interaction as a fundamental basis of human experience and the world-constituting quality this interaction entails. While this is an attempt to roughly formulate a theoretical foundation for videogame experience more generally, we focus especially on the relation between the body and videogame sound.

2. BODILY PRESENCE IN THE GAMEPLAY

To paraphrase Graeme Kirkpatrick (2015, p. 111), the central paradox of gameplay is that it is a physical activity of manipulating the controller and following the events unfolding on the screen, yet we talk and feel about it as if we were acting *in* the game. This sense of inhabiting the game has been considered as a question of player's identification with an avatar, through which one may enter the world presented by the game. A prevalent line of thought has centered on the degree of realism or the gameworld's visual fidelity to the real world, which has been criticised as a too narrow way to understand the involvement in gameplay. For example, James Newman (2002) has pointed out that the enjoyment of the videogame playing is not about visuals but about kinesthetic involvement: Instead of identifying with the avatar, the player embodies the character as a sort of vehicle or equipment, that is "as a set of capabilities, potentials and techniques" the game offers for the player. Presented this way, the core of a player's presence in the gameworld is about having an effect on what happens in the game, which does not even require an avatar to be identified with.

While Newman's characterisation of the avatar as a "vehicle" controlled by the player is helpful in centering the gameplay on activity instead of visuals, it might downplay the role of direct bodily involvement in the game. As Daniel Black (2015) has argued, the idea of "vehicular embodiment" is still entangled with the Cartesian dualism by positioning the player as disembodied cogito controlling the game character. Black points out that the gameplay is not experienced as a sort of distanced problem solving using a digital character but is indeed often a visceral and body-involving experience.

Another way of approaching player embodiment is to consider how our sense of being-in-the-world is grounded on our capabilities for action. From the enactive perspective (Varela et al., 1993), action and perception are not different processes but rather unified under the idea of fundamentally bodily sensemaking. Simply stated, the idea is that our understanding, our perceiving the world as meaningful for us, is grounded on our bodily capabilities of interacting with our environment. This can be illustrated by considering what we perceive as affordances, that is, possibilities for action related to our sensorimotor capabilities (Gibson, 1986). Essentially, in this view, perception is an active and bodily process of making sense of the world.

The basis for this kind of bodily perception lies in the enactively coupled relations between our motor action and sensory stimulus, in other words, sensorimotor contingencies (Noë, 2006). At the very basic level, this refers to how, for example, our vision of objects changes as we turn our heads or how our experience of sounds changes as we move closer or farther from the sound source. While videogames arguably provide another "level" to these contingencies, the basic principle can be thought as being essentially the same: we come to associate our bodily action with the actions in the game not by "high-level" cognitive inference but because of the lawful dependencies between our actions and what is happening in the game.

Concerning videogame sound, Karen Collins (2013) has highlighted the relation between sound and action, and how it facilitates player embodiment, through the concept of synchresis. Originating in film studies, synchresis refers to how simultaneous sound and image are perceived as a single phenomenon, as if having a common source (Chion, 1994). As Collins (2013) has suggested, in the case of interactive media such as videogames, it is more apt to consider sounds to be fused with action rather than with image, in what she terms kinesonic synchresis. What we may consider as lawful relations between the actions of the player and the sounds perceived in the game, players are in direct, embodied interaction with the game sounds and may thus "extend" themselves in the game. Moreover, while the player embodiment in the game is most clearly illustrated with the congruence between player actions and sounds, arguably every event-related sound is also embodied in the sense that they are experienced in terms of the player's capabilities for action: the way we make sense of the sounds is through our embodied understanding of how they relate to action (see Krueger, 2009).

From the enactive perspective, the core of the player's presence in the game is grounded on the possibilities of interacting with the game, that is, manipulating the controller in a way that has effect on the game. In this sense, the mapping of player controls need not to bear resemblance to realism, as long as our actions and perceptions are related to each other in a lawful manner, which allows us to make sense of the gameworld through our bodily understanding of gameplay interactions. While, in the enactive view, this kind of interactive bodily sensemaking is the basis for all our experiences, the characteristic feature of videogames is the agency it grants for the player. The concept of agency could allow for insightful comparison between videogames and other types of media (see for example Crick, 2011; Black 2017) but in this paper we consider it in regards to how the possibility of meaningful interaction in the game gives rise to the constitution of the game as a space.

3. CO-CONSTITUTED GAMEWORLDS

The characterisation of gameworld in terms of inhabiting a fictious space of gameplay activities aligns with the enactive perspective. For example, the activity of listening to music has been considered as an exploration of spatial organisation of the work (Krueger, 2009). For the enactive view, however, the idea of gameworld as pre-given is problematic (for a similar critique from an aesthetic perspective, see Kirkpatrick 2011). Instead, one of the main ideas of the enactive approach is that we constitute, or bring forth, our world as a meaningful space through interacting with it. Actually, a more apt term would be co-constitution, because as the player turns the gameworld into a meaningful place, at the same time the player also constitutes herself/himself as an agent in that world.

Again, leaving the visual side aside, the gameplay activity can, at its core, be considered as an exploration of how the game works (Kirkpatrick, 2011). At this level, the exploration is about the mechanics and rules: What kind of actions are meaningful in the sense that they have an effect in the game and relate to what the game invites us to do. We may consider the core of the gameworld to be this kind of space for affordances: A place that permits certain kinds of actions and restricts others, and encapsulates a rule-based normativity with regard to the desirability of actions. As affordances tie the agent and the world together, this world of possibilities for action also brings forth the agent with the game-related capabilities for action.

The Player Involvement Model of Gordon Calleja (2007) points to a similar notion of "dual natured" involvement by relating player immersion with player incorporation. While immersion refers to the experience of inhabiting a virtual world, incorporation has to do with the other aspect of this process, which is the internalisation of the gameworld, with all its kinesthetic, ludic, narrative, spatial etc. dimensions, by the player. In respect to sound, Mark Grimshaw (2008) has discussed how the sounds in an FPS-game facilitate immersion by situating the player within the acoustic ecology of the game. By using the concept of ecology, instead of a more usual environment, Grimshaw highlights a holistic view of the game in which the gameworld includes also the players and their relationship to the environment.

This characterisation of the co-constitution of the gameworld and the player within it can be contrasted with the ideas of player being transported or extended into the gameworld. In contrast to suggesting a transference of a pre-given agent to the pre-given world, the co-constitutive view is based on the idea that the constant activity in itself keeps the understanding of the world in a constant state of flux, being based on our fundamentally bodily possibilities of action within it, that is, enacting our experience. This highlights how our sense of self and world are not that fixed but rather entangled with our capabilities for action and, importantly, always "in the making" (see Black 2017).

To further elaborate the relation between the gameworld and the real world we might return to the very basic notion about videogames as technological activities. As Don Ihde (1990) has argued, technologies change the way we experience our world: They reveal certain aspects and hide others, frame things differently and extend our abilities. By mediating our relation to the world, being entangled with our sensemaking abilities, technologies change our sense of self and our experience of the world (see Verbeek, 2015). We might continue on this line by considering Alva Noe's (2015) view of technology as very broadly "skillful activity", which includes not only tools but also practically every activity that is characterised by organization (from listening to music, conversing, nurturing etc.). In this sense, our everyday life consists of a series of technological activities, our habitual ways of doing, which structure our worlds and ourselves.

4. CONCLUSION

Seeing player embodiment through the enactive approach grounds the gameplay experience on the player's sensorimotor interaction with the game. Through this interaction, the player brings forth the gameworld as a space for possibilities for action and a sense of oneself as a capable actor within that space. In contrast to objective space (merely considering physical dimensions), the gamespace is here considered as *lived space* that incorporates the imagined embodied experiencing of gamespace into the physical presence.

While this view shares several ideas already highlighted in the discussions of player embodiment and immersion, such as the central role of action and agency, malleability of the sense of self and the "dual-nature" of involvement as immersion and incorporation, there are, however, two points that are especially pronounced in an enactive approach. The first of these concerns the fundamental role of bodily action in understanding and experiencing. This means that our way of making sense of the world is by bodily action and this gives the basic structures for all our experiences (see Johnson 2007). The second point is that the sensemaking activity is co-constitutive by its nature: We are not "ready" actors in a "ready" world but rather constantly creating the world as a meaningful place through our interaction with it. This point can be linked to the more general tendency of "reframing" or "organising" our sense of self and of the world through technology, and our will to submit to the rules and logic of a game by adopting a lusory attitude.

It can be argued that this kind of view is stretching the enactive ideas too far from the very primordial sensorimotor interactions they originally relate to. Indeed, it seems unlikely that the sense of our digital embodiment could simply be equated with our sense of embodiment in the real world, at least in the sense that we would confuse these two with each other (see Farrow & Iacovides 2014). Moreover, the framing of our experiences as fundamentally world-constituting sensorimotor interaction (at least at the level discussed in this paper) blurs the differences between our involvements in different kinds of media. Nevertheless, the enactive idea of grounding the experience in world-constituting bodily activity may provide a fruitful starting point for considering the "level" of these differences, as well as the role and nature of "higher" cognitive processing usually treated in representationalist terms (e.g., our narrative, imaginative or pictorial involvement) from a non-Cartesian perspective.

ACKNOWLEDGEMENT

This work is funded by Kone Foundation (grant number 201908388).

REFERENCES

Black, D., 2017. Why can I see my avatar? Embodied visual engagement in the third-person video game. *Games and Culture*, 12(2), 179-199.

Calleja, G., 2011. *In-game: From immersion to incorporation*. MIT Press.

Collins, K., 2013. *Playing with sound: a theory of interacting with sound and music in video games*. MIT press.

Chion, M., 1994. *Audio-vision: Sound on screen*. Columbia University Press.

Crick, T., 2011. The game body: Toward a phenomenology of contemporary video gaming. *Games and Culture*, 6(3), 259-269.

Farrow, R., & Iacovides, I., 2014. Gaming and the limits of digital embodiment. *Philosophy & Technology*, 27(2), 221-233.

Gibson, J.J., 1986. *The Ecological Approach to Visual Perception*. Lawrence Erlbaum Associates.

Grimshaw, M. N., 2008. Autopoiesis and sonic immersion: Modelling sound-based player relationships as a self-organizing system. *Proceedings of The 6th Annual International Conference in Computer Game Design and Technology*. The school of Computing and Mathematical Siences – Liverpool John Moores University.

Ihde, D., 1990. *Technology and the Lifeworld: From Garden to Earth*. Indiana University Press.

Johnson, M., 2007. *The meaning of the body: Aesthetics of human understanding*. University of Chicago Press.

Kirkpatrick, G., 2011. *Aesthetic theory and the video game*. Manchester University Press.

Krueger, J., 2009. Enacting musical experience. *Journal of Consciousness Studies*, 16(2-3), 98-123.

Newman, J., 2002. The myth of the ergodic videogame. *Game studies*, 2(1), 1-17.

Noë, A., 2006. *Action in perception*. MIT press.

Noë, A., 2015. *Strange tools: Art and human nature*. Hill and Wang.

Varela, F. J. et al, 1993. *The Embodied Mind: Cognitive Science and Human Experience*. MIT press

Verbeek, P. P., 2015. Beyond interaction: a short introduction to mediation theory. *Interactions* 22, 26–31.

A REVIEW OF NARRATIVE APPROACHES IN ELECTRONIC GAMES

Yi-Peng Li and Jia-Qi Li
Faculty of Humanities and Arts, Macau University of Science and Technology, 999078, Macau China

ABSTRACT

There is always heated discussion among academic researches around whether electronic games are standard narrative carriers. Undeniably, electronic games have its own narrative characteristics. However, there is few studies on the narrative approaches of electronic games. Different narrative approaches would cause different feelings among players. Perhaps the in-depth study of narrative approaches can bring new inspiration for the topic. This paper has reviewed different opinions against the narratives of electronic games. In future studies, I plan to further explore how different narrative approaches could affect players and games, and how to choose the right narrative approaches for different types of games.

KEYWORDS

Electronic Games, Narratives, Media

1. ELECTRONIC GAMES ARE NARRATIVE

In studies of the narratives in games, different researchers hold different opinions toward issues related to “whether games are narrative” and "could games be narrative".

Some scholars believe that electronic games are obliviously narrative. Jesper Juul, associate professor of the School of Design of the Royal Danish Academy of Fine Arts, stated that “games are narrative” for three reasons when discussing the relevance between electronic games and narratives: everything is narrative and can be displayed narratively. most games feature narrative introduction and background; games have narrative characteristics. [Jull, 2005] In this regard, Janet Murray believes: "Games are all stories, including abstract games like chess and Tetris." [Murray, 2003] According to Julian Kucklich, games and literature have obvious similarities. Although the analogy between the gaming process and the reading process has oversimplified games to some extent, some electronic games do better than common games in storytelling. In this light, electronic games can be regarded as a cross-category of traditional narrative literature and games. [Kucklich, 2003] Concerning this, Craig A. Lindley holds a similar view. He believes that electronic games have many similarities with media forms such as media like TV dramas, TV news, and movies. They all have a narrative structure, and the difference is that the narrative structure of electronic games not only consists of story systems or fact elements, but also involves three basic symbol systems based on time structure: game, model and narratives. [Lindley, 2004].

2. ELECTRONIC GAMES ARE NOT NARRATIVE

Some researchers, on the contrary, believe that electronic games are not narrative or the narratives in electronic games are not indispensable. In relevant studies, Jesper Juul not only pointed out the three reasons for the standing that “games are narrative”, but offered three reasons for "games are not narrative": narrative media ecology consists of movies, novels and narratives, not games; compared with narratives, time plays a different role in games; readers or the audience’s relationship with the story world is different with that between players and games. Although many games have the characteristics of a certain form of narratives, it could not be concluded that games are equivalent to narratives. More importantly, although traditional narrative media, namely, novels, movies, and dramas, can be converted into each other, electronic games cannot completely restore and reproduce any of them. The convertibility between different media forms is a major narrative characteristic. [Jull, 2005] According to Peter Brooks (1984), the biggest difference between electronic games and traditional narrative media like novels and movies lies in the fact that the goal setting of games is always more important than the setting of stories. He believes that narrative is related to desire, and the purpose is to stimulate readers' desire to explore the unknown ending. The story of a video game is not the most important, because the ending is often already known. But it is always achieving the already-known ending that become the players' greatest pleasure. In a discussion on "simulation" and "narratives", Gonzalo Frasca (2003) stressed that the narratives of electronic games are not the most important, and the goal should not surrender to achieve narrative purposes. In games, gameplay is the priority that needs to be emphasized, not narrative.

3. ELECTRONIC GAMES ARE PARTIALLY NARRATIVE

Some scholars take a middle ground, believing that games are partially narrative. These scholars generally believe that when exploring the narrative characteristics of electronic games, one should firstly recognize the nature of games and the difference between narratives and games. Espen Aarseth (1997) once said: “If you confuse games with narratives, regarding the two indistinguishable, you are actually ignoring the essential attributes of the two. Though the difference might be ambiguous, there are still some important overlaps" Julian Kucklich (2003) pointed out that the narrative characteristics of electronic games has extended the gaming nature of games, and can be regarded as an integration of traditional narratives and games. Majewski (2003) held that the focus of studies should be the relationship between games and narratives. There are many problems to be settled when combining the two. Richard Bartle emphasized that the discussion on the narrative characteristics of electronic games should be take the category of games as the basis. Not all electronic games are narrative, and the narrative characteristics of RGPs are relatively obvious. [Bartle, 1985]

As for recent studies, Professor Hartmut Koenitz from the University of Hong Kong stated in a paper published in 2019 that researchers hold different opinion over the narrative potential and scope of electronic games mainly for lack of common understanding of the definition of “narratives”. The “experience dimension” of a scholar might be the “narratives” of another scholar, while the "level design" of a developer might be the "narratives" of the audience. Since a widely accepted definition of "narratives" is still absent, he encouraged scholars and professionals engaging in video game narratives to further study the definition and underlying assumptions. [Koenitz, 2018].

4. CONCLUSION

Although there are still various opinions over the narrative nature of electronic games, it is undeniable that electronic games, serving as a new narrative carrier that boasts some of the characteristics of traditional narratives, contain diversified narrative elements and unique interactive narrative features. In the future, I will probe into the influence different narrative approaches may have on players’ emotions, and how to choose the right narrative approaches for different categories of games.

REFERENCES

Craig A. Lindley, 2004. N*arrative, GamePlay, and Alternative Time Structures for Virtual Envlronments.T*IDSE, P183_194.

Espen Aarseth, 1997. *Cybertext: Perspectives on Ergodic Literature, Baltimore: John Hopkins University Press,* P4.

Gonzalo Frasca, 2003. *Sim Sin City: some thoughts about Grand Theft Auto3,* in Game stodies 1, http:/www.gamestudies.org/0302/frasca/.

Hartmut, Koenitz, 2018. *“Narrative in electronic games”.* Encyclopedia of Computer Graphics and Games. Edited by Newton Lee, Springer.

Jakub Majewski, 2003. *The Orising Video Game Narrative.* p. 58.

Janet Murray, 2003. "*FromGame_ Story to Cyberdrama "in Noah Ward_ rip_ Fruin and Pat Harrigan, ed. FirstPerson: New Media as Story, Performance, and Game.* Cambridge and London: The MIT Press, p. 2.

Jesper Jull, 2005. G*ames telling stories? [M].Handbook of electronic game studies,* Cambridge, p. 219.

Julian Kucklich, 2003. P*erspectives of electronic Game Philology.* Game Studies, http://www.Gamestudies.org/0301/kuchlich/.

Julian Kucklich, 2003. *Perspectives of electronic Game Philology.* Game Studies, p. 92.

Peter Brooks, 1984. R*eading for the Plot. New York: Vin-tage,* P40- 41, P52.

Rjehard Bartle, 1985. *Interactive Multi-Player electronic Games.*UK: Essex. p. 45.

AUTHOR INDEX